Places of Pain and Shame

Places of Pain and Shame is a cross-cultural study of sites that represent painful and/or shameful episodes in a national or local community's history, and the ways that government agencies, heritage professionals and the communities themselves seek to remember, commemorate and conserve these cases – or, conversely, choose to forget them.

Such episodes and locations include: massacre and genocide sites, places related to prisoners of war, civil and political prisons, and places of 'benevolent' internment such as leper colonies and lunatic asylums. These sites bring shame upon us now for the cruelty and futility of the events that occurred within them and the ideologies they represented. They are, however, increasingly being regarded as 'heritage sites', a far cry from the view of heritage that prevailed a generation ago when we were almost entirely concerned with protecting the great and beautiful creations of the past, reflections of the creative genius of humanity rather than the reverse – the destructive and cruel side of history.

Why has this shift occurred, and what implications does it have for professionals practising in the heritage field? In what ways is this a 'difficult' heritage to deal with? This volume brings together academics and practitioners to explore these questions, covering not only some of the practical matters, but also the theoretical and conceptual issues, and uses case studies of historic places, museums and memorials from around the globe, including the United States, Northern Ireland, Poland, South Africa, China, Japan, Taiwan, Cambodia, Indonesia, Timor and Australia.

William Logan is UNESCO Professor of Heritage and Urbanism and Director, Deakin University, Melbourne. His research interests include world heritage, Asian heritage and heritage and human rights. His recent publications include: *Hanoi: Biography of a City* (2000), *The Disappearing 'Asian' City* (2003) and *Vientiane: Transformation of a Lao Landscape* (2007, co-author).

Keir Reeves is a Monash Research Fellow at Monash University. His research interests include: Chinese-Australian history, Asian history and heritage, heritage studies, mining history and cultural landscape analysis. He is contributing co-editor of the recent publication *Deeper Leads: New Approaches to Victorian Goldfields History* (2007).

Key Issues in Cultural Heritage
Series editors: William Logan and Laurajane Smith

Also in the series:

Intangible Heritage
Laurajane Smith and Natsuko Akagawa

Places of Pain and Shame

Dealing with 'difficult heritage'

Edited by
William Logan and
Keir Reeves

Routledge
Taylor & Francis Group

LONDON AND NEW YORK

First published 2009
by Routledge
2 Park Square, Milton Park, Abingdon, Oxon OX14 4RN

Simultaneously published in the USA and Canada
by Routledge
270 Madison Ave, New York, NY 10016

Routledge is an imprint of the Taylor & Francis Group, an informa business

Typeset in Garamond by
Bookcraft Ltd, Gloucestershire
Printed and bound in Great Britain by
CPI Antony Rowe, Chippenham, Wiltshire

British Library Cataloguing-in-Publication Data
A catalogue record for this book is available from the British
Library

Library of Congress Cataloging-in-Publication Data
Places of pain and shame : dealing with "difficult heritage"/
edited by William Logan and Keir Reeves.
  p. cm.
  1. Cultural property—Cross-cultural studies.
  2. Collective memory—Cross-cultural studies. 3.
  Shame—Cross-cultural studies. I. Logan, William Stewart,
  1942– II. Reeves, Keir.
CC135.P59 2008
363.6'9—dc22   2008028855

ISBN10: 0–415–45449–2 (hbk)
ISBN10: 0–415–45450–6 (pbk)
ISBN10: 0–203–88503–1 (ebk)

ISBN13: 978–0–415–45449–0 (hbk)
ISBN13: 978–0–415–45450–6 (pbk)
ISBN13: 978–0–203–88503–1 (ebk)

Contents

Illustrations

Figures

Tables

Contributors

Dr Bronwyn Batten is a Senior Policy Officer in the Culture and Heritage Division of the NSW Department of Environment and Climate Change. Her chapter is based on PhD research at Macquarie University, Sydney, on the interpretation of sites of 'shared' indigenous and non-indigenous history.

Chou Ching-Yuan is a history researcher at the Taipei Women's Rescue Foundation. She was educated at the Freie Universität, Berlin, St John's University, New York, and Tamkang University, Taipei.

Dr Joost Coté teaches Asian Studies and History as well as Heritage Studies at Deakin University, Australia. His research interests are in postcolonial theory and cultural history focusing on late nineteenth-, early twentieth-century colonial and nationalist discourses in Indonesia and Australia.

Ai Kobayashi is completing her doctoral thesis on the eminent Australian political scientist, William Macmahon Ball, at the School of Historical Studies, University of Melbourne.

Dr Michael Leach is a Senior Lecturer in Politics at Swinburne University of Technology, Melbourne, Australia. He is a political scientist with a long-standing research interest in nation-building and national identity in Timor-Leste.

Spencer Leineweber is a Professor of Architecture and Director of the Heritage Center at the University of Hawaii, Honolulu. She teaches studio and architectural history in the graduate program.

Dr Jane Lennon, AM, is a member of the Australian Heritage Council and principal of a heritage consultancy service based in Brisbane, Queensland. Her PhD at Deakin University focused on the protection of cultural landscapes.

Dr William Logan is Alfred Deakin Professor and holds the UNESCO Chair in Heritage and Urbanism at Deakin University. His current research interests are Vietnamese heritage and the interface between heritage and human rights.

Dr Colin Long is an urban historian with interests in Vietnamese, Lao and Cambodian history and heritage, as well as Australian urban history and the heritage of Communism. He lectures and conducts research in the Cultural Heritage Centre for Asia and the Pacific at Deakin University.

Dr Sara McDowell lectures in Geography at the University of Ulster, UK. Her PhD entitled Representing Memory, Power and Identity: An Examination of Northern Ireland's Cultural Landscape sought to unravel the representation of memory in Northern Ireland through detailed analysis of the memorial landscape.

Dr David Nichols is lecturer in urban planning in the University of Melbourne's Faculty of Architecture Building and Planning. He has published on planned community space and buildings, urban activism and grassroots democracy, and the work and lives of twentieth-century Australian planning innovators.

Dr Angel David Nieves is an Associate Professor in the Africana Studies Program at Hamilton College, Clinton, New York. He completed his PhD in architectural history and Africana studies at Cornell University in 2001.

Dr Qian Fengqi is a research fellow with the Cultural Heritage Centre for Asia and the Pacific, Deakin University, Australia. Her research interests are in cultural heritage policies, management and interpretation, with the focus on China and East Asia.

Dr Keir Reeves is Monash Research Fellow at Monash University. Recently he was an Australian Research Council Postdoctoral Fellow in the Cultural Heritage Unit, School of Historical Studies, University of Melbourne. He is currently undertaking research into the cultural landscapes of central Victoria, Australia, and heritage and tourism in Indochina.

Dr Yushi Utaka is Associate Professor at the University of Hyogo. His research interest is in heritage conservation, with a special focus on the Asian social context. He was previously a researcher at University of Science, Malaysia, and the National University of Singapore.

Dr Sara Wills is a lecturer in Australian Studies at the University of Melbourne who has taught and published widely on Australian migration issues. Arriving in Australia as a teenager in the 1980s, she has a particular interest in cultures of migrant memory.

Katie Young is Assistant Director, International Aviation Industry Policy Section in the Australian Department of Transport and Regional Services, and is undertaking a PhD in Heritage Studies focusing on the management of Auschwitz-Birkenau.

Dr Bart Ziino is an Australian Research Council Postdoctoral Fellow in the School of History, Heritage and Society at Deakin University. He is currently researching Australian civilian experiences of the Great War, 1914–18, through personal records.

Acknowledgements

The editors would like to thank Matthew Gibbons and Lalle Pursglove at Routledge for their good advice and patience during the preparation of the volume, which grew out of a Discovery Grant project funded by the Australian Research Council, and to Fiona Erskine at Deakin University for her assistance. Most of the figures in the volume are photographs taken by the chapter authors, but others are published courtesy of Hiroshima City Government (Fig. 2.3), *The Bulletin* (Fig. 6.3), the Taipei Women's Rescue Foundation and its volunteer photographers (Figs 7.1–7.4), Antara New Service (Fig. 8.5), Hawaii State Archives (Fig. 14.1) and Dr Graeme Tuer (Fig. 15.2).

Introduction
Remembering places of pain and shame

William Logan and Keir Reeves

Most societies have their scars of history resulting from involvement in war and civil unrest or adherence to belief systems based on intolerance, racial discrimination or ethnic hostilities. A range of places, sites and institutions represent the legacy of these painful periods: massacre and genocide sites, places related to prisoners of war, civil and political prisons, and places of 'benevolent' internment such as leper colonies and lunatic asylums. These sites bring shame upon us now for the cruelty and ultimate futility of the events that occurred within them and the ideologies they represented. Increasingly, however, they are now being regarded as 'heritage sites', a far cry from the view of heritage that prevailed a generation ago when we were almost entirely concerned with protecting the great and beautiful creations of the past: reflections of the creative genius of humanity rather than the reverse – the destructive and cruel side of history. Why has this shift occurred, and what implications does it have for professionals practising in the heritage field? In what ways is this a 'difficult' heritage to deal with?

This book has been conceived as a cross-cultural study of sites representing painful and/or shameful episodes in a national or local community's history and the ways that government agencies, heritage professionals and communities themselves seek to remember, commemorate and conserve these cases of 'difficult heritage' – or, conversely, choose to forget them. The book brings together scholars and practitioners from six countries to explore these questions, using case studies of historic places, museums and memorials in the United States, Northern Ireland, Poland, South Africa, China, Japan, Taiwan, Cambodia, Indonesia, Timor-Leste (East Timor) and Australia. The team of authors includes architects, historians, geographers, political scientists and public policy specialists. That they are all heritage practitioners in a variety of ways underlines the multidisciplinarity that is now recognised as necessary for the development of heritage management teams able to produce cohesive heritage management plans and strategies.

The book considers the ways in which these historic sites and their significant heritage values can be and are being interpreted and conserved through planning and management interventions. According to Teresa Leopold (2007: 1), it is the manager of a site who has the most impact on its interpretation through the way in which he/she decides what to say and what to leave out. But heritage practitioners also need to listen to the affected community's views of the site's significance and management practices are contingent upon how the site is held in the public memory. An effective management plan for such places must be based on an analysis of the way in which the events for which heritage sites are said to be significant are remembered. Sometimes sites gradually change as memories of the past fade or are distorted; even sometimes, it is argued, sites should be actively changed where they merely aid the remembrance of the perpetrators of pain and shame rather than the victims.

It is important, therefore, to determine what aspects of the past are being ignored or poorly represented in the interpretation of the heritage sites. But sometimes whole sites may be missing from the public consciousness and hence from heritage registers, perhaps because the public in question does not want to remember the values associated with such places. Kenneth Foote (1997: 33) in his book on landscapes of tragedy in the United States raises the issue that many sites that played a significant role in the evolution of American society could now be lost from the collective memory and no longer marked at all. The question of what has and has not been marked is important. As Elie Wiesel, Nobel Prize winner, said: 'The executioner always kills twice, the second time with silence' (cited in M. Bouchenaki 1999: 1).

Heritage places are commonly *lieux de mémoire*, acting, as Pierre Nora (1989) suggested, as sites harbouring memories that serve to maintain a group's sense of connection with its roots in the past. Such places have political functions, used and abused by governments (Graham *et al.* 2000) for reasons that can be both benign and malign in intent and effect (Logan 2007). A frequent motive is nation-building, which accompanies the formation and strengthening of states. Governments encourage particular memories and provide rituals and venues for memorialisation, which may be benign if such actions promote the development of tolerant states and societies based on human rights.

In many cases, however, state authorities engage in retelling history, inventing traditions and celebrating heritage in ways that serve their own interests, which are often as crude as maintaining a grip on power. Connerton (1989:1) refers to this as the 'wilful distortion' of collective memory by governments, a distortion strategically aimed at manipulating the collectivity by manipulating its history, by 'explaining' its history in order to win support for a particular set of policies or for the maintenance of their hegemonic power in the present social order. For the British historian, Eric Hobsbawm (1997:5), it is in nationalistic politics that wilful distortion is at its worst, and certainly the history of wars and of colonialism shows the centrality of this propaganda ploy of distorting the past. But memory distortion and the fabrication of myths also occurs commonly in postcolonial situations where the creation of national identity is necessary to achieve political and cultural cohesion.

The contestability of memory has implications for the way particular cultural heritage sites have evolved over time. This in turn has implications for contemporary understanding and management of the built environment and sites of significance. Ashworth and Tunbridge (1996: 21) regard atrocity heritage as 'particularly prone to many types of dissonance'; however, while atrocity relates to the worst experiences of inhumanity, all places of pain and shame reveal dissonances, since there are always perpetrators and sufferers and their perceptions inevitably differ radically.

Growing world interest

There is a growing interest in the heritage associated with pain and shame at both international and national levels. At the international level, Paul Williams (2007) sees a 'seemingly unstoppable rise of memorial museums' (p. viii) as a 'global rush to commemorate atrocities' (Williams 2007). UNESCO listed Auschwitz as a World Heritage site in 1997 and the Hiroshima Atomic Bomb Dome in 1997. Robben Island, the site of Nelson Mandela's imprisonment, was inscribed in 1999. The UNESCO Bangkok Office sees the forced migration of peoples as a useful new theme leading to new places being considered for World Heritage listing. Such a thematic approach, and this theme in particular, has value as a way of putting into operation its 'Global Strategy' of shifting the balance of the World Heritage List away from Western Europe and North America. The slave depot island of Gorée in Senegal was an early inscription (1978). The Australian Government submitted its convict sites as a serial site nomination in 2008 using this theme, and work is being done on the Shimoni caves in Kenya (Kiriama 2005) and other sites associated with the slave trade.

At the national level, the impress of tragedy and violence on landscape has been studied by scholars such as Foote (1997) categorising public responses to violence and tragedy in the United States in terms of sanctification, designation, rectification, and obliteration (pp. 7–8). In 2002 Australia ICOMOS and University of Tasmania co-hosted a conference at the Port Arthur convict prison site entitled 'Islands of Vanishment'. The conference theme was described as exploring the nuances of meaning and memory of such heritage places, which 'tell us much about our origins, history and past way of life. They also resonate with strong emotional themes of tragedy, injustice, endurance and sometimes redemption' (University of Tasmania 2002). It was at this conference that David Lowenthal presented his 'Tragic Traces on the Rhodian Shore' paper in which he outlined a variation on Foote's categories.

What drives this interest in places of past pain, shame, humiliation and the macabre? Clearly, 'atrocity tourism' is booming, a point that led Ashworth and Hartmann (2005) to revisit the management of atrocity sites for tourism. As Katie Young explains in her chapter in this book, more than a million tourists visit Auschwitz-Birkenau annually. Anne Frank's House in Amsterdam, the Daniel Libeskind-designed Jewish Museum in Berlin and other Holocaust memorial sites and museums are also major tourism destinations. Stasimuseum in the central East German Ministry of State Security in Berlin-Lichtenberg is another tourist attraction focusing on the more recent Cold War past. Is it to feel the collective shame, if not the personal pain?

It is said that, paradoxically, we are personally comforted by misfortune falling on others; we are the lucky ones, the survivors, the chosen. How could this apply to genocidal atrocities, the enormity of which one would hope is overwhelming to anyone with any degree of sensitivity? Holocaust sites are visited by Jewish families devastated by the Nazi regime but also by vast numbers of others with no personal connection. Have people become so desensitised by the pictures of horrific war scenes on television news, by Hollywood 'adventure stories' and body-blasting electronic games that sites such as these become mere entertainment or sites to tick off on the world tour? Governments, of course, back such tourism because it generates foreign revenue. Two hundred thousand people per year now travel to Australia's Port Arthur. The pain and shame can be lost in the celebration of other, more commercial, values at sites that have become major tourist attractions.

Battlefield tourism has boomed, as Ryan's 2007 book demonstrates. Governments, military groups and people who lost family members and close friends in wars over the last century have an interest in keeping memories alive, and war-related tourism to places like Flanders, Gallipoli and the Thai–Burma Railway has grown enormously in recent decades. The need to honour those who perished in World War II is clear and the various commemorations of the end of World War II, as well as the Vietnam War and other more recent conflicts, mean much to people today. Excavating the remains of soldiers missing in World War I over 90 years ago is less understandable since almost no-one alive today has first-hand connections with these men. It is of concern that the continuing focus on more distant conflicts may represent the use of heritage by governments wishing to shape social values along jingoistic lines, readying the population for new wars.

The question of at what point memories can be allowed to fade and memorialisation end is a complex and difficult one. So, too, is the question that faces some communities where it is seen to be important for community identity reasons to keep memories alive but where the generations which experienced the pain and suffering are passing away. How do such communities keep alive the memories for subsequent generations? Heightened commemorative activities, including university and public seminars, the writing of plays and novels, the making of films and television programmes, and the production of museum exhibitions, even the building of new memorial museums, have been among the strategies adopted. According to writers such as Hamilton (1994) and Huyssen (1995), much of this has arisen in response to debates in Germany, France and Italy about World War II and, not surprisingly, Jewish scholars and artists have been at the forefront of much of this activity.

Book structure: the experience of pain and shame

The aim of the authors of this book is to broaden the interpretation of their case study sites, to take into account their multiple and contested ownership, and to unpack the different layers of meaning. The case studies range in age, size, historical origins and societal response. At one extreme, some places of pain and shame have come to be regarded with the passage of time as having a quasi-sacred status, often as reminders of the bitter stages of a society's evolution, and warnings of the potential that human beings have for inhumane actions towards one another. Sometimes, these places may come to be regarded as sites of an individual's or group's transcendence over the conditions of unjust treatment in times of war or of resistance to cruel and oppressive political regimes. In such cases there may be little or no dispute about their heritage significance, although the processes of achieving their effective interpretation, documentation and long-term protection remain difficult.

At the other end of the spectrum the book includes some places not celebrated until recently because of their association with pain and suffering in the past. Often today's communities are ashamed of these episodes or fear that probing into them may reopen divisions within the community. Such places frequently become the subject of calls for their demolition in order to erase the shame and fear associated with them. For this reason there is an urgent need to assist in clarifying the processes of identifying, documenting and, where appropriate, physically protecting significant sites that are threatened with obliteration.

In terms of typology, the case studies represent four major kinds of 'difficult' heritage places. Thus Part I of this volume offers five chapters that document the emergence, evolution and current state of massacre and genocide sites, while Part II includes four places related to war, either wartime internment camps or war memorials. Part III considers four civil and political prisons, and Part IV introduces places of 'benevolent' internment. There is not always a clear-cut distinction between the types, so that a place like Hiroshima (Chapter 2) is both a massacre site in which thousands of civilians were killed and a war-related place the bombing of which was justified on military strategic grounds by the perpetrators. The heritage in Timor-Leste flows out of a mixture of international war, massacres and civil strife. Hoa Lo Prison in Hanoi (Chapter 11) survived long enough to have performed several roles – a political prison under the French colonial authorities but later a war-related place housing downed American pilots during the Vietnam War.

Massacre and genocide sites

Qian Fengqi's chapter on the Nanjing Massacre Memorial examines the contested and highly politicised process of remembering/denying and interpreting this site of extreme violence, and explores the heritage of intra-Asian postcolonialism and the internationalisation of the rape of Nanjing through the construction and promotion of the Nanjing Massacre Memorial. The chapter shows that public commemoration of the atrocity throughout the twentieth century highlights the shifting attitudes towards what is remembered and how heritage practitioners interpret past violence in the present day. In neighbouring Japan, Yushi Utaka analyses, through a case study of Hiroshima, how the death of a city is remembered and memorialised. Initially the Hiroshima Peace Memorial was ground zero, yet with time it has become a global shrine for peace with a contentious world heritage listing. This transformative process has in one respect reclaimed the site from its association with atrocity, and in turn enabled a less pervasive sense of remembering the bomb to endure in effect 'moving beyond difficult memories of the past' and to contribute to a reappraisal of Japanese national identity.

Katie Young's contribution on Auschwitz-Birkenau reviews the increasingly complicated heritage significance of a key genocide site. The contestability of interpreting heritage sites associated with pain and shame is examined with reference to the Polish resistance. A contrast to this is the case study of Anlong Veng associated with the genocide in Cambodia. Here Colin Long and Keir Reeves examine the recent efforts to make Anlong Veng, the last bastion of the Khmer Rouge and the site of Pol Pot's grave, into a heritage tourism destination. While the Cambodian government sees tourism as a way of reintegrating this desperately poor region back into a nation finally at peace, Long and Reeves argue that such a strategy reveals how limited are the economic development options for many developing nations. Anlong Veng's Khmer Rouge sites are presented in a historical and moral vacuum that does nothing to commemorate the atrocities committed in the movement's name: guides around some sites openly talk of their approval of Pol Pot and Ta Mok, the movement's military leader.

Both Long and Reeves' chapter and Young's chapter highlight the intersection of political and heritage agendas. However Anlong Veng remains under-researched and the authors' data is mostly limited to rally drivers' accounts and journalists' short political/travel stories. Furthermore the Cambodian conflict is recent, not only in respect of the genocide, but also in that the Khmer Rouge itself was active as recently as 1999. In another contrast with Auschwitz-Birkenau, Brownyn Batten's chapter examines the emotional power of an Indigenous massacre site, Myall Creek, that is older and smaller and, like Anlong Veng, little known by the general public outside the locality itself. This is partly explained by the tendency of postcolonial settler societies to adopt a stance of silence towards treatment of Indigenous Australians in relation to nineteenth-century frontier atrocities.

War-related sites

Ai Kobayashi and Bart Ziino explore the enduring contested nature of the Pacific war through the interpretation of the Japanese War Cemetery in the New South Wales town of Cowra. They uncover a hidden history of a little known war episode and show the difficulties faced by a local community in facilitating a process of healing and reconciliation through an overt attempt to memorialise a site of difficult heritage so soon after the conclusion of the war. This is also a feature of Michael Leach's chapter on Timor-Leste where the independence war against Indonesia is barely over and civil unrest between competing internal groups continues. Leach discusses the independence struggle itself as cultural heritage, focusing on efforts to conserve key Falintil sites. As well as the difficulties deriving from the country's extremely limited resources, complexities result from the contestation over memories of the past held by the Portuguese and Indonesian colonial powers and the various communities within Timor-Leste. The key argument is best left in his own words: 'The cultural heritage landscape reflects a major fault line in post-independence politics, in that the contribution of younger East Timorese nationalists in the struggle for independence remains relatively neglected.'

The chapters by Chou Ching-Yuan and Joost Coté deal with the efforts to remember and memorialise the treatment of women in wartime, a subject that has to date received relatively little attention in heritage literature. In her study of Taiwanese comfort women during World War II, Chou explores the taboo of remembering and interpreting a site typified by systemic sexual violence, rape and exploitation of women, and the process of denial by the aggressor. Reading one of the sites – a cave in Shuiyuan Village – as a heritage site enables the sequence of events and victims' memories to emerge, in the process facilitating a redemptive process restoring honour as well as enabling the truth of the horror to emerge through a physical interpretation of the cave site. Coté's case study lies further south in Java. He uses the reading of internment sites as places of individual pain and national shame as the means to interpret the heritage of World War II women victims in Indonesia generally and to show the contestability of the past for constructions of national memory in the present day.

Civil and political prisons

The focus of the book shifts in Part III to civil and political prisons. The work of Michael Ignatieff (1978) is useful in order to establish why it came to be considered just, reasonable and humane to immure prisoners in solitary cells. Between 1770 and 1840 this form of carceral discipline 'directed at the mind' replaced a cluster of punishments 'directed at the body' – whipping, branding, the stocks and public hanging. The appearance of a new style of authority within the walls obviously must be linked to changes in class relations and social tactics outside the walls. Hence a study of prison discipline necessarily becomes a study, not simply of prisons, but of the moral boundaries of social authority in a society undergoing capitalist transformation.

Broader and longlasting implications for British and Australian societies followed through the introduction of a policy in which criminals were transported to remote convict settlements in the Antipodes. When the French adopted a similar policy, similar continuing links developed between metropolitan France and antipodean New Caledonia. In her chapter on Port Arthur, Norfolk Island and New Caledonia, Jane Lennon explores the global nature of the convict experience by an investigation of extensive management plans and the importance of site interpretation. Between 1848 and 1863 Port Arthur was a place for recidivists and political prisoners, a prison within a prison. Port Arthur has always been a place where visitors are moved emotionally, sometimes to tears, one of few such cathartic locations in post-settlement Australia. Like Myall Creek, there are various levels of significance as Port Arthur is an important foundation for Tasmanians' shared sense of identity, evoking intense, and at times conflicting, feelings about who they are and their place in the world.

In his chapter Angel David Nieves investigates the intersection of heritage, politics and public memory in modern South Africa. He analyses places of pain as tools for achieving social justice, particularly in the nation's townships. Nieves contends that today communities struggle still to acknowledge their ignored or hidden histories. Sara McDowell's chapter is set in a different geographical and cultural hemisphere and yet the struggle to find interpretations of the past that encourage the development of a common identity is in many ways similar. She reads Long Kesh (also known as the Maze prison) as a place of pain and shame through an examination of the physical site and its master plan for redevelopment. She outlines both the politicisation of prisoners that flowed in large part from their prison employees' subjective experience of injustice and experience of the penal system. This intangible heritage was reflected physically in the architecture of the site which McDowell sees as confirming the prison's objective to oppress.

The proposal to make a place that housed some of the world's most dangerous terrorists and symbol of sectarian bloodshed into a new national sports stadium has generated much controversy. Some want to keep the prison as a microcosm of the conflict that will both enable reflection on past struggles and help to build future peace. One local politician from the Sinn Fein party, Paul Butler, went further to claim that 'Long Kesh is on a standing with Robben Island, Auschwitz and the Berlin Wall and we cannot afford to lose that history' (Smith 2003). A representative of the Northern Ireland Museums Council, on the other hand, explained that while her organisation recognises the need to preserve the site for future generations, it might be too early to turn it into a museum. Logan's Hoa Lo case study is similar in that the prison complex had outlived its usefulness, but, since Vietnam is one of the few remaining communist states with highly centralised political and administrative structures and a tradition of top-down decision-making, proposals to redevelop the site, turning part of it into a museum, were put forward without opposition and, therefore, quickly implemented. That was in the 1990s, however; since then 'creeping pluralism' has made it more possible for public officers to make statements about the past, including within the Hoa Lo museum, that reflect divergent interpretations.

'Benevolent' internment camps

Part IV sees the focus of study shift to 'benevolent' sites of incarceration where people have been incarcerated 'for their own good'. Examples include mental institutions and infectious disease control areas. The work of Michel Foucault reminds us of the psychological cost and social stigmatisation that occurs with benevolent incarceration. He argued (1991: 198), for instance, that 'the leper gives rise to rituals of exclusion, which to a certain extent provided the model for and general form of the great confinement.... The leper was caught up in the practice of rejection.' In her chapter 'Beauty springing from the breast of pain', however, Spencer Leineweber highlights how sites of benevolent incarceration, such as her case study site of Kalaupapa on northern Molokai in the Hawaiian Islands, can be read as a site of pain and shame. Human trauma is not always as easily identified as it is in most of the other cases in this volume and, when it was proposed that the Kalaupapa peninsula should become a national park, the residents were adamant that they wanted to stay on and that their settlement be left 'undisturbed and uncommercialized' (Yong 2003). The patients wanted visitors to know about not only the segregation and suffering of Kalaupapa, but also the lives of the patients. For the residents the process of reclaiming the dignity of their personal story is an important aspect of interpreting the site for future.

Just as some people questioned the opening up of a leper colony to the general public as a national park, so too, in their case study of the Kew Asylum in Melbourne, Keir Reeves and David Nichols indicate that many people find uncomfortable the way in which this iconic Victorian-era 'lunatic asylum' has been put to new uses, in this case as a middle-class residential complex. Nevertheless the adaptive re-use project appears to have been successful and the authors suggest that 'the consolations of the development's cost and exclusivity' cushion [the new occupants] ... from what otherwise might be oppressive or sinister associations with madness and its treatment'.

In the book's final chapter, Sara Wills highlights a tension that resonates through many chapters of this book – a tension between the known and the unknown, the member of the group and the stranger. Esses *et al.* (2001: 390) read out from this personally experienced tension to see a wide gap between social ideals and policies in support of multiculturalism and those relating to global openness, observing that 'prejudice and bias not only toward minority groups within a country but towards immigrants from other countries still characterize the attitudes of many individuals and nations still carefully restrict immigration'. Although these observations are about Australian society, ideals and policies, they have relevance to many countries around the world, especially in the aftermath of New York's Twin Towers catastrophe in 2001. Wills examines the consistent official denial of racial discrimination in Australian immigration administrative systems and argues that refugee detention centres are effectively prisons (see also Jupp 2002: 8). She contrasts the Woomera refugee centre, only recently closed, with the Bonegilla migrant camp of the post-World War II years and, in doing so, she shows how the cultural politics of emotion is a way that certain histories remain alive. National shame, Wills concludes, is tied to a history of individual migrants hurting. This situation where the personal is also political occurs commonly throughout the case studies in this book and has important implications for the process of heritage interpretation and memorialisation.

Implications for professional practice

Drawing on sites from different areas and cultural contexts the book is intended as a cross-cultural comparative study that identifies heritage values of these 'difficult' places and explains the ways in which these values can be interpreted and conserved. The case studies in the book have been organised according to the commonality of experience, which is not, of course, to suggest that all cases are equal or even similar in the degree of barbarity displayed by the perpetrators. The case studies also show the way that societies and heritage professionals have responded differently to the difficult sites in their midst. It is very clear that the interpretation, conservation and management of former places of pain and shame present a particular set of challenges for heritage practitioners. Like all professions, the heritage profession does not operate in a vaccuum; its individual members and, more slowly, its institutions respond to shifts in community attitudes and interests – in this instance to the growing urge to explore memory, to remember the past, to re-interpret old stories to suit new times and to commemorate and memorialise.

But a discourse has developed within the profession itself which has a powerful momentum of its own. From an initial monumental approach heritage protection activities moved into heritage precincts with the Loi Malraux 1962 and English towns following the Civic Amenities Act 1967. The powerful World Heritage system was established in 1972, with its dual focus on natural and cultural places. By the 1990s attempts to move away from the Eurocentric concentration on castles, cathedrals and historic towns led the World Heritage Committee to begin inscribing cultural landscapes. UNESCO under Director-General Koïchiro Matsuura then broadened the concept further by venturing into the listing, protection and encouragement of intangible forms of cultural heritage – essentially performance skills – again hoping that this would better serve those parts of the world not well represented in the tangible heritage lists and programmes. This trajectory is reflected in global, national and local heritage conventions, laws and guidelines and in the heritage education programs in universities.

The broadening of the cultural heritage concept with which this book deals – a broadening that allows heritage claims to be made for places of pain and shame, the ugly side of history – reflects both the shifts in community interests and the trajectory of change within the profession. But such broadening requires a new philosophical grounding. A key issue raised is whether there are limits to what places from the past we should keep, and, if so, what they are. Part of the difficulty flows from the general adoption of an anthropological definition of culture by UNESCO and the World Heritage system: when all forms of social behaviour can be regarded as part of one's 'culture', setting limits on the concern and purview of the cultural heritage profession becomes problematic. Thus even political behaviour like Ku Klux Clan rituals can be seen as a cultural manifestation – one example of many cultural forms held to be important by communities and groups within various countries. It was no doubt simpler when cultural heritage had a narrower definition focusing on the exotic, the traditional and the artistic – but then that fails to capture the complexity and richness of human existence.

How would we justify the exclusion of places promoted by their local communities or governments? Recourse to the principles of human rights is one way, but this does not cover all cases (Logan 2007, 2008). In their chapter on Anlong Veng, Long and Reeves offer a further answer, arguing that 'the purpose of heritage preservation in the case of places of pain and shame is to commemorate the victims' and therefore 'there is little role for the preservation of perpetrator sites'. Young's chapter highlights another requirement of good professional practice in dealing with difficult heritage places – the need to take into account all of the victims of pain and shame associated with a place and to find ways for all to explore their memories and have their stories told. Former director of the World Heritage Centre, Bernd von Droste, once commented that 'Some sites are so difficult to manage that they are not managed.'[1] In the case of some sites with various, contrasting meanings to different racial and ethnic groups no-one dares manage on behalf of all the stakeholders. Multireligious sites in many parts of the world are also challenging, especially where the ownership and control has moved from one religion to another in the past. How do heritage professionals act as mediators in situations where values conflict? While the professional response might be to look for ways to see the sites as 'shared heritage' or at least to tell parallel interpretative stories about them, often the national or communal politics does not allow this. Cemeteries require sensitive treatment, too. For some religions a cemetery needs management; for other religions burial places are left alone. In the case of genocide sites, the crime against the Jews was so great that other victim groups feel displaced. What sort of training is required when dealing with stakeholders for whom the place remains a source of acute anguish? Young tells us about recent moves to allow a co-existence of values, although it is fair to say that many of the difficulties of dealing with the concentration and death camps at Auschwitz-Birkenau have been side-stepped by a managing the site principally as a place to educate future generations in how societies should not behave.

Given the complicity of governments in perpetrating episodes of pain and shame, it is not surprising that many today continue to resist efforts by community groups and heritage professionals, either within the country concerned or at an international level, to explore the past, to tell a fuller story, especially one that focuses on the victims. There is always a danger that only those places that reflect the official interpretation of historical events are likely to be commemorated and that those places that do not reflect the ideology of the regime in power or the dominant social, ethnic or racial group are neglected. How do heritage professionals respond in such circumstances? Accepting work under such regimes may be seen by critics as sharing in their complicity. In some cases it may be appropriate to continue working in the hope that the political situation will improve and the full significance of the sites of pain and shame can be revealed.

Many of the case studies in this volume demonstrate the need for heritage practitioners to take into account the broader ideological role that heritage sites have and to recognise that official interpretations will vary over time. Qian, Utaka and Logan see close but changing links between state ideology and museum and memorial policies in China, Japan and Vietnam respectively. Nieves, McDowell and Leach deal with situations in South Africa, Northern Ireland and Timore Leste where conflict continues to break out or the memory of it is still raw. Heritage conservation activities under such circumstances can usefully become tools of conflict management, helping to build in a sense of shared national identity. National economic conditions are also important and heritage protection is clearly more difficult in less developed countries, such as Timor-Leste, Cambodia, Bosnia or Kosovo, especially when the heritage sites are places of pain and shame and the objects of ambiguous public sentiment. It is difficult sometimes for heritage professionals to recognise that heritage conservation is of low government priority in the face of extreme poverty and it is important to find ways to use heritage projects to generate employment in physical restoration and maintenance and through pro-poor cultural tourism.

Another set of difficulties raised in several chapters of this book relates to changes in the level of significance attributed to sites. Sometimes the local community may refuse to accept national or world interest in their past. Norfolk Island, one of the convict settlements discussed in Lennon's chapter, initially waged a campaign against being included in a convict serial sites nomination to the World Heritage Committee, fearing the political implications this would have. Batten describes the moves afoot to make a place that has been primarily of local significance, Myall Creek, into a national site representing all Aboriginal massacre sites. She is concerned that the detail, accuracy and emotion of the local story may be lost in the process. Wills discusses the Bonegilla migrant camp that is now portrayed as representative of Australian migrant camps in general. The Cowra war cemetery discussed by Kobayashi and Ziino has assumed international status by becoming a site representing reconciliation between once warring nations. In many ways it is a model of best professional practice, although it would appear that Japanese and Australian visitors, while politely acknowledging one another, interpret the site differently and may take away different messages.[2] Chou's cave in Taiwan seems to be valued more highly by a national group, the Taipei Women's Rescue Foundation, than by the local community, necessitating an awareness-raising campaign among local residents if conservation of the heritage site is to be sustainable. Leineweber's chapter shows how it is possible, with sensitive consultative and planning processes, for the local community to maintain a satisfactory degree of control over the reclassification of their site as a national park, its opening up to the geneal public and associated publicity and commercialisation that this will entail.

In other instances it is at the national government level, rather than within the community, that resistance to heritage inscription and protection schemes occurs. Changes of government can, of course, change the situation, as with the way in which the Woomera refugee internment camp in South Australia might be considered as 'heritage' by the Howard Government and its successor, the

Rudd Government (elected 2007). Sometimes a national community can agree that a site reflecting a painful episode in its history should be protected but the site is located in another country. Coté's internment sites in Indonesia are a case in point: there is national shame about the treatment of Dutch female civilians during World War II and Dutch authorities are permitted a role in memorialising those who suffered. In Vietnam, the French and Australian dead from the Battle of Dien Bien Phu and Vietnam War are permitted to have official memorial sites, but not yet the Americans. The Dutch and Commonwealth dead are honoured at war cemeteries and memorials along the Thai–Burma Railway, even though the railway is an almost forgotten episode in Thai history producing little if any emotional response on the part of most Thai visitors. That the Australian Government was able to construct the Hellfire Pass memorial museum reflects the generally strong bilateral relations between the two countries rather than any great emotional commitment to the war heritage, which is essentially seen as non-Thai. On the other hand, the Australians tended to commandeer the Hellfire Pass story, and its initial museum interpretative strategy had to be substantially modified following objections from other countries whose citizens suffered along the railway.

Foreign professionals can avoid or at least minimise problems such as these by adopting a sensitive cross-cultural negotiation approach in all stages of the commemoration process, remembering that they are working on someone else's land. The same requirement applies, in fact, to all heritage conservation practice where groups from different jurisdictions are involved. This means that, among other things, the education of heritage professionals in universities and other training organisations must include how to deal with stakeholders for whom the particular heritage site remains a source of acute anguish and where various different yet equally valid interpretations can be made. Interaction with the community is indispensable. So, too, is recognition that the context in which professionals work is political. Heritage conservation is a form of cultural politics; it is about the links between ideology, public policy, national and community identity formation, and celebration, just as much as it is about technical issues relating to restoration and adaptive re-use techniques. This view of heritage and its implications for practice is one of the many fundamental issues explored by the authors in this book.

Notes

1 Comment made when chairing a session at the conference on 'Heritage Education: Capacity Building in Heritage Management', Brandenburg Technical University, Cottbus, Germany, 15 June 2006.
2 This possibility was suggested by Dr Keiko Tamura, Project Manager, Australia–Japan Research Project, Military History Section, Australian War Memorial, in a personal communication, Canberra, 23 June 2008.

References

Ashworth, G.J. and Hartmann, R. (2005) *Horror and Human Tragedy Revisited: The Management of Sites of Atrocities for Tourism*, New York: Cognizant Communication.

Ashworth, G.J. and Tunbridge, J.E. (1996) *Dissonant Heritage: Management of the Past as a Resource*, Chichester: Wiley.

Bouchenaki, M. (1999) 'Breaking the silence: Sites of memory', *The World Heritage Newsletter*. Paris: UNESCO, 23 (Sept–Oct): 1.

Connerton, P. (1989) *How Societies Remember*, Cambridge, UK: Cambridge University Press.

Esses, V.M. *et al.* (2001) 'The Immigration Dilemma: The Role of Perceived Group Competition, Ethnic Prejudice, and National Identity', *Journal of Social Issues* 57(3): 389–412.

Foote, K.E. (1997) *Shadowed Ground: America's Landscapes of Violence and Tragedy*, Austin: University of Texas Press.

Foucault, M. (1991) *Discipline and Punish: the Birth of the Prison*, translated by Alan Sheridan, London: Penguin.

Graham, B., Ashworth, G.J. and Tunbridge, J. (2000) *A Geography of Heritage: Power, Culture and Economy*, London: Arnold.

Hamilton, P. (1994) 'The knife edge: debates about memory and history', in K. Darien-Smith and P. Hamilton (eds), *Memory and History in Twentieth-Century Australia*, Melbourne: Oxford University Press.

Hobsbawm, E. (1997) *On History*, London: Weidenfeld & Nicolson.

Huyssen, A. (1995) *Twilight Memories: Marking Time in a Culture of Amnesia*, London: Routledge.

Ignatieff, M. (1978) *A Just Measure of Pain: The Penitentiary in the Industrial Revolution, 1750–1850*, 1st edn, New York: Pantheon Books.

Jupp, J. (2002) *From White Australia to Woomera: The Story of Australian Immigration*, Cambridge: Cambridge University Press, 2002. Reprint, 2003.

Kiriama, H.O. (2005) 'Archaeological Investigation of Shimoni Slave Caves', in B. Zimba, E. Alpers, and A. Isaacman (eds), *Slave Routes and Oral Traditions in Southeastern Africa*, Maputo: Filsom Entertainment, Lda.

Leopold, T. (2007) 'A proposed code of conduct for war heritage sites', in C. Ryan (ed.), *Battlefield Tourism: History, Place and Interpretation*, London: Elsevier.

Logan, W.S. (2007) 'Closing Pandora's Box: Human Rights Conundrums in Cultural Heritage Protection', in H. Silverman and D. Fairchild Ruggles (eds), *Cultural Heritage and Human Rights*, New York: Springer.

Logan, W.S. (2008) 'Cultural Heritage and Human Rights', in B.J. Graham and P. Howard (eds), *Ashgate Research Companion to Heritage and Identity*, Aldershot, UK: Ashgate Publishing Ltd.

Smith, R. (2003) *Can Maze Jail Escape Demolition?: Expert to Rule on Listed Status*, The News Letter (Belfast), 23 August. Available from http://www.encyclopedia.com/doc/1G1-106796738.html (accessed 23 August 2003).

University of Tasmania (2002) *Islands of Vanishment Conference*. Available at http://www.arts.utas.edu.au/islands/structure.html (accessed 20 June 2008).

Williams, P. (2007) *Memorial Museums: The Global Rush to Commemorate Atrocities*, London: Berg.

Yong, J. (2003) *Last Days of a Leper Colony*, CBS News.com, 22 March 2003. Available from http://www.cbsnews.com/stories/2003/03/22/health/main545392.shtml (accessed 22 March 2003).

Part I

Massacre and genocide sites

Chapter 1

Let the dead be remembered
Interpretation of the Nanjing Massacre Memorial

Qian Fengqi

The 'Memorial Hall for the Victims of the Nanjing Massacre by Japanese Invaders to China' (hereafter referred to as the Nanjing Massacre Memorial or the Memorial) is the first memorial in China commemorating Chinese victims of Japanese atrocities during World War II. Since its construction in 1985, this Memorial, designated by Central Government as a national site for patriotic education, has reportedly received over 10 million visitors (Nanjing Massacre Memorial official website).

The massacre remains large in the memory of Nanjing citizens. A negative event tends to impact people in such a way that it leaves a deep 'scar' in people's memory. This is because, psychologically, 'memory for traumatic and highly emotional negative events tends to be reasonably accurate and better retained over time than is memory for more routine experiences' (Goodman and Paz-Alonso 2006: 234). Yet in Freud's view, strong unpleasant emotions might be actively suppressed and inaccessible to consciousness. In his book *Justice and Reconciliation: After the Violence*, Andrew Rigby (2001: 1) observed that it would seem obvious that most people want to forget past pain and, therefore, opening up the past may not be the best way of healing. So how difficult is it for a society to discard, or to retain past traumas such as the Nanjing Massacre, even some seventy years after its occurrence?

The Nanjing Massacre is known worldwide, having attracted activists and campaigns in the West following the phenomenal sales of Iris Chang's *The Rape of Nanjing: The Forgotten Holocaust of World War II* in 1997. It is a core historical issue affecting Sino-Japanese relations, reflected in the controversy over Japanese history textbooks (Askew 2002). In reviewing Masahiro Yamamoto's 2000 book *Nanking: Anatomy of an Atrocity*, David P. Barrett (2003) contended that the focal points of dispute regarding this massacre were the number of people killed and the placing of responsibility. Japanese views regarding the scale of the massacre are widely divided. According to historian Hata Ikuhiko of Nihon University, people holding different views on this issue fall into three categories based on political orientation and assessment of the number of Chinese killed: radicals (the 'massacre faction'); conservatives (the 'illusion' faction); and moderates (the 'in-between' faction) (Hata 1998). In his analysis of controversies about the Nanjing Massacre, Masahiro Yamamoto tags groups of people in the debate as 'extreme traditionalists', 'moderate traditionalists', 'moderate revisionists', 'extreme revisionists' and so forth. His research shows that opinions in Japan about the number of victims vary from 300,000 or more, held by 'extreme traditionalists', to 50, held by 'extreme revisionists' who deny that the Nanjing Massacre ever happened at all (Yamamoto 2000: 254).

The attempt to deny the Nanjing Massacre by the 'illusion faction' caused severe concern in China. This reached a height in 1982 when, following a bill conceived in 1981 to tighten government control over school textbooks, the Japanese Education Ministry screened history textbooks to make sure they played down reference to Japanese aggressive behaviour during the Asia-Pacific War (1934–45) (Yoshida 2000: 84). In response to the textbook controversy, a series of actions were taken on the Chinese side. These included officially protesting against the Japanese Education Ministry's attempt to water down the content about Japanese aggression and wartime atrocities such as the Nanjing Massacre, publishing research findings on the massacre, introducing an annual commemorative ceremony on the anniversary of the fall of Nanjing, as well as building the Nanjing Massacre Memorial.

This chapter attempts to identify changes of attitude in China towards this atrocity; the identity of the victims; the objectives of the current interpretation of the massacre; and the internal and external factors contributing to the changes. It begins with a review of the way in which memories of the massacre were treated in China before the 1980s. The construction of the Memorial is examined with regard to the internal and external political environments, and the dispute between China and Japan over the textbook controversy. The interpretation of the massacre at the Memorial is then examined by analysing the rationale of the architecture and the exhibitions, and assessment is made regarding the message being communicated.

Discussions in this chapter relate to the status of the Memorial as at June 2006. The current site was erected in 1985 and renovated in 1995 but the site is being extended from mid-2006 and is due to be re-opened in December 2007, marking the 70th anniversary of the fall of Nanjing to the Japanese invaders. At the time of writing, the renovation project is still underway.

Memories of the Nanjing massacre

In July 1937 the Chinese and Japanese troops opened fire on each other at Lu Gou Qiao (Marco Polo Bridge) near Beijing. This event, known internationally as the Marco Polo Bridge Incident, ignited full-scale Japanese aggression in China as well as the all-nation resistance to the aggression, referred to as the Anti-Japanese War, which ended with the Japanese surrender in 1945.

For months after the Marco Polo Bridge Incident, the Japanese military thrust southwards to expand its occupation of China. Having taken control of Shanghai, the Japanese troops began pushing towards Nanjing, the Chinese capital at the time. The occupation of Shanghai and the invasion of Nanjing encountered fierce resistance from the Chinese army, but the defence of Nanjing was doomed. On 13 December 1937, Nanjing fell to the Japanese. The following six weeks or so witnessed atrocities that were later known as the Nanjing Massacre or the Rape of Nanjing, conducted under the pretext of searching for and executing Chinese soldiers. During this period of time, hundreds of thousands of Chinese, including civilians, were killed. Properties were looted and destroyed, and women were assaulted.

According to the judgement on the war crime of Tani Hisao by the Nanjing Military Tribunal in 1947, 300,000 people were killed in this massacre (Hu 2006: 389).[1] Mass burials began early in 1938 when the worst of the massacre eased. There were about 13 major mass burial sites, mainly scattered on the western side of Nanijing near the Yangtze River, where many bodies were disposed of.

Joshua Fogel (2000) stated that these atrocities have never been accorded the importance or status they warrant in modern history (Fogel 2000: 1–2). Indeed, over the decades, China, Japan and the international community said little about the Nanjing Massacre, a situation referred to by Caroline Rose (2005: 36) as 'collective amnesia'. Until the 1980s, memories of the massacre seemed to be buried with the victims. Public commemoration of the event was rare.

It has to be understood that up to the early 1980s, memories of the Anti-Japanese War in China were shaped by the strategic imperatives and official ideology of the time. Bob T. Wakabayashi (2007: 3–4) listed some contributing factors to the amnesia about the Nanjing Massacre until the 1980s: the Nationalist regime's priority after the war was to eliminate its Communist rivals; the Communist Party, after taking over power in 1949, was preoccupied with consolidating its regime as well as internal and external problems such as the Korean War, famine, the Sino-Soviet split and the traumatic Cultural Revolution. Official propaganda focused on the Chinese people's fight against the Japanese, and their ultimate victory over Japanese aggression. Discussions about the victimisation of China were discouraged. Records show that in the 1960s when a group of Nanjing-based historians conducted research on this massacre, their work could not be published, one of the historians being accused of stirring up national hatred against the Japanese people (Yang 1999).

There were more intrinsic factors contributing to this lack of attention and public commemoration. National pride and the determined self-reliance policy of the Chinese government during the post-1949 era are counted by researchers as key factors influencing the Chinese government's position on the past until the 1980s (Eykholt 2000, Fogel 2000). With the founding of the People's Republic of China, Mao Zedong announced that China would no longer be subject to insult and humiliation. In the early 1950s, China was engaged in building a new national identity, anxious to shake off the image of the 'sick man of East Asia [*dong ya bing fu*]'. Ideological campaigns during that period aimed to consolidate the legitimacy of the new regime and to raise the confidence of the nation. The focus of history education at the time was on class struggle, promoting a spirit of nationalism and heroism. This official interpretation of the past was in turn epitomised by numerous memorials to honour revolutionary heroes and martyrs nationwide. The 'Monument to the People's Heroes' in the middle of Tian'anmen Square, for example, was erected in 1958. As the inscription on the structure states, the monument is dedicated to 'those who gave their lives for the cause of Chinese revolution between 1840 and 1949'. In 1961 the first list of national heritage properties was released by the Central Government, and of 180 listed sites 33 were 'revolutionary relics'. In Nanjing, until the 1980s the official commemorative site was the 'Revolutionary Martyrs' Memorial' at Yuhuatai (the Rain Flowers Terrace), listed as national heritage in 1988. It is a cemetery for those who died as heroes for the revolution. In contrast, sites of the Nanjing Massacre were not marked until the 1980s, and not until 2006 were they listed as national heritage (Chinese State Administration for Cultural Heritage official website; Jiangsu Province Administration for Cultural Heritage official website).

During the 1950s and 60s, China was also troubled by border conflicts and saw foreign invasion as imminent. People were told to be prepared for war. While monuments to revolutionary heroes could boost national morale, past tragedies such as the Nanjing Massacre might create fear among the public about war. Memories of the past were therefore filtered so that victories were enlarged and highlighted whereas bloodshed and death were played down.

Policies regarding the past, as Caroline Rose observed, 'are the product of political situations and judgement of the time, and are open to manipulation or bargaining' (Rose 2005: 47). Revolutionary fever gradually cooled in the 1970s and China began to improve relations with the West as well as Japan. International recognition of Beijing as the sole legitimate government of China was a priority. The re-establishment of the Sino-Japanese relationship and the signing of the Sino-Japan Communiqué in September 1972 were significant diplomatic landmarks. While urging Japan to face up to its war crimes in China during the World War II, China chose to renounce its demand on Japan for war reparation.

The Nanjing Massacre, however, remained a bitter chapter in Nanjing's history, inflicting painful and shameful memories among its citizens. During this massacre, civilians, particularly women and children, died helplessly, but afterwards, memories were usually suppressed, partly because people preferred not to dwell on the trauma. When mass graves were located at Jiangdongmen, and bone deposits of victims unearthed during a test excavation, site workers were very distressed and felt reluctant to dig further. They decided to seal up the graves because 'they didn't want to reopen the scar in their memories' (personal communication with Director of Public Works, Jianye District, Nanjing, October 2005). As mentioned above, government manipulation of societal memory also discouraged any obsession with past misery. Officials preferred stories of resistance and fighting to those of bitterness and suffering. Alongside the promotion of national pride and revolutionary heroism, personal tragedy appeared pathetic and insignificant, even embarrassing, especially for the female victims who survived atrocities and sexual abuse.

1980s: memories of pain and shame versus the government's new agenda

Official narratives of the Anti-Japanese War were moderated in the 1980s and became more inclusive and objective. As well as glorious stories of victory, less heroic aspects of the war – including casualties and civilian suffering – were increasingly revealed to the public. Reports and monographs about atrocities by the Japanese troops were released as official documents, literature, arts and mass media. Sites of atrocities were identified and protected, and memorials in honour of victims of Japanese aggression were erected. Apart from the Nanjing Massacre Memorial, a number of other memorials and museums were identified, such as the Memorial Hall of the Chinese People's Anti-Japanese War at Lu Gou Qiao, and the site of the Japanese Germ Warfare Unit 731 in Harbin.

Such a change in attitude could be seen as a response to the political circumstances at home and abroad. Internally, the Chinese government began to allow China's victimisation to be discussed more freely, and encouraged research. The public was urged to learn from the past, particularly from tragedies such as the Nanjing Massacre, and to be aware that 'backwardness invites aggression'. In a sense, national humiliation serves as a catalyst boosting nationalism. In his research paper, William Callahan (2004: 202) noted that self-understanding in China had shifted from communism to nationalism and that Chinese nationalism today is largely based on national insecurity. 'Chinese nationalism is not just about celebrating the glories of Chinese civilization; it also commemorates China's Century of National Humiliation. Humiliation has been an integral part of the construction of Chinese nationalism.' Heroism and victimisation are inseparable antipodes complementing a collective identity. David Lowenthal (1996: 59–74) observes that, while martyrdom unifies a nation, misery forges lasting bonds. Fogel contends that a negative instance links an ethnic group in victimhood and bonds them in a way that cannot be questioned (Fogel 2007). Remembrance of the Nanjing Massacre is parallel to the government's search for a unifying ideology in the post-reform era: patriotic nationalism helping to achieve the government's reform and 'opening up' agenda. With China opening to the world, the Communist Party's ideological dogma was for the first time challenged by the influx of liberalism, individualism and consumerism. The rise of a market economy saw the collapse of the established value system. The government was concerned with the loss of traditional morality, the swelling of egoism and ignorance of Chinese history among the young generation. A patriotic campaign was seen by the top leaders as a valid substitute for the unpopular Maoist practice of class struggle, and seemed more effective in uniting the nation.

Externally, re-opening memories of past atrocities like the Nanjing Massacre signalled China's security concerns, especially its fear of the revival of Japanese militarism, which was deepened by the textbook controversy to be discussed in the following section.

The construction of the Nanjing Massacre Memorial

The remembrance of the Nanjing Massacre in China can be seen as nurtured by a range of factors. Apart from the need for patriotism education, the textbook controversy contributed to embedding the massacre in public memory on a national level, as noted by historian Yoshida Takashi (2006: 113).

In 1972, the Sino-Japanese diplomatic relationship was normalised. China valued highly the new relationship, seeing it as a major diplomatic achievement. Over the following decades, 'close neighbours separated only by a strip of water [*yi yi dai shui de ling bang*]' became a catchphrase connoting not only the geographic but also cultural closeness between the two countries; friendship was the keynote dominating Chinese media reports about Japan. However, Hidenori Ijiri, an East Asia expert, has pointed out that decades after the re-establishment of diplomatic friendship, both China and Japan still feel sensitive regarding their past, bitter confrontations (Ijiri 1996). Memories of the Nanjing Massacre resurfaced after the textbook controversy in 1982, when the Japanese Ministry of Education tried to play down Japanese war conduct when screening school textbooks. The textbook controversy was by no means an isolated episode, as it occurred in the context of the right-wing faction in Japan calling for the revision of the history between 1931 and 1945. It was regarded by Ijiri as the most serious dispute in Sino-Japanese relations in the two decades following the re-establishment of diplomatic relations. The textbook controversy and the later Japanese revisionist claim that the Nanjing Massacre was a fabricated story were soon made known to the Chinese populace, provoking street demonstrations and other forms of public protest. Letters were written by survivors of the Nanjing Massacre, families of the victims, as well as university students and staff, to leaders at municipal, provincial and national levels, demanding the establishment of a memorial dedicated to the victims of the Nanjing Massacre. One of the protestors was quoted as saying in his letter to the Nanjing municipal government, that 'the blood drenched history of the Nanjing Massacre should be inscribed on the soil of Nanjing' (Zhu 2005).

The director of the Nanjing Massacre Memorial, on the Memorial's official website, contends that the construction of the Memorial was a response to the urges of both the public and the leadership (Zhu 2005). Indeed, the public voice exerted considerable influence on the building of a commemorative structure for the Nanjing Massacre, but the decision to build the Memorial was made at a much higher level. In 1982 when the textbook controversy was at its peak, Deng Xiaoping, China's supreme leader at the time, suggested that a monument should be erected to emphasise the fact of the Japanese invasion of China. In Deng's words, China 'should erect memorials to engrave the fact of Japanese invasion in response to attempts by Japanese politicians to cover up Japan's war crimes in China' (Zhu 2005).

The Nanjing Massacre left 13 major burial sites in Nanjing, but until the 1980s there was little commemoration in honour of the massacre victims and the burial sites were left unmarked and unattended. No purposeful excavation had been conducted, although some mass grave pits were opened up accidentally, and bone deposits and other remains of massacre victims were unearthed. Usually the bones and remains were reburied or relocated so that they would not be disturbed again. As time passed, the burial sites faded from public memory. Despite oral and written records, the locations of mass burial pits were hard to track down and many might have been lost.

The Nanjing Massacre Memorial is located at Jiangdongmen in the Western suburb of Nanjing. Records show that it is one of the 13 major massacre and mass burial sites. Jiangdongmen used to be a small town outside the city wall and a fairly remote place. To the east of the town was Jiangdong Creek, with some swamps alongside.[2] During the invasion campaign, a number of massive shell craters were created through Japanese air raids. In the northeast corner of the town was a military jail run by the Nationalist army. It was recorded that on 16 December 1937, large groups of captured Chinese soldiers and civilians, who had been temporarily detained in the jail, were taken out and executed in the open field between the town and the swamps. The bodies of the dead were left unattended for a month or so until they were collected and buried by the Red Swastika Society and other charities in early 1938. Some of the bodies were buried in the shell craters, which served as convenient grave pits (Zhu 2002).

For decades, Jiangdongmen remained a somewhat remote, underdeveloped suburb of Nanjing. With the expansion of the city of Nanjing, Jiangdongmen urbanised rapidly. Compared with other massacre sites, Jiangdongmen was close to the city proper and was the most accessible. As development pushed ahead, it became hard to locate the mass burial graves of the Massacre victims. When the decision was made to build the Memorial, intensive research was organised in order to locate the site. Specialists from the Nanjing Cultural Relics Administration conducted test excavations and a burial pit was soon opened up and bone deposits unearthed. It was confirmed that the conditions of the pit were in accordance with the burial records made in early 1938. The site having been located, a foundation stone for the Memorial Hall was laid on 13 December 1983, to commemorate the fall of Nanjing 46 years before. Construction began in 1984, designated as one of the key projects of the year. The mayor of Nanjing at the time took direct charge of the project and construction progressed quickly. On 15 August 1985, the 40th anniversary of Japanese surrender in World War II, the construction was complete and the site was opened to the public. In 1995, phase two of the project was completed, with more structures and exhibitions added to the original site. These included a cross-shaped sign pole inscribed with the date of the fall of Nanjing (Fig. 1.1), a group sculpture named 'catastrophe in an ancient city', a wall for mourning, an evidence exhibition, and a small cinema. Further additions were made to the site in 2002. These included a gigantic bell named 'Peace' and a pavement engraved with the footprints of some witnesses. In 2003, a bronze panel, mounted on a marble wall, was inscribed with a poem by Wang Jiuxin, entitled 'Wild Snow,' dedicated to victims of the Nanjing Massacre.

Figure 1.1 Sign pole at the entrance of the Memorial bearing the dates during which the Nanjing Massacre occurred. (Source: Qian, F.Q)

Since the opening of the Memorial, further archaeological discoveries have been made. In April 1998, another burial pit was discovered by the site staff. After confirmation that the skeletons belonged to the Massacre victims, the pit was protected and a new exhibition was built *in situ*.

In 1999, a submission by the Memorial's designer, Professor Qi Kang, was forwarded to the Chinese People's Political Consultative Conference, a national political advisory body, for the extension of the Memorial. Seven years later, in 2005, ground was broken for the extension project. Among new additions to the site will be a green open area named Peace Park to emphasise the theme of the memorial. This project attracted a total investment of 493 million Yuan (US$62 million) (Wu 2006a), and will enlarge the original site by three times to cover an area of 7.4 ha (Wu 2006b).

The Nanjing Massacre Memorial: interpretation of the massacre

W. Scott Howard (2003: 50–1) argues that landscapes of memorialisation, while embedded with the memories of the past, have more to do with the present and future than with the past. While enacting the work of mourning, they

> manifest an imaginary world where the tragic past may be transformed into the desired present and/or future…. Memorials, unlike monuments that strive toward historical closure, concern the ongoing struggles of the living who confront losses that have yet to reach points of resolution.

The Nanjing Massacre Memorial was built amidst disputes between China and Japan regarding historical issues. As shown previously, its construction enjoyed strong government endorsement and is regarded as an important vehicle communicating the government's position on these issues. Apparently this building was intended to counteract the right-wing voices in Japan, who claimed that the Nanjing Massacre was an illusion, by presenting and interpreting the atrocities committed by Japanese invaders in Nanjing.

The Chinese idiom, 'The past, if not forgotten, will guide the future [*Qian Shi Bu Wan, Hou Shi Zhi Shi*]', inscribed on marble panels at the Memorial, underlines the objective for constructing the site. The Memorial, like other structures of this kind, was built as a place where the public memory about past tragedy and humiliation is acknowledged and activated. It is meant to be a site where, in Howard's words, 'we may place our sorrow in order to return with renewed strength to the known, imperfect world' (Howard 2003: 47). A memorial of this type is not only concerned with the past, but also with the present and future, and related to vital issues confronting both the governments and the populace of the two countries involved. For these reasons, the interpretation of the Nanjing Massacre involves emotions and compassion and represents what is referred to as 'hot cognition' of the past event (Uzzell 1989: 33–4), rather than being 'cool' and detached.

The Memorial was declared one of 'China's top ten architectural works of the 1980s'. Professor Qi Kang, an eminent architect and architectural educator in China, had been commissioned to create the design. A Nanjing native himself, Qi was exposed to the terror of the war at the age of six. Writing about his design, Qi Kang (Qi 1997: 8) argued that it was, and had to be, infused with compassion:

> Designers often find themselves remote from the historical past. But a designer should put his feeling in his interpretation of the past event … In order to commemorate the tragic event of Nanjing Massacre and to educate

Figure 1.2 The number of people that China insists were killed during the Nanjing Massacre is engraved on the wall of the Memorial. (Source: Qian, F.Q)

future generations, we tried to create an atmosphere, ... and to present the historical truth with some kind of metaphor and analogy, also to enact the past with a manmade scene.

The architecture of the Memorial, according to Qi Kang, adopts a classical style. It features a landscape where life and death are placed in contrast, and projects the identities of the victim and the perpetrator. The exterior of the memorial hall, together with its settings and art work, utilises strong symbolism embodying pain and sufferings.

The Nanjing Massacre Memorial Hall comprises three sets of interpretations: architectural monuments and other artwork including sculptures and reliefs; the display of the bone deposits of the Nanjing Massacre victims coupled with the open burial pit discovered in 1998; and the exhibition of other objects as massacre evidence.

The verdict of 300,000 victims, reached by the Military Tribunal in Nanjing in March 1947 (Hu 2006: 389) and supported by the mainland Chinese scholarly community (Li and Sabella 2002: 35),[3] was inscribed on the stone wall facing visitors soon after they enter the Memorial, together with the word 'victims' in Chinese, Japanese and English (Fig. 1.2). The figure was further highlighted after the 1995 renovation with the addition of a sculpture to the site, whose abstract shape spells out the number 300,000. The inscription of the victim number, according to the designer, was inspired by the top authority of the Nanjing municipal government of the time, who initially suggested that the 300,000 figure be painted over the site in red to symbolise the bloodshed (Liu 2006).

Figure 1.3 Promotional poster impression of the New Memorial Hall interior after the renovation in 2007. (Source: Qian, F.Q)

Special building materials and colour tone were utilised to symbolise the tragic loss of lives during the Massacre. Around the entrance to the exhibition 13 small rocks are purposefully placed, each representing one of the 13 burial sites across Nanjing. At the exhibition hall, a stairway leads to a gravel-covered open field referred to as 'Graveyard Square', which is scattered with a few dead trees. This carefully elaborated landscape has various connotations. According to the architect and the management of the memorial, the gravel-covered square represents barrenness and death, but also symbolises the sandy ground of the actual massacre and burial site at Jiangdongmen. Since the 1995 renovation, more art work has been added to the Memorial. This includes three groups of reliefs depicting scenes of atrocity and mourning. To the left, inside the gate, are marble panels engraved with the names of some of the victims that have been retrieved (obviously a full victim list will never be possible). In 2002, before the 65th anniversary of the fall of Nanjing, a new pavement was laid, which comprised 222 bronze panels engraved with footprints collected from surviving witnesses of the Massacre, each footprint being accompanied with the signature of the survivor.

On one side of 'Graveyard Square' is a small exhibition hall, whose eerie exterior resembles a coffin of Chinese style, which again reminds visitors of death. Scent sticks contributed by visitors burn at the entrance, a Chinese ritual in tribute to the deceased. Inside the hall is the exhibition of victims' bone deposits that were unearthed on the site. Interviews with Nanjing residents, conducted in October 2006, suggest that this exhibition, together with the open mass grave pit at its side, is regarded by visitors as the most striking scene of the Memorial. Replacing the abstract symbolism of the architecture and art work, here a real place and objects allow the visitors' gaze to lock onto the scene of death.

The main exhibition hall houses objects and artefacts presenting visitors further details of the massacre. This exhibition, called 'Exhibition of Historical Evidence', is arranged under various themes, including atrocities by Japanese troops, the international aid, the Japanese surrender and the trials of war criminals, as well as confessions by former Japanese soldiers. Photos are displayed showing scenes of killing, torture and sex assaults, many of which are gruesome and disturbing. They are accompanied by objects such as a gasoline tank, nails and bayonets used by the Japanese soldiers in the massacre. Under the heading of 'The past, if not forgotten, will guide the future', books, articles and news reports are displayed as evidence of the atrocities.

Confessions by former Japanese soldiers and items expressing regret from Japanese visitors are highly appreciated in China. In the exhibition hall, written confessions and apologies by former Japanese soldiers and visitors are carefully placed for easy viewing. Flowers and artefacts presented by Japanese visitors are displayed at conspicuous spots. Behind the mass grave pit is a stone tablet engraved 'Atonement', presented to the Memorial by an aged Japanese visitor whose identity remains anonymous.

To Nanjing citizens, the best-known Japanese war veteran is probably Shirō Azuma, known as the 'conscience of Japan' (Wu 2007). Azuma served in the Japanese Imperial Army in 1937. In 1987 he published his wartime diary to make public the atrocities committed by Japanese troops in China. He was sued for libel in 1993, and ultimately lost the case. In February 1999, two months after he lost the lawsuit, a special exhibition was launched at the Memorial to show support. Azuma's diary was displayed, together with documents and archives and witness statements related to its publication and the lawsuit. The curator of the Memorial recalled that:

> The special exhibition was attended by Shirō Azuma himself, researchers and officials from both provincial and municipal governments. Visitors contributed their signatures on a banner that read 'Shirō Azuma , you have the support from people of Nanjing'.
>
> (Zhu 2007)

David Lowenthal (1996: 75) contends that atrocities are invoked not only to forge internal unity but also to enlist external sympathy. Given both the internal and external factors that provide the context in which the Memorial was established, it can be argued that it was built on the one hand to urge the nation to learn from history, and on the other to urge Japan to face up to its war conduct so that the tragedy will not be repeated, and to gain moral support from the international community for this stance. However the interpretation of the Memorial is not free from controversy and remains problematic.

Since the 1980s, research on the Nanjing Massacre has flourished. The government's 'opening up' policy, together with rapidly increasing globalisation, has led to a changed research environment in which major historical issues are being revisited and new findings achieved. In 2005, Sun Zhaiwei published his current research into the Nanjing Massacre. Compared with the conventional position held in past publications of this kind, which attributed the massacre entirely to the brutality of the Japanese troops, Sun's research encompasses a broader scope, investigating a set of complex factors that contributed jointly to the tragedy. These factors included the morality, the logistic faults, the military tradition and the psychology of the Japanese troops on the one hand, and poor coordination among the Chinese defending troops, failure to withdraw the remaining Chinese troops from Nanjing, and the consequent mixing of combatants with civilians on the other. Regarding the number of victims, Sun affirms the 300,000 figure, arguing that the actual number could be even higher if killings in the area of Greater Nanjing were taken into account. Nevertheless, Sun (2005: 274–6) agrees that inconsistency and duplication did exist in the statistics 70 years ago, and that there remains room for further investigation and revision in this matter.

Academic research on the Nanjing Massacre is becoming more rational and independent, with historians agreeing that the focus of the interpretation of the massacre should be on 'making sense of history' (interview with Director of the Research Centre for Nanjing Massacre, Nanjing Normal University, October 2006). In other words, their research is going beyond the question of 'what happened during the massacre?' to enquire 'why did the massacre happen?' However, the Memorial's interpretation of the massacre does not necessarily reflect this shift of research focus, as it remains very much centred on the question of 'what happened during the massacre'. The multi-dimensional enquiry advocated by historians seems missing in the interpretation of the massacre by the Memorial. Striking images are being impacted on the audience at the site. Massacre and torture are presented through item displays and photographs (some obviously too gruesome for a young audience). The poem 'Wild Wind', inscribed on the wall of the site, is very realistic in its depiction of atrocities, including even cannibalism by the Japanese soldiers. It remains emotion-fuelled and is therefore, as noted by Daqing Yang (2000), emotion-stirring. Inspecting the role of public emotion in Sino-Japanese relations, Wan Ming (2006: 156) notices the process of the development of national emotion and is concerned that due to the socialisation of emotions, the current generation of young people in China appears to have become even more emotional about Japan than the previous generation.

The interpretation of the Memorial, together with that of other war museums in China, has caused new international disputes. News reports claim that the conservative Japanese lawmakers launched a campaign in June 2007 urging China to remove photographs and exhibits from museums that they say distort the truth about Japan's war record, claiming that some exhibits and photographs at Chinese war museums are fake. China reacted promptly to this accusation, denying that photographs exhibited at Chinese war memorials have an anti-Japanese bias. On 14 June 2007, *China Daily* reported that at a regular news conference, a

Chinese Foreign Ministry spokesman contended that the displays reflect what really happened and that Japanese critics should face up to historical facts.

In 2006, the mass burial sites left by the Nanjing Massacre were listed as national heritage by the Chinese government. Since 1996 comments and submissions have been made suggesting the site should bid for the World Heritage listing. These comments and submissions are based on the argument that the atrocity is comparable to the Holocaust and the Hiroshima bombing in terms of the scale of casualty, and that the site in Nanjing deserves a World Heritage status, given that the Genbaku Dome of Hiroshima and Auschwitz-Birkenau Memorial have both been inscribed as World Heritage sites. The extension of the Memorial site is therefore speculated by the media as a step towards that end.[4]

Conclusion

In their 1996 book on 'dissonant heritage', Tunbridge and Ashworth noted the experience of atrocity in the building of a group identity. They observed (p. 107) that a political identity, underpinned by a victim-group identity built around an atrocity such as the Holocaust, could be a powerful means to obtain foreign support, to achieve internal coherence, and prevent a recurrence. The phrase engraved on the wall of the Memorial reflects the Chinese stand on the memories of the past atrocity, 'the past, if not forgotten, will guide the future'. By safe-guarding memories of the massacre, the Memorial is intended to achieve a number of officially set goals. The first goal is to reach a determination in the nation for self-strengthening. The slogan 'Backwardness invites aggression' is being rein-forced through the interpretation and communicated to the public. This helps to achieve a national coherence and to further legitimate the government's 'opening up' agenda. The second goal in commemorating this massacre (as well as other atrocities) aims to reinforce the 'never again' promise from Japan. Thirty years after the Sino-Japanese Communiqué, China still fears a revival of Japanese militarism and remains sceptical about Japan's sincerity about peace. Likewise, Japan remains afraid of the escalation of national emotions against Japan among the Chinese populace. The third goal aims to internationalise the Memorial and memories of the massacre. The proposal for the World Heritage bid, whether it is to be put into action or not, reflects the intention to further internationalise the Nanjing Massacre and its memories, as well as competing for the status of one of the major tragedies in World War II, alongside the Holocaust and atomic bombing.

Joshua Fogel (2007: 273–4) believes that today's younger generation in China choose to focus on China's victimisation at the hands of foreigners. He refers to this generation as the 'Fourth Generation', whose members somehow face a crisis of identity. They 'have championed China's status as a victim', Fogel concludes, 'in order to compensate for the very insecurity produced by their lack of anything substantive on which to build an identity'. This is probably true. It is noteworthy, however, that China's past victimisation is often utilised by the government to project the country's present status as a rising power. In this sense, the new-found national pride is bolstered by thoughts that the Nanjing Massacre is being inter-nationalised. It is also arguable that the demand for Japan to face up its wartime behaviour and to make a 'never-again' promise, apart from anything, reflects China's confidence that it is equal to any nation in the world.

Distrust and fear between China and Japan have been addressed by Chinese and international researchers whose work aims to identify historical responsibilities, and to establish a framework within which a common, trans-national understanding about the shared past can be achieved (Sun 2005, Yang 1999). In China, research on the Nanjing Massacre is now moving beyond the tragedy into a multi-dimen-sional enquiry in order to make sense of history. By comparison, the interpretation at the Nanjing Massacre site remains somewhat single-minded, functioning mainly as a vehicle to communicate public emotion and government positions.

The Nanjing Massacre Memorial has the highest profile of its kind in China, and has so far successfully won large government funding. However it has to be noted that not all the sites of this kind are properly protected. In fact, simulta-neous with the extension of the Nanjing Massacre Memorial is the erection of commercial high rise buildings adjacent to the site, and their impact on the site and its environs is self-evident. While 13 December becomes a public commem-oration day in Nanjing, and commemorative ceremonies are being held each year, both public and official attitudes and approaches towards this heritage of pain and shame are still in a process of change.

Notes

1 This figure was cited in the indictment against Lieutenant General Tani Hisao by the Nanjing Military Tribunal, 10 March 1947.
2 The creek no longer exists. It was filled up in the 1990s.
3 For example, leading researcher Sun Zhaiwei, Jiangsu Academy of Social Science and Vice President for the Nanjing Massacre (see Sun 2005: 177–265).
4 See for example, the Shanghai daily newspapers *Jie Fang Ri Bao (Jiefang Daily)*, 11 March 2004 and *Wen Hui Bao* (*Wenhui Daily*), 11 March 2004.

References

Askew, D. (2002) 'The Nanjing Incident: Recent research and trends', *Publishing on the Internet, Electronic Journal of Contemporary Japanese Studies*. Available online at: http://www.japanesestudies.org.uk/articles/Askew.html (accessed 14 May 2007).

Barrett, D.P. (2003) 'Nanking: Anatomy of an Atrocity (Book Review)', *Canadian Journal of History*, 38:1, 169–70.

Callahan, W.A. (2004) 'National Insecurities: humiliation, salvation and Chinese nationalism', *Alternatives: Global, Local, Political*, 29:2, 199–219.

Chinese State Administration for Cultural Heritage official website. Available online at: http://www.sach.gov.cn (accessed 25 May 2007).

Eykholt, M. (2000) 'Aggression, Victimization, and Chinese Historiography of the Nanjing Massacre', in Fogel, J.A. (ed.) *The Nanjing Massacre in History and Historiography*, Berkeley, CA: University of California Press, pp. 11–68.

Fogel, J.A. (2000) 'Introduction', in J.A. Fogel (ed.), *The Nanjing Massacre in History and Historiography*, Berkeley, CA: University of California Press, pp. 1–10.

Fogel, J.A. (2007) 'The Nanking Atrocity and Chinese Historical Memory', in B.T. Wakahayashi (ed.) *The Nanking Atrocity 1937–38: Complicating the Picture*, New York: Berghahn Books, pp. 267–83.

Goodman, G. S. and Paz-Alonso, P.M. (2006) 'Trauma and Memory: Normal versus Special Memory Mechanisms', in B. Uttl *et al.* (eds) *Memory and Emotion: Interdisciplinary Perspectives*, Malden, UK: Blackwell Publishing, pp. 233–58.

Hata, I. (1998) 'The Nanjing Atrocities: Fact and Fable', *Japan Echo*, 25:4, 47–57.

Howard, W.S. (2003) 'Landscapes of memorialisation', in I. Robertson and P. Richards (eds), *Studying Cultural Landscapes*, London: Hodder Arnold, 47–70.

Hu, J.R. (ed.) (2006) *Nanjing Sheng Pan [Judgment at Nanjing]*, Nanjing: Jiangsu Renmin Chu Ban She.

Ijiri, H. (1996) 'Sino-Japanese Controversy since the 1972 Diplomatic Normalization', in C. Howe (ed.), *China and Japan: History, Trends and Prospects*, Oxford: Oxford University Press, 60–82.

Jiangsu Province Administration for Cultural Heritage. Available online at: http://www.jscnt.gov.cn/pub/jscnt/jscnt_wwbl/ (accessed 25 May 2007).

Lowenthal, D. (1996) *Possessed by the Past: The Heritage Crusade and the Spoils of History*, New York: The Free Press.

Li, F. and Sabella, R. *et al.* (eds) (2002) *Nanking 1937: Memory and Healing*, New York; London: M.E. Sharpe, Inc.

Liu, W. (2006) 'Ping Min Jian Zhu Shi Qi Kang' [Qi Kang: A People's Architect], *Ren Wu*, 2006:3, 51–7.

Nanjing Massacre Memorial official website: www.nj1937.org (accessed 25 May 2007).

Qi, K. (1997) *The Process of Architecture Design – Selected Works of Qi Kang 1980–1997*, Beijing: Zhong Guo Jian Zhu Chu Ban She.

Rigby, A. (2001) *Justice and Reconciliation: After the Violence*, Boulder; CO: Lynne Rienner Publishers.

Rose, C. (2005) *Sino-Japanese Relations: Facing the Past, Looking to the Future?*, New York: RoutledgeCurzon.

Sun, Z. (2005) *Cheng Qing Li Shi: Nanjing Da Tu Sha Yan Jiu Yu Si Kao [Clarifying Historical Facts: the Study and the Reflection on the Nanjing Massacre]*, Nanjing: Jiangsu Ren Min Chu Ban She.

Tunbridge, J.E. and Ashworth, J.G. (1996) *Dissonant Heritage*, Chichester; New York: J.Wiley.

Uttl, B. *et al.* (2006) 'Memory and Emotion from Interdisciplinary Perspectives', in B. Uttl *et al.* (eds), *Memory and Emotion: Interdisciplinary Perspectives*, Malden: Blackwell Publishing, 1–12.

Uzzell, D.L. (1989) 'Interpretation of War and Conflict', in D. L. Uzzell (ed.), *Heritage Interpretation: The Natural and Built Environment*, London: Belhaven Press, 33–47.

Wakabayashi, B.T. (2007) 'The Messiness of Historical Reality', in B.T. Wakabayashi (ed.), *The Nanking Atrocity 1937–38: Complicating the Picture* New York: Berghahn Press, 3–25.

Wan, M. (2006) *Sino-Japanese Relations: Interaction, Logic and Transformation*, Washington D.C.: Woodrow Wilson Center Press.

Wu, J. (2006a) 'Nanjing plans to improve environment for memorial', *China Daily*, 27 February 2006, 3.

Wu, J. (2006b) 'Renovation Details of Memorial Hall Revealed', *China Daily*, 27 September 2006, 3.

Wu, J. (2007) 'Nanjing Pays Tribute to "Conscience of Japan"', *China Daily*, 6 January 2006, 3.

Yamamoto, M. (2000) *Nanking: Anatomy of an Atrocity*, Westport, Connecticut, and London: Praeger.

Yang, D. (1999) 'Convergence or Divergence? Recent writing on the rape of Nanjing', *The American Historical Review*, 104:3, 842–65.

Yang, D. (2000) 'The Challenges of the Nanjing Massacre: Reflections on Historical Enquiry', in J.A. Fogel (ed.), *The Nanjing Massacre in History and Historiography*, Berkeley, CA: University of California Press, pp. 133–180.

Yoshida, T. (2000) 'A Battle over History', in Yang, D. (2000), 'The Challenges of the Nanjing Massacre: Reflections on Historical Enquiry', in J.A. Fogel (ed.), *The Nanjing Massacre in History and Historiography*, Berkeley, CA: University of California Press, pp. 133–180.

Yoshida, T. (2006) *The Making of the 'Rape of Nanking': History and Memory in Japan, China and the United States*, New York: Oxford University Press.

Zhu, C. (2002) *Qin Hua Ri Jun Nanjing Da Tu Sha Jiangdongmen Wan Ren Ken Yi Zhi de Fa Jue Yu Kao Zhen* [*The Excavation and the Research Inspection of the Mass Grave Pits at Jiangdongmen during the Nanjing Massacre by the Japanese Troops Invading China*], Nanjing: Jiangsu Gu Ji Chu Ban She.

Zhu, C. (2005) 'Nanjing You Zuo Weiren Deng Xiaoping Chang Dao Jian Li de Jinianguan (A Memorial Hall in Nanjing Initiated by the Great Man Deng Xiaoping)', *Publishing on the Internet*, Official website of Nanjing Massacre Memorial. Available online at: http://www.nj1937.org (accessed 29 May 2007).

Zhu, C. (2007) 'Wo Yu Dong Shi Lang Jiao Wang Shi San Nian' [A Thirteen-year Acquaintance with Shiro Azuma], *Publishing on the Internet*, Zhong Guo Hua Qiao Chu Ban She. Available online at: http://book.sina.com.an/nzt/history/his/woyudoshilangfiao/index.shtml (accessed 20 June 2007).

Chapter 2

The Hiroshima 'Peace Memorial'
Transforming legacy, memories and landscapes

Yushi Utaka

Hiroshima: a legacy of recovery

The recent publication *Wounded Cities: Destruction and Reconstruction in a Globalized World* edited by Jane Schneider and Ida Susser (2003) considered the nature of 'wounded cities' around the globe. Its case study chapters show us how our cities have been hurt both physically and socially by terrorism, conflict and war, political disorder, crime and drugs, uncontrollable expansion, and environmental pollution. Examining the situation closely, the degree of woundedness is not identical or controllable and it sometimes seems to bode the death of a city. In the aftermath of the September 11 onslaught on the United States of America and the subsequent spread of terrorism, we were informed that we are now living our everyday life in fear of violence or death that can be neither accurately described nor predicted. Rich or poor, male or female, strong or weak, there are no exceptions: all are equal in the grave.

However, despite the fact that our bodies experience physical death, our memories and wisdom continue to be handed down to our successors. People's difficult memories recall their pain or shame and offer us the challenge of learning new lessons in order to develop new wisdom and conquer ill fortune. In this sense, it could be argued that two cities in Japan – Hiroshima and Nagasaki – represent among the most powerful lessons of the 'deaths of a city'.

Hiroshima: recovery from death

Hiroshima expanded as a castle town during the Edo period and experienced further growth as a modern industrial city as well as a centre of military logistics thereafter. On 6 August 1945, Hiroshima experienced the world's first and worst atomic catastrophe, caused by the atom bomb attack by United States armed forces. In addition to causing, in an instant, thousands of deaths and the total destruction of the city's rich urban fabric, many people suffered serious atomic radiation effects. Some continue to be hospitalised even today.

Immediately after the catastrophe, it was said that, 'for at least 70 years, no grass and tree would grow' (*The Mainichi Newspapers*, 23 August 1945). However, this

Figure 2.1 Visitors at the Dome on a cloudy morning. (Source: Y. Utaka)

was not true. Notwithstanding the tragedy above, nowadays in Hiroshima beautiful flowers bloom profusely, gentle breezes ripple the surface of the rivers, and people enjoy their lives in the downtown area in exactly the same place where the tragedy of the thousands of deaths took place just over 60 years ago. Sometimes the tragedy represented by the A-Bomb Dome fades entirely from people's imaginations.

Indeed, today Hiroshima is a lively and growing city, declared an 'International City of Peace and Culture' expressing the idea of global peace through Hiroshima's experience of pain and the difficult memories of wars that are handed down to coming generations. Hiroshima's places of destruction are functioning as challenges for the future and are creating new hope for recovery within the phenomena of the age of 'wounded cities'. In other words, if we are able to truly learn from the experiences of the catastrophe that befell Hiroshima, it should be almost impossible to fall into another tragedy of such enormous scale: there would be '*No more Hiroshimas*'[1].

Transforming the legacy of Hiroshima: place and memories

In Japanese, Hiroshima is written in several different ways, using different characters, although always said with the same pronunciation. Generally, the old form characters recall the imperialistic, pre-war, military legacy of the city; the new form characters are associated with a democratised and mediocre city among other post-war cities in Japan; while the katakana characters emphasise the city of peace and anti-nuclear movements (Yoneyama 1999: 82–3).

Pre-war expansion and targeted city

After the start of the Meiji Period, Japanese society aggressively implemented modern development policies, a response that represents the beginning of the headlong fall into Japanese imperialistic expansionism in the Asia-Pacific region. Under these socio-political circumstances, the Sino-Japanese War (1894–95) was the first case of modern Japanese international war, and Hiroshima expanded as one of the most important strategic military cities. In fact, as a provisional military headquarters many key institutions were allocated to Hiroshima, such as the Hiroshima Imperial Headquarters. In the neighbouring Kure City, Japan's largest naval docks launched a number of vessels and battleships during the wars, including the largest battleship ever built, *Yamato*. A large number of soldiers were deployed from Hiroshima's Ujina Port to the battlefield; the city thus represented a departure from this world for many of them.

The Hiroshima Prefectural Industrial Promotion Hall was the official name of the building that stood on the site of the A-Bomb Dome (*Genbaku Dome* in Japanese) prior to the bombing. This five-storey building with a 25m-high dome is located on the riverbank of the Motoyasu River; it was designed by the Czechoslovakian architect Jan Letzel (1880–1925) and its construction was completed in 1915. After the official opening, it functioned as an attractive venue, not only for industry-related, but also arts and educational exhibitions that effectively contributed to provincial socio-cultural development. At the same time, Hiroshima also became a provincial centre of education and cultural institutions.

The hall was located in Hiroshima's largest business and commercial district along the busy Old Saigoku Highway. The unique T-shaped Aioi Bridge was located on the northern bank of this area; unfortunately, the Allied Forces had identified Hiroshima as a military city and this bridge was selected as the target for the dropping of the atomic bomb. On 6 August 1945, at 8:16am, the city was completely destroyed by the detonation of the atomic bomb 'Little Boy', and 140,000 people are believed to have died. Almost all of the houses were completely destroyed within a two-kilometre radius from the hypocentre. The district known as Nakajima Town was directly beneath the hypocentre and almost entirely vanished except for a few stronger structures, including the structures of Hiroshima Prefectural Industrial Promotion Hall – the A-Bomb Dome.

Enhancing democratic features – post-war-reconstruction

Immediately after the bomb fell, many rescue teams were assembled and deployed, but nevertheless a high level of residual radiation was indicated within the city and radioactive rain soon fell. The Hiroshima City Government instigated a City Reconstruction Bureau in 1946. Despite desperate efforts towards urban and social reconstruction, it is recorded that people struggled with serious disorder and delays caused by a lack of finance and manpower. In 1949, the Hiroshima Peace Memorial City Construction Law was implemented and the city was re-designed according to modernist planning approaches. Under this legislation, a reconstruction plan was implemented, designing a new urban infrastructure and with a financial proposal not only to facilitate restoration to the city's pre-war state, but also to realise the legacy of a democratic reborn Hiroshima and Japanese nation.

Immediately after the introduction of the new reconstruction legislation, the Hiroshima city government organised a design competition – The Peace Park and Exhibition Hall Design Competition – for newly proposed urban facilities above the destroyed Nakajima Town. The modernist architects Kenzo Tange[2] and his associates won the first prize in that design competition. In his design Tange proposed a strong visual axis through the park focusing on the A-Bomb Dome and including the 'Monument of Peace', which he designed with *piloti* and massive reinforced concrete building blocks that exactly mirrored the work of his modernist contemporaries.

Tange's approach in this competition also shows us clearly his thinking with regard to the new era of democratic Japanese society. He described his concept of design as follows:

> Peace is not naturally obtained easily for us from nature and gods. We need to fight and acquire our peace strongly and practically.... To realize this understanding of peace, first of all, we are going to develop and construct this museum as a factory of peace.
>
> (Tange 1949)

But despite the fact that his works were widely accepted as great advances in architectural development, various objections were raised from the intelligentsia internationally. Tange's works were sometimes said to reflect his opportunistic attitudes towards the imperialists during the war and his quick conversion into a democratic modernist after the war. The critic Shouichi Inoue (2006: 304–6) traces how Tange was inspired to create his winning design proposal for the Peace Memorial. Inoue points out that Tange had been greatly influenced by Le Corbusier's 1932 Palace of Soviets design proposal. He had also maintained the design approach previously developed in 1942 for the Memorial Statue of the Greater East Asia Co-Prosperity Sphere design competition organised by the Architectural Institute of Japan under the nationalistic sponsorship of Japanese construction industries.

Notwithstanding this, Inoue acknowledges that the A-Bomb Dome was saved from demolition by the contribution of Tange's Peace Park design that provides a visual focus on the A-Bomb Dome. This was an important achievement since, in the early stages of the reconstruction in Hiroshima, the majority of public opinion indicated that the A-Bomb Dome gave people flashbacks of negative memories and pain and there was some support for the idea of demolition and re-development of the site. Tange succeeded therefore in encouraging the preservation of the A-Bomb Dome (Fujimori 1998) even though this land had not been officially registered for many years.

The period after the war was one of drastic socio-political change following the introduction of the democratic constitution and social modernisation by the Supreme Commander of the Allied Powers. Japanese society had just returned to a normal frame of mind from the wartime imperialistic fervour. Japanese architects and planners including Tange were groping in the dark to establish their design methodology and applied their espoused modernism to represent the newborn Japan. Additionally, there was no doubt that Hiroshima's urban reconstruction process focused on its physical appearance with respect paid to the landscape of the A-bomb Dome and people's memories. Diverse experiences and views about Hiroshima are now unified in Kenzo Tange's axis that connects the A-Bomb Dome, Peace Park and Hiroshima's new urban fabric. In 1966 the Hiroshima City Government officially declared its intention to preserve the A-Bomb Dome and a public fundraising campaign was begun. In 1967, the preservation project committee carried out the first phase of a series of preservation projects that included structural reinforcement of the Dome and chemical treatment of the cracked building surfaces (Hiroshima City 1997: 102).

While architects and planners were developing their own theories about how to realise the city as a symbol of peace, Hiroshima was also beginning to play the role of an incubator of narratives of peace. A number of peace movement groups were established and the experience of Hiroshima became a driving force for creative expression among a wide field of artists – in music, movies, literature and animation. Be they requiems or literary rage, many of the new expressions gave personal impressions about the experience of Hiroshima. Kenzaburo Oe is one such artist: awarded the Nobel Prize for Literature in 1994, he continually discusses the meanings of Hiroshima (see, for example, Oe 1965).

However, with political turbulence among peace activists, these groups underwent a constant alignment and realignment because of their different observations about the Hiroshima experience and their political backgrounds. Additionally, appeals from Hiroshima to the global community have been sometimes questioned: can Hiroshima be allowed to stand alone as a place of victims or should it be recognised as also an assailant – a military city from which Japan invaded neighbouring countries during the war.[3] As Yoneyama (1999: 22–3) notes, the Memorial Cenotaph in Hiroshima, located at the centre of Tange's visual axis in the Peace Memorial Park, carrying the famous epitaph –'Repose ye in Peace, for the error shall not be repeated', was always questioned about its exact meaning: who should be called to reflect on the past?

From time to time, Hiroshima has been described as contrasting with the city of Nagasaki which was struck by another atomic bomb on 9 August 1945. The cities are sometimes described as 'Hiroshima is angry and Nagasaki prays'; it is believed that they have different socio-cultural backgrounds. In fact, within its predominantly Buddhist or Shinto environment Nagasaki's society has been much influenced by Christianity.

Symbolising global peace – the 'world' heritage

After the completion of the Peace Park, the A-Bomb Dome itself was not officially registered – it was called just a 'no-number land lot'. The ruin still has a high risk of collapse because of its burned structure and its instability in this earthquake-prone country. An initial appeal for the A-Bomb Dome's preservation was made as early as 1947 when the city was suffering hunger and disorder. It is said that the authorities and ordinary people recognised the significance of the A-Bomb Dome but they had a huge number of urgent matters to attend to for the essentials of people's lives and safety at the time. In fact, Japanese society maintained a strong desire to see 'an end to the post-war period' which was officially stated in 1956 when Japan began to experience high economic growth, epitomised by the holding of the Tokyo Olympic Games. Additionally, during the post-war period, Japanese society was in political disorder and was governed according to the detailed instructions of the United States and her allies in a context of the strengthening Cold War. Thus, official recognition of the phenomenon of 'Hiroshima' had to be done carefully until the restoration of diplomatic relations between the previously belligerent countries.

Immediately after the Japanese government accepted the Convention Concerning the Protection of World Cultural and Natural Heritage in 1992, the Hiroshima Municipal Assembly adopted a proposal for the A-Bomb Dome to be submitted as a candidate for World Heritage nomination. Subsequently, citizen's groups added their support to the proposal and it was eventually adopted by the National Congress of 1994. A year later, the Japanese government designated the A-Bomb Dome on the National Historic Sites under the Law for the Protection of Cultural Properties and in 1996 the Hiroshima Peace Memorial (Genbaku Dome) was listed as a UNESCO World Heritage site.

During the nomination process of the Hiroshima Peace Memorial, the assigned advisory body, ICOMOS, outlined the significance of the place as follows:

> Firstly, the Hiroshima Peace Memorial, Genbaku Dome, stands as a permanent witness to the terrible disaster that occurred when the atomic bomb was used as a weapon for the first time in the history of mankind.
>
> Secondly, the Dome itself is the only building in existence that can convey directly a physical image of the tragic situation immediately after the bombing.
>
> Thirdly, the Dome has become a universal monument for all mankind, symbolizing the hope for perpetual peace and the ultimate elimination of all nuclear weapons on earth.
>
> (ICOMOS 1995: 115)

Following this official evaluation by ICOMOS, the Hiroshima Peace Memorial was eventually inscribed on the World Heritage List under Criteria (vi) at the 20th World Heritage Committee meeting.[4] At the meeting, both the People's Republic of China and the United States of America stated their objections to Hiroshima's listing. Hiroshima itself not only figures in domestic conservation debates, but also, now a city of 'world' heritage, Hiroshima invites wider foreign perspectives that require political correctness and diplomacy with multiple state parties.

World heritage 'buffer zone': enhancing the legacy of Hiroshima

The A-Bomb Dome is located in the middle of high-rise buildings and a busy commercial district that is much the same as ordinary downtown areas in many Japanese cities. The 'core zone' of the World Heritage site is 0.4 hectares. The stated 'buffer zone' includes the Peace Memorial Park compound, the water surface of the nearby rivers and the built-up areas along the riverbanks. Since 1983 Hiroshima city has designated under municipal urban planning legislation two different landscape-control guidelines for the area surrounding the park. The design guidelines cover details of building design, including colour, materials, signboards, etc. All stakeholders within the designated area are required to inform the planning department in order to obtain development permission for proposed construction work or alternations that will affect the cityscape. However, these design guidelines are not backed by official orders and enforcement; they are only effective in that they offer limited advice to the stakeholders. Nevertheless, not a small number of these stakeholders readily accept these design guidelines. For example, a building standing beside the riverbank changed its rooftop signboard to a smaller version with a moderate colour. Such stakeholder choices reveal a stricter sense of design guidelines than those promulgated by the current municipal authorities. In particular, owners of commercial buildings are relatively sensitive to the visual impression experienced by park visitors; generally, visitors expect to spend a quiet time in the park. Even if unsuitable development is proposed, the municipal planning department can only provide advice without enforcement. However, under the highly secured Japanese licence-based administrative culture, the local authorities still hold many cards that indirectly change stakeholders' mindsets.

The author continues to hear comments that reveal how the public in general accept Hiroshima's cityscape and urban development. For example, on an extremely hot day, the author was chatting with an elderly gentleman who works as a gate controller of private car parking lots in the city centre when suddenly he looked around at the buildings surrounding his parking lots and muttered:

> See, there are a lot of new shiny buildings surrounding the Genbaku Dome – A-bomb Dome. We, the people of Hiroshima have worked hard. The day August 6, the entire town was gone. We started from almost nothing to build everything you can see now. It was a long struggle.

Despite the uncountable difficulties of rebuilding the city and recovering from physical and psychological pain, surprisingly the old man's observation seems to be silently shared by many Hiroshima locals. They accept that the lively growing city is evidence of their efforts for recovery and from time to time observe the A-Bomb Dome as a contrast to this.

On the other hand, sharp criticisms have been raised continually about the surrounding landscape, especially the buildings standing around the park. For example, a young urban planning expert from another city views all of these buildings as obstacles to the plea for peace: 'We should demolish several buildings that are located near the A-Bomb Dome. All of them are obstacles to pleas for peace.' Recent landscape debates triggered by a residential flats development near the A-Bomb Dome clearly reveal the issues (*The Chugoku Shismbun*, 23 March 2006). When the municipality approved a development plan for a 14-storey, 44m-high private housing project, many interest groups criticised the decision arguing that the flat development will be unsightly and an obstacle to the plea for peace. Immediately after this criticism was raised, the municipal government announced a revision of planning guidelines that establishes new height controls.

Following the introduction of new height controls, the local authority has not received strong objections from stakeholders, despite the fact that the issues have been discussed in the respective media nationwide and have been talked about a lot by experts. Nevertheless, following the announcement of new municipal height controls, the issue spread to a re-think of the whole surrounding environment, as epitomised by the following recommendation sent in a letter from ICOMOS Japan to the Prime Minister of Japan and local authorities:

> 2. To see the planned demolition of the Shōkōkaigisho building as a recognition that obstruction of the view and spatial integrity of a World Heritage Site is a diminution or dilution of its cultural value and to ensure that any future use of this area will strengthen the outstanding universal values of the World Heritage Site.[5]

In this recommendation letter, the Shōkōkaigisho building – the Hiroshima Chamber of Commerce and Industry Building – is singled out. Undoubtedly, this building stands near Tange's focal axis and almost overlaps visually with the A-Bomb Dome, viewed from the park compound that is always targeted in landscape debate in Hiroshima.

On the other hand, this modernist-designed, award-winning building has served Hiroshima's regional development since 1965 when Hiroshima was on the path towards urban reconstruction.[6] Functionally, the building has always been occupied by leading companies and institutions that were invited and supported by Hiroshima's local society, including, since 2003, the Hiroshima Office of the United Nations Institute for Training and Research. From the view of the windows of this building, the A-Bomb Dome and Peace Memorials are clearly visible. There is no doubt that the vista from this building indirectly contributes towards many kinds of important discussions and decisions taken among social leaders in Hiroshima, those people who contributed to post-war Hiroshima's economic and industrial reconstruction and development. Recently, the Hiroshima Chamber of Commerce

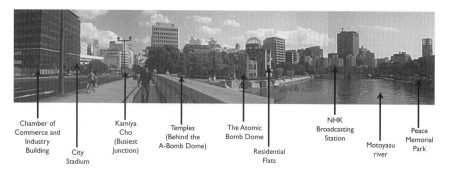

| Chamber of Commerce and Industry Building | | Kamiya Cho (Busiest Junction) | Temples (Behind the A-Bomb Dome) | The Atomic Bomb Dome | | NHK Broadcasting Station | | Peace Memorial Park |

Figure 2.2 Surroundings of the A-Bomb Dome and Park, from the targeted T-shaped 'Motoyasu Bridge'. (Source: Y. Utaka)

and Industry announced their own Hiroshima urban revitalisation plan that targets specific means of implementing reconstruction, including the building itself which was diagnosed as lacking sufficient earthquake resistance, following a recent revision of legal building standards (*The Chugoku Shismbun*, 14 January 2006).

The Park has been surrounded by prime institutions within the buffer zone that essentially served the people of Hiroshima during the post-war reconstruction period: the Chugoku Shimbun Newspaper Building (eight storeys) on the west bank has played a role in conveying the message of 'Hiroshima' and peace internationally; the Tutiya Hospital (nine storeys) on the south side is an important medical institution; also there are a school, hotels, many offices and residential flats. All of these properties have their own invisible narratives and memories that might be recognised as a part of the history of Hiroshima's post-war reconstruction.

Walking around the always perfectly purified park compound, people are naturally fascinated by Tange's focal axis to the A-Bomb Dome. It is a special place associated with global peace for visitors who expect their experience of peace to be strongly felt here. In contrast to the perfectly preserved A-Bomb Dome and core zone – where time has frozen since 8:16am, 6 August 1945 – lies the modern city of Hiroshima. Arguably, the city is nothing unique with its surrounding realities of an ordinary Japanese city – snail-like street trams, traffic jams, hamburger shops, love hotels, forgotten bicycles, kissing lovers and lonely pensioners. However, these sorts of mixed realities represent the evidence of people's daily efforts and the living city of Hiroshima.

Contemporary Hiroshima: beyond the distant memories

Officially, the Hiroshima City Government has been campaigning since the 1970s for the city to become a City of International Peace and Culture. It is, however, a difficult concept upon which to base a campaign, people not being able to under-

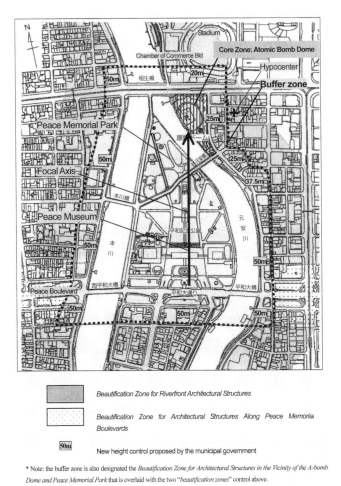

Figure 2.3 Hiroshima A-bomb Dome and surroundings. (Courtesy of Hiroshima City Government)

stand how it relates to their daily life. Consequently it is the A-Bomb Dome and the Peace Memorial that have been expected to be the symbols of a new legacy for Hiroshima, a new heritage moving beyond the difficult memories of the past.

The Peace Memorial Museum: exhibiting the memories and reputation

Currently, the Hiroshima Peace Museum is under a review process with regard to its future development. Actually, visitors enter the museum from the east wing, recently added to the museum exhibition, and proceed to the east wing's exhibition, which includes a pre-war history of military Hiroshima and the invasions of neighbouring countries. They then proceed to the exhibition of damage caused by the atomic bomb in the main building through overhead bridges connecting both the main building and the annex building. This layout was implemented after a sensitive debate about Hiroshima's historic reputation and the question of whether Hiroshima was only a victim of war or an assailant of war, especially to neighbouring Asian countries. After these criticisms were raised in domestic and international forums, the museum decided to add a new exhibition space in the east annex building where the city's pre-war history could be explained.

According to a report made by the museum, officially a museum visit will take around three hours, but in fact the visit takes only 45 minutes on average. It is said that some contents of the exhibition are too appalling for young eyes (Ogino 2002: 63). The latest plan approved by the committee shows that another entrance is proposed in order to provide more choice for visitors about what they want to see, depending on the time available, and to provide more space for meditation after they visit the museum (Hiroshima City Government 2007).

The Peace Memorial Museum is not only a functioning exhibition, but also provides educational programmes with actual survivor-storytellers (mainly for schoolchildren) who describe how they experienced the tragedy. Sufferers or survivors – Hibakusha – continue to talk about their tragic experiences to visitors, especially young students who visit Hiroshima on their school excursions. Actually, according to the museum department, there are around thirty survivor-storytellers contributing to this museum programme who provide presentations over 1,900 times a year. These fresh recollections are delivered without any official direction,[7] but survivor-storytellers are careful in recollecting their memories and selecting their words to explain to the young who are part of the wealthy post-war generation. The museum is also currently collecting survivors' voices in digital format for future use.

The Peace Memorial Park: enhancing its status as a 'holy place'

The Municipal Ordinance for Urban Parks defines the use of Hiroshima's park spaces and the Peace Memorial park compound comes under the supervision of the Greenery Promotion Department. One of the ideas behind the signing of this ordinance was that this park needs to be appreciated as a holy place. Additionally, there are some behaviour codes in the park: for example, small chorus groups are accepted, but brass bands are not allowed (*The Chugoku Shimbun*, 27 April 2004). In fact, almost all of the park's lawn spaces are designated as natural nurseries and people are prohibited from entering them. However, there are interesting pictures taken in 1984 that show a number of families in front of the Memorial Cenotaph enjoying a picnic and relaxing in the same way as in other ordinary parks in Japan (*The Chugoku Shimbun*, 31 April 2004). Of course, this kind of legislation exists only as a safeguard for extreme behaviour among the well-mannered Japanese population. However, it has been questioned whether it is being too protective to maintain the 'holy place'. Some feel it should be more natural with people doing their daily activities.[8]

Recently, in 2002, the Hiroshima National Peace Memorial Hall for the Atomic Bomb Victims opened following the announcement of new support legislation for war victims in Hiroshima. Kenzo Tange Associates designed this memorial hall. The building is buried deep within the grounds of the park, without any interruption to the park's spatial settings and landscape, designed originally by Tange some sixty years ago. From the entrance to the memorial hall, visitors are led along a spiral path deep underground to see pictures of victims and hear the voices of survivors. Visitors feel enclosed and feel memories of the past as if transmitted from the dark earth. It also clearly shows the concept of the park as a horizontal expanse and the memorial hall as a vertical place to ponder on memories and feelings from the past. Hiroshima's complex of peace memorials has obtained another icon to help it attain the status of 'holy place'.

The war against vandalism and apathy

At the same time as the park has gained more characteristics of holiness, this quiet park has also become a place of vandalism: not a small number of memorial cenotaphs – the park has over 40 monuments – have been continually attacked in recent years. In 2003 a drunken university student set fire to a large number of paper cranes that were presented in memory of the victims by students and visitors. After this spate of vandalism, the municipality provided monitoring cameras to prevent more incidents. These are not only for the monuments but also for people who fear to walk through the park at night even though they believe they live in the safest country in the world. On the other hand, the park, especially the area in front of the A-Bomb Dome, is a most attractive place where many interest groups make their public appeals. Arguably, the appearance of the A-Bomb Dome contains stronger metaphors that encourage people to appear in front of it. Nevertheless, it may be that this extraordinary visual environment tends to make people more aggressive when they explain their story.

Hiroshima is now facing another social change – aging. In reality, Japanese society is facing silent changes in its demographic pattern. At the present time, elderly people (aged 65 years and over) make up around 20 per cent of the total Japanese population (Japanese Statistical Bureau 2000). Furthermore, an overall population decrease has not abated in recent years. Of course, this tendency is also now clearly seen in the number of *Hibakusha*, as the victims of the atomic bombing of Hiroshima and Nagasaki are widely known in Japan. The sufferings of the Hibakusha are still a matter of sensitivity and are sometimes concealed deep within the memories of this society. Cruel social prejudices have been observed against Hibakusha; for example, marriages with the sufferer's kin have often made people afraid of developing hereditary disorders caused by radioactivity.[9]

6 August is of course the most important remembrance day for Hiroshima. This particular day is sometimes also noted for its meteorological singularity of fine summer weather and heat, as was the case in 1945. Thousands of people attend this Memorial Day and hotels in the city are nearly fully occupied by visitors at this time. In the days leading up to the 6 August memorial, industrious newspaper journalists often prepare articles for the *Hati Roku* (Eight–Six, or 6 August) special issues that touch enlightened readers. However, sometimes among locals, this day is just seen as a summer festival to help pass a hot day (Kuroshima 2003).

Raise up the spirit: the battleship Yamato and submarine Akishio

Recently, the neighbouring Kure City in Hiroshima Prefecture opened the municipal Kure Maritime Museum – known as the Yamato Museum. This museum has an exhibition of maritime engineering and modern merchant ships as well as that of a huge model of the battleship *Yamato*, real *Zero-Sen* fighters, and the 'human torpedo', *Kaiten*. In the following year, the Japan Maritime Self-Defence Force opened the JMSDF Museum in front of the Yamato Museum. This museum has an outdoor exhibition where a retired JMSDF submarine *Akishio* exposes her huge body in front of the popular neighbouring shopping complex *YOU-ME-TOWN* and the JMSDF Kure port with many real vessels.

Both these newly opened museums show how Kure's modern-contemporary engineering development has contributed practically to Japanese post-war reconstruction and successful economic development, as well as to maintaining peace globally. Historic continuities are clearly shown from the pre- to post-war and are never divided. Despite a worry about a lack of visitors, prior to opening, the museums have gained more and more visitors with long queues observed during weekends. Recently, among Japanese people the *Yamato* has been highlighted in the media; in fact, new films related to the battleship have proven very popular in respective cinemas.

However, there have been several criticisms raised about the success this formerly depressed, post-industrial and military city has gained in attracting new visitors. An article found in the *Asahi Shimbun* said that it focuses too much on exhibiting war weapons and vessels (Amano 2007). Kure City's Communist Party Councillors group questioned the municipal assembly, with party representative K. Tamatani arguing that 'this is a revival of the legacy of military Kure once again. This is not a marine time museum. This is a military museum' (*Kure Municipal Assembly Record* 2002). On the other hand, observations welcoming these museums in Kure city said that Kure city is a part of Hiroshima Prefecture and, although located some distance from the 'holy land' of Hiroshima city, it encourages visitors effectively to think about the meaning of war and the achievement of post-war efforts.

Recently the public have come to recognise that Japan is now changing towards an economically divided 'gap society' as a consequence of her long years of

Figure 2.4 Museums in Kure City, Hiroshima Prefecture (JMSDF Museum and Submarine *Akishio* on left; Shopping Complex YOU-ME-TOWN on right). (Source: Y. Utaka)

economic recession in the 1990s following the collapse of the Japanese 'bubble economy'. The unemployment rates have risen significantly, especially among the younger generation aged in their late 20s–30s – those people sometimes called the 'lost generation'. Unfortunately, some unemployed people are already expressing their desperation, even saying they are waiting for another war. A radio talk show entitled 'Is war the permanent part-timer's dream?', scripted by three permanent part-time workers, contained the following chilling statement:

> War makes Japanese society more fluid and demolishes the rigid social order. If we live under prejudice or shame in a peaceful society, we would prefer to suffer difficulties which are equal upon everyone in another war.
>
> (Hayano 2007)

Sixty years after the A-Bomb day, the singular weather peculiarity still means that every year there is very likely to be a clear sky and summer heat in Hiroshima. However, something seems to be changing the climate in Japanese society.

The city of living hope: establishing the new legacy of Hiroshima

Recently, in 2007, the Hiroshima Peace Memorial Park was designated as a Place of Scenic Beauty (Meisyou) and the Peace Memorial Museum as an Important Cultural Property [*Zyuuyou Bunkazai*] under the supervision of the Japanese heritage conservation act – the Law for the Protection of Cultural Properties. This is the first case in which the 'Important Cultural Property' nomenclature has been given to a post-war property, such properties previously understood to be of lower priority for legal protection. Another property designated in the same year, 2007, is also located in Hiroshima: the Hiroshima World Peace Memorial Cathedral designed by the architect Tohgo Murano and constructed thanks to the donations of a Christian believer. This theoretical endeavour of the Japanese heritage protection system encourages us to extend our historical thought from memories of bygone years to nearer days. Younger heritage sites will serve as memory stepping-stones that can help people develop more powerful images of the past. Of course, this will also help to prevent memories from weathering, deteriorating and being fabricated.

Hiroshima has been encouraged repeatedly to remind people of her tragedy and to keep on questioning the pre-war experience. It has successfully preserved the most highly significant historical structures and sites using specific protection policies and incorporated artefacts in well-maintained museums. The city speaks eloquently of its recovery through the contrast of the A-Bomb Dome and the new urban landscape and people's lives within it. Recently, locals have started talking about survivor buildings in cities, and the Hiroshima City government provides relatively supportive policies to conserve these survivor buildings in keeping with people's everyday lives. This will encourage us to think that our heritage and histories exist not only to recall our past, but also to provide continuities into the future.

Conclusion

In Hiroshima, the number of foreign visitors is increasing year by year and the city is being observed from their different point of views. For example, a visitor from a country that had recently experienced wartime tragedy talked of his impression of Hiroshima:

> In my country, we are all now living in a place like Hiroshima's core zone (the compound of the preserved A-bomb Dome). Historically, we were a rich country, but after the wars everything has gone. One day, I would like to invite you and friends in Hiroshima to my country, when we have rebuilt our cities like the lively Hiroshima of today.

Hiroshima is still relevant and significant as a symbol of hope around the globe where not a small number of cities are still wounded. Crowded and alive, quiet and steady, the scenery of Hiroshima's everyday life gives us great visions of unlimited possibilities. Hiroshima is the city of living hope.

Notes

1 The phrase 'No more Hiroshimas' was penned by Wilfred Burchett in the conclusion to his article 'The Atomic Plague' published in London's *Daily Express*, 5 September 1945.

2 Kenzo Tange (1913–2005), architect, attended Hiroshima High School and graduated from and served in the architectural school of the University of Tokyo.
3 The poet Sasako Kurihara raises questions, for example, about an Army Division that was deployed from Hiroshima that committed a massacre in Malaysia during the war (see Kurihara 1992).
4 Selection Criteria (vi): to be directly or tangibly associated with events or living traditions, with ideas, or with beliefs, with artistic and literary works of outstanding universal significance.
5 The recommendations came out of the '*ICOMOS symposium, World Heritage Convention and the Buffer Zone*', organised by ICOMOS Japan and ACCU, 29 November 2006.
6 The Shōkōkaigisho Building was awarded the BCS Prize from the Building Construction Society Japan in 1967. It was designed by Nikken Sekkei and constructed by the Fujita Co.
7 However, in Nagasaki, an association of an extra-departmental body of the Nagasaki City Government sent a letter to survivor-storytellers instructing them not to incline towards any particular political direction (*The Asahi Shimbun*, 3 May 2006).
8 *The Chugoku Shimbun*, 28 April 2004.
9 This kind of social prejudice was observed as early as in the 1960s (Lifton 1967: 198–204).

References

* Titles translated by the author for references and notes published in Japanese.

Amano, T. (2007) Newspaper article in *The Asahi Shimbun*, 21 May 2007.
Fujimori, T. (1998) *Architect Kenzo Tange and his Works in Hiroshima*, Public Lecture at Peace Memorial Museum.*
Hayano, T. (2007) 'Political Nippon', newspaper article in *The Asahi Shimbun*, 18 June 2007.*
Hiroshima City (1997) *Record of the Nomination of the World Heritage Listing of the Genbaku Dome*, Hiroshima City Government.*
Hiroshima City Government (2007) *Redevelopment Proposal for Hiroshima Peace Memorial Museum*, Hiroshima City.*
Inoue, S. (2006) *Dream and Fascination of Totalitarianism*. Tokyo: Risosha.*
International Council on Monuments and Sites (ICOMOS) (1995) *Document of Advisory Body Evaluation, Hiroshima Peace Memorial – Genbaku Dome*, Paris: ICOMOS.
Kure Municipal Assembly Record, No. 06, 20 March 2002.*
Kurihara, S. (1992) *Questioning Hiroshima*, Tokyo: Sanichi Shobou.*
Kuroshima, K. (2003) Newspaper article in *The Shikoku Shimbun*, 10 August 2003.
Lifton, R.J. (1967) *Death in Life: The Survivors of Hiroshima*, New York: Random House.
The Mainichi Newspaper, 23 August 1945.
Oe, K. (1965) *Hiroshima notes*, Iwanami.*
Ogino, M. (ed.) (2002) *Sociology of Cultural Heritage: From the Louvre to Genbaku Dome*. Tokyo: Shinyousha.*
Schneider, J. and Susser, I. (eds) (2003) *Wounded Cities: Destruction and Reconstruction in a Globalized World*, Oxford: Berg.
Tange, K. (1949) *Interviews*, Shinkentiku, vol. 10.
Yoneyama, L. (1999) *Hiroshima Traces: Space, and the Dialectics of Memory*. Berkeley: University of California Press.

Chapter 3

Auschwitz-Birkenau
The challenges of heritage management following the Cold War

Katie Young

During its reign of terror the Nazi Party systematically exterminated six million Jews, alongside five million people from other communities and 'races' it designated as inferior. At the core of the Nazi Party's Final Solution policy were the Auschwitz-Birkenau concentration and extermination camps. Auschwitz, the concentration camp where many people, including Polish political prisoners and Soviet prisoners of war, were incarcerated, is situated within the medium-sized Polish town of Oswiecim. Located three kilometres from Auschwitz, among farming land and adjacent to the small village Brzezinka, is Birkenau, the concentration and extermination camp that was primarily used by the Nazis to kill Jews.

This chapter explores the development of the camps as 'heritage sites', focusing in particular on the consequences of their being declared a museum during the period when Poland was under Communist rule. During this period the museum espoused the regime's doctrine and rhetoric and sought to use the site as a vehicle to glorify Poles' martyrdom and resistance against fascists. The Nazi Party had ravaged Poland and the Polish, who they deemed sub-human. The country suffered the most devastating casualties of the war, proportionately greater than any other country, their losses estimated to be between 1.8 to 1.9 million (non-Jews) and nearly 3 million Polish Jews (United States Holocaust Memorial Museum n.d.). The museum's Polish focus constrained its ability to present the history of the Holocaust and the stories of all communities who were affected by the camps. The chapter explores how Poles and Jews have claimed custodianship toward the camp and contested its identity and history.

It is a critical time for the camps. As the memory of the Cold War fades it can no longer be used as an excuse for the deteriorating state of the camps today. The camp buildings and artefacts stand desperately in need of protection as their deterioration is further compounded by an endless stream of visitors and inadequate funds for upkeep. Despite these limitations the camps' significance remains unquestionable and most visitors overlook the limitations of presentation; indeed most have life-affecting experiences at the site.

The camps' Cold War history: the Auschwitz State Museum

In 1947 the Polish Communist Government created the Auschwitz State Museum (ASM). The ASM's enabling legislation declared that the site would predominantly commemorate the 'martyrdom' of the Polish nation and its people (Dwork and Van Pelt 1996: 364). Its mandate cast, the ASM would be a stark reminder of the inherent dangers of fascism, and as Cole (1999: 99) observes 'a comforting reminder of the "liberating" presence of the Soviet Union'. In devising its exhibitions the ASM merged and blurred the history of both camps, enabling Auschwitz to assume Birkenau's identity as a place of absolute destruction. While many Poles were murdered at the camps, this fact was exaggerated by rhetoric and ill-conceived research, including the Soviet Extraordinary State Commission's death toll of four million people (Van Alstine 1996). At the ASM the histories of many communities imprisoned or executed at Auschwitz-Birkenau, especially Jews, were either not presented or marginalised.

The State did not entirely discount the execution of Jews at Auschwitz-Birkenau; however their suffering was not considered unique, their fate being the same as Polish prisoners (Huener 2003: 53). Consequently the exhibitions were fervently nationalistic, were limited in scope, and suppressed the history of the Holocaust. For example the ASM's 1986 official guidebook failed to explain the history of the Holocaust, the word 'Jew' not making it into print (Tanay, cited in Rittner and Roth 1991: 100). The ASM neglected Birkenau, under the guise of implementing a policy of limited disturbance, doing very little to protect the space (Huener, cited in Holian 2005; Dwork and Van Pelt 1996: 363; Auschwitz-Birkenau State Museum, n.d.). For the most part Birkenau and Buna Monowitz (the main slave labour camp in the area) were left to deteriorate. Birkenau's fences fell into disrepair and farm animals grazed at the site. Consequently visitors' attention was easily captured by the redeveloped and exhibited Auschwitz. During the 1960s and 1970s the museum increased its activities and began to engage with the international community, sending many of its exhibits abroad. Interest in Auschwitz in Poland culminated at this time through the visit of Pope John Paul II to the camps and its 1979 World Heritage listing; yet during this period few international visitors could visit the camp.

The camps' post-Cold War history

As the Cold War came to a close at the end of the 1980s, the operation of the museum was examined and in 1989 a working group was established to assess the future of the museum. It was decided that it would remain a state institution, reporting to the Polish Minister of Culture and National Heritage. The organisation was re-branded as the Auschwitz-Birkenau Museum and Memorial (ABMM), the new title reflecting the importance of the camp complex as a whole. Today various iterations of this name appear throughout the camp's website and official documents. Most recently the annual report used the title 'Memorial Auschwitz Birkenau State Museum', whereas the website uses 'Memorial and Museum Auschwitz Birkenau'. Several advisory councils and boards, composed of representatives from across the globe, were instituted to inform the activities of the museum and the International Centre for Education about Auschwitz and the Holocaust. Founded in 1990 the International Auschwitz Council (IAC) was established as the main advisory body. In 2000 its authority was elevated when it was selected to advise Poland's Chairman of the Council of Ministers on all the former Nazi extermination camps and other Holocaust memorials in Poland (Auschwitz-Birkenau State Museum, n.d.).

During this period, especially in the early 1990s, many international visitors and stakeholders converged at Auschwitz-Birkenau. For many communities it was the first opportunity to visit the camps to mourn lost friends and family. What they discovered at the camps was far removed from the history they had learnt and, in the case of survivors, from the hell they had lived through. When Primo Levi returned to Auschwitz in 1982 he found the site to be 'static, rear-ranged, contrived' (Gruber 1992: 38).

One of the earliest efforts to amend the Cold War era rhetoric at the camps was the effort by the ASM to rectify the incorrect death toll presented to visitors. Devised by the Soviet State the figure was far removed from international consensus. The rigorous key studies by Piper and Wellers found the toll to be in the order of 1–1.4 million victims, with Piper indicating that 960,000 Jews, 70,000–75,000 Poles, 21,000 Gypsies, 15,000 Soviet prisoners of war and a further 10,000–15,000 other nationals died at the camps (see Cole 1999: 107, Jarmen 1999). In the mid-1990s the sites' key memorial was corrected to read 'one and a half million men, women, children and infants', its Cold War title 'the International Monument to the Victims of Fascism' was also changed to 'the Monument to the Victims of Auschwitz Concentration Camp' (Young 1994: 136). The memorial's plaques were rewritten in nineteen languages, recognising the diversity of the victims of Auschwitz-Birkenau and acknowledging that the people killed were 'mainly Jews from various countries of Europe' (Gilbert 1998: 147).

At Auschwitz, national pavilions are housed in several barracks. These are places where countries and communities can recount the experiences of their citizens or members at the camps. Originally, only pavilions displaying the experiences of Communist countries were permitted. Slowly new pavilions representing other communities were allowed. Heuner has termed this period from the late 1960s onwards as the museum's internationalisation phase (Heuner, cited in Holian 2005). Today many countries and communities are represented by national pavilions, including France, the Netherlands and Russia. The opportunity for visitors to learn about the experiences of their countrymen and women has been an important development at the camp. Through these revisions the increasing number of international visitors could clearly see the intent of the Final Solution Policy and the central, prominent role of Birkenau in its execution. This was fundamental to acknowledging the rationale for the camps and to providing an evidence-based account of the Holocaust at Auschwitz-Birkenau.

Yet many Poles did not primarily identify Auschwitz-Birkenau as a site of the Holocaust and the revisions proved unsettling and disorientating. For some Poles the onset of international visitors and communities connecting with the camps were perceived as a threat. The ASM was a firmly embedded Polish nationalist memorial and Auschwitz-Birkenau was entrenched in the Polish sense of self. In 1995 a Polish Government survey on Auschwitz observed that a collective grief about the camps was shared among its citizens, akin to that of a personal family tragedy (Steinlauf 1997: 141). Considering the devastation inflicted upon Poland and its people during World War II, the survey's findings and the Poles' reactions are understandable. However the survey also captured the effect of the State's suppression of Holocaust history in Poland: barely 8 per cent of those surveyed associated Auschwitz-Birkenau with the martyrdom of the Jews. The upset and contestation were highlighted at the 50th liberation anniversary of the camps in 1995 when Jews, Poles and other stakeholders argued over proceedings and one journalist questioned 'who was the host and who was the guest?' (Steinlauf 1997: 142). The confusion was personalised by a Polish Auschwitz survivor who reflected that '25 years ago they were the centre of attention, but today … only an addendum' (Gilbert 1998: 140). However by 2000 Poles' understanding of the Jewish experience at Auschwitz-Birkenau had increased by 30 per cent (Jarmen 2000).

Visiting the Auschwitz-Birkenau Museum and Memorial

Today many people visit the camps, on bus tours, for educational purposes or on pilgrimage. Each day the long line of buses makes the one hour journey from Krakow to Oswiecim. Arriving at the camps mid-morning, visitors can partake in the standard site tour. Indeed, participation is compulsory for groups although only optional for the independent visitor. The first part of the tour, lasting approximately an hour and a half, shows visitors Auschwitz, including several of the camp's thirty red-brick, three-storey barrack buildings, the 'Arbeit Macht Frei' gate and the devastating wall of death. After a short break, visitors spend an hour and a half at Birkenau. Key sites of the tour include the gas chamber ruins, the gate house and the International Monument memorial. In the time available at Birkenau the tour is unable to take in much of the camp. Further arrangements can be made to take longer tours and those not in groups can explore the camps by themselves; however most will undertake a visit similar to that described above. There is still limited transport between the camps, especially during non-peak times. The standard visit in itself is undeniably a valuable experience, and for most a truly moving and affecting event in their lives. Yet despite visitors' encounters, the site as currently presented and the standard tour as delivered remain problematic.

The visitors' encounter with Auschwitz: confused and congested

While the political dynamics have changed, the legacy of the ASM looms large at Auschwitz. The ASM demonstrated a haphazard approach to heritage management, some barracks were altered significantly to display camp artefacts, while others were preserved only poorly. Because many of the ASM's installations remain unchanged at the ABMM today, historical misrepresentations, skewed presentations and dilapidated exhibitions continue to undermine and distort visitors' engagement with the camp. Lennon and Foley (2000: 57) observe how the barracks today are presented without a 'chronological or coherent orientation or guidance to the history of the camp'. It is easy to miss a key exhibit or find it closed. The information plaques lack detail and visitors are prone to bypassing the tired displays. However the ASM was fulfilling its aforementioned legislated mandate to concentrate on the Polish experience of resistance and martyrdom at Auschwitz. The same cannot be said for the ABMM, which has been slow to rectify the state of the museum installations. In July 2007 the ABMM's governing authority, the IAC, committed to addressing the problems of the museum's exhibitions. The redevelopment will be a lengthy undertaking, in the meanwhile ad hoc adjustments are made and the museum's limitations persist.

The value of the national pavilions is also hampered. Scattered among the barracks and often with different opening hours, the better resourced pavilions expose the skewed history and deteriorating displays in the museum installations. There has also been disagreement between curatorial groups. For example the ABMM is currently in discussions with Russia over its pavilion exhibition (Haaretz 2007).

The standard tour is inherently flawed. Most tours start at Auschwitz in the morning, and most at the same time. Consequently, the number of visitors trying to see the site is concentrated in the one time slot and the camp becomes crowded. In some buildings, due to wear and tear, only a small number of visitors can enter certain spaces; for example the basement prison cells. While a practical necessity, this leads to bottlenecking and also imposes time constraints for visitors when in the areas. The similar/more serious limitations of the tour at Birkenau are discussed later in the chapter.

Distorted emphasis

The 'Arbeit Macht Frei' gate, pictured in Fig. 3.1, is a prominent feature of the camp, encountered by visitors at the start of the standard tour. Many write about their interaction with the gate, one traveller noting that 'the most intimidating, as well as most significant thing was just entering through the gates' (Teramae 2002). Yet its position and prominence is problematic for several reasons. The gates were moved throughout the war. They do not represent the demarcation of the camp boundary as many visitors understand it to be. When visitors pass through the

Figure 3.1   A busy morning at Auschwitz, visitor groups commence their tour nearby the Arbeit Macht Frei gate. (Source: K.Young, 2005)

gates they are in fact already well inside the main camp's boundaries (Dwork and Van Pelt 1996: 359–60). The tour's design, including the presentation of the gates, suggests that Auschwitz is the start of the Holocaust story, whereas the majority of prisoners were sent directly to Birkenau, their stories being markedly different from those of Auschwitz prisoners. Between 1942 and 1944 the first seminal encounter that the Auschwitz prisoners had with the camp was initiation or processing in the prisoner reception centre, not passage through the gates.

The prisoner reception centre at Fig. 3.2 represents a crucial means to understanding the history of the camp and yet its functions have never been fully exhibited and interpreted. It also provides context to the gates. Constrained by limited funds, the ASM converted the building to house administration offices and visitor reception facilities, an arrangement which persists today. Dwork and Van Pelt (1996: 363) suggest that this building redevelopment ideologically suited the ASM and assisted the museum to focus its exhibition on Polish martyrdom and resistance efforts. For many prisoners the initiation process of tattooing, shaving and having belongings confiscated was devastating and disempowering; it crushed their hope and resilience. If this experience was exhibited in the reception centre it would have detracted from the resistance theme presented throughout the museum. The ongoing omission of the building from the museum tour negates an in-depth exploration of the experience for visitors.

As a visitor reception centre the building becomes congested as visitors purchase tour tickets, consume beverages and use the bathrooms. Cole (1999: 110) laments how the building has 'silently become the place of Auschwitz land's tourist initiation'. Its history suppressed, the building now insulates visitors from their imminent tour of the camps. In addition to housing exhibitions and national pavilions, the Auschwitz barracks and other buildings also accommodate memorials, archives and preservation workspaces. The ABMM's demand for usable space has outweighed the contemplation of the camp's preservation, thereby affecting the camp's authenticity and long-term preservation. This dilemma continues, with the potentially promising news that the ABMM plans to revise and redevelop its museum exhibitions being complicated by its intent to use the camp's barracks rather than a new, purpose-built space to house the exhibition.

The most prominent example of misrepresentation at Auschwitz is its reconstructed gas chamber. During the war a makeshift gas chamber was developed at Auschwitz, first in the camp's prisoner block and then inside the crematorium (Dwork and Van Pelt 1996: 364). The crematorium gas chamber was experimental, devised to manage the increasing influx of Soviet POWs. The crematorium was abandoned in 1942 and subsequently altered to function as an air raid shelter (Dwork and Van Pelt 1996: 293–294, 364; Hartman, cited in Dwork and Van Pelt 1994: 239). It was not used for mass extermination in the context of the Final Solution Policy. Damaged before the end of the war the ASM reconstructed the building to resemble its earlier incarnation as a gas chamber. With visitors kept away from Birkenau, the ASM intended the chamber to assume an identity that was not entirely its own – the final and telling element of the catastrophic story.

There has been limited discussion at Auschwitz about the history of the reconstructed crematorium and its detailed features are difficult to determine today. The absence at the site of a clear and defined account of the crematorium's origins and functions enabled Holocaust denier David Cole to acquire varied 'historical' accounts about the building from museum staff (The Nizkor Project 2007). Across denier websites the 'fake chamber argument' features prominently (for example, Focal Point Publications 24 June 2003; Stormfront 1999). The history of the building as presented at the site and on the ABMM's website remains vague. With accuracy and honesty its history should be disclosed across the various media where visitors may encounter the site.

Exhibiting the Holocaust

Throughout the museum exhibitions the stories of prisoners' lives are overshadowed by the history of their deaths. This is best exemplified by the museum's mass exhibitions of prisoners' belongings. Hair, prosthetic limbs and suitcases are some of the belongings on display; the mustiness is penetrating. Yet at Auschwitz the number of personal belongings on display, while confronting, represents only a very small portion of the belongings confiscated from Auschwitz prisoners. Minimal if any documentary information is provided to give context to the display. Showing the items en masse can be effective in prompting visitors to contemplate the scale of Auschwitz's operations, but in this way it also distances visitors from the experiences of the individual prisoners. The collection's decrepit state also reveals the museum's preservation struggle and further undermines the items' importance as belongings rather than relics.

There are some limited glimpses into the lives and personalities of the people imprisoned in the camps on display at Auschwitz, as, for example, in the artwork drawn on the walls by inmates. Yet these are more incidental than a strategic consideration *per se*. It is essential to provide a substantial exploration of the murderous operations at Auschwitz-Birkenau; however, exhibitions tackling the death of individual prisoners and the suppression of their identity should not condemn their memory to the same fate.

The visitor's encounter with Birkenau: a quiet space and a vast place

Much of Birkenau's infrastructure was destroyed by the Nazis when they deserted the camp in January 1945, and then by the Soviets upon liberation later that month on the 27th. All that remains are mostly ruined buildings, including the gas chambers. However, the ASM's ideological disregard for Birkenau spared it from the reconfigurations and renovations undertaken at Auschwitz. The unadulterated presentation of the camp provides relief to those grappling with their emotions and also to those struggling with the state of preservation and exhibitions at Auschwitz. Today the ABMM website states that Birkenau is the most important part of the camp complex (Auschwitz-Birkenau State Museum n.d.). While the absence of much intervention has left Birkenau appearing more authentic, there are many preservation challenges at the camp. For example, the camp's barbed wire and concrete post fence is deteriorating and it is a considerable task preserving this immense artefact. Another large and costly project is to preserve the gas chambers, but this is especially complicated by rising groundwater.

It seems that the value of Birkenau for most visitors is experiential rather than informative (in the traditional sense of a museum and its documentary-like presentation of information). The enormity of Birkenau's ruins and fields stuns most visitors; the space, the stark silent barrack chimneys, the rail tracks and the silhouette of the gate house. There is limited interpretation, though there are excellent information boards situating historical photographs in their physical location. To walk alone at the camp can be a profound experience, though visitors must be willing to look beyond the immediate shelter of the crowds. Holocaust museums and memorials globally have attempted to replicate this type of encounter, possibly best exemplified by the distorting corridors of the Berlin Jewish Museum and the silent stones of the Monument to the Murdered Jews of Europe, also in Berlin.

At Birkenau there is an absence of barriers and attendants. This arrangement, while of benefit to the visitor, presents a significant risk to the preservation and integrity of the site. Museum Spokesman, Jarek Mensfelt, pointed out to one journalist visiting Birkenau that underfoot were 'not stones, bones' (Johnson

Figure 3.2   Taken from the Birkenau gate house, the photograph captures the main route visitors take through the camp. At the end of the rail tracks near the tree line are gas chambers, crematoria 2 and 3, and the International Monument to the Victims of the Auschwitz Concentration Camp. (Source: K. Young, 2005)

2007). Some visitors can and do walk away with parts of the camp, the rectification of which is a most pressing matter.

The standard tour described earlier is brief and superficial considering the size of the site and the number of potential exhibits. The memorial process for many visitors is expedited in an effort to make the late afternoon buses back to Krakow. For most though, visiting the key sites may be enough, the history apparent and grief real. After all, visitors have spent a day, of sorts, at the camp. If visitors do go beyond the key sites they will discover many overlooked pertinent spaces integral to the camp's history. These include the earliest gas chamber sites and the devastating ponds of ashes. The tour fails to take in an excellent post-Cold War museum exhibition about the camp, housed in its sauna.

The sauna exhibition

Opened in 2001, the sauna exhibition balances the aforementioned paradox of how to present the Holocaust; confronting the mass horror but not losing sight of the individual. The final room of the exhibition is filled with personal photos of people murdered at the camp. Brought into the camp by the prisoners themselves, the photos survived through the efforts of prisoner resistance groups.

Through the photographs, Leon Wieseltier explains that 'we remember what they wished to remember; and in the memory of their memory, they live'(Brawarsky 2001). To exhibit what the prisoners believed was important provides a valuable means to overcoming the paradox and making a connection beyond the horror of systematic murder. For many, making the connection with just one of the one million is profound.

The personalisation of an exhibition also counters an experience and a history that has become prone to stereotype – the Oscar-worthy, uplifting but devastating story of the pyjama-clad concentration camp prisoner. Many Holocaust museums now present personal stories alongside the historical account, and often survivors themselves act as guides at the museums and memorials. Given the shortcomings of the museum exhibition at Auschwitz, the sauna and its exhibition should be included in the standard camp tour.

Memorialisation at Auschwitz-Birkenau

Auschwitz-Birkenau has numerous roles to fulfil and communities to cater for. Auschwitz has long been identified as a museum, a busy place. In contrast Birkenau, the world's largest cemetery, is a witness to genocide. First through neglect, and then choice, it has been reserved as a desolate space where communities can come in solitude to grieve and remember. In the 1950s an international design competition for a Birkenau memorial was held. Although a design was chosen it was never installed following protest from survivors who had difficulty with it; the design also contravened the camp's governing legislation. As with this occasion, making decisions today about how to present the camps is a complex and lengthy process especially because of the many parameters and stakeholders involved. Preserving the authenticity of the sites is a major concern when determining how to present the site, as so too the interests of camp survivors. The ABMM heritage management quandary will evolve as time passes and attitudes change, as new preservation techniques are developed and as survivors pass away.

Religious memorialisation has figured prominently at the camps. In 1982 the International Council of Christians and Jews denied a request from a Carmelite order of nuns to establish a permanent place of Catholic worship at the camps. The Council recognised that Jewish and Catholic relations at the site were fragile. Importantly, it acknowledged that religion was not a facet of the lives of many survivors, their families and friends. For many it was at the camps that they had relinquished their faith. For Alexander Donat, 'God was not present at our indescribable predicament. We are alone, forsaken by God and men' (Donat, cited in Gutman and Berenbaum 1994: 32). Yet in 1984, with the approval of some Catholic Church leaders and Polish Government officials, a Carmelite convent was founded in the World Heritage-listed Auschwitz theatre building (Rittner and Roth 1991: 5). Located adjacent to the current demarcation of Auschwitz's boundaries, the theatre had been used in the war as a storehouse for Zyklon B, the gas crystals used in the exterminations. In 1987 the International Council reiterated that the nuns should leave the camp and that at Auschwitz 'everyone will be able to pray there according to the dictates of his own heart, religion and faith' (Rittner and Roth 1991: 22). The nuns resisted relocation.

Against a backdrop of political upheaval, many Poles, feeling isolated and discontented, sought to reclaim their history and faith at the camps. They rallied behind the efforts of the nuns and fostered further support for the activities of the Catholic Church at the camps. In a relatively short period of time Auschwitz-Birkenau became a battleground as stakeholders contested their right to representation. Catholic and Jewish communities attacked one other verbally, and in one instance physically, with such ferocity that it was surreal given the setting.

The Church identified two Catholic martyrs murdered at the camps. These selections are viewed by Jews and other commentators more broadly as problematic (Foxman and Klenicki 1998, Van Biema 1998), and so too the establishment of individual camp memorials. The presence of a large cross also led to conflict between Jews and Poles. A related local campaign saw hundreds of small crosses deposited at the camps, the situation further exacerbated when Polish school children, in an attempt to mend relations, fixed Stars of David to the crosses, the perceived subjugation of Jewish religious iconography leading to further conflict. The convent matter became an international crisis with Poland and Israel casting slurs at one another in the global arena. Poland's Cardinal Glemp 'tactlessly called on Jews to stop using their influence in the media to push Poland around' (*The Economist* 1990). This was followed by Israel's Prime Minister Yitzhak Shamir's vehement attack claiming 'Poles sucked anti-Semitism in with their mothers' milk' (ibid). It took eleven years to resolve the matter of the convent's occupation and the nuns were relocated to new premises in Oswiecim.

The story of the convent illustrates that memorialisation, particularly where religion is involved, is not an easy path to navigate. Through dialogue, particularly at the local level, the two groups began to work towards conciliation. A key means to facilitating learning and empathy between the parties was the establishment in Oswiecim of several Jewish and Catholic community centres, where education and cross-cultural dialogue now figure prominently. When visitors of either faith come to Oswiecim they can find, in the community, a place where they can pray, seek dialogue and education. With dialogue comes tolerance and at the camps the visible presence of Catholic memorialisation remains, including the crosses outside the theatre and individual memorials. It is difficult to determine whether Jewish communities and other stakeholders have accepted these symbols and shrines or just resigned themselves to their presence, wanting to avoid further damage to one another and the site.

Auschwitz-Birkenau and Oswiecim

Oswiecim is a medium-sized town of more than 40,000 people, while the adjacent Brzezinka is a small village. In the pages of history, and by their physical proximity, the towns and the camps are inextricably linked. Nazi atrocities were

Figure 3.3 Taken from the Birkenau gate house the photograph shows the proximity of Brzezinka to the camp. (Source: K.Young, 2005)

not confined by the camps' perimeter fences; scars left by the Nazi regime reach far into the towns, by the river and along the rail tracks. Auschwitz literally neighbours Oswiecim residences and several camp buildings are now used for public housing. At one point there is little more than a small wire fence separating houses from the camp. Visitors encounter outdoor furniture and washing lines while touring the site.

Emerging from the Cold War there was little acknowledgement or awareness from the international community of the camps' and towns' co-location, and the inherent predicament this presented. Many visitors ponder how Oswiecim residents could live where they live. Yet for most residents this is home, their family heritage. It is also a town of public housing and many residents battle against financial hardship. Oswiecim underwent considerable post-Communist regime political and socio-economic upheaval. Experiencing long periods of recession, the town's unemployment rate increased from 6.7 per cent in September 1996 to 17.25 per cent in 2001 (Ministry of Interior and Administration, Republic of Poland 2002). The town is subject to planning protocols and zoning restrictions which further inhibit growth (Jarmen 2006).

It was over several planning developments that the association was made between town and camps, in particular proposals to build a supermarket opposite Auschwitz and to house a disco in a slave labour tannery. In both cases international commentators and the popular press readily and repeatedly cast Oswiecim as opportunistic and heartless to pursue such development opportunities. When articles like 'Death Goes to the Disco' brought Oswiecim's quandary to the attention of *New York Times* readers (Groff-Palermo 2001), few commentators acknowledged the town and the needs of its community. Furjan, a younger member of the community told of his struggle: 'if we listen to what people tell us what we should do,' he says, 'then we'd be a city always in mourning' (Hammer 2000: 49). The arguments against the Oswiecim developments pointed to both moral and physical degradation of key historical buildings and surrounds. The rejection of these developments appeared arbitrary to many in town and it is clear that the role of the international community in dictating how Oswiecim should operate made more difficult an already complex predicament.

Matters of buffer zones and protection of key heritage sites are undoubtedly important. However sentencing Oswiecim to a standstill is not a constructive solution. In 2000 the town held a conference exploring its status, development challenges and camp boundaries (Polski 2000). Oswiecim is a town with a history and community that reaches far beyond World War II. The Oswiecim website reflects the struggle: 'Let us to present you the over 8-centuries history of Oswiecim, of an ancient Piast's castle situated on Sola river, its present day and possibilities of development' (Miasto Oswiecim n.d.). Demonstrating its determination to reclaim its heritage and identity Poland sought to change the camp's World Heritage listing inscription from 'Auschwitz Concentration Camp' to 'Former Nazi German Concentration and Death Camp Auschwitz-Birkenau'. The World Heritage Committee agreed the change was required 'in order to promote adequate historical understanding of its creation' (UNESCO World Heritage Centre n.d; PAP–aki/kan 2006).

Oswiecim continues, however, to struggle financially despite an ever-increasing number of visitors. Two key limitations for Oswiecim persist: on the one hand, it is located too close to the camps, deterring touring holiday-makers who arrive in the town as part of their itinerary from wanting to stay on; and, on the other hand, it is not so remote from Krakow that visitors need to stay. Visiting the camps, for most, will remain a day trip. These are not necessarily bad things, but rather facts that Oswiecim will need to take into account as it devises a forward strategy. That said, with a million visitors coming to the camps last year, to capture just a fragment of the market would provide new opportunities for the town as a whole. A key challenge will be to make the town an accessible and obvious place to stay. Facilitating the visits of students at the educational and religious centres in Oswiecim would seem to represent the best opportunity for Oswiecim to foster its development and financial security. It is important to stress that Oswiecim is not looking for a windfall. Initial funding provided for the town in Poland's Governmental Strategic Programme for the Oswiecim Area 1997–2001 was directed towards basic infrastructure, including roads and lighting. The programme for 2002–2006, recognising the problems outlined above, incorporated the following four priorities: (1) bringing order and development to the areas around the State Museum Auschwitz-Birkenau; (2) improving transport accessibility of Oswiecim to pilgrims and tourists, commuters and investors;

(3) conducting educational activities in Oswiecim related to the commemoration sites and the issue of human rights, international relations and peace; and (4) increasing the attractiveness of Oswiecim and its surroundings for tourists. The programme thus far has brought about some positive achievements, though funding limitations are repeatedly cited in reviews of progress.

Oswiecim represents a significant partner in the task of maintaining the integrity of Auschwitz-Birkenau. The challenges are ongoing, and in some instances appear to be irresolvable. Yet Oswiecim and the ABMM have made steady efforts to bridge the gap, including ABMM-run intern and education programmes for the community. Important as it is for the town to reclaim its identity, its future is alongside the camps, not in contest with them or disenfranchised by the influx of visitors. Engaged with the ABMM, Oswiecim is best placed to provide visitors to the camps with insight into the experiences of their families and countrymen and women through the presentation of personal stories stripped of ideological rhetoric and intent. Greater engagement at the camps by the community will build a bridge connecting visitors to the town, potentially providing the financial injection it needs.

Conclusion: next steps

The struggles of Auschwitz-Birkenau are far greater and more complex than other Holocaust museums. It is an atrocity site, a cemetery whose boundaries reach beyond the museum doors. The camps' identities have been the subject of much of the discussion in this chapter. Matters of perception, memorial contests, the use of the Auschwitz camp and its buildings, Oswiecim town planning and the influence of Communist rhetoric have deprived the site of its rightful evidence-based heritage and have bred confusion about the site's purpose.

Stakeholders in their contests with one another overlooked the sanctity of each and every human life lost at the camps; no prisoner's experience at the camps should be marginalised. Their history at the camps must be presented with accuracy, their suffering with honesty and humanity. The devastating statistics relay a history of suffering unique to the Jews. But the Polish experience at the camps must also be presented, potentially with a more extensive interpretation focusing on the experience of Poles in the region. Auschwitz-Birkenau's significance is on a global scale, but removing it from a local context must be avoided. Oswiecim in particular and the people of Poland identify strongly with the camp. They are the camps' caretakers and primary sponsors and their importance should not be underestimated. The current exhibition on Poland's experience is busy and tired and warrants revision to ensure the experiences are relayed in a professional, accurate and personal manner; engaging to both local and international visitors. The trend of Holocaust museums to engage Holocaust survivors as guides or hosts of exhibition spaces could be replicated in the Polish exhibition space to further stimulate visitors' engagement. The post-war history of the camp also warrants exhibition.

The preservation and exhibition task at the camps is immense; both need to be addressed urgently. The ABMM receives core funding (approximately 50 per cent of its income) from the Polish Government, while income generated by the museum contributes most of the remaining 50 per cent, with a small contribution from private donors. In 2006, the budget of the Auschwitz-Birkenau State Museum totalled 21 million Polish zloty (PLN) (approximately €5.2 million euro). By contrast the United States Holocaust Museum and Memorial (USHMM) cost approximately $US168 million to construct, including $US78 million for the exhibits. It has a base operating budget of $US69.7 million for the financial year 2007 or approximately €52 million (USHMM n.d; USHMM 2005). The Memorial to the Murdered Jews of Europe (MMJE) in Berlin was constructed at cost of €27.6 million with €12.8 million on the Information Centre alone (MMJE n.d.). In short, when compared to the funding received by key Holocaust memorials and museums elsewhere the funding for Auschwitz-Birkenau is clearly insufficient.

The current use of the sites and the order in which visitors encounter them significantly influences the visitors' regard for the camps, which is not necessarily a due or fair reflection of their histories. Untangling the presentation of the camps' histories should allow stakeholders to more clearly identify places of significance for them personally and their communities. The Auschwitz camp site in many ways has acquired the mantle for the Auschwitz-Birkenau camp complex as a whole. This is where tours start, beverages are purchased and the history of the camps is exhibited; visitors see a lot, but what they can't experience without reservation or distraction is Auschwitz itself. The camp's history and its physical condition are compromised by the site's presentation. The Auschwitz site could relay more effectively its history and communicate in its entirety the Polish experience at the camp if the visitor facilities and the museum exhibitions were relocated to a purpose-built space separate from the camp. Alternatively if this task is too great, even moving the museum's Birkenau exhibitions to Birkenau would assist. Birkenau is undeniably the primary site of the Holocaust, a fact not missed by visitors. That said, much of the Birkenau landscape is overlooked by visitors. In order to never forget the atrocities of the Holocaust Birkenau should be experienced in its entirety. What is crucial for the future is the visitors' ability to connect with the site and the history of the Holocaust. The design of the standard tour must be revisited.

The ABMM approach to museum management at Auschwitz has limited the potential engagement and education of visitors. Its museum exhibition, a mere extension from the time of the ASM, has perpetuated misrepresentations and confounded many. Despite the considerable work that remains to be undertaken at the site, it is important to acknowledge the progress that has been made in recent times. The appointment of new Director Piotr M.A. Cywiński in July 2006 has brought momentum to the ABMM, best illustrated by the decision to publish the first ever ABMM Annual Report. The Museum in July 2007 hosted the Remembrance, Awareness, and Responsibility Conference. Through these undertakings greater transparency has been cast upon the operation of the museum and a recognition has been made by the museum that it needs to do better than the current tired displays and deteriorating buildings. Hopefully the ABMM can move beyond operating with limited funds and the indecision that have stifled its potential and its universal obligation to present the camps' histories in an unadulterated fashion. As the ABMM moves forward it remains critical that the sentiment espoused by General Telford Taylor at the Nuremberg trial should resonate: 'we cannot here make history over again. But we can see that it is written true' (The Nizkor Project 2002).

References

Auschwitz-Birkenau State Museum (n.d.) *Dates in the History of the Memorial and Museum*. Available online at http://www.auschwitz.org.pl/new/index.php?language=EN&tryb=stale&id=425 (accessed 17 June 2007).

Auschwitz-Birkenau State Museum (n.d.) *The Establishment of the Museum. Its History and Present State*, Auschwitz-Birkenau State Museum. Available online at http://www.auschwitz.org.pl/new/index.php?language=EN&tryb=stale&id=426 (accessed 17 June 2007).

Brawarsky, S. (2001) 'New book chronicles what Auschwitz prisoners brought with them, and how they wanted to be remembered', *Jewish Week*, Online Posting 23 March: Available online at http://www.thejewishweek.com/news/newscontent (accessed 1 May 2002).

Cole, T. (1999) *Selling the Holocaust: from Auschwitz to Schindler: How history is bought, packaged, and sold*, New York: Routledge.

Dwork, D. and Van Pelt, R.J. (1994) 'Reclaiming Auschwitz', in G.H. Hartman (ed.), *Holocaust Remembrance: the Shapes of Memory*, Oxford: Blackwell Publishers.

Dwork, D. and Van Pelt, R.J. (1996) *Auschwitz, 1270 to the present*, New York: Norton.

Focal Point Publications (2003) *Real History on Auschwitz and a Startling Confession – Auschwitz Museum Officially Admits Gas Chamber is a 'Reconstruction'*, Global Vendetta. Available online at www.fpp.co.uk/docs/irving/raddi/2003/ 230603.html (accessed 12 June 2007).

Foxman, A. and Klenicki, L. (1998) 'The Canonization of Edith Stein: An Unnecessary Problem', Anti-Defamation League, online posting (October). Available at http://www.adl.org/opinion/edith_stein.asp (accessed 16 November 2007).

Gilbert, M. (1998) *Holocaust Journey: Travelling in search of the past*, London: Phoenix.

Governmental Strategic Programme for the Oswiecim Area 2002–2006, 27 November 2002. Ministry of Interior and Administration, Republic of Poland.

Groff-Palermo, S. (2001) 'Death Goes to the Disco', *New York Times*, 1 January 2001.

Gruber, R.E. (1992) *Jewish Heritage Travel: A Guide to Central and Eastern Europe*, New York: John Wiley & Sons.

Gutman, Y. and Berenbaum, M. (eds) (1994) *Anatomy of the Auschwitz Death Camp*, Washington D.C.: Bloomington.

Haaretz (2007) 'Poland, Russia clash over Auschwitz memorial to Russian war casualties', *Haaretz.com* online posting 5 April. Available at http://www.haaretz.com/hasen/spages/845874.html.

Hammer, J. (2000) 'Auschwitz: Dancing on old graves, A controversial disco sparks a tense holocaust debate', *Newsweek*, 136, 9 October: 49.

Holian, A. (2005) *Review of Jonathan Huener, Auschwitz, Poland, and the Politics of Commemoration, 1945–1979*, H-German H-Net Reviews, online posting (October). Available at www.h-net.msu.edu/reviews/showrev.cgi?path=63151148317223 (accessed 7 May 2007).

Huener, J. (2003) *Auschwitz, Poland, and the Politics of Commemoration, 1945–1979. Polish and Polish-American Studies Series*, Athens: Ohio University Press.

Jarmen (1999), Franciszek Piper – Fritjof Meyer, 'Die Zahl der Opfer von Auschwitz. Neue Erkenntnisse durch neue Archivfunde', Auschwitz-Birkenau State Museum, online posting (12 December). Available at http://www.auschwitz.org.pl/new/index.php?tryb=news_big&language=EN&id=563 (accessed 10 June 2007).

Jarmen (2000), *Polish Perceptions of Auschwitz: Who sees what?* Auschwitz-Birkenau State Museum, online posting (31 January). Available at http://www.auschwitz.org.pl/ new/index.php?tryb=news_big&language=EN&id=18 (accessed 10 May 2007).

Jarmen (2006) *Regulatory Plan for the Grounds and Immediate Surroundings of the Auschwitz-Birkenau Death Camp Being Prepared for UNESCO. The Position of the Auschwitz-Birkenau State Museum*, Auschwitz-Birkenau State Museum, online posting (10 June). Available at http://www.auschwitz.org.pl/new/index.php?tryb=news_big&language=EN&id=1139 (accessed 10 June 2007).

Johnson, C. (2007) 'Fight against time to preserve Auschwitz', Sydney Morning Herald, online posting (31 January). Available at http://www.smh.com.au/news/travel/fight-against-time-to-preserve-auschwitz/2007/01/31/1169919380731.html (accessed 31 January 2007).

Lennon, J. and Foley, M. (2000) *Dark Tourism: The attraction of death and disaster*, London: Continuum.

Memorial to the Murdered Jews of Europe (n.d.) *Frequently Asked Questions* Foundation Memorial to the Murdered Jews of Europe, online posting. Available at www.holocaust-mahnmal.de/en/faqs#cathead10 (accessed 3 June 2007).

Miasto Oswiecim (n.d.) *Oswiecim*, Miasto Oswiecim, online posting. Available at http://www.um.oswiecim.pl/pl/index.php (accessed 12 June 2007).

The Nizkor Project (2007) *Shofar FTP Archive File: Dr Franciszek Piper Correspondence*, The Nizkor Project, online posting (8 February). Available at www.nizkor.org/ftp.cgi/people/p/piper.franciszek/press/daily.texan.1093 (accessed 30 May 2007).

PAP–aki/kan (2006), *UNESCO Heritage Committee Approves Measure to Change Name of Auschwitz Camp*, Auschwitz-Birkenau State Museum, online posting (12 July). Available athttp://www.auschwitz.org.pl/new/index.php?tryb=news_big&language=EN&id=107 (accessed 17 June 2007).

Polski, D. (2000) *Does Oswiecim Have a Future? A Conference on the City's Problems*, Auschwitz-Birkenau State Museum, online posting (31 October). Available at http://www.auschwitz.org.pl/new/index.php?tryb=news_big&language=EN&id=206 (accessed 12 June 2007).

Rittner, C. and Roth, J.K. (eds) (1991) *Memory Offended: The Auschwitz Convent Controversy*, New York: Praeger.

Steinlauf, M.C. (1997) *Bondage to the Dead: Poland and the Memory of the Holocaust*, New York: Syracuse University Press.

Stormfront (1999) *March of The Titans – A History of the White Race, Chapter 64: The Racial State – The Third Reich, Part Three Auschwitz – Extermination or Labor camp*, Ostara Publications, online posting. Available at http://www.stormfront.org/whitehistory/Auschwitz.htm (accessed 12 June 2007).

Teramae, M. (2002), *A Visit to Auschwitz*, online posting. Available at http://www.eurotrip.com/destinations/auschwitz.html (accessed 31 May 2002).

The Economist (US) (1990) 'The peace of Auschwitz. (How to honour the people who died at Auschwitz; Poland)', Vol. 314, No.7645, 55–57.

UNESCO World Heritage Centre (n.d.) *30COM 8B.12 – Changes to Names of Properties (Auschwitz Concentration Camps)*, UNESCO, online posting. Available at http:// http://whc.unesco.org/en/decisions/987.

United States Holocaust Memorial Museum (2005) *Frequently Asked Questions*, United States Holocaust Memorial Museum, online posting (18 January). Available at http:// www.ushmm.org/research/library/faq/details.php?lang=en&topic=06#08 (accessed 11 June 2007)

United States Holocaust Memorial Museum (n.d.) *Poles: Victims of the Nazi Era*, United States Holocaust Memorial Museum, online posting. Available at http://www.ushmm. org/education/resource/poles/poles.php (accessed 15 November 2007).

Van Biema, D. (1998) 'A Martyr – but Whose?' *Time*, online posting (19 October). Available at http://www.time.com/time/magazine/article/0,9191,989351-2,00.htm (accessed 16 November 2007).

Young, J.E. (1994) *Texture of Memory: Holocaust Memorials and Meaning*, New Haven: Yale University Press.

Chapter 4

'Dig a hole and bury the past in it'

Reconciliation and the heritage of genocide in Cambodia

Colin Long and Keir Reeves

Those who have visited sites of commemoration associated with the Nazi Holocaust will be familiar with the power of those places to stimulate strong and distressing emotions. A persistent sense of the evil of the genocidal acts performed there combines with a mournfulness born of awareness of great suffering, loss and trauma. Although the interpretative and memorial strategies employed at Holocaust sites vary, there is an overwhelming sense of respectful commemoration of the victims of Nazi persecution in all cases. There is also a necessary clarity of message: one is left in no doubt about the identity of victims and perpetrators or about the extent of the evil committed. In the case of Cambodia a debate continues over the full extent of deaths as a result of the Khmer Rouge regime but credible estimates range between 1.5 and 2.5 million (Kiernan 2005).

The emotions stimulated by a visit to the last bastion of the genocidal Khmer Rouge regime at Anlong Veng in northern Cambodia, and the messages conveyed at the tourist-historical sites there, on the other hand, are much less clear and much more disturbing. This lack of clarity raises a further question for Cambodian heritage tourism officials specifically, and for cultural heritage practitioners more generally: is it appropriate to commemorate or interpret contested sites of pain and shame such as Ta Mok's compound at Anlong Veng?

There are two key problems in considering Anlong Veng from a heritage tourism perspective. The first is the site's inadequate infrastructure. Second, and perhaps more important, is the temporal proximity of the Khmer Rouge period, and the still open wounds that afflict Cambodian society. Cambodia has yet to recover from the Khmer Rouge trauma. Because of this it is extremely difficult to interpret and promote the site in any objective, non-politicised or constructive capacity.

Put simply the violence of the recent past is still too raw and the impact of the genocide too difficult a topic to broach in terms of public commemoration. This has resulted in an amnesia about the recent past in Anlong Veng and its hinterland communities. This is unsurprising given that the region has the dubious honour of being the last stronghold of the Khmer Rouge. Furthermore, the Byzantine nature of Cambodian politics means that it is intensely difficult to contextualise these sites historically and to interpret them without causing offence to powerful lobbies within the region. Ultimately we argue that the current attempts to create a tourism industry concentrating on a heritage strategy emphasising sites associated with the Khmer Rouge have come before this place of pain and shame has been historically contextualised and the necessary process of healing has occurred.

Anlong Veng represents an interesting case study of a place of pain and shame, highlighting broad issues about the transformation of places associated with extensive violence into heritage sites. It represents a key site within a much broader landscape of violence in Cambodia, including the better known Tuol Sleng prison in Phnom Penh and also its killing field, Choeung Ek, to the north of the city. However it is at the Anlong Veng site that one is invited to wonder what the role of heritage is in these areas. Does it exacerbate or absolve the events of the past? Or is it part of a constructive dialogue of reinterpretation of the recent past with the broader aim of reconciliation in present day Cambodia?

We first visited Anlong Veng in November 2005, arriving from Thailand through the border crossing at Sa Ngam on a drizzly, surprisingly cool day. The border crossing is a ramshackle collection of huts and small traders' stalls lining a muddy path. It has a distinct backwoods, isolated feel, understandable given it was only opened for legal transit in November 2003, and links Thailand's Sisaket province to one of the most under-developed areas in Cambodia, which was controlled until 1999 by remnants of the Khmer Rouge. The presence of sand-bagged machine gun nests on the Thai side of the border only adds to the sense of entering a wild, possibly dangerous place.

Given that the only other people crossing the border when we arrived were Cambodians in the back of pick-ups, heads swathed in *krama*, the ubiquitous scarf of Cambodian peasants, our presence caused some bemusement among the border guards, especially since we were on foot. A Cambodian border policeman offered us a lift (for a fee) to Anlong Veng, some 15km away, and since there was no other obvious means of going any further (certainly no public transport), we gratefully accepted.

The border crossing is at the top of the Dangrek escarpment, near the remains of a number of residences of former Khmer Rouge leaders, including Pol Pot, a military post of the area's former Khmer Rouge commander, Ta Mok, and Pol Pot's grave site itself. The road to Anlong Veng is currently under construction, and on this day was little more than a mud slide, negotiable by only the most skilled drivers in four-wheel drives; fortunately our border policeman was one of those.

Our impressions of the frontier crossing, and our perilous descent down the mountain, created a sense of anticipation that bordered on foreboding which was dramatically heightened when we stopped at Ta Mok's house on the outskirts of Anlong Veng town. Ta Mok was, during the period of Khmer Rouge control of Cambodia (the period of Democratic Kampuchea – DK), a member of the Standing Committee of the Party Central Committee and the Secretary of the southwest zone and later of the north/central zone, as well as Chief of the General Staff (Fawthrop and Jarvis 2005: 264). After the Vietnamese ousted the Khmer Rouge in 1979, Khmer Rouge forces retreated to six areas mostly bordering Thailand, from where they received Thai, Chinese and Western support to continue

Figure 4.1 The house of Ta Mok the 'Butcher', now a heritage museum in Anlong Veng. (Source: C. Long)

an insurgency that wreaked immense destruction on Cambodia until the final demise of the movement in 1999. Ta Mok, whose reputation for ruthlessness is reflected in the epithet 'The Butcher', took control of the band of mountains to the north of Siem Reap, with his headquarters at Anlong Veng. As other Khmer Rouge strongholds fell or surrendered to government forces in the 1990s,[1] the remaining Khmer Rouge leaders, including Pol Pot and Democratic Kampuchea defence minister, Son Sen, joined Ta Mok at Anlong Veng.

Here the Khmer Rouge leaders, increasingly isolated and desperate, fell on each other for one last time. Nothing if not consistent, the small band of surviving leaders embarked on a final round of violent purges in 1997: Pol Pot ordered the murder of Son Sen and his family, which in turn sparked Mok to arrest the former Brother Number One and subject him to a people's court. Duly convicted, Pol Pot was sentenced to house arrest and died the following year in a hut near today's border crossing (Short 2004: Ch. 12). His body was hastily cremated and his ashes heaped into a pile, with a scrappy corrugated iron roof to protect it from the rain, and bottles planted in the earth as a border. It is a tawdry monument to one of the greatest murderers of the twentieth century.

Ta Mok's house is the most intact and substantial of the 28 tourist-historical sites in the Anlong Veng area. In fact the house compound consists of three structures on a man-made isthmus jutting into a lake that Mok created by damming a stream. While locals point to the benefits of a fish supply created by the lake, its value to Mok as a security barrier is obvious. At the entrance to the isthmus is the Anlong Veng Tourism Office, housed in a wooden hut and infrequently open.

Our vehicle jolted to a halt in a grove of trees beside Ta Mok's house. Several young men sidled up to us, one engaging our driver while another sought four dollars from us as an entrance fee. One of the men was soon identified to us as a guide and we followed him towards the buildings. Just in front of the main house is a large open-sided shed with a concrete floor, where several people squatted in conversation, casting us frowning glances. Here, too, were two small steel cages, recognisable from news footage and photos in books as the 'tiger cages' used by the Khmer Rouge as jungle prison cells (on a subsequent visit a guide confirmed that they had been used to hold people, but only 'traitors' to the Cambodian nation).

As we entered the house a most extraordinary scene developed. A mini-van pulled up among the trees, disgorging a wedding party – bride, bridesmaid, groom, best man and groomsman – all clad in improbably impeccable white. Our guide ushered us into Ta Mok's house. The place is a rough two-storey concrete and timber structure with tiled floors and almost devoid of furniture. In fact its only decoration consisted of four naïve murals, revealing much of the essence of the Khmer Rouge's ideology. On the first floor, an end wall features a peeling mural of Angkor Wat portraying an idyllic Khmer society against the backdrop of a lurid sun-rise. Upstairs a colourful map of Cambodia painted on a wall shows the country divided into provinces; neighbouring Thailand and Laos are indicated, but southern Vietnam, what is known to the Cambodians as Kampuchea Krom and was, until the eighteenth century, part of the Cambodian kingdom, is a grey, unidentified wasteland. Flanking the map are other murals, one of a jungle scene and another of what is taken to be the nearby temple of Preah Vihear. The absence of readily-identifiable ideological symbols seems at first glance rather odd, until one remembers that, particularly in its latter days, the Khmer Rouge tried to portray itself above all else as the defender of an historic Khmer essence (hence Angkor Wat, the temple and the jungle) against the depredations of aggressive foreigners – chiefly the Vietnamese.

We noticed the wedding party entering the house where they began to pose in front of the murals for photographs. We asked the bride if we could take some photos of her too, but she turned away unsmilingly, and the party continued to ignore us. A number of men loitered apparently aimlessly about the house. They were clearly not visitors, but what exactly was their association with the site was unclear. Their presence was somewhat unsettling.

At this instant something akin to a tempest sprung up, slashing across the lake and driving sheets of rain horizontally through the open windows of the house. The bizarreness of the scene – a photo shoot of a wedding party in the former house of a man now in prison awaiting trial on charges of genocide, sullen men loitering, and an atmospheric sound and light show courtesy of the weather – provided an interpretative experience of this site of pain and shame that no museum curator could ever hope to create.

The storm quickly passed, and within minutes the grey tranquillity of this strange Cambodian day had returned.

> 'Why', we asked our guide, 'would people wish to have their wedding photos taken in such a place?'
> 'Because', he replied, 'they think that Ta Mok was a good man, who provided much for the local people.'
> 'And what', we asked, 'do you think of Ta Mok?'
> 'Yes, he was a good man.'
> 'And do you know where he is now?'
> 'Yes, he is in Tuol Sleng prison.'[2]

Our sense of unease was rapidly turning to a feeling of repulsion as we realised that we were surrounded by unreconstructed former Khmer Rouge cadre: had the wedding party, we wondered, so resplendent in white in an area otherwise caked in a brown layer of mud and poverty, been the children of high-ranking Khmer Rouge leaders who still live in the area?

We examined the rest of the site quickly, not daring to enter the foul-stinking rooms under the houses – were they garages or bomb shelters, as our guide suggested, or prison cells, as our driver thought? – and, the feeling of ghoulishness becoming overwhelming, decided to leave. Does Anlong Veng, we pondered as our driver cheerfully raced us towards Siem Reap, offer anything worthwhile to the visitor seeking understanding and commemoration of the Khmer Rouge genocide?

Subsequent visits to Anlong Veng produced similar experiences: the same sense of a tragic past being exploited with little thought or care, the void created by a lack of interpretation filled by uneducated former Khmer Rouge with their own highly distorted understanding of Cambodian history. The questions inevitably arise: why is Anlong Veng being developed as a tourist attraction? Does the preservation of these former Khmer Rouge sites help in the understanding and commemoration of Cambodia's traumatic history? Why do we want to preserve such sites? To prevent forgetting? To aid in reconciliation? Can sites like Anlong Veng perform the latter role? In traumatised societies what is most important – justice or reconciliation? If the latter, does the preservation of sites of trauma help in achieving reconciliation?

In the most prosaic sense, the development of Anlong Veng as a tourist-historic site is part of an attempt by the Cambodian government to reintegrate the area back into a nation finally at peace. It is part of an economic development programme that has also seen the area opened up by roads, especially the one linking the town to Cambodia's tourist epicentre at Siem Reap, the location of the Angkor World Heritage site, and the creation of a border crossing with Thailand. It is envisaged that Anlong Veng will eventually provide an overland route from Bangkok to Siem Reap: the vision of tens of thousands of tourists passing through the town on the way to Angkor must have local officials rubbing their hands and thinking of ways to get them to stop. The former Khmer Rouge sites appear to be the area's chief historical resource, but plans are also afoot for the construction of a casino.

Although Anlong Veng is only a few hours by road from Siem Reap, its isolation from the project to rebuild the national community after the collapse of the Khmer Rouge regime in the face of the 1978 Vietnamese invasion should not be underestimated. Together with Pailin and other Khmer Rouge holdouts until the 1990s, Anlong Veng still remains tenuously integrated into the nation. Ex-Khmer Rouge officials retain positions of authority in all former Khmer Rouge strongholds, and a large proportion of Anlong Veng's population consists of ex-Khmer Rouge cadre or soldiers. The prominent monument at the crossroads in the middle of Anlong Veng town celebrates the construction of the roads that serve to physically reintegrate the area into the nation. If the development of the town's heritage sites is intended to reintegrate it into the national historical discourse, it is far less successful.

If the Cambodian People's Party (CPP) Government in Phnom Penh hopes to reintegrate Anlong Veng into the nation, what message does it want portrayed through the area's heritage sites, and is that message being adequately conveyed? Here we must briefly touch on a debate that is of overwhelming importance to contemporary Cambodia: the debate about the correct response to the Khmer Rouge (Linton 2004). Which is more important to contemporary Cambodia – justice or reconciliation? Since its earliest days, the People's Republic of Kampuchea (PRK) regime, and subsequently the government of the CPP, offered the hand of reconciliation to the Khmer Rouge, which was prepared to abandon opposition to the government and renounce its involvement with Pol Pot's forces. Large numbers of low-level Khmer Rouge soldiers and cadre took up the opportunity, the desertions increasing rapidly into the 1990s as Prime Minister Hun Sen offered amnesty to remaining Khmer Rouge leaders if they brought their forces back into the national fold. Although Pol Pot himself was never offered amnesty, other extremely high-ranking Khmer Rouge leaders, including former DK Foreign Minister Ieng Sary, one-time DK Head of State, Khieu Samphan, and Brother Number Two, Nuon Chea, benefited from a policy that offered to forget their pasts if they 'sincerely reformed' and 'created feats on behalf of the Revolution' (that is, on behalf of the PRK regime) (from the decree-law establishing a 'Revolutionary People's Trial of the Genocide Crime of the Pol Pot-Ieng Sary Clique', cited in Heder, 2002: 190).

On the surface the amnesty policy appears to have been very successful in breaking the back of the Khmer Rouge insurgency, and the organisation, deserted of most of its leaders and their troops, finally collapsed in 1999. Hun Sen continually points to this success to justify the policy. But considerable disquiet remains, both inside Cambodia, and particularly within the international human rights advocacy system, about the absence of any judicial accounting for the crimes of the Khmer Rouge (Linton 2004; Fawthrop and Jarvis 2005). By abandoning the Khmer Rouge in its dying days, despite decades of service to its murderous programme, leaders such as Nuon Chea and Khieu Samphan managed to avoid punishment for their actions for many years. Only recently, with the arrest of Nuon Chea in September 2007, has there been any commitment to bring some leaders to trial: exactly how many will eventually face court remains to be seen. Hun Sen has argued that achieving peace and national 'reconciliation' is more important than a strict judicial accounting and punishment for perpetrators. Just what Hun Sen means by 'reconciliation', however, is problematic. His definition appears to consist of 'integration' of the former Khmer Rouge back into the nation and the absence of armed conflict. Having achieved this reconciliation, he believes that the proper treatment of the country's traumatic history is to 'dig a hole and bury the past in it' (Linton 2004: 12). Given that Cambodia's history of genocide is most starkly manifested in the familiar images of exhumed mass graves, Hun Sen's words are insensitive at best, somewhat sinister at worst.

Heder (2004) makes a strong point about the political nature of Hun Sen's approach to integrating the Khmer Rouge. He argues that just as the models for judicial practice in Cambodia – French colonial 'justice' for Vichy collaborators after World War II, and post-Khmer Rouge Vietnamese People's Courts – were primarily concerned with the political needs of the accusers rather than achieving justice and a true accounting for the past, Hun Sen's system of 'integration' and 'reconciliation' of Khmer Rouge has been primarily about increasing the power of first the PRK regime and then the subsequent CPP government. Rather than any system of official judicial accountability, it is Hun Sen who has determined who should or should not be punished, and in the process demonstrated that the key measure of 'integration' into the nation is loyalty to the CPP regime.

In deciding how to deal with the Khmer Rouge past, the government has paid scant attention to the wishes of the Cambodian people. In an important survey of the attitudes of Cambodians to the Khmer Rouge past, the Documentary Centre of Cambodia, a non-government organisation dedicated to recording and preserving the history of the Khmer Rouge regime and to compiling information that might be used in any trials of former Khmer Rouge, found that respondents were not interested in a truth commission along the lines of the South African Truth and Reconciliation Commission; what they wanted was some sort of trial process, which would lead to

> a public coming to terms with the past, a symbolic formal act played out in the courtroom, where the Khmer Rouge/CPK and their philosophy will be brought into the open through trials of the leaders…It seems that the symbolism of the legal process involves the once powerful being brought down to size, underlining that an era of extraordinary cruelty and abuse of power is really over, with symbolic lessons for today's leaders…[The former Khmer Rouge leaders] would have the opportunity to confess and apologise should they so wish, but would be once and for all vanquished through a judicial process that leads to conviction and punishment.
>
> (Linton 2004: 26)

In contrast to this clear desire for a trial, the government's attitude to the Khmer Rouge has been confusing for ordinary Cambodians. On the one hand they are told that the Khmer Rouge was responsible for the most heinous crimes. On the other they are told that reconciliation with them is the price of peace, even if 'reconciliation' means digging a hole and burying the past in it. Much of the

PRK's and CPP government's focus, too, has been on portraying the Cambodians as the victims of a small, genocidal clique of leaders, thus absolving the bulk of the population, including the not-insubstantial number of ordinary Khmer Rouge cadres and soldiers, of guilt. The problematic nature of contemporary commemoration in Cambodia is illustrated by the 'Day of Hate', or 'Day to remain tied in anger', held annually on 20 May, although not formally promoted by the government since the Paris Peace Accords. It marks the day in 1973 when the Khmer Rouge adopted the policy of total agrarian collectivisation. When it was originally established, the day was used to focus the people's anger against the Khmer Rouge, who were still fighting at the time. Heder argues that the Day of Hate was less a day of culturally appropriate commemoration than an attempt by the government to reinforce the dominant narrative that the Khmer Rouge period was the result of a small group of evildoers victimising the overwhelming majority of Cambodians (Linton 2004: 63–4).

Confusion about approaches to the past is replicated in sites of remembrance in Cambodia. The major site of commemoration is Tuol Sleng, the Khmer Rouge prison and torture centre in suburban Phnom Penh, and its associated killing field at Choeung Ek, on the edge of the city. Both sites are powerfully confronting. Both were established as places of commemoration by the Vietnamese when they displaced the Khmer Rouge in 1979. One of their very clear functions was to display to a world that – except for the Soviet Union and its allies –was opposed to Vietnam's intervention the horrors of the Khmer Rouge regime that the Vietnamese had brought to an end. Just as the PRK and CPP would subsequently do, the interpretation at the sites sought to blame a small group of leaders – the 'Pol Pot-Ieng Sary Clique' – for the corruption of Cambodian communism and the descent into genocidal madness.[3] In more recent years this interpretation has become more nuanced in Tuol Sleng at least, where new exhibits explore the thoughts and motivations of low-level perpetrators as well as victims. The earlier, simplistic message about the culpability of a small clique of leaders has been opened up to a degree, and the full tragedy of the Cambodian trauma has been exposed in a way that is more shocking and distressing than the propagandistic treatment that characterised the site's early interpretation, and that still characterises the interpretation at Choeung Ek.

Nevertheless, the stark brutality of Tuol Sleng and Choeung Ek leave the visitor in no doubt that these are sites of commemoration of the victims of a great crime. The opening up of interpretation at Tuol Sleng to an attempt to broaden the identification of perpetrators and to an exploration of their motivations does not weaken the powerful message of condemnation of the crimes of the Khmer Rouge and of sympathy for their victims. In a sense Tuol Sleng and Choeung Ek continue to bear witness to the crimes of the Khmer Rouge that largely continue to go unpunished, their raw exposure of the brutality of the Cambodian communists demanding some form of accountability. In a country where the history of the Khmer Rouge period is virtually not taught in schools (see Fawthrop and Jarvis 2005: 147; and Kiernan 2004), such sites can also play an extremely important public education role.

As places of interpretation and commemoration of the Khmer Rouge past the sites at Anlong Veng are far more problematic. Here Hun Sen's strategy of 'reconciliation' and 'integration' plays out in an utter failure of interpretation and a complete surrender of moral responsibility for commemoration of the past to the exigencies of development and reintegration of the Anlong Veng region into the nation.

We are conscious here that our reading of the Anlong Veng sites diverges substantially from that of Timothy Dylan Wood, who has perhaps spent more time than anyone studying the Anlong Veng area. Wood believes that the Ministry of Tourism views the tourist-historical sites at Anlong Veng as a resource for economic development of the town, and the reintegration of the area's former Khmer Rouge soldiers and their families.[4] However, at the same time, he argues, the Ministry seeks to impose 'a singular, true representation of history as well as its (authentic) restoration/reconstruction' (Wood 2006: 185):

> The tourism arrangement, which involves the local elites as participants in the decision-making bodies or actively supportive on-lookers, appears as an extension of the Prime Minister's iron grasp. This material configuration becomes the basis for the implantation of a victor's history that confirms and promises the continued existence of this hierarchy. Drawing on its faith in tourist revenue as a foundation, the government demonstrates a keen ability to manage its former enemy while simultaneously (and by means of) producing a tourist area.
>
> (Wood 2006: 18)

The problem with this interpretation is the lack of evidence on the ground. The profound problem with Ta Mok's house, with Pol Pot's grave, is the lack of adequate interpretation, and the lack of control over the messages being conveyed at these sites. The visitor does not get a sense of victor's history. The guides do not stick to the official narrative and there is no alternative source of interpretation: no signage, no leaflets, no guidebook. Can anyone imagine being given a guided tour of Hitler's bunker by former SS soldiers and being told by them that Hitler was a good man because he got the trains running on time? Of course not. But that is, in effect, the closest parallel to what the visitor is expected to accept at Anlong Veng.

Anlong Veng seems to us to demonstrate, not the government's 'keen ability to manage its former enemy', as Wood claims, but the extent to which Hun Sen's CPP regime has abandoned the search for justice and truth in order to achieve its version of reconciliation and peace. Integrating Anlong Veng into the nation through tourism development, with little attempt to control the interpretation of the area's historic sites, serves Hun Sen's purpose of bringing the former Khmer Rouge back into the national fold, but without any demand that they acknowledge guilt or pay penance.

The Hun Sen regime's desire to achieve its version of reconciliation and peace is an important explanation of the disjuncture between what Wood sees as the Ministry of Tourism's desire to control the interpretation of Anlong Veng's

Figure 4.2 Pol Pot's grave. (Source: C. Long)

historic sites and the reality of their interpretation. But there are other factors in operation here too.

The failure of interpretation, as we see it, indicates the extent to which Cambodia remains, in fact, a fractured and fragmented country. Former Khmer Rouge leaders continue to exercise considerable power in a number of regions, and at all levels of government. Hun Sen's strategy of ignoring individuals' former activities with the Khmer Rouge so long as they now pledge allegiance to the CPP has encouraged this lack of accountability for past actions and the persistence of regional autonomy. While the Ministry of Tourism may have a clear sense of how it wants the Anlong Veng sites interpreted, its ability to implement its vision in a far-flung province inhabited by substantial numbers of former Khmer Rouge is obviously lacking. Lack of expertise and funding clearly also restrict the Ministry. A well-developed interpretation plan for the Anlong Veng sites would cost more money than the Ministry can afford, and, as places like Choeung Ek demonstrate, the practice of heritage interpretation remains under-developed in Cambodia. This is, of course, understandable in a country where there are far more pressing claims on the government's limited budget and on the activities of international aid agencies.

One of the fundamental failures of interpretation practice demonstrated in Anlong Veng has to do with the lack of understanding of the difficulties associated with perpetrator sites as sites of commemoration. By 'perpetrator sites' we mean places associated purely or primarily with the perpetrators of pain and suffering – Hitler's bunker, the statue of Felix Dzerzhinsky in Moscow, Stalin's dacha, Saddam's palaces – rather than places associated with their victims – Auschwitz, Tuol Sleng, gulag camps, Robben Island, the Berlin Wall, to name a few. Given that all heritage practice involves the making of judgements about what is worthy of preservation and what stories are to be told through preservation, we see no difficulty in stating that if the purpose of heritage preservation in the case of places of pain and shame is to commemorate the victims, then there is little role for the preservation of perpetrator sites. Heritage preservation is not about preserving all of the past – it is about remembering aspects of the past which we believe worthy of remembrance. As controversial as it may sound, it is extremely difficult to see how the preservation of Anlong Veng's sites as *heritage sites*, particularly in their current interpretation-free state, contributes anything to the understanding of the Khmer Rouge period or to the commemoration of that period's victims.

Often it is much harder to divide victim and perpetrator sites, and in such cases the responsibility borne by those entrusted with interpretation is heavy. Even more problematic are places associated with a hated regime or a regime widely acknowledged as having perpetrated great injustices, but which are not directly implicated in painful or shameful events. Here we can think of Nazi-era buildings still standing in Berlin, or the Stalin-era skyscrapers such as the Moscow State University, replete with communist decoration, that dot Moscow's landscape, or even the Moscow Metro. Debates about the preservation of such places have raged with varying outcomes in most of the countries emerging from traumatic pasts, especially in the post-communist countries of Europe. The contenders tend to divide into two camps. Those arguing for preservation have frequently made the case that the structures, through their design and association with memories, provide an important reminder of the nature of the system and historical period from which they derive. Such structures or places serve as a safeguard against forgetting, and thus as a form of warning about the possibility of repetition, and as a means of commemoration. It is also claimed that one of the typical characteristics of the regimes of which they are symbolic was contempt for the past; thus we should not replicate the behaviour of the defeated regime by setting out to destroy all of its traces (Hoffman-Axthelm 1993; Light 2000; *Moscow Times* 2002; MacDonald 2006). On the other hand, opponents of preservation have argued that in order to move on to the future, it is necessary and right to remove the symbols of the rejected past. Each political system, it is argued, must construct a landscape that reflects its own values and aspirations.[5]

We believe that the sites at Anlong Veng fall clearly into the category of perpetrator sites but that the parameters within which we must interpret their meaning are clear and agreed by virtually all parties: their relationship to the genocide perpetrated by the Khmer Rouge. Do these sites further understanding of the Cambodian genocide or help in the commemoration of the victims? The answer, we believe, is no. There seems to be a clear understanding in other cases where commemoration of the victims of crimes of the nature and scale perpetrated by the Khmer Rouge is seen as the *raison d'être* of heritage preservation that perpetrator sites are inappropriate commemorative sites – Germany is the best example (Fulbrook 2002). The failure to recognise this in Cambodia is the result of the confused approach to historical accountability and justice that filters from the top down (in fact, as Linton shows, many ordinary Cambodians are much less confused about the need for a proper accounting for the past than their political leaders).

The failure also derives from poorly developed understandings of heritage interpretation and preservation practice. The problem in Anlong Veng is that the imperative of economic development through tourism has led to the hasty and ill-considered incorporation of historic sites into a heritage tourism strategy which Cambodia is not professionally equipped to manage. The national government's desire to stimulate development in the Anlong Veng region and thus to reintegrate it into the nation is entirely laudable. However, the choice of tourism development as a primary strategy reveals the extent to which tourism has become embedded in international development thought as a panacea for developing countries. In fact, the reliance on tourism reflects the lack of legitimate development options open to struggling countries like Cambodia in the context of an international system strongly loaded against them, and the lack of innovative thinking and commitment to meaningful and sustainable development exhibited by political elites and international development organisations. The contrast with the treatment of Nazi-related sites in Germany demonstrates that even in the treatment of genocidal histories there are great disparities between the wealthy and the poor.

The Anlong Veng sites raise some difficult questions about the purpose and nature of heritage interpretation and preservation. Contemporary interpretation practice, at least in the West, has tended towards the opening up of meanings, the rejection of didacticism and the promotion of multiple stories and self-discovery. But how appropriate is this approach in cases involving places of pain and shame?

Wood seems to fall into the relativist trap with his concern for the voices of Anlong Veng locals to be heard in the interpretation of the Khmer Rouge sites:

> The Anlong Veng museum project provides a glimpse into the logic underlying aspects of government development initiatives. First, the processes by which the government and its various affiliates have amassed data and pursued representations (by tour guides) demonstrates the fixing of a particular narrative, operating as 'truth' and achieved at the expense of the perspectives and participation of locals who were actively involved with the ousted forces of Democratic Kampuchea.
>
> (Wood 2006: 190)

The involvement of locals in development projects is quite appropriate in normal circumstances, as most international aid agencies now recognise. But this politically correct approach to development practice is simply inappropriate in the interpretation of the Anlong Veng sites. Why should interpretation take into account local perspectives if locals believe that Ta Mok and Pol Pot were good men? Do former Khmer Rouge have the right to have their understanding of history seriously considered in interpreting the Cambodian past? How are the

Figure 4.3 Khmer Rouge figures sculpted out of rock on the road descending from the Dangrek Escarpment near Anlong Veng. (Source: C. Long)

perspectives of former Khmer Rouge to be weighed against the perspectives of other Cambodians who suffered because of the actions not only of the Khmer Rouge leaders, but also of Anlong Veng locals who followed those leaders?

In the end we are forced to contemplate the questions that we raised early in this chapter: why do we want to preserve such sites? To prevent forgetting? To aid in reconciliation? Can sites like Anlong Veng perform the latter role? In traumatised societies what is most important – justice or reconciliation? If the latter, does the preservation of sites of trauma help in achieving reconciliation? Does the preservation of these former Khmer Rouge sites help in the understanding and commemoration of Cambodia's traumatic history?

Our conclusion, which does not come easily to us as heritage professionals committed to our field and to the power of heritage as a force for remembrance, is that preservation of the Anlong Veng sites does little or nothing to further understanding or commemoration of Cambodia's tragic and painful past. To wipe them from the heritage and tourism map would not be to encourage a culture of forgetting. Tuol Sleng and other such sites, together with the everyday reality of Cambodian trauma and, hopefully, the trials of the remaining leaders, ensure that the Khmer Rouge period will not be forgotten. Forgetting Anlong Veng's Khmer Rouge sites, though, will contribute to a culture of true reconciliation by ensuring that the message about the Khmer Rouge period is clear and untrammelled by moral and historical relativism, by emphasising above all else the voices of the victims and silencing the perpetrators once and for all.

Notes

1 The central government's strategy of offering amnesty to Khmer Rouge leaders who surrendered and offered their forces up for integration back into mainstream Cambodian society was very successful in splitting the movement and hastening its demise; the legality and morality of the amnesties is another question altogether. For an extensive discussion of the strategy and associated legal and moral issues, see Linton 2004.
2 In fact Ta Mok died in captivity just seven months after this visit, apparently from a stroke.
3 Signage at the Choeung Ek site still speaks in propagandistic tones about the 'Pol Pot-Ieng Sary clique'.
4 Wood (2006: 183) reports that the area was once home to 16,000 Khmer Rouge troops and their families.
5 Two interesting examples of sites that have provoked debates of this kind are the Moscow Hotel in the Russian capital and the Palast der Republik, the former Parliament of the GDR in Berlin. In both instances, preservation advocates lost. In the German case, the plan is to reconstruct the Berliner Stadtschloss, which was demolished to make way for the Palast.

References

Fawthrop, T. and Jarvis, H. (2005) *Getting Away with Genocide: Elusive Justice and the Khmer Rouge Tribunal*, Sydney: UNSW Press.

Fulbrook, M. (2002) *German National Identity After the Holocaust*, Cambridge: Polity Press.

Heder, S. (2002) 'Hun Sen and the Genocide Trials in Cambodia: International Impacts, Impunity and Justice', in J. Ledgerwood (ed.), *Cambodia Emerges from the Past*, DeKalb, IL: Center for Southeast Asian Studies, Northern Illinois University.

Hoffman-Axthelm, D. (1993) 'The demise of Lenin Square', *Daidalos*, XLIX: 122–9.

Kiernan, B. (2004) 'Coming to terms with the past: Cambodia', *History Today*, September: 16–18.

Kiernan, B. (2005) 'Barbaric crimes of a mystical communism seen through its own eyes', review of *Pol Pot: The History of a Nightmare*, by Philip Short, *Times Higher Education Supplement*, 25 February.

Light, D. (2000) 'An unwanted past: contemporary tourism and the heritage of communism in Romania', *International Journal of Heritage Studies*, 6 (2): 145–60.

Linton, S. (2004) *Reconciliation in Cambodia*, Phnom Penh: Documentation Centre of Cambodia.

MacDonald, S. (2006) 'Words in stone: agency and identity in a Nazi landscape', *Journal of Material Culture*, 11 (1/2): 105–26.

Moscow Times (2002) 'Keep Iron Felix on scrapheap of history', Editorial, September 18: 10.

Short, P. (2004) *Pol Pot: The History of a Nightmare*, London: John Murray.

Wood, T.D. (2006) 'Touring memories of the Khmer Rouge', in Ollier, L.C.P. and Winter, T. (eds), *Expressions of Cambodia: The Politics of Tradition, Identity and Change*, London: Routledge.

Chapter 5

The Myall Creek Memorial
History, identity and reconciliation

Bronwyn Batten

Well-travelled Australians often speak of what it feels like to walk in places steeped in history; what it is like to climb a set of stone stairs in Italy, knowing that those same stairs have been scaled daily since the 1500s. An even more powerful experience is to stand at the site of significant events – events that changed the trajectory of history, or shaped nations for decades to come. It is this phenomenon that calls numerous Australians to Gallipoli every year. There is an intense desire to understand our history, but more than that, there is an inner need to let the stories held in the land speak to us: to feel the power of these places, to hear the messages they hold for us.

The site of the Myall Creek massacre appears on the surface to be a typical rural vista. Golden grasslands recede into the distance; the odd gum tree dots the landscape. It is a scene of rural tranquillity. Perhaps it is this contradiction – the

Figure 5.1 Myall Creek today. (Source: B. Batten)

picture of tranquillity the site presents in contrast to the painful history that lies beneath its surface – that cuts to a visitor's soul. The power of the Myall Creek site is considerable. One cannot help but feel the indelible stain the massacre has left on the land. It is this power that creates the potential to deliver a number of significant messages and experiences of the site. It would be difficult for anyone to leave the site emotionally unaffected. How this power is utilised, and for what purpose, is the main topic explored in this chapter.

Brief historical overview

The Myall Creek Massacre occurred on 10 June 1838 and is one of the most widely known accounts of a massacre targeting Aboriginal people in Australian history. In particular, the conviction and hanging of seven white men brought the case considerable notoriety.

The Myall Creek Station was established by Henry Dangar in 1837 (Stubbins and Smith 2001: 2). In May 1838, a group of approximately fifty Aboriginal people from the Wirrayaraay tribe were warned to move on from a nearby station in fear of their safety. At the invitation of a convict stockman at Myall Creek, they moved there, and for the next few weeks the station hands at Myall Creek developed close relationships with the group. On 10 June 1838 most of the male Aborigines at Myall Creek went to help cut bark at a neighbouring station. It was there that they learnt of a party of armed stockmen who were patrolling the area. The male Aborigines went back to warn the others but arrived too late (Reece 1974: 37).

The armed group consisted of ten or twelve stockmen. One of the Myall Creek convicts also took part in the massacre, despite having had amicable relationships with the Aboriginal party. Another convict refused to be party to the activities and later gave evidence in court against the stockmen. Only two boys aged about eight or nine managed to escape the massacre (Stubbins and Smith 2001: 3). The day after the massacre the murderers returned to the site to burn the bodies. They also tracked down and murdered most of the Aboriginal men who had been absent cutting bark.

The massacre was reported by a local landholder. An inquiry into the incident identified ten suspects (Stubbins and Smith 2001: 7). There was considerable publicity over the trial of the men, most of it supportive of them (Stubbins and Smith 2001: 8). *The Herald* put forward the argument that, as Aborigines did not improve the land but merely occupied it like animals, the land was not worked as God had intended it to be, and so '[the murderers] were therefore really protecting the property of the white man, carrying out a task that was really the government's responsibility' (Waldersee 1979: 72). The jury declared the men not guilty. A second hearing was, however, achieved by the prosecution.

It was at the second trial (where only seven of the original ten accused were tried) that the men were found guilty. The men were not found guilty of a 'massacre', but rather the murder of an Aboriginal child. This was because the remains of a child's skull was the only firm evidence available as most of the evidence was destroyed.

The testimony of the convict as to the massacre was largely dismissed, and no Aboriginal testimony was allowed (Stubbins and Smith 2001: 10). The seven men were executed on 18 December 1838. The conviction was probably aided by pressure being placed on the Governor of New South Wales (NSW) from humanitarians in England over the rights of Aborigines (Waldersee 1979: 72). Without this shift in attitude towards Aborigines, the Government may not have acted so decisively against the accused.

Memorial background

The idea of creating a memorial to the massacre dates back to at least 1965 when Len Payne, a resident of Bingara (the town near Myall Creek), tried to gain support to 'erect a memorial which would take the form of a symbolic gate on the site of the massacre' (Jesuit Publications 2003). The idea was condemned by one letter written to the local paper stating that 'The whole idea was ill-conceived, unconsidered, mischievous and an insult to the Bingara people' (Stubbins and Smith 2001: 11). As a result of the publicity no memorial was erected at the site.

To some extent this decision can be seen as a product of its time. In the 1968 *Boyer Lectures* the anthropologist W.E.H. Stanner discussed what he termed 'The Great Australian Silence' (Stanner 1991: 27). Robert Manne (2003: 2) argues that what Stanner meant by this is often misunderstood. Manne writes:

> Stanner did not mean that scholars and others had failed to show an interest in traditional Aboriginal society... What Stanner meant was that both scholars and citizens had, thus far, failed to integrate the story of the Aboriginal dispossession and its aftermath into their understanding of the course of Australian history, reducing the whole tragic and complex story to ... a 'melancholy footnote'.

But the 'silence' was unlikely to last long (Stanner 1991: 27). Indeed in 1970 Charles Rowley effectively broke the 'silence' with the publication of his three-volume study *The Destruction of Aboriginal Society, Outcasts in White Society* and *The Remote Aborigines* (Manne 2003). The story of Australia's post-contact history, at least in historical discourses, was beginning to be told. It would still be some time however, before traumatic events like the Myall Creek Massacre would begin to be memorialised and interpreted within the Australian landscape (Batten 2004).

In 1998, a descendant of one of the Myall Creek massacre survivors, Sue Blacklock, initiated a 'one-off' reconciliation conference at Myall Creek and it was at this event that a decision was made to erect a permanent memorial (Stubbins and Smith 2001: 11–12). A committee was formed to oversee the project and regular meetings were held. From the outset, perhaps because the effects of negative criticism against the previous attempt to erect a memorial had been so detrimental, the committee established a firm rationale for the need for a memorial. The grounds for erecting the memorial as tabled at the meeting are listed below.

> If we and our descendants are to live in peace ... then we have to tell and acknowledge the truth of our history. It is not that all our history is bad, but the bad must be acknowledged along with the good, if we are to have any integrity. There is a code of silence surrounding the massacres.
>
> We want Australia to be an inclusive society... This cannot happen until the history includes the stories of how Aboriginal people as well as non-Aboriginal people experienced the history.
>
> We owe it to those who died defending their country and families, or died as innocent victims of vengeance, to create a memorial which reminds us of their part in our common history.
>
> It is important to acknowledge the people who acted for justice in the story....
>
> We are not pointing the finger at the people of Myall Creek or Bingara. The massacres were all over the country.
>
> (Stubbins and Smith 2001: 12)

An additional reason for establishing such a firm rationale was that the memorial project coincided with a period of time when the so called 'history wars' were flourishing in Australia (Macintyre 2003). Kelly (2003: 8) writes that in Australia, it was in 1992 during the time of the Keating government that history was 'harnessed... for his [Keating's] political purpose' and was thus taken into the public arena. A rebuttal against this manoeuvre came from senior opposition parliamentarian John Howard (who would later become Prime Minister). Howard utilised the work of the historian Geoffrey Blainey who had formulated the notion of 'black armband history', which essentially argued that historians (and Keating) had taken an excessively negative and unjustified view of the development of the Australian nation.

Australia's post-contact Aboriginal history took centre stage at the height of the history wars. In particular the focus was upon how responsible the Australian nation is for the actions of the past. Keith Windschuttle caused considerable friction in historical circles with the publication of a series of articles in *Quadrant* in 2000 and 2001 and volume one of *The Fabrication of Aboriginal History* in 2003. In *The Fabrication of Aboriginal History* he argues that 'the settlement of Australia was basically benign and that the destruction of Aboriginal society was a consequence of ... disease ... primitive dysfunctionality and the criminal proclivities of the Aborigines' (Macintyre 2003: 221). Counter-arguments to Windschuttle's work were put forward in a series of books and articles that responded to his publication, such as *Whitewash*, edited by Robert Manne.

At the time that the Myall Creek Memorial was beginning to be established therefore the issue of how Australia's Aboriginal history was interpreted and presented was politically charged in the extreme. The Memorial Committee was thus particularly conscious of gaining the necessary support for their project and of ensuring the memorial was established in an inclusive manner. To this end, descendants of the Wirrayaraay were consulted as to how the project should continue (Stubbins and Smith 2001: 12). They were given the option of continuing the project themselves, or of involving both Indigenous and non-indigenous people. There was unanimous support for it being a jointly managed project (Stubbins and Smith 2001: 12), and from that time, the memorial project began to increasingly take on board aspects of shared history and reconciliation. In June 1999 the statement that the memorial 'is also for the purpose of reconciling Aboriginal and non-Aboriginal people' was added to the list of grounds for erecting the memorial (Stubbins and Smith 2001: 13). The memorial had begun to take on the role of commemorating not only a specific historical event, but to function as being representative of broader aspects of Australian history.

The Opening Ceremony for the memorial was held on 10 June 2000, a year that was marked by other reconciliation events held across Australia. These events aimed to recognise the impact the course of Australian history has had on

Figure 5.2 Example of the small boulders with plaques. (Source: B. Batten)

Figure 5.3 The final large boulder at the 2003 memorial ceremony. (Source: B. Batten)

Aboriginal people. The Opening Ceremony at Myall Creek was unique in that it brought together 'in an emotional personal reconciliation three descendants of the murderers with several descendants of those who were massacred' (Brown 2003). The descendants on both sides held official roles in the ceremony.

As it stands today, the memorial consists of a winding trail on which small boulders are placed at regular intervals with plaques revealing (in both Gamilaraay, the language of the Wirrayaraay, and English) the history of the massacre. A final large granite boulder surrounded by crushed white granite acts both as a memorial to the dead and as a touchstone for the past. The plaque on the final boulder states:

> In memory of the Wirrayaraay people who were murdered on the slopes of this ridge in an unprovoked but premeditated act in the late afternoon of 10 June, 1838.
>
> Erected on 10 June 2000 by a group of Aboriginal and non-Aboriginal Australians in act of reconciliation, and in acknowledgement of the truth of our shared history.
>
> We remember them.
>
> Ngiyani winangay ganunga.

Myall Creek: Pilgrimage and reconciliation

When visiting the Myall Creek Memorial many Australians experience a personal pilgrimage into the Australian past and our national identity. The memorial also triggers or strengthens many Australians' commitment to reconciliation. The origins of the 2000 memorial are steeped firmly in the national reconciliation movement. The ABC Radio National programme *Perspective* featured a piece by the Rev. John Brown (co-chair of the Memorial Committee) in June 2003 which reinforces this view. In the programme he stated that 'Because of its notoriety, this massacre is representative of all the massacres that occurred across Australia' (Brown 2003). Brown went on to explain that this was the reasoning behind the invitation for all those who attended the dedication (opening) ceremony to bring a stone or rock to contribute to the memorial. 'They symbolize the fact that this memorial commemorates the shared history of all of us' (Brown 2003). Myall Creek portrays a history for all Australians. Accordingly, Brown encouraged listeners of *Perspective* to visit the memorial freely, regardless of whether it was an official ceremonial occasion. 'The memorial is worth a visit at any time for all people travelling in Northern New South Wales' (Brown 2003). He also suggested that 'Because of its representative nature, the Memorial should be recognized as a site of national heritage significance' (Brown 2003).

A discussion section posted on the Myall Creek Memorial Committee website features a letter from Ted Stubbins in mid 2002 discussing what direction the Memorial Committee should now take having achieved the establishment of the memorial. Stubbins writes that the committee's initial objectives were to develop a 'fitting memorial' for those who were killed or suffered as a result of the events at Myall Creek, and to show 'solidarity with the Aboriginal quest for truth and justice' (Stubbins 2002). In establishing the memorial the committee also hoped to 'cause the people of the New England/North West to confront the largely unspoken and unacknowledged history of atrocities and injustices... [to ideally] lead to better relations between Aboriginal and other Australians in this area' (Stubbins 2002). The committee wanted visitors to make the leap from the specific history of the massacre, to a broader regional – and ultimately a national – narrative. The third point that Stubbins raises is of particular relevance to the process of establishing the memorial as a national monument in the eyes of all Australians – somewhere that they should visit at least once in their lifetime as part of their own personal pilgrimage in coming to terms with and acknowledging aspects of the past. Stubbins writes that the committee felt that 'in recognition of the massacre being a uniquely well-documented signal event in Australian history', they should 'develop a high and continuing profile for the memorial. The memorial would serve as a national acknowledgement and as a means of educating succeeding generations' (Stubbins 2002). Stubbins felt that they had succeeded in developing an appropriate memorial and that the annual ceremonies were gradually reaching out to and educating the people of the New England and North West Regions of NSW. He believed, however, that the majority of visitors from outside the New England/North West Regions were people who had a prior interest in reconciliation. He writes:

> In order to achieve its potential as an agent of national acknowledgement and education, the memorial needs to attract large numbers of Australians, many of whom have little or no knowledge of the history of contact between Aboriginal people and new comers. There needs to be a continuing effort to promote the memorial so that it attracts large visitor numbers. For instance, it should be on the itinerary of the average person who sets out on his/her round Australian trip… Just as the Stockman's Hall of Fame is a permanent iconic reminder of aspects of Australia's colonial pastoral past, the Myall Creek Memorial needs to have an indelible niche in the national consciousness.
>
> (Stubbins 2002)

How the Memorial Committee could go about increasing public awareness of the memorial was the focus of further discussions on the website and at committee meetings. The preparation of a professional report and plan of action was one suggestion (Stubbins 2002). A grand vision of working with an Aboriginal Land organisation to try to acquire the Myall Creek Station was also put forward (Riddell 2002). A descendant of one of the men convicted of murder at Myall Creek, Des Blake, was fairly pessimistic of the potential for the memorial to be a site of such well-known national significance, stating that for this to occur realistically:

> …the attraction has to be situated near a town… [with] good facilities. At this time Bingara doesn't meet these requirements… It needs to be on a tourist route… I don't believe the highway…is a main tourist route… [and] the attraction needs to be something the average Australian is interested in. Unfortunately I do not believe that enough people would be interested to make any further major development a feasible project. The main visitors would probably be schools or people who are really interested in Reconciliation. Present facilities are probably adequate for this.
>
> (Blake 2002)

Whether furthering the status of the site is achievable or not, at a Committee Meeting in October 2002 resolutions were put forward to try to increase awareness of the site. It was suggested that corporate sponsorship of the site be sought and tour operators such as Oz Experience be contacted with details of the site. A resolution was made that:

> The central focus of future activity should be on education. Myall Creek Memorial is representative of all massacre sites. In Australia we are inclined to bury and forget what we ought to remember. This is a place for truth-telling. This is the massacre which of all massacres stands out. This is an event

which changed the history of Australia, because for the first time people were brought to justice for the massacre. This is where the education about our shared history should take place.

(The Myall Creek Memorial Committee, 2002)

At the gathering following the 2004 Memorial Ceremony a representative from the Department of Environment and Heritage was invited to speak about the newly established National Heritage List and the process for nominating the Myall Creek Memorial Site. The Memorial Committee were excited about the possibility of having the memorial formally identified as a site of national heritage significance. It was felt that formal listing could only increase the memorial's status and thus the nation's awareness of the Myall Creek massacre and so the Committee prepared a nomination for the site. The Minister for the Environment announced at the Annual Memorial Ceremony on 7 June 2008, the 170th anniversary of the massacre, that the site had been added to the National Heritage List (Garrett 2008).

Since 2002 the Myall Creek Memorial Committee has been determined to portray Myall Creek as a site of national significance, as a site for all Australians to visit. Will a formal assessment process of the site concur with the Committee's passionate belief that this is a site of truly national significance? Time will tell. Visitor perspectives of the site, however, can shed light on the ways in which Australians perceive the site and the values they place on it.

Participant survey

To explore why people come to the site, where they are coming from, and what their experiences of the Memorial Ceremony are, a short survey of those attending the Memorial Ceremony in June 2004 was conducted. A copy of the survey is reproduced in Table 5.1. Of the approximately 150 people who attended the memorial service in 2004, forty completed the survey.

The results of Question 1 revealed that well over half of those attending the ceremony were from the New England or North West Regions of New South Wales. For the main part, therefore, it could be argued that the event is still largely attracting a regional, and not a national, attendance. Only two other states/territories were represented – Queensland and the Australian Capital Territory – but their participant numbers were insignificant. A factor influencing the origin of those attending is the narrow publicity that the event received. By contrast, in 2003 several reconciliation email lists advertised the upcoming event and a wider participation was achieved.

Two responses to Question 2 were equally popular: attending the event is important for reconciliation, and attending the event is important to help build community relations. The fact that the latter response was so popular may be a result of the number of attendees from the local region, but is also a clear indication that the event is still largely one of regional rather than national importance.

Table 5.1 Copy of the 2004 Visitor Survey.

1 Where did you come from (e.g. what town/state/country do you normally reside in) to attend the Myall Creek Memorial Ceremony in 2004?

2 What were the *main influences* which made you decide to attend the Myall Creek Memorial Ceremony in 2004? (tick which ever box/es apply and feel free to add any additional comments on the lines given or over the page):

    ☐   I am participating in a role in the ceremony.

    ☐   A friend or relative is participating in the ceremony.

    ☐   I am representing my place of employment or organisation

    ☐   I feel that it is an important part of the reconciliation process to acknowledge the darker aspects of the Australian past.

    ☐   I feel I need to develop a better understanding of Australia's history, and thought my attendance at the ceremony might help me to achieve this.

    ☐   I think it is an important event for the local community, bringing both Indigenous and non-indigenous people together and so I wanted to show support.

    ☐   I have a direct link to an ancestor who was involved in the events at Myall Creek in 1838 so I feel it is a part of my personal history.

    ☐   Other (please feel free to expand on your reasons in the lines below)

3 (Optional) How did you feel after attending the 2004 Myall Creek Memorial Ceremony?

The high number of respondents ticking the reconciliation box is unsurprising given that, as Des Blake suggested (as discussed earlier in this chapter), those choosing to attend the event are likely to have a strong interest in reconciliation.

Six respondents gave 'Other' answers. One respondent from Inverell indicated that his/her family had never attended the event before but felt that it was something that they should do and bring their children to. This respondent noted that 'we will be back next year', adding to the idea that the event becomes a kind of pilgrimage for some attendees. This idea was also backed by another respondent from Tamworth who had 'attended this gathering since 1998' with his/her partner and it was something that they would continue to try to do.

Other explanations focused on a desire to express a personal response for the need for reconciliation. For example, one respondent from Warwick, Queensland, wrote 'I need to come here today to stand as a person speaking against the evils done to the gentle owners of this land. I stand with those healing the wrong and bless their efforts.' Some respondents noted that they regularly attended, or expanded on the organisations or work places that they were representing (e.g. World Vision Australia), or why they felt a personal link with the event (e.g. they had lived locally all their life or they had descended from those involved in the massacre).

Question 3, an optional question asking how respondents felt after attending the ceremony, received 35 responses (87.5 per cent of all respondents). These mostly focused on being emotionally moved by the ceremony and feeling a renewed enthusiasm for reconciliation. Many responses noted that the event provided an almost spiritual experience:

> It is a very moving place. Always feel a sense of 'spirituality' after being at the 'Rock'.
>
> (Respondent from Warialda)

> A stronger link to the land and its Aboriginal people. It was in a sense a 'Holy-Walk' of sadness yet hope, especially when the students from their respective high schools said their responses to each other.
>
> (Respondent from Oatlands)

> I feel glad that I came – it is a public statement of support for reconciliation. It makes me glad to see so many Aboriginal people here for this ceremony each year. To see the direct descendants of those who perpetrated the massacre is a wonderful thing too.
>
> (Respondent from Narrabri)

> This is an important moment each year to re-tell the shared history and engage others in the significance, including the lack of education offered by our education system to discover the truth.
>
> (Respondent from Canberra)

> As always a religious/spiritual experience. Thank you.
>
> (Respondent from Moree)

> This is my third visit. I need to continue to come each year to refresh my commitment to reconciliation.
>
> (Respondent from Moree)

> I felt that I wanted everyone else at school, my friends, everyone, to know the true history of Australia.
>
> (Respondent from Inverell)

Thus the experience for many of those who responded to the survey at the 2004 event was a spiritual, almost personal pilgrimage or journey of understanding into the Australian past and its role in the present. The Myall Creek Memorial Committee has sought to create this kind of experience and is continuing to promote the memorial and the associated ceremony held each June to increase its status from regional to national recognition and importance.

Discussion

The Myall Creek Memorial and the annual Memorial Ceremony held at the site raise a number of interesting questions, particularly in relation to a single massacre story being used to represent a broader historical relationship and a related process of reconciliation. This chapter focuses on the memorial's status. In particular, the question of whether the memorial will ever reach a stage of development where it has achieved nationwide recognition as a significant historic site and become a 'must see' destination. Offshoot questions associated with this are how, if the site's status is increased, can its integrity be preserved, and how can it remain a site of 'historic pilgrimage'? With increased patronage, could Myall Creek become a site that merely satisfies morbid curiosities rather than achieving meaningful engagement with the past? Perhaps a more pertinent question is whether it is indeed desirable for the site to be marketed as a site that is representative of the history of massacres in general in Australia. Both sides can easily be argued for.

When used broadly to educate about Indigenous/non-indigenous relations across Australia, the Myall Creek massacre does help to explain the culture of silence that developed surrounding massacres in Australia. The frequency or severity of massacres did not necessarily cease or decrease across the nation as a result of the Myall Creek convictions but rather were driven further underground so that often the only evidence that remains of these events is regarded as 'folklore'. Revealing the background to the culture of silence aids understanding as to why the scepticism over the existence of massacres in Australian history has developed. In this respect, the Myall Creek site can therefore play an important role in educating Australians broadly about the past. Clearly there are benefits in bringing to the Australian public a broad understanding of the past. There is the potential to aid the reconciliation process as visitors to the site can see how the history of Myall Creek may be mirrored in other states and territories across Australia.

There is an inherent danger, however, in using the story of the Myall Creek Massacre to raise awareness of massacres across Australia. The danger is that the general may override the specific. Is this a necessary trade-off to further the cause of reconciliation in Australia? If so, can the Myall Creek story sit under the banner of promoting 'truth-telling' in history as the Myall Creek Memorial Committee desires? How thorough (and truthful) a history can be told when we seek to generalise the events to broadly explain a darker period of history? These are complex issues. It is a fine line to walk promoting truth-telling in history through the establishment of one site as being representative of all others. If the accuracy of the Myall Creek story is lost under the broad-brush approach, the promotion of reconciliation and acknowledging our 'shared history' may be threatened by the failure to acknowledge the complexity of the Myall Creek story.

By emphasising the story of Myall Creek as being a story that was repeated in many places across Australia some of the individuality and intricacies – the detail of the Myall Creek story – are easily lost. For this reason, it is important that the promotion of the Myall Creek site continues to be carried out with the support of the descendants of the Aboriginal people so they can ensure the local story of their ancestors is not lost at the expense of establishing a national narrative. Above all, it must be remembered that the Myall Creek Memorial is a memorial to the 28 Wirrayaraay men and women who were murdered in 1838. Not only is this necessary out of respect for the dead, it is the sober reality that gives the site its emotional power, and enables the Memorial to act as a site of reconciliation more broadly. It is a place where unspeakable events occurred, and a place where history must be remembered. This is the touchstone that must be retained if the Myall Creek site and the Memorial Ceremony are to maintain their credibility.

There are also other aspects of the specific history of the Myall Creek site that should not be lost in the move to promote the site as broadly representative of Australian history. These aspects provide important lessons about the past that extend beyond using the site as a means of breaking the culture of silence surrounding the massacres and the darker side of Australian history. For example, Campbell (1978) discusses some exceptions to the dominant trend of Indigenous/non-indigenous relations in the New England/North West Regions at the time of the Myall Creek massacre, adding to the complexity of the historical picture. He writes, for instance, about the Everett brothers, who:

> came to New England in 1838 – during the violent era on the tableland. The local Aborigines helped them choose a fine tract of land…. The Everetts learned the local Aboriginal dialect, and mutual trust, respect and honesty prevailed between the representatives of the two races on [the property] as they do today (1969). The Everetts were employing Aborigines as stockmen and house servants with great success and satisfaction at a time when other settlers viewed the 'no hoper savages' with contempt and hatred…. They overcame the incompatibility of values and ways of life by deep interest, broad sympathy and respect for the humanity of the natives.
>
> (Campbell 1978: 9)

The issue of whether or not the Myall Creek Memorial is a good model for other potential memorials at historic sites across Australia is also worth exploration. The establishment of the Myall Creek Memorial Committee with both Indigenous and non-indigenous representation from the outset provides an important model for others interested in establishing similar memorials or interpretation programmes. Where a site involves the history of multiple groups, an equitable outcome is to have representation from all relevant stakeholders. The Myall Creek Memorial Committee has taken the concept of representation one step further, however, by insisting that the make-up of their committee consist of 50 per cent

Indigenous and 50 per cent non-indigenous members (Rev. John Brown, 2004 – personal comment at the Annual Myall Creek Memorial Committee Meeting). This equality of representation may be integral to achieving an appropriate balance between representing the specific history of the site (and in particular honouring the dead) and dealing with the darker aspects of Australian history more broadly.

Conclusion

The Myall Creek Memorial Committee has a vision: to harness the power of the Myall Creek site – the call to action people feel after visiting the site – to further reconciliation and to foster a better understanding of the Australian past. It is a noble vision, but a complex and sensitive task. Myall Creek has enormous potential to be a focal point for reconciliation and an aid to understanding Australian history – to harness this potential it is necessary to ensure the site maintains its integrity; that is, its essential character and purpose. First and foremost the site must be treated as a memorial to the 28 Wirrayaraay men and women who were murdered in 1838 – it must retain its individual story. Secondly, the site must retain its rural tranquillity, which allows the history beneath its surface to be felt first-hand. A major factor in the significance and power of the place is its landscape: gum trees and golden grasslands. These things are a catalyst for reflection, and as such, can be a catalyst for reconciliation.

In the years to come the Myall Creek site may strengthen its status and truly become a place of national significance where people come from all over Australia to make a pilgrimage into the past and their national identity. With careful treatment, the individual history of the Myall Creek site can be retained, allowing the site to retain its integrity, while acting as a trigger for Australians to further the cause of reconciliation. By visiting Myall Creek, Australians can pass through the past, in order to get to the future.

References

Batten, B. (2004) 'Monuments, Memorials and the Presentation of the Indigenous Past', *Public History Review*, Vol. 11, 100–21.

Blake, D. (2002) *Extract from a letter to John Brown*. Available online at http://www.myallcreekmemorial.com.au/Minutes.html (accessed 20 August 2003).

Brown, J. (2003) *The Myall Creek Massacre* (Transcript. Available online at http://www.abc.net.au/talks/perspectiv/stories/s870787.htm (accessed 29 April 2004).

Campbell, I.C. (1978) 'Settlers and Aborigines: The Pattern of Conflict on the New England Tableland 1832–1860', in *Records of Times Past: Ethnohistorical Essays on the Culture and Ecology of the New England Tribes*, Ethnohistory Series 3, Canberra: Australian Institute of Aboriginal Studies.

Garrett, P. (2008) Media Release: Myall Creek Massacre Recognised 170 Years On. Available online at http://www.environment.gov.au/minister/garrett/2008/pubs/mr20080607.pdf (accessed 11 June 2008).

Jesuit Publications (2003) 'The Myall Creek Memorial', *Madonna* September/October 2003. Available online at http://www.madonnamagazine.com.au/articles/0309pike.html (accessed 20 October 2003).

Kelly, P. (2003) 'Our Rival Storytellers', *The Weekend Australian*, September 27–28: 8.

Macintyre, S. (2003) *The History Wars*, Carlton, Victoria: Melbourne University Press.

Manne, R. (ed.) (2003) *Whitewash: On Keith Windschuttle's Fabrication of Australian History* (esp. Introduction pp. 1–12), Melbourne: Black Inc. Agenda. Available online at: http://evatt.labor.net.au/publications/papers/109.html (accessed 11 November 2007).

The Myall Creek Memorial Committee (2002) *Minutes of the Public Meeting Held at the Myall Creek Memorial Hall, 19th October 2002*. Available online at: http://www.myallcreekmemorial.com.au/Minutes.html (accessed: 20 August 2003).

Reece, R.H.W. (1974) *Aborigines and Colonists*, Sydney: Sydney University Press.

Riddell, C. (2002) *Comments on 'What Next'* (Discussion Section on Website). Available online at: http://www.myallcreekmemorial.com.au/Minutes.html (accessed 20 August 2003).

Stanner, W.E.H. (1991) *After the Dreaming (1968 Boyer Lectures)*, Crows Nest, NSW: Australian Broadcasting Corporation.

Stubbins, T. (2002) *Where Next?* (Letter). Available online at http://www.myallcreekmemorial.com.au/Minutes.html (accessed 20 August 2003).

Stubbins, T. and P. Smith (2001) *The Myall Creek Massacre: Its History, Its Memorial, and the Opening Ceremony*, Bingara: The Myall Creek Memorial Committee.

Waldersee, J. (1979) 'The Myall Creek Massacre: The Execution of Seven Unfortunate Men', in J. Waldersee, *Historical Perspectives*, Chevalier Press: Kensington, NSW.

Part II

Wartime internment sites

Chapter 6

Cowra Japanese War Cemetery

Ai Kobayashi and Bart Ziino

In death, soldiers remain subjects of their nations, subject to the politics and passions of war and the machinations of peace. So too are their resting places subject to those politics. At Cowra, in provincial New South Wales, a unique burial ground contains the bodies of more than five hundred Japanese prisoners and internees of the Second World War. Around half of them were killed in the course of a mass escape attempt at Cowra Prisoner of War camp in August 1944. Yet it is not necessarily this event that makes the cemetery unique. Rather its significance lies in the way it catalyses personal and national memories of the Pacific war, showing where those memories contend and compete.

This chapter examines the ways in which Japanese and Australians have negotiated their painful memories at this place. The events at Cowra are not entirely unique – a similar riot at Featherston, New Zealand, in 1943 also resulted in numerous deaths – but the narratives drawn around the event mark the Cowra Japanese War Cemetery as a crucial place in attending to the pain of war and the shame of lost honour. For Cowra people the Japanese dead are integral to a narrative of forgiveness and redemption; for former inmates and families of the dead the cemetery offers consolation, and some affirmation of identity, against a national memory of the war not yet sympathetic to their experiences. For the Japanese government the existence of the cemetery represented a normalising of diplomatic ties, though less a confrontation with the nation's wartime past, or with the experiences of some of its own citizens. 'Reconciliation' is perhaps not the correct word to attach to what has happened at Cowra over the past sixty years. The Japanese war cemetery is a shared site of pain: not just Australians trying to 'understand' the Japanese, but a Japanese expression of their own, often difficult, memories of conflict and grief.

In 2004, on the sixtieth anniversary of the breakout, Cowra citizens added a further monument to an identity built on international understanding. The 'Peace Pathway' points both backwards, to a history of goodwill and bridge building, and forwards, to the hope of cultural understanding between peoples. The pathway is one in a series of fixtures dedicated to a story of putting aside differences or, as the fiftieth anniversary commemorations proclaimed, 'Making Friends'. We might call this the Cowra narrative: a story that explains the meaning of past events, with a strong moral core. At the heart of the story is a genuine act of goodwill: in the early years after the war, men of the Cowra sub-branch of the Returned Services League (RSL) undertook the care of local war graves, including Australian, German and Italian graves, before extending that care to Japanese graves. A local guidebook explains: the 'honourable manner' in which former soldiers in Cowra maintained Japanese graves saw 'the hand of peaceful reconciliation ... extended through this respectful treatment. ... The aftermath and the memory of the breakout have become a healing and unifying influence between two once-opposing nations' (Cowra Tourism Corporation 1999: 6). The making of a permanent Japanese cemetery in 1964 seemed to confirm the sentiment that 'it was senseless to go on with the hatred' (*Cowra Guardian* (CG) 3 August 1994: 3). The aim of this chapter is not to expose the Cowra narrative, but to point to the ways in which an examination of the Japanese war cemetery is not just about 'making friends', but about the difficulties of coming to terms with the past, personal and national.

The cemetery is the key fixture of the Cowra narrative, though it was not always secure in that position. For Australians the cemetery needs to be understood not simply in terms of the breakout: its development at Cowra reflected a wider difficulty in coming to terms for those who had learnt to hate the Japanese, who had suffered by war against them, or who called on a history of anti-Asian sentiment to fuel their anxieties and hatreds over three and a half years of conflict. To Australians, the Japanese war dead remained objects of enmity. We see this clearly in Japanese proposals in 1954 to retrieve and commemorate their dead in the Pacific theatre. Australia aside, the bodies of almost a quarter of a million Japanese soldiers lay scattered across the battlefields of South-East Asia. The intention to mark the sites of their deaths with stones bearing the ambiguous English translation 'In memory of those who fell in World War II with ardent prayers and hope for the eternal peace of the world' drew censure from the Australian government, and ensured that they were changed.

The response may be understandable, but it also offered an opportunity for some evaluation of the state of relations between Australia and Japan. 'A.V.B.', an Australian in Japan, thought the Australian government's attitude a petty continuance of wartime hostilities. 'The filing of a protest against the inscription', he asserted, 'appears to indicate an Australian view that the Japanese dead scattered throughout the southern islands merit posthumous punishment' (*Asahi Shinbun*, 12 January 1955. National Archives of Australia (NAA): A1838/1, 1510/3/38/1 Part 2). Such attitudes fed into an increasing Japanese sentiment that Australians held too strongly to their wartime prejudices. The *Nippon Times* editorialised, in relation to a separate issue, that:

> Even the passing of a decade has failed to heal the wounds left by the past war. This has been due in part to a regrettable tendency on the part of some jingoistic Australian newspapers to rekindle the wartime hatred for Japan whenever possible.
>
> (*Nippon Times*, 13 January 1955. NAA: A1838/1, 1510/3/38/1 Part 2)

The polarisation implied by these responses does not mean that some did not see the possibilities for a more honest appreciation of sensibilities on either side. 'An Australian', another expatriate in Japan, responded by pointing out that 'Improved relations between two countries require an honest admission on both sides of past mistakes, and an honest effort to rectify them' (*Asahi Shinbun*, 17 January 1955. NAA: A1838/1, 1510/3/38/1 Part 2). Too many people in Japan were too willing to believe themselves sinned against, 'An Australian' thought, rather than accept some responsibility for Australian attitudes, which nevertheless had 'historical reasons'. The Japanese dead of the war, though ten years past, retained the symbolic potency of those antagonisms.

For the Japanese, the problem was both diplomatic and deeply emotional. 'The collection of remains from the battlefields of the Pacific War has been an outstanding problem since the end of the war', observed the *Asahi Shinbun* in January 1955. 'Bereaved families are distressed' (*Asahi Shinbun*, 12 January 1955. NAA: A1838/1, 1510/3/38/1 Part 2). Thousands of mourning Japanese families spent the decade after the war unaware of final resting places, but certain in the knowledge that final rites and rituals had been denied the dead. When the mission prepared to depart early in 1955, mourners sent more than two thousand 'comfort items' to be scattered or buried where the dead were presumed to lie. They sent locks of hair, letters, Buddhist images and rice cakes. Weeping women were reported at the wharf delivering liquor and food for the dead, while some 'asked the mission members to take cans of water because their men were reported to have died of thirst' (*Sydney Morning Herald* (SMH), 13 January 1955: 3). While some might hope to have the ashes of their loved ones returned to them, most could not expect such comfort. As it was for those Australians who lost their loved ones abroad, Japanese mourners also experienced a dislocated grief, in which they were unable to offer repose to the souls of their dead.

At Cowra in 1944, survivors of the breakout were able to begin to offer those rites. The dead were first of all concentrated just outside the camp, where surviving prisoners assisted in making identifications. As they prepared the dead for burial, they made their own gestures of comfort and farewell. An Australian guard observed them: 'the survivors picked up cigarettes and lit them, then put those cigarettes between the fingers of their dead friends' (Nakano 1983: 105–6). Australian officials reported that the dead were buried 'with all due respect and reverence', though only the single fatality among Japanese officers received the honour of having his funeral attended by Australian and Japanese officers. Transferred to another prisoner of war camp, survivors constructed a monument, within which were sealed the names of the dead, and around which prayers were offered for their souls.

The Japanese military code (*Senjinkun*) attached great shame to those captured in battle. Fidelity to that code helps to explain the breakout as an opportunity for honourable death (Carr-Gregg 1978; Gordon 1978; Bullard 2006). The effect of the code at home was to deny that POWs even existed. Relatives of POWs were led to understand that their loved ones had died in action. Many of those in Cowra were mourned even as they continued to live. Those who would return from Cowra came to their families as ghosts, and often faced their own graves in local plots. One of these was Masaru Moriki who returned to his home on Shikoku Island to confront not only his family, but his own grave:

> Many grave posts were erected in a line. Among them I saw 20–30 new posts. I prayed for each one of them starting from the east end. Many childhood friends had become grave posts. … After a while I stood in front of my own grave. I stood there for a long time.
>
> (Moriki c. 1998: 65)

Confronting the reality of Japanese prisoners was made difficult not only by official pronouncements that they had died in action, if indeed they had died, but by the continuing effects of the *Senjinkun* on governmental and personal levels. Even after it officially acknowledged former prisoners of war with pensions in 1952, the Japanese Ministry of Welfare was reluctant to report the fate of those who died in captivity to their families. Equally, private resistance to the truth also existed. In 1954 the Ministry began to seek out families of dead prisoners, but ceased after locating only a few. It had found, Moriki says, that some families could not accept a different fate for their loved ones to that which they had begun to accept: 'We have told the children that their father was killed in action courageously, so we can't tell them now that he died in a POW camp' (Moriki c. 1998: 66).

Such sentiments were not necessarily general among survivors or grieving families. Unpicking the experience of prisoners of war in post-war Japan has been a slow and difficult process administratively and emotionally. As they returned to their homes and reintegrated with the living, Moriki's comrades divided between those who chose to reveal their prisoner status, and those who preferred to conceal that past. Among the latter, it seems, that sense of shame persisted, and Moriki has estimated that more than half of those who returned refused to acknowledge their captivity at Cowra, even to their death. Most did not respond to Moriki's attempts to contact survivors. Of those who did, a lot

> sent back terse letters telling me never to get in touch with them again. I wasn't surprised. After all, some of them had not even told their own families, and here I was asking them to join an organisation that would commemorate their captivity.
>
> (Gordon 1994: 11)

Even after almost fifty years, some POWs hesitated to speak publicly about their experiences, preferring to use pseudonyms when they did so (Nagase and Yoshida 1990: 81, 196–7).

Yet there were also those survivors who were driven by their experience and their mourning to embrace an identity as former prisoners of war. For these men and their sympathisers, the dead at Cowra were crucial. They formed the Cowra

Kai, or Cowra Memorial Club, which sought to acknowledge the experience, and commemorate the dead. These people recast the events at Cowra as tragedy. The key figure in the establishment of the society was Ichijiro Do, an older man than most veterans, who had held reservations about the breakout. In 1965, he called the event an 'abominable incident' in which, fortunately, his life was spared. Another veteran wrote anonymously to a newspaper in 1964, recalling 'those days of tragedy' (*CG*, 15 January 1965: 3; 4 August 1964: 11). Both men were responding to the development of the cemetery at Cowra, an event and a site that gave impetus to their desire to engage with their past.

A Japanese war cemetery at Cowra was never a certainty. The Japanese government had made overtures in 1947 toward the cremation and return of the remains of Japanese prisoners and internees from Australia, but Australian authorities deferred this plan pending the conclusion of a peace treaty. With the treaty in 1952 came Australian government concerns that the Japanese government should remove the bodies, but at this time, the Imperial War Graves Commission was in the midst of negotiations to establish a permanent Commonwealth War Cemetery at Yokohama, and the matter was not pressed. Though the federal government had granted the Cowra RSL trusteeship of the cemetery in 1948, it remained concerned about the ultimate disposition of Japanese bodies in Australia. In 1953, Secretary of the Department of the Army F.R. Sinclair thought it 'most desirable that the Japanese be permitted to repatriate the remains contained in these graves' (Memo 12 March 1953. NAA: A1838/1, 1510/3/38/1 Part 1). When nothing had changed several years later, Cowra's returned men pressed authorities for resources with which to care specifically for the graves of former prisoners and internees. Their local and personal concerns, however, were not reflected by the government, which continued to regard those graves as an impermanent fixture in the Australian landscape.

The matter resumed in 1957, propelled not only by bureaucratic desire to conclude the issue, but by the ongoing personal pain of those who mourned their dead. Toshiaki Natsume, a former internee in Australia, wrote to the *Asahi Shinbun* to

> express a hope that the remains of my fellow-countrymen who are sleeping on foreign soil may be brought back to Japan where their bereaved kinsfolk are patiently waiting. If this is not possible, I hope that at least a little soil may be brought back.
> (*Asahi Shinbun*, February 1957. NAA: A1838/1, 1510/3/38/1 Part 3)

Though Japanese authorities responded to Australian overtures at this time, the issue once again lapsed. The question of Japanese bodies in Australian territory, it seems, awaited the much larger resolution of relations between the two countries, both on official and private levels.

That kind of normalising of relations had been gathering momentum over the course of the 1950s, as the peace treaty and trading relationships began to overturn certain immigration restrictions and, to a lesser extent, the prejudices hardened in the war (Nagata 2001: 231–6). The political shifts of the period would have similar effects on the politics of the dead. Early in 1963, Japanese representatives in Australia began to discuss again the ultimate treatment of the dead. They spoke now, however, of leaving them in Australian soil. Part of the impulse was administrative: conceding that for the most part the names recorded on graves were aliases, officials realised that the return of particular remains to families would be almost impossible. A Japanese reporter in Australia told his audience that 'the only alternative seems to be to hold a collective memorial service in Cowra for the repose of the souls of these unidentified P.O.W.s' (*Asahi Shinbun*, 15 January 1963. NAA: A1838/1, 1510/3/38/1 Part 3). Yet the Japanese dead were spread further across Australia, in the Northern Territory, South Australia, and Victoria. With the assistance of the Department of External Affairs, the Japanese ambassador contrived to request that all Japanese dead be concentrated at Cowra, where they would be cared for at the cost of the Japanese government. Drawing a lineage of goodwill and respect, ambassador Saburo Ohta was careful to thank the Commonwealth War Graves Commission and the Cowra RSL for almost twenty years' maintenance of the site (Ohta to Barwick 3 June 1963. NAA: A1838/1, 1510/3/38/1 Part 3).

Ohta might have endorsed the basis of a developing Cowra narrative, but open debate in Sydney's *Daily Telegraph* showed that the idea of a Japanese cemetery in Australia was far from universally acceptable. Though the war had been over for almost twenty years, 'and much of the bitterness has ebbed', J. McNaughton insisted that 'there are some things that cannot be forgotten'. A Japanese cemetery would be 'desecration indeed' (*Daily Telegraph*, 24 January 1963: 2). J.R. Evans asked if others could forgive Japanese treatment of Australian prisoners: 'I can't' (*Daily Telegraph*, 30 January 1963: 2). Former prisoner of the Japanese J.P. Carey asserted that a memorial at Cowra would be 'an insult to every soldier who fought the Japanese' (*Daily Telegraph*, 28 January 1963: 2). In response, D.J. Helleur accused dissenters of nurturing enmity with a people who were already tending to Australian dead at Yokohama, and a nation whose trade was fundamental to Australia's economic health (*Daily Telegraph*, 25 January 1963: 2). G.J. Wood was more embracing again. The Japanese who died in a brave and legitimate bid for freedom, he declared, 'have just as much right to an honoured burial place as our own dead' (*Daily Telegraph*, 31 January 1963: 2). The exchange showed that some attitudes had mellowed, and that some Australians could acknowledge a Japanese memory of loss, pain and grief. Yet it also showed that many Australians' personal memories of pain occasioned by the war could not accommodate such expressions of shared experience.

Even in Cowra the efficacy of forgiveness was not uncontested. Responding to his colleagues, 'P.B.I.' suggested that some of Cowra's fervour for good relations with Japan came from their interest in trade as a wool-growing district. More importantly, he added that he personally had not been able to achieve forgiveness:

In my humble opinion, the current catchcry 'forgive and forget' went out with muzzle loading weapons. I, for one, cannot forget nor can I forgive. ... Maybe I am living in the past, but I had a number of friends who died and were killed needlessly and who have now not the opportunity to live in the past.

(*CG*, 8 November 1963: 4)

While the past continued to give pain, permission for the Japanese government to proceed with the cemetery at Cowra was granted on 14 October 1963, as Japanese Prime Minister Ikeda toured the country. The land would be vested in the Commonwealth War Graves Commission. Defying those like 'P.B.I.', Brigadier A.E. Brown, who headed the Anzac Agency of the Commonwealth War Graves Commission, tied the cemetery to Australia's future in Asia. He prophesied that while 'Australians and Asians were different in their ways ... the time would come when Australians' thinking would have to be altered very considerably' (*CG*, 18 August 1964: 5).

The work of making the cemetery at Cowra permanent began in May 1964 with the relocation of more than two hundred sets of Japanese remains from other parts of Australia. Altogether five hundred and twenty three bodies were concentrated at Cowra. The design of the expanded cemetery was placed in the hands of Japanese architect Shigeru Yura, who had recently been teaching at the University of Melbourne. Yura's plan reflected the principles of Japanese garden design: low concrete plinths represented the rows of graves, into which would be set brass name plaques. Within the low walls, 'mottled pathways, stepping stones, and cream pebbles and black basalt' offset the graves. At the entrance stood a stone lantern, donated by the president of the Mitsui company. On the black basalt pillar was inscribed the bald statement: 'In Memory of Japanese War Dead'. This was the first official Japanese war cemetery outside Japan and like Australia's cemeteries abroad, it attempted to cater to the needs of those who grieved at a distance (Ziino 2007).

Japanese mourners remained keenly aware of developments at Cowra, yet none would be present at the cemetery's inauguration on 22 November 1964. A columnist in the *Asahi Shinbun* attributed the situation to an insensitive government attachment to the view that bereaved families would rather believe that their loved ones had died in battle than as prisoners. 'The idea that "prisoners of war were cowards" should have disappeared by now,' they wrote. 'There must be family members who do not care what people may say about POWs and who want to go to Australia to offer flowers' (*Asahi Shinbun*, 21 November 1964. NAA: A1838/1, 1510/3/38/1 Part 3). C.H. Clark, of the Australian Embassy, thought that the number of attendees remained low because many still did not wish to be identified as former prisoners. So too he believed that bereaved relatives remained absent 'preferring it to be thought that their relatives died in action' (C.H. Clark 24 November 1964. NAA: A1838/1, 1510/3/38/1 Part 3). In Tokyo, twenty former prisoners of war gathered at the Yasukuni Shrine to mark the occasion. The *Asahi Shinbun* reported that it was 'the first time in twenty years

Figure 6.1 Entrance to Japanese War Cemetery, Cowra. (Source: B. Ziino)

for most of them to see each other' (*Asahi Shinbun*, 22 November 1964. NAA: A1838/1, 1510/3/38/1 Part 3). While only a few might have attended such a public commemoration, many bereaved Japanese took comfort from the ceremonies. Haruhisa Fukushima, a survivor of the breakout, had already written to a Japanese newspaper when he heard about the preparation of the cemetery, glad to observe that 'The war is over and those unfortunate Japanese now rest in peace.' (*CG*, 4 August 1964: 11). The Cowra Memorial Club raised funds in order to have camellias planted at the cemetery. Ichijiro Do believed that the action 'gave comfort to our comrades' souls' (*CG*, 15 January 1965: 3).

In the event, several hundred people attended the ceremony in Cowra, though neither the Prime Minister nor the leader of the Opposition were present. A few days before the ceremony, the Chiefs of Staff of the three services had all declined to attend, and substitutes had quickly to be found. Outside Cowra, indeed outside the cemetery, the response seemed muted. A *Sydney Morning Herald* reporter described the scene in those terms: 'The wind shook the eucalypts and a little dust eddied outside the cemetery boundaries as the appropriate words were spoken' (*SMH*, 23 November 1964: 9). The 'appropriate words' were spoken by Ohta, who said that the cemetery reminded them all of the 'blackest period in Japanese–Australian relations'. For their part, the Australian speakers attempted to alleviate the Japanese war dead of some of their difficult political baggage. Brigadier Brown 'was saddened by the fact that these young men who were now lying in peace had only been doing their duty as they saw it'. Former

Figure 6.2 Japanese War Cemetery, Cowra. The central monument is inscribed 'In Memory of Japanese War Dead'. The graves are arranged and marked on the plinths behind. (Source: B. Ziino)

soldier A.J. Oliver, now mayor, implicated Australians directly in giving meaning to this site. The people of Cowra, he said, 'would accept the responsibility of remembering the Japanese war cemetery as a place of special significance to all Japanese people' (*CG*, 24 November 1964: 1). An anonymous Christmas card to Oliver, from 'A Japanese', thanked the people of Cowra for establishing the cemetery, and referred to the personal pain of the bereaved: 'Their families must be very happy and grateful about it' (*CG*, 12 January 1965: 1). To further salve that pain, Sydney's small Japanese community arranged for a Buddhist blessing of the cemetery shortly after its inauguration.

The new publicity permitted some families to discover for the first time the fate of their loved ones. The Kochi-Cowra Association, under Masaru Moriki, held its first memorial service at the Kinren-temple of Ino-cho on 5 August 1965, and members of the association personally sought out other survivors and families of the dead for subsequent annual commemorations. Moriki observed the bereaved at the services: 'Aging fathers and mothers and brothers and sisters cried for joy that they finally knew the last moments of their loved one' (Moriki c. 1998: 67). The existence of a formal cemetery gave impetus for pilgrimages to the gravesite. While no Japanese mourners or survivors had been present at the opening of the cemetery, in the following year the Ministry of Welfare subsidised three family representatives to undertake a pilgrimage.

THE VIETNAM TEACH-INS   AUGUST 7, 1965

The Bulletin

INCORPORATING THE AUSTRALIAN FINANCIAL TIMES

JAPAN AND AUSTRALIA
Twenty Years After

日本人戦没者之墓

Japanese War Cemetery, Cowra, N.S.W.

Figure 6.3 Buddhist ceremony conducted shortly after the dedication of the cemetery, 1965. *The Bulletin*'s headline suggests the broader historical and political context of commemoration at Cowra. (Source: *The Bulletin*)

As Mr Okazoe, of the Kochi-Cowra association, prepared to leave, Moriki asked him to place before the graves water from home, dried bonito (fish), and a pebble from the local beach, 'as an offering from home and a eulogy from the survivors'. Okazoe duly did so, and returned with photographs of the graves, and pebbles from the former campsite. In 1983 Takanori Kojima, whose brother had committed suicide shortly prior to the breakout, travelled with his wife and sister to offer prayers at the grave. He also brought an offering from his brother's fiancée, Nobuko Yamashita, who had asked that a lock of her hair be placed in the grave. Such personal acts reflected the cemetery's immediate role as a site for expressing and coming to terms with grief, as much as it reflected the broader politics of the war.

While the cemetery may have eased a certain pain of grief for Japanese mourners and participants, at the same time it opened a new commemorative dialogue, which the people of Cowra would actively harness and shape. In Cowra too, memory-making was both a private and public process. The memory of the breakout itself was for a long time a local phenomenon, given the Australian government's suppression of the details. Even acknowledging Australian loss in the breakout had been a difficult process, though several years after the war two Australians were posthumously awarded the George Cross for their bravery. Appreciation of Japanese loss was a much more difficult issue, given that the cemetery was a reminder both of the event and of broader wartime animosity. Yet as Bridget Stockdale has observed, 'Rather than attempting to bury the politically contentious and little-understood trauma within an otherwise quiet historical narrative, Cowra used it to spawn a program of reconciliation activities that has assigned it a unique place in the history of Australia–Japan relations' (Stockdale 2006: 3).

The reconstruction of wartime memory in Cowra has in some ways been an obvious process, if we chart it through its major fixtures. In 1965, local authorities commenced a 'Festival of Nations' under the initiative of Mayor Oliver. The main theme of the Festival was 'International Understanding'. Representatives of the guest nation – of which Japan was first in 1966 – were invited to the Festival, where the cultures of the country were introduced and people in Cowra and a wider Australian public were encouraged to participate. The festival worked to articulate further the symbolism of the cemetery – tolerance, reconciliation and understanding – and in 1970 Cowra's relationship with Japan was reinforced by the inauguration of a school exchange programme.

The patronage and gratitude of Japanese veterans and authorities – especially royalty – helped to confirm Cowra's emergent sense of identity as a place of healing and reconciliation. In January 1971 Prince Mikasa, brother of Emperor Hirohito, visited Cowra with Princess Yuriko to place a wreath at the cemetery and plant a tree. The *Cowra Guardian* celebrated the moment as 'the first official royal visit in Cowra's history' (*CG*, 12 January 1971: 3). By the time Crown Prince Akihito and Princess Michiko visited in 1973, Cowra had hosted five members of the Japanese royal family, as well as numerous diplomats. These royal visits, however, crystal-lised a discrepancy between official Japanese appreciation of the Cowra people's dedication to commemorating Japanese war dead, and a failure to induce reflection on Japan's own wartime past. At the official reception, Prince Mikasa said 'I believe Cowra will always have [a] unique place to the Japanese people' because there was 'a small area of land set aside as a Japanese Cemetery'. Akihito two years later repeated almost the same phrase: 'Cowra held a unique place in the hearts of the Japanese people because of its care of the Japanese cemetery.'

Such comments suggest the government's appreciation of the care of the Japanese War Cemetery. Yet the story is not so simple as to speak of 'reconciliation' between former enemies. Other kinds of reconciliation have been overlooked in Japan. The Japanese public know little about the experience of the prisoners of war in general and what happened in Cowra in particular, and so these comments – full in sentiment but light in content – played to separate audiences. They gave the impression that POWs' experiences had been integrated into the national past, when such a process had hardly taken place in Japan. Few if any of the princes' comments reflected specifically on the events of August 1944, and certainly not on Japan's own treatment of prisoners. Akihito was impressed by 'the Australian humanitarian attitude to mankind', and insisted that: 'The tragedy of war should not be forgotten, but it should be turned into something good' (*CG*, 11 May 1973: 8). These phrases were polite enough to acknowledge and appreciate Australians' treatment of the Japanese dead, but at the same time obscured Japanese unwillingness to confront the nation's wartime experience.

Nevertheless, at the same time as the visits of Japanese royalty, the meaning of Cowra's commemorative activity took a more consistent shape and tone. Following Akihito's visit, a Sydney reporter interpreted the cemetery as 'more than just the final resting place for Japanese dead'. Now it represented 'a living memorial to a friendship built from bitterness. Casting aside prejudice and hatred, Cowra people have sought to understand the Japanese people' (*SMH*, 9 August 1973: 12). Further fixtures of Cowra's emergent memory industry embraced this sense of mission. Local businessman Don Kibbler developed the idea for a Japanese garden and cultural centre not just to complement the cemetery, but as a direct extension of it. Even thirty years after the war there remained some antagonism: 'Most people in Cowra', recalled former Mayor Barbara Bennett, 'knew somebody who had been a prisoner of war in Japan or who'd been killed by the Japanese' (Colhoun 19 March 2003). Still, there was sufficient support to see it proceed, and designer Ken Nakajima intended that the garden provide solace for the spirits of the dead, both Japanese and Australian. In 1988, a new avenue of cherry trees between the cemetery and the gardens linked the two. In 1992, Cowra also received Australia's World Peace Bell from the United Nations, usually reserved for capital cities – a tangible acknowledgement and recognition of Cowra's effort to promote itself as a centre of 'peace, international understanding, and friendship' (*CG*, 1 August 1994: 5).

By the fiftieth anniversary of the breakout, in 1994, Cowra had established an identity in its dedication to this code. At its heart remained the cemetery and the moral tale attached to it. As organiser of 1994's fiftieth anniversary commemorations, Jan Munday located that sense of identity in reconciliation and understanding, and invoked the cemetery as its materialisation: 'From as early as

1948, International Understanding became part of Cowra, when the local RSL members decided to tend the graves of the Japanese Prisoners who were buried at the edge of the town' (*CG*, 3 August 1994: 5). Prime Minister Paul Keating offered his own affirmation of the narrative: 'At a time when many other Australians were not ready to do so, the people of Cowra chose to pursue reconciliation and healing' (*CG*, 3 August 1994: 2).

Former prisoners attending the celebrations embraced the message, but also testified to what they saw as the failure of the Japanese government to acknowledge their experiences. Cowra POWs have attained some little public exposure through unofficial means: memorial services, personal memoirs, at least one novel, and the proceedings of a seminar conducted in 1989, which a number of former prisoners attended. These accounts have struggled to find a place in a mainstream Japanese understanding of the past: in 2004 journalist Yasuo Tsuchiya testified to a fundamental lack of knowledge of a war with Australia, let alone the Cowra incident. The dead at Cowra, he felt, desired that he should write about them (Tsuchiya 2004: 11–13). This alienation is evident in former prisoners' exclusion of Japanese officialdom from their accounts of reconciliation with their pasts. Silences are significant: none, for instance, comment at all on royal visits to Cowra. At the fiftieth anniversary commemorations in Cowra, former prisoners similarly excluded the Japanese government from their memories, or otherwise implicated them as agents of resistance to their reintegration with Japanese society. Masatoshi Kigawa, Chairman of the Cowra Association in Japan, embraced the Cowra narrative as a story of honourable Australian activity:

> The Australian government kindly prepared a cemetery for the Japanese soldiers who died during this time, entombed them. And set up a grave-post for every one of them. I would like all of you to know that we deeply appreciate the Australian government. We should have come here earlier to pay a visit to the graves of our comrades-in-arms.
>
> (*CG*, 10 August 1994: 5)

In Kigawa's mind it was Australians who, through the cemetery, facilitated POWs' coming to terms with their 'shameful' experiences, and saved their memories from suppression. That he does not acknowledge the Japanese government's role in establishing the cemetery is telling. Masaru Moriki, also present, went further than Kigawa, as he criticised the Japanese government's lack of enthusiasm for reconciliation with the experience of POWs. The Japanese government, he thought, 'should officially apologise for what happened 50 years ago' (*CG*, 10 August 1994: 5). Certainly Moriki meant an official acknowledgement of what happened to the POWs in Cowra and the culpability of the *Senjinkun* in creating the situation. His demand crystallises the unreconciled aspect of the Japanese POWs' living memory.

The willingness of Cowra people to honour the Japanese dead also exhibits a willingness to reckon with the past, and with the politics of the dead. The Cowra narrative, which urges forgiveness and understanding, speaks not only of events at Cowra in 1944, but of the much greater struggle to meet the pain of the brutal conflict in the Pacific during the Second World War. That process is incomplete. Those directly affected still contend with their painful pasts. They continue to embody competing impulses to hate, forgive and understand. Former prisoner of war Rowly Richards distinguished between his particular captors and the Japanese people, but still felt that 'It's not so much a question of forgiveness as of understanding. We should try to understand different cultures and their history.' Ray Brown, captured on Ambon, went to Japan in 1967, journalist Tony Stephens says, 'to try to understand the Japanese'. Brown still struggles with forgiveness, though he believes he has mastered hatred. Maureen Devereaux, whose brother perished as a prisoner at Sandakan, professes that she still can't forgive (Stephens 2005: 14).

As a place of pain, the significance of the Japanese war cemetery emerges through confronting and teasing out such personal complexities. Here too in a wider context, of national and international contention over reconciliation of wartime actions and experiences, do we find a place in which memories can be negotiated. For at political levels too, the issue is unresolved. On the sixtieth anniversary of the end of the Second World War, Australian Prime Minister John Howard spoke, in the presence of the Japanese ambassador, of how Australian prisoners of the Japanese faced 'years of forced labour, starvation and brutality at the hands of a cruel enemy'. In Tokyo that day, Japanese Prime Minister Junichiro Koizumi apologised for the suffering inflicted in Asia by Japanese aggression: 'Humbly accepting this fact of history, we again express our deep remorse and heartfelt apology and offer our condolences to the victims of the war at home and abroad.' Doubts persist in the minds of victims as to the sincerity of Japanese apologies, while they have little or no recourse to compensation claims, when Japanese leaders continue to visit the Yasukuni shrine, and when the Japanese education system continues to marginalise the nation's wartime history. Cowra POWs count themselves among those victims of marginalisation in the national memory; Australian veterans and their families continue to feel the need for a frank admission of Japanese brutality and an expression of contrition. In Cowra, at least, the Japanese war cemetery offers a place where two peoples can confront and negotiate the pain of that past on personal and public levels. This process is begun, but it is not likely to be resolved within the lifetimes of those most intimately affected.

References

Asahi Shinbun (newspaper), 12 January 1955; February 1957; 15 January 1963; 21 November 1964; 22 November 1964.

Bullard, S. (2006) *Blankets on the wire: The Cowra breakout and its aftermath*, Canberra: Australian War Memorial.

Carr-Gregg, C. (1978) *Japanese prisoners of war in revolt: The outbreaks at Featherston and Cowra during World War II*, St Lucia: University of Queensland Press.

Colhoun, T. Interview with Barbara Bennett, Cowra, 19 March 2003. Available online at: http://ajrp.awm.gov.au/ajrp/ajrp2.nsf/cowrapages/NT0000EF7E?openDocument (accessed 27 September 2005).

Cowra Guardian (newspaper), various dates 1963–94.

Cowra Tourism Corporation (1999) *The Cowra Japanese Gardens*, Cowra: Cowra Tourism Corporation.

Daily Telegraph (newspaper, Sydney), 24–31 January 1963.

Gordon, H. (1978) *Die Like the Carp!*, Stanmore: Cassell.

Gordon, H. (1994) *Voyage from Shame: The Cowra Breakout and Afterwards*, St Lucia: University of Queensland Press.

Memo 12 March 1953. NAA: A1838/1, 1510/3/38/1 Part 1.

Moriki, M. (c. 1998) *Cowra Uprising: One Survivor's Memoir*, Masaru Moriki.

Nakano, Fujio (1983) 'Cowra Revisited', *Geo: Australasia's Geographical Magazine* 5: 102–11.

Nagase, T and Yoshida, A. (eds) (1990) *Kaura Nihonhei horyo*, Tokyo: Aoki Shoten.

Nagata, Y. (2001) '"Certain Types of Aliens": The Japanese in Australia, 1941–1952', in P. Jones and V. Mackie (eds), *Relationships: Japan and Australia, 1870s–1950s*, Parkville: History Department, University of Melbourne: 217–39.

National Archives of Australia: A1838/1, 1510/3/38/1 Part 1; A1838/1, 1510/3/38/1 Part 2; A1838/1, 1510/3/38/1 Part 3.

Nippon Times, 13 January 1955. NAA: A1838/1, 1510/3/38/1 Part 2.

Ohta to Barwick 3 June 1963. NAA: A1838/1, 1510/3/38/1 Part 3.

Stephens, T. (2005) 'Let's forget about it', *Sydney Morning Herald*, 11 August, 14.

Stockdale, B. (2006) 'Localising Internationalism': Cowra's Festivals of the Lachlan Valley, 1965–1971, unpublished BA (Hons) Thesis, Department of History, University of Melbourne.

Sydney Morning Herald (newspaper), 13 January 1955: 3; 23 November 1964: 9; 9 August 1973: 12.

Tsuchiya, Y. (2004) *Kaura no Kaze/The Breeze of Cowra*, Tokyo: KTC Chuo Shuppan.

Ziino, B. (2007) *A Distant Grief: Australians, War Graves and the Great War*, Crawley: University of Western Australia Press.

Chapter 7

A cave in Taiwan

Comfort women's memories and the
local identity

Chou Ching-Yuan

In the early 1990s, the history of the Taiwan comfort women surfaced. With the help of women's rights activists and many civil society groups, their ordeals were publicised in Taiwan, the memory of each individual being documented by newspaper articles, books and documentary films. The comfort women's ordeals during the war became a part of the public memory of the Japanese colonial era in Taiwan. Innocent young women had been deceived and exploited, but their suffering continues into the present. Women's rights activitists used the mass media to expose their ordeal and the Taipei Women's Rescue Foundation (TWRF) organised public testimony meetings at the campuses to introduce the stories of comfort women. It was estimated that the TWRF had held about 300 meetings at universities and high schools up to 2007. Many young students said that they felt the pain of the Taiwanese comfort women after hearing their public testimonies. However, their memories were not to go unchallenged in Taiwan. In 2001, a Japanese political cartoonist, Kobayashi Yoshinori, published *On Taiwan*, a series of manga texts in which he voiced the opinion that the Taiwanese comfort women were volunteers. Some 250,000 copies were sold in Japan and, when a Chinese translation was published in Taipei later in 2001, comfort women survivors and their sympathisers organised rallies to have the book banned in Taiwan.

In 2006, 17 women's cultural heritage sites were selected around Taiwan island (see National Cultural Association and Fembooks 2006).[1] Most of those sites emphasise women's attributes and successes in Taiwanese society, except the site at Shuiyuan Village, in the east coast Hualian County, which is about the suffering of aboriginal Taiwanese comfort women at the hands of an imperialist power. This chapter examines the Hualian women's cultural heritage site as a place of pain and shame by outlining the history of Taiwan's aboriginal tribes under Japanese rule and the movement demanding apologies and compensation from Japan for the comfort women in Taiwan. The chapter also considers how best to position and preserve the memories of young aboriginal women's pain in the collective memories of the Japanese colonial era both within and outside the Shuiyuan community.

Taiwan under Japanese rule

After its defeat in the Sino-Japanese War in 1894, imperial China ceded control of Taiwan to Japan in the Treaty of Shimonoseki in 1895. At that time, about 45 per cent of Taiwan, mainly in the western and coastal regions, was under Han Chinese control while the regions of the interior and the east were under the control of various aboriginal tribes. The relationship between the two groups was good. From 1895 to 1945, the highest authority in colonial Taiwan was the Office of the Governor-General (OGG) in Taipei. The chief of Home Affairs was the primary executor of the OGG's policies. In Taiwan, Japan concentrated on economic exploitation and its territorial ambitions, with raw materials, rice and sugar being the main export products. The control of Taiwan was mainly through educating people thoroughly in the Japanese language. Throughout the colonial era, this policy never wavered.

The first twenty years of Japanese rule in Taiwan were marked by many acts of armed resistance from both Han Chinese and the aborigines. A quick contingent of military Governor-Generals was sent to Taiwan to suppress the uprisings. The Japanese set up the 'National Language Schools', public primary schools and instructional institutes, all with instruction in Japanese.

In 1919, a system of civil governorship was established and the attention of the colonial authority turned more fully to the economic and political exploitation of China and Southeast Asia. Several corporations were set up backed by the Japanese colonial government, such as the Taiwan Colonial Trade Development Corporation in 1936. To meet the needs of Japanese colonial development, Japan pursued an 'assimilation' policy between 1919 and 1937, under which the Taiwanese were taught to know their duties toward imperial Japan. In the process, many public schools and vocational schools were established.

From 1937 to 1945, the OGG sought to maximise productivity in agriculture, develop industries serving the military, and mobilise natural and human resources for the war effort. To this end, the colonial government sped up the process of Nipponisation (otherwise known as the Kominka Movement). During this period, the colonial authority promoted Shintoism, the 'National Language Family', adoption of Japanese names, and the Japanisation of customs and practices in Taiwan generally. Every child had to attend Japanese school and speak Japanese at home. After the outbreak of the Pacific War, the government encouraged Taiwanese to volunteer for the imperial army. In 1945, a full-scale draft was ordered and school children were also mobilised for the war effort.

The colonial policy was successful. Both Han Chinese and aborigines were securely under the control of the Japanese government. From 1937 to 1945, over 207,000 Taiwanese youths volunteered or were drafted into the Imperial Japanese Army or worked for the various corps in China and Southeast Asia (Qi 2007: 88). It was estimated that approximately 300,000 Taiwanese in total were conscripted while the total number of deaths among Taiwanese soldiers ran to over 30,000 by the end of the war (Pan 1998).

The aborigines in Eastern Taiwan under Japanese rule

In the late nineteenth century, the plains aborigines, living on the west coast, were almost completely assimilated into Chinese society. The unassimilated aborigines lived mainly in the interior and eastern Taiwan. At the beginning of the Japanese colonial period, Japan adopted a segregation policy which isolated the aborigines in the mountain region, using outposts, modern weapons, a telegraph network and security cordon to confine them. This territory was called the 'Barbarian land'. The tribal people on the Barbarian land were not allowed to interact with Han Chinese.[2] Japan's eventual goal was to control the land and to ensure the labour force. Hence colonial authority's policy toward the tribal people was to assimilate them through suppression and re-education.

The largest aboriginal tribe in Taiwan, the Truka[3], is located in eastern Taiwan, including Hualian County. It was still a hunter society in the late nineteenth century and it was the last to submit to Japanese rule. At that time most of the Truku lived in the lightly populated mountainous areas of central and eastern Taiwan. From 1896 to 1919, the Truku rebelled several times because of the aggressive Japanese appropriation of tribal land and enforcement of policies directed against tribal customs and practices.[4] In 1907, under the 'Barbarian Children Special Education Program', all tribal children had to learn Japanese in the so-called 'Barbarian Children Schools'. In 1909 a 'Five Year Policy for Managing the Barbarians' was drafted to suppress the aborigines further. Accordingly, police outposts were established in every village and Japanese policemen were put in charge of education, trading, migration and the judicature. Aboriginal children at schools were instructed by policemen to be loyal Japanese subjects. Under this policy, traditional practices were banned, such as headhunting, young women were no longer allowed to tattoo their faces, traditional festivals were shortened and only Shinto shrines were allowed to be erected in the tribal areas.

From 1910 onwards, many Japanese families migrated to Hualian County. The OGG committed huge funds to agricultural migration from Japan to Hualian. The vocational education for tribal youths was concentrated on developing expertise in modern agriculture, poultry and nursing, and helping to increase productivity and supply cheap labourers for Japanese corporations in the surrounding areas. In September 1914, 42 police stations were set up in the Truka tribal homeland. There were about 96 Truku *she*, the smallest tribal unit, living around the Taroko region in 1917 (Xia 2005: 106). The high mountain *she* were gradually forced to relocate closer to the plains. In 1918, many Truku *she* resettled in the area, later named Xiulin Town, located in the northern part of Hualian County.

The largest anti-Japanese uprising in the colonial era was led by the Truku chief, Mona Rudao, in October 1930. Over 300 tribal men assaulted a sports festival held by the Wushe (Musyaji) Elementary School. In the uprising, 134 Japanese nationals and two Taiwanese were killed, and 215 Japanese nationals were injured. Further raids were conducted on police outposts, post offices and Barbarian management offices. In response, the Japanese retaliated with its modern arsenal. The crackdown on the uprising took about two months and the Truku were forced to resettle elsewhere.

After the Wushe Incident, the colonial government sped up its assimilation policy and lengthened primary education for the aborigines. In 1937, the Japanese colonial authority began a stronger social-political programme to enforce Japanese customs, rituals and identity on the aboriginal youth. Shortly after the outbreak of war in Asia, the Japanese military in Taiwan used the 'Act of Mobilisation for Japan' to mobilise the aboriginal males and females to work for the Japanese military in Taiwan. At the end of 1941, many aboriginal youths, with many drawn from the Truku, volunteered for the Japanese war efforts.[5] Takasago Volunteer Units were sent to China and Southeast Asia as labourers or guerrilla fighters (Qi 2007: 88).

Japanese military in Hualian, 1937–1945

From 1895 to 1945, Japan had stationed a large number of troops at geographically important locations on a more or less permanent basis. After 1937 Taiwan became a transport station, sending Japanese troops, Taiwanese labourers and supplies to the south. Given Japan's needs for military resources, the colonial government devised a new development scheme for Hualian. In 1938, a new harbour was completed in Hualian by Taiwan Development Company, executing the OGG's economic policies. Hualian became the base for the wartime military industry.

Prior to August 1945, Japanese barracks and camps were concentrated in the areas surrounding Hualian Port. The number of Japanese soldiers around Hualian was approximately 11,000 (Liu 1997: 119–21). From 1938 to 1945, military supply factories were set up by the Japanese Imperial Army. In November 1943, the vocational institutes at Hualian Port were transformed into a weapons factory (Lo (ed.) 1983: 22, 24). In 1944, the Hualian harbour and surrounding areas were constantly raided by the Allied air force. The Japanese military had to send supplies and weapons further into the mountain region to be stored in caves. Therefore, some Japanese troops began to be stationed at several villages in Xiulin Town.

When the Allied forces took over the Japanese military bases at Xiulin Town in 1946, the names of four warehouses, which stored large amounts of food, medical, veterinary supplies and ammunition, were found in the military documents (Liu 1997: 246): Rongshu Warehouse, Banyan Warehouse (Mqmqi in Truku), Tongwenlian Warehouse (Tmuann in Truku) and Sabodang Warehouse (Saboda in Truku).

Using the 'Act of Mobilisation for Japan', local Japanese policemen stationed at these warehouses recruited many young aboriginal females to help with housekeeping around the camps. Japanese abused those young females at the same time. However, it was not until fifty years after the end of World War II that some of the abused women recognised publicly that they had been the victims of Japanese military sexual slavery.

Asian comfort women activities

The first comfort stations were set up in Shanghai when Japan began its invasion of China following the Manchuria Incident in 1931. To summarise expert research on the subject (see Chu 2004; Su 1999; Yoshimi 1995), the Japanese military set up comfort stations for the following reasons: (1) to stabilise and calm the soldiers, thereby increasing their combat power; (2) to help in maintaining discipline and prevent rapes, hence avoiding international condemnation; (3) to prevent venereal disease; (4) to stop any leak of military secrets; (5) to allow anger to be vented against women from enemy countries; and (6) to relieve soldiers' fear of war and death. It was seen as a military necessity and the comfort women were regarded as strategic assets for the Japanese Army.

In 1937, after Japan had entered into fully fledged war against China, steadily expanding its occupied territories there, the army began to set up comfort stations in different parts of China. The women came from mainly China, Japan, Korea and Taiwan. When Japanese troops advanced into Indochina in 1940 and expanded to other Southeast Asian countries, they also set up comfort stations as part of the military deployment. Comfort stations were set up in all the territories occupied by Japan, including Taiwan. The Japanese army kidnapped young females from home and transferred them to comfort stations abroad (never in their home countries). Several Korean women testified that they were transported from Korea to comfort stations at various locations, including Zhanghua (Chung-Hwa) and Xinzhu (Hsinchu) where Japanese troops were stationed (Howard 1995: 88, 95, 143).

In 1991, The Korean Council for the Women Drafted for Military Sexual Slavery by Japan[6] received a telephone call via its hotline from Ms Kim Hak-soon, a former comfort woman in Korea. Subsequently, 214 Korean female victims have come forward. In December 1991, Ms Kim and three other Korean women went to Tokyo District Court to file a lawsuit against the Japanese government, demanding a formal apology and compensation. Soon after, in January 1992, Yoshimi Yoshiaki, a history professor who had done a vast amount of research since the late 1970s on Japan's role and responsibility for the Asia-Pacific War, discovered wartime documents in Japanese Self-Defence Agency archives, showing that the Japanese Imperial Army was directly involved in planning and running comfort stations. The findings were published in the *Asahi Shimbun* (Daily News) on 12 January 1992.

In February 1992, Ms Ito Hideko, a former member of Japan's House of Representatives, discovered three telegrams in the library of the Japanese Self-Defence Agency. One, dated 12 March 1942, required shipping permits from the Japanese Imperial Army to allow fifty 'comfort personnel' to transfer to Sarawak, Borneo. These fifty comfort personnel had been conscripted by the Japanese Military Commander in Taiwan at the request of the Southern Region Headquarters. Subsequently, the Southern Region Headquarters indicated that these fifty comfort personnel were overworked and requested an additional twenty personnel. The third telegram also sought travel permits and the request was again granted.

The three telegrams proved beyond doubt that during the war, Taiwanese women were sent to the frontline to serve as sexual slaves for the Japanese Imperial Army. This discovery triggered actions by the comfort women movement in Taiwan. On 20 February 1992, the Taipei Women's Rescue Foundation (TWRF, or Women's Rescue Foundation of Taipei) established a comfort women hotline. Several hundred calls were received and their claims of wartime experiences were investigated by the TWRF in cooperation with scholars, historians and government officials. Fifty-eight women have been conferred with the status of comfort women forcibly drafted by the Japanese military prior to 1945.

The Japanese government could no longer deny the involvement of its military in managing comfort stations. Prime Minister Kiichi Miyazawa issued an apology to Korean survivors during a trip to South Korea. In 1995 the Japanese government established a private foundation to compensate the victims of Japanese military sexual slavery.

Ms Wang Ching-feng, then director of the TWRF, campaigned with government agencies for an in-depth study of the Taiwan comfort women issue and for the founding of the 'Special Committee for Taiwanese survivors of Japanese sexual slavery'. As a result of the TWRF campaign, the Ministries of Foreign Affairs and of the Interior, Taipei and Gaoxiong city governments and Taiwanese provincial governments worked with the TWRF to set up a team to represent Japanese military sexual slavery survivors in Taiwan, assisting the victims in demanding an official apology and compensations from the Japanese government. At the same time, the team also raised funds successfully from the Taiwan government to enable the provision of financial and medical support. The media and TWRF kept the comfort women and their stories in the public arena. In addition, Taiwanese comfort women and activists cooperated with survivors and organisations from South Korea, the Philippines and the Netherlands to campaign on the human rights issue internationally.

Based on interviews with Taiwanese survivors, eyewitness reports, memories of Taiwanese soldiers and declassified documents, it was estimated that the number of Taiwanese comfort women is about 2,000 or more (TWRF 1999: 38). The number of Taiwanese comfort women drafted to work overseas peaked after the outbreak of the Asia-Pacific War. From the historical documents, Taiwanese scholars were able to establish that the deceptive ways of recruitment involved high-level Japanese military personnel and colonial officials as well as business figures in Taiwan.[7] Another way of recruiting women in Taiwan was through local brokers who would deceive young girls into believing they were simply going to do chores for restaurants or teahouses in South China or Southeast Asia. After arriving at the designated locations, the girls were forced to provide sexual services to the soldiers and others. From the backgrounds of the 58 known cases, it can be deduced that most of them were from impoverished families with little education or simply illiterate. They usually had to work for a living or had been supporting families from a young age. In wartime Taiwan, jobs were difficult to get. Therefore, the wages promised by the brokers were attractive to them.

The Taiwanese public knew that there had been three types of sexual violence committed by the Japanese army prior to 1945. The first type concerns the systematic establishment of comfort stations in urban areas. Yoshimi (1995) suggests that there were four kinds of comfort stations: military-controlled comfort stations; military-controlled comfort stations with a civilian front; civilian-run comfort stations providing services to the armed forces; and civilian brothels. Women from Korea, Taiwan, Japan and other countries were sent to these kinds of comfort stations.

The second type is mostly found in rural areas where strong anti-Japanese sentiment persisted. Japanese soldiers looted, kidnapped and raped local women by official sanction. The best study is done by the 'Association of Finding the Truth of the Sexual Violence committed by the Japanese Army' which spent many years researching and documenting the Japanese wartime atrocities at Yuxian, Shanxi Province (Institute of Taiwan Japan Studies 2007: 47–9, 122–6). The victims were usually local women.

The third type of sexual violence is a mixture of the two types mentioned above. Japanese soldiers committed mass rapes when on punitive operations, but also used comfort stations regularly in the urban areas.

In the first part of the 1990s, the images of those poor Taiwanese women abused by Japanese soldiers were brought to and stayed at the forefront of public consciousness. When the Taiwanese comfort women denounced the Asian Women's Fund in 1995, the public stood behind them. Novels and books about their sufferings were published and photographers took photos of them. But some wondered why there was not more material to reinforce the images and keep the public interest going. Would more victims come forward in Taiwan? These questions would be answered in 1996.

The aboriginal comfort women in Taiwan

On 7 September 1996, a preliminary meeting for the 'Asia Pacific Post-war International Conference' was held in Hualian City for former Taiwanese soldiers, surviving descendants of the soldiers and nurses in the Hualian region.[8] Several aboriginal women from Shuiyuan Village attended the meeting as family members of the soldiers. Soon after, seven aboriginal women petitioned the Ministry of Foreign Affairs and other government agencies to recognise their status as Taiwanese comfort women.

The investigations were conducted by scholars and the TWRF and their status as comfort women was confirmed in November 1996. The total number of the aboriginal petitioners was 16. Of these, 12 had been determined as genuine after interviews and investigations and 11 decided to seek compensation, the twelfth having denied being a comfort woman. Another petitioner could not be confirmed as a comfort woman; and two petitioners rejected the petition for family reasons (Wang and Chiang 1997).

The 16 petitioners came from the three major aboriginal tribes in Taiwan: one from the Bunun tribe, seven from the Atayal tribe and eight from the Truku tribe

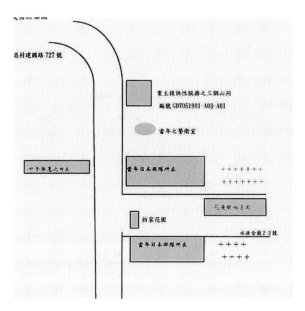

Figure 7.1   Map of Shuiyuan Village (Alang Sakura in Truku language) in 1945 drawn from the memories of the aboriginal comfort women. The grey shaded buildings are (from top): the Japanese military warehouse GDT051901-A03; the police station, the Japanese military camp, and the second military camp. (Source: Chou, TWRF)

(ibid.). The only aboriginal who had been a comfort woman abroad was Li Wen Hung-Shih who gave a public testimony in 1996. She was born in a Bunun *she* in Gaoxiong, South Taiwan. In 1941, she was approached by a Japanese policeman who promised to arrange for her to visit her husband in Hong Kong, where he had been conscripted to work as a guard at an ammunition warehouse. She was abducted while landing at Hong Kong harbour and taken to another barrack to cook and launder during the day and provide sexual services to Japanese soldiers at night. She felt that, 'as a married woman, it was filthy and shameful for her sexual organs to be touched by men other than her husband' (TWRF 2005: 156–7). Ms Li Wen finally told her husband about her past in Hong Kong on his deathbed in 1984.

Of the 12 aboriginal comfort women, only one was victimised outside Taiwan and the remaining petitioners were all victimised in their villages. During the schedule of interviews in various parts of Taiwan, the investigators found out that most of the places where the petitioners had been victimised were Japanese military camps, some of which had since been destroyed, while others were still occupied by the army. The Truku women's victimisation sites were located at three military warehouses at Xiulin Town, Hualian County, and one of the warehouses, a cave at Shuiyuan Village, was almost intact. Without going inside the

Figure 7.2 The cave at Shuiyuan Village, Xiulin Town, Hualian County in 2005. (Source: TWRF volunteer photographer Shen Chun-fan)

cave for nearly fifty years, several Truku petitioners could still tell the investigator the interiors and exact places where they were raped.

The caves at Xiulin town

Xiulin Town (Alang Bsuring in Truku) is located in a mountain region in the northernmost part of Hualian County. It has abundant forest, water and mineral resources. After 1918, the Japanese colonial government forced most of the Truku tribes to relocate from the central mountain regions to this area. The Barbarian Management Bureaus, police stations and several Barbarian children's schools were set up at this region (Sun 2007: 341). Xiulin comes under the jurisdiction of Hualian County and is the County's largest town. In 2005, there were 4,299 families with total population of 15,099. Most of the local residents are Truku aborigines whose families had been resettled from the Central mountain region during the Japanese colonial period (Sun 2007: 323).

The cave is located at Saboda, the source of the Mei-Lun River and site of a water treatment plant, Shuiyuan Village (Pajiq in Truku), Xiulin Town, Hualian County. It was a warehouse used to store weapons and supplies for the Japanese Army and its military inventory number, GDT051901-A03, is still on the wall. The cave is the only known comfort station remaining in Taiwan. Here the young aboriginal women used to wash clothes for the Japanese soldiers at the brook during the day and were raped by the soldiers every night until the war's end. It was formerly owned by the Defence Department; today it is the property of the Council of Indigenous Peoples.

Table 7.1 Basic information on the eight Hualian aboriginal comfort women.

Name	Place of birth	Place of residence	Education	Status at the time	Age	Conscripted for	Place & time of victim	Family conscripted
Chun-fang	Banyan	Banyan	Elementary school	married/3 children	31	laundry, sewing	Banyan 1945–6	brother
Michiko	Banyan	Banyan	Elementary school	unmarried	17	laundry, sewing	Rongshu 1944–6	brothers
Mei-Yue	Xiulin			married/children	22	laundry, sewing	Rongshu over 1 year	husband
A-Hou	Xiulin			unmarried	19	washing, cleaning	Over 1 year	
Ab02	Mountain	Hong Ye		unmarried	19	washing, cleaning		
Xiu-Lan	Mountain	Hong Ye	Nursing training	married /1 daughter	21	odd jobs		husband
Hsiu-Feng	Taroko mountain	Hong Ye	5 years	unmarried		restaurant	Hong Ye 1944–5	brother
Fanf-mei	Mountain		Elementary school	engaged	13	floor sweeping	Shui Yuan 1945	fiancé

Sources: Data collected by TWRF, unpublished; Wang and Chiang 1997.

The Shuiyuan community was quite surprised by the news at the end of 1996 that the village housed victims of the Japanese sexual slavery during the wartime period. By the 1990s there were several comfort women in the village. The village had grown and residents lived along both sides of the Mei-Lun River. The majority of the comfort women found manual jobs in Hualian City or other urban areas. But there were several theme parks along the river and many families ran bed and breakfast establishments during the tourist season. There were restaurants and a grocery store. Several residents had greenhouse businesses. Catholic and Protestant churches shared the Christian believers in the village and across the river there was a Buddhist medical school. Walking along the village streets, one could hear Japanese, Truku, Fujian dialect and Mandarin Chinese spoken. The Truku comfort women at Shuiyuan spoke Japanese and Truku only.

Of the eight Truku comfort women who had been victimised at three different caves, several characteristics were shared among them. They all came from poor families, for instance, and had had no opportunities to leave their home villages. Some had had family members conscripted as soldiers, while others had been recruited by local Japanese policemen or were conscripted to work odd jobs around the military camps. They were brought to the caves to be abused after having worked at the camps for over three months. Afterwards, they were told to keep silent about what had happened at the caves.

Truku customs required young women to remain pure before their parents arranged suitable spouses. During the interviews or group therapy sessions, the women expressed shame and the feeling of being unclean or dirty; because of this, they were afraid of speaking in the village. Only one out of the eight Truku survivors lived outside the village after the war. They all kept quiet about their fate during the wartime and suffered alone or with their fellow victims. Their villages were isolated from the outside. For all these reasons, they came forward much later than did the Han Chinese comfort women survivors.

Conclusion

On 17 August 1999, nine former comfort women from Taiwan, including one from Xiulin, filed a lawsuit at the Tokyo District Court, demanding an official apology and compensation from the Japanese government. The suit was turned down in October 2002, the Tokyo Supreme Court rejecting the lawsuit again on 25 February 2005. Since 2005, the TWRF has worked with the National Cultural Association in promoting the deserted cave at Shuiyuan as a historical site for women in Taiwan. The TWRF promoted the historical significance of the site to the public and mobilised college students to visit the site and talk with the remaining local survivors. In addition, the TWRF planned to erect a human rights monument in front the entrance and clear the interior and surrounding areas for future exhibitions. It was hoped that by creating a real historical space to memorialise the comfort women's story, the memories might live longer.

Figure 7.3 The cave in August 2006. (Source: Shen Chia-Ming, one of the university students who attended the comfort women public testimony)

Both organisations petitioned the owners of the cave and surrounding land, the Council of Indigenous Peoples, to have the site released. The TWRF invited aboriginal chiefs, officials, local historians and residents to participate in the project. They faced many difficulties from the community and the outside world. Some residents rejected the idea of the memorial site being in their backyard on the grounds that it would deter economic development. The local leaders and shop owners hoped to develop tourism to relieve unemployment and could not see the benefit of protecting such a difficult historical site. Money had been pouring into the theme parks and businesses. Therefore, when college students from Taipei visited there, they saw local homeless people defacing the exterior of the cave with paint. The space outside was occupied by homeless people and old furniture with graffiti in red Chinese characters: 'Welcome to the Bed and Breakfast'. There was more graffiti on the wall in Chinese characters.

In 2005, 1,147 out of the total 1,315 Shuiyuan residents were Truku (Sun 2007: 323). They had a strong sense of tribal identity and took pride in being the offspring of Mona Rudao, a heroic anti-Japanese fighter.[9] In recent years, Ms Chin May, a legislator of Truku identity, went to Yasukuni Shrine with the Takasago volunteers and descendants to bring the spirits of dead tribal comrades. Through her actions, the Takasago volunteers were painted as the victims of Japanese military might in the public mind (Simon 2006). This image is particularly popular within the local community.

Today, the TWRF is faced with at least three extremely sensitive and difficult questions. The first is how to merge the two different images of Taiwanese comfort women into one. As Jan Assmann (1992) suggests, collective memories persist through monuments, or words spoken in the community. Outside the Shuiyuan community, the difficulty is also how to merge the popular image of a young woman facing unspeakable violence against her in a foreign country and the image of the aboriginal comfort woman, and then bring them together to the site of a deserted cave. Secondly, how can the women's cultural heritage site and the commemoration of the hero, Mona Rudao, be brought together so that a stronger symbolic reminder of the comfort women's suffering is achieved. The TWRF's task is now to merge all the images and memories into one, so that the cave becomes the symbol of all the sufferings in Taiwan's colonial history. The third issue is how to promote the heritage site without the TWRF being seen as an external force manipulating or monopolising the public memories held by the tribal communities. Answers to all three questions will depend on encouraging those for whom the memories are personal to take the lead in determining what happens, when and how.

Notes

1 Two out of the seventeen sites are located in eastern Taiwan, one being the cave at Shuiyuan Village, Huanlian; another is the Puyuma Women's festival (Pinyin: Beinan-zu) in south-eastern Taiwan. Only three sites out of 17, including the two above, are about the history of aborigines in Taiwan.

2 A Truku woman, at Xiulin Town, recalled that 'Japanese policemen called me loudly as Truku Barbarian at public ... Policemen prohibited Truku girls marrying Han Chinese' (see Sun 2007: 448).

3 The Truku tribe, often romanised as 'Taroko', is also sometimes referred to as Sediq, a subgroup of Atayal. It received recognition as the twelfth aboriginal tribe in Taiwan on 15 January 2004 (Sun 2007: 621).

4 For example, the Xincheng incident in 1896, the Weili incident in 1905 and in 1914 the Taroko Incident, where the Japanese colonial authority mobilised 20,000 polices and soldiers to suppress 3,000 Truku warriors. It is described in the *Xiulin Xianzhi* (Lo 2007) as the Taroko–Japan War.

5 They were told by the Japanese police that 'fighting for the Japanese Empire is a noble deed, and sacrificing in combat is the highest honour to the Volunteers' families' (Institute of Taiwan Japanese Studies 2007: 47).

6 The council was established in 1990 as an organisation for activists and researchers to fight for the rights of former comfort women in South Korea. With survivors and activists, it began the Wednesday Demonstration every week at noon in front of the Japanese Embassy in Seoul.

7 Some documentation proves that the recruitment of the women was partly carried out through a government-sponsored corporation, the 'Taiwan Colonial Trade Corporation'. A document shows that at least three merchants were entrusted with the work of accompanying the recruited females to Hainan Island in the late 1930s (see Chu 2001: 204–9).

8 The conference itself was held in Tokyo on 9–10 August 1996, with representatives from over ten countries from Asia and the USA. The Taiwan delegation consisted of soldiers, comfort women and their descendants, nurses and aborigines.

9 After two long days of conference in May 2007, Ms Chin May took a group of more than forty Japanese and Korean participants to a tour to visit the Mona Rudao Monument at Wushe and commemorated his struggle against Japanese aggression.

References

Assman, J. (1999) *Das kulturelle Gedächtnis: Schrift, Erinnerung und politische Identität in frühen Hochkulturen*, München: Beck.

Chen, J. (2000) 'Sexual Slaves Speak Out Against Injustice', *Sinorama*, January.

Chu, T.-l. (2004) *Lishi de Shangkou: Taiji weianfu koushu lishi jihua chengguo baogaoshu* (History scars: Report of comfort women's oral histories in Taiwan), Taipei: TWRF (in Chinese).

Chu, T.-l. (2001) *Collection of documentations on Taiwan Comfort Women*, Tokyo: Fuji Bookstores (in Japanese).

Howard, K. (ed.) (1995) *True stories of the Korean comfort women*, New York: Cassell.

Institute of Taiwan Japanese Studies (ed.) (2007) *Report on the Forced Labours and Sexual Slavery of the Japanese Imperialism*, Taipei: Institute of Taiwan Japanese Studies (in Chinese).

Kobayashi Yoshinori (2001) *On Taiwan: New Arrogant-ist Manifesto SPECIAL*, Tokyo: Gosen.

Liu, F.-H. (1997) *The Japanese Army in Taiwan: military deployment and key activities, 1895–1945, vol. I.*, Taipei: Academia Historica (in Chinese).

Lo, H.-l. (ed.) (1983) *Hualian Xianzhi (Hualian Annals)*, Taipei: Ch'eng-Wen Publishing Co (in Chinese).

National Cultural Association and Fembooks (eds) (2006) *Women's Footprints: Women's Cultural Heritage Sites in Taiwan*, Taipei: Fembooks Publishing House.

Pan, K.-c. (1998) *Hsinchu Man, Japanese Soldier, War Experience*, Chifeng: Tang Publisher (in Chinese).

Qi, J. (2007) *Drafters, Labors and the Japanese Imperialism in Taiwan*, in Institute of Taiwan Japanese Studies (ed.) *Report on the Forced Labours and Sexual Slavery of the Japanese Imperialism*, Taipei: ITJS (in Chinese).

Simon, S. (2006) *Formosa's First Nations and the Japanese: from Colonial Rule to Postcolonial Resistance*, in *Japan Focus*, available online at: http://japanfocus.org/products/details/1565 (accessed 25 June 2007).

Su, Z. (1999) *Studies on Comfort Women*, Shanghai: Shanghai Publishing (in Chinese).

Sun, D. (2007) *Xiulin Xiangzhi* (The Annals of Xiulin Town), Xiulin: Xiulin Township office (in Chinese).

Tao, D.-G. (1988), *Dianxi Kangri Xuezhan Xieshi*, Taipei (in Chinese).

Wang, Ching-Feng and Chiang, Mei-Fen (1997) *Aboriginal Taiwan comfort women in the Taiwan region: case analysis study*, available online at: http://taiwan.yam.org.tw/womenweb/conf_women/conf_abo.htm (accessed 25 June 2007).

Women's Rescue Foundation of Taipei (TWRF) (1999) *Report on Comfort Women in Taiwan*, Taipei: Taiwan Commercial Press.

Women's Rescue Foundation of Taipei (TWRF) (2005) *Silence Scars: History of Sexual Slavery by the Japanese Military – A Pictorial Book*, Taipei: Business Weekly Publications, Inc. (in Chinese).

Xia, Z. (2005) *The Youth in the Iron Box: Stories of Taiwan Comfort Women*, Taipei: the Bookzone (in Chinese).

Yoshimi, Y., translated by Suzanne O'Brien (1995) *Comfort Women: Sexual Slavery in the Japanese Military during World War II*, New York: Columbia University Press.

Chapter 8

Postcolonial shame
Heritage and the forgotten pain of civilian women internees in Java

Joost Coté

This chapter considers the question of whether sites of colonial wartime civilian internment can constitute heritage sites, and if so on what terms. Central to this discussion is the experience of the suffering and humiliation of colonial white women. These women were isolated from their menfolk, subject to the arbitrary authority of Asian male conquerors and vulnerable to the attitudes of the Indonesians who had been colonised by Europeans prior to the conquest of the Japanese during World War IIbetween November 1942 and September 1945. The chapter argues that this experience constitutes a specific historical moment of individual, national and international – as well as global – significance.

The issue of civilian wartime internment camp experience involves, of course, significantly more than just questions of heritage. There is, for instance, the important question of crimes against humanity, in particular the issue of the so-called 'comfort women', the forced prostitution of incarcerated civilian women (Sajor: n.d.). Arguably also, the privileging of white female civilians in this discussion belittles the pain and suffering of millions of indigenous women and men under wartime conditions. Nor is this chapter concerned with POW camps or the experience of national militaries. One aim here in focusing on wartime civilian internment is to disengage the obvious nationalist motivation that is generated by 'uniformed history' from the experience of civilians neither prepared for nor directly involved in (even if complicit with) the projects of 'warring nations' (Fuijiana *et al.* 2001: 4).

Globally, memorialisation of war dead and pilgrimages to war-related sites can be regarded as one of the more extraordinary manifestations of a resurgent (if not politically manipulated) nationalism. This typically involves iconic sites where, on the one hand, private memories can be nationalised and, on the other, where representations of nationalism are able to be effectively 'spiritualised' and ingested by pilgrims.[1] That these sites (and memories) are linked to national military operations, and gain further significance by being linked to broader supra-national histories – world war, the end of Empire, decolonisation, nationhood – provides them with immediate public legitimacy. At the same time the personal narratives that adhere to them are reinforced by being framed by their association with military operations and confirmed by intra-generational story-telling within families.

Commemoration of World War II in Asia, as Dirlik (2001) suggests, is a 'perilous exercise': war is never a single event and the very specificity of the term 'World War II' conflates the trajectories of a variety of national experiences – and wars. Conventional terminology elides the sharp separation between the 'European' and the 'Asia-Pacific' war but more importantly, in regards to the latter, the distinction between the Japanese–American war and the numerous wars of national liberation with which this intersected. There was not one war but many wars and these were experienced differently by a variety of peoples both within and outside the national frameworks that these events also helped define. There is not one historical chronology of events, but separate sequences of events that extend well beyond the confines of 1941–1945. For many, in colonised Southeast Asia, World War II was not *the* war. In the case of Indonesia, difficult as the years of Japanese occupation were for ordinary Indonesians, the real war came later.

Current practices of memorialisation tend to conflate the gaps that exist between private experience and collective (nationalist) memories, and elide the significant differences in meaning that separate the different national narratives which intersect at iconic sites or in historical moments such as war. Furthermore, not only does the 'unofficial' suffering of civilians in such times typically fail to 'compete' with that of national heroes but the shame of either imperial or freedom fighters, or the pain of colonisers or colonised hardly registers in postcolonial or post-imperial memories. Commemoration of such moments, then, can potentially be responsible for a whole new set of 'victims' – victims of history.

Christina Twomey (2008) suggests that this 'amnesia' 'has more to do with the ambivalent legacy of colonialism than it does with the limited languages of war'. This clearly applies to European civilian women internees in Japanese occupied Dutch East Indies, whose 'ambiguous position' lies not only in their civilian status in a context overlain with nationalist and militaristic symbolism but in the ideological ambiguity that surrounds their pain and suffering in a postcolonial age. Historiographically, the moment of private pain experienced by this population of over 300,000 – over one third of whom are estimated to have been interned as civilians – represents an issue of some significance. It concerns the end of a 350-year European settler society with roots in the Indonesian archipelago going back generations, augmented by sojourning *totoks*, 'career migrants' from the Netherlands. Primarily ethnically Dutch, a significant majority were of mixed European and Indonesian parentage, a large proportion of whom while speaking Dutch had never seen the Netherlands (Bosma and Raben 2003; Taylor 1983). Many were intimately involved in 'colonisation', in maintaining colonial rule where this was increasingly contested by an Indonesian nationalist movement broadly supported by the indigenous population. Like other exogenous communities spawned by European imperial expansion in Southeast Asia expunged from the post-war historical stage by the Japanese occupation, the fate of this community therefore lies at the heart of the process of decolonisation and at the foundation of national emancipation.

In postcolonial times the experiences of European colonial settlers have lacked clear definition. Specifically, they have failed to generate any positive historical

Figure 8.1 Dutch field of honour, Kalibanteng. (Source: J. Coté, 2007)

capital either at a national or international level. Indeed, to the contrary, colonialism and colonial entities have been widely reviled both in the 'liberal West' and
the postcolonial East; only recently has historical discourse begun to investigate the
phenomenon more objectively. In the case of the Dutch colonial community of
the former Dutch East Indies, since the war neither Indonesia nor Japan have been
interested in recognising or recalling to present memory this group's experience.[2]
In the case of the Netherlands, the 'Asian war' was not separately commemorated
nationally till 1980, and a national 'Indisch' war memorial not established till 1988
(Steijlen 2005; Locher-Scholten 1999).[3] At about the same time, the maintenance
of, and pilgrimages to, the seven Dutch war cemeteries – *erevelden* or 'fields of
honour' – in Indonesia has been officially promoted.[4] However, these memorials
and 'fields of honour' are primarily identified as the final resting places of Dutch
casualties of war: of the Japanese attack, of Japanese POW deaths and of the casualties of the post-1945 attempt to suppress Republican Indonesian forces. Little
separate significance is accorded the experience of civilian internees of more than
40 civilian internment camps who survived, while those who perished are included
indiscriminately as the victims of war.[5] This emerging history, therefore, which
conjures up intensely personal memories, may well represent a case where remembering private experiences generates the excavation of public and national histories;
where commemoration of private pain leads to the recognition of public shame.

The heritage of internment camp experience

While all Dutch war cemeteries in Indonesia include the remains of civilian victims, only one, Kalibanteng, in Semarang, is specifically recognised as a memorial to civilian internees, and specifically the women and child victims of Japanese occupation. The cemetery, dominated by the 'tomb of the unknown woman',[6] remembers the women victims of four internment camps in and near the city of Semarang – Ambarawa, Banyu Biru, Lampersari and Karangpanas – which by the end of 1944 had come to house women from throughout Central and Eastern Java.[7] Later the remains of the victims of boys' internment camps were brought here as well.[8] Although Kalibanteng also contains the remains of civilian men – many named crosses indicate these were elderly civilian males – from the beginning it was designated as a memorial to women

> whose courageous conduct and proud bearing during the war and the Japanese occupation of Indonesia gained the appreciation and admiration of both Dutch people and foreigners, and, simultaneously the memory of the countless women together with the hundreds of children who lost their lives in Japanese concentration camps.
>
> (Oorlogsgravenstichting 1999: 41)

While not the actual site of an internment camp, here we come closest to where the specificity of civilian victimhood can be remembered in a single location; where both the individual pain of the civilian experience (including the loss of loved ones – mothers, aunts, grandmothers, sisters, daughters) and the national shame (imperial loss, human rights violations, murders) mediated by the opprobrium related to colonialism and the rhetoric of Asian emancipation and the nationalist struggle can be memorialised.

But cemeteries represent somewhat abstract sites of intangible heritage. Of the total of eight Dutch war cemeteries in Indonesia, only two mark actual sites of the wartime events that produced the casualties so honoured: the Ambon international war cemetery established on the site of a large Japanese POW camp, and Ancol, near Jakarta, the site of a notorious Japanese place of execution, which has been dedicated as a final resting place for all victims of Japanese execution in the archipelago. In all other cases, the actual sites where civilian internment was experienced have been obliterated either by the process of post-war economic development or simply by the process of forgetting. Any visitor or Indonesian of the post-war generation today can walk through the laneways of Kampung Sompok or Lampersari in Semarang, for instance, completely unaware of the experience of thousands of women and children who lived among these very streets and inside the extant pre-war houses that remain. Meanwhile an accumulation of numerous autobiographical accounts, archived and published diaries, and some recent historical research, together with the healing of time, have made an objective recognition of the significance of that experience a possibility. Privately, as the

Figure 8.2 Monument to women, Kalibanteng cemetery (Source: J. Coté).

generational community involved itself nears the end of its life, it worries that its history will be forgotten, (Coté and Westerbeek 2005; Westerbeek 2007).

The question that therefore needs to be asked is, should the personal pain of these non-combatants be isolated from its present nationalist, and military context? Can we expect the memory of this painful history – experienced on a large-scale and by a civilian community complicit in the denial of national emancipation; perpetrated by an army claiming thereby to liberate a people from colonial oppression; and supported by the founders of the nation that benefited from this 'event' and which must legislate in regard to any heritage project on its territory – can this be given specific, international, public recognition? Should these victims, not of war but of 'decolonisation', attract recognition in a post-colonial age? Should we expect the three nations, which have invested such national importance in the history surrounding this private pain, be asked to recognise their mutual complicity in this suffering?

The recent turn in 'heritage discourse' towards memorialising sites and experiences of public 'tragedy' and suffering suggests that it is at least reasonable to contemplate. Even if the realisation remains problematic, the experience of the largest single civilian European community to be incarcerated in the course of the Asia-Pacific War has some claim to consideration as heritage.

The experience of internment

There is little doubt that the Indonesian archipelago's natural resources were the target of the Japanese military's southward push.[9] But it also had a related aim of challenging European imperialism and, after the surrender of the East Indies government on 8 March 1942, Japanese occupation forces began to quickly implement a policy of eliminating the European cultural presence from its newly conquered territories. Apart from the prohibition of the Dutch language and the closing of Dutch financial and educational institutions, this involved dealing with the civilian European population. The solution arrived at defined the experience of European civilian women internees.

Several general conclusions can be drawn from the history of Dutch civilian internment during the Japanese occupation of the East Indies.[10] In the first place this Japanese policy for containing and obliterating European influence in Indonesia was as much a measure to achieve maximum propaganda impact as it was a security issue – it appears not to have been effectively pre-planned, nor uniformly or immediately instituted. The places of incarceration were neither uniform nor initially available or for the most part purpose-built. Complete implementation of an internment policy took till the end of 1943, was developed through trial and error, and varied in its impact between camp commanders and over time. First-hand accounts indicate that harsher conditions followed the eventual transfer of civilian camp administration to military control at the beginning of 1944, and that inmates suffered increased deprivation in the last twelve months primarily as a result of a process of camp consolidation and general food scarcity rather than (although not to the exclusion) of the brutality of guards (Jansen 1988; Boissevain and Van Empel 1981).[11] In hindsight, the experience within camps can be seen to have been directly or indirectly related to Japan's faltering military situation, and deteriorating food and manpower resources in the latter part of the war. As such, apart from their incarceration and their immediate subjection to Japanese army surveillance, in general terms European civilian internees probably suffered worse physically only in degree compared to the surrounding Indonesian community beyond the wire (Kratoska 2005; Sato 1994; Jansen 1988).[12]

The emotional and physical experience of internment was structured by an apparently rational organisational framework developed and imposed by the Japanese civil administration in the course of its first eighteen months. Derived from regulations governing military POW camps, this was largely defined by three sets of procedures set out in three key documents: Regulations No. 7 and No. 33 issued by the local Jakarta-based Japanese military command of 11 April and September 1942 respectively and in parallel local camp regulations retro-spectively summarised and given official imprimatur by a central Tokyo-based Japanese War Ministry document of November, 1943 (Van Velden 1963: 548–75 [Appendixes 1–3]).

The first of these regulations required all non-Indonesian, male and female 'enemy subjects' – that is, all those non-combatant, non-government personnel not immediately imprisoned as prisoners of war – to register and swear an 'oath of loyalty' to the Japanese army. This process required registrants to present their birth certificate (*asal usul*) indicating their family lineage,[13] and pay a registration fee of 150 guilders. In turn, registrants were issued with an identification paper or certificate (*pendafteran*) that indicated whether they were *totok* (of pure Dutch parentage) or *Indo* (of mixed Dutch-Indonesian or Chinese parentage). The second regulation, issued in September, defined those who were to be interned, and had the effect of enforcing a division in the colonial European community between Europeans and Indo-Europeans. While also affecting men, the regula-tion had a primary impact on the wartime experience of non-indigenous women and children.

Japanese policy regarding Eurasians was a complex of pragmatic and ideo-logical principles. Its aim was to promote Eurasian identification with their Indonesian rather than their European heritage, and, it has been suggested, to employ this segment of the population in the administration and exploitation of the country in the future. In practice it essentially implied that those who could demonstrate they had a degree of Indonesian parentage – in Java this applied to approximately 100,000 individuals previously classified as European – initially remained free after registering (Van Velden 1963: 440–51). This effectively determined for them an ambiguous future existence in occupied Java outside internment camps. Subsequent re-registration procedures involved a gradual refinement of racial categorisation according to which the number subject to internment was gradually expanded (De Jong 1985: 849).

But the main immediate impact of the September 1942 regulation was to resolve the problem confronting the Japanese administration of what was termed 'unaccompanied European women' – women whose menfolk had been killed in military action or had become POWs. They were now to be placed in what might, to reflect the Japanese rhetoric, be termed 'protective custody'.

A consequence of the internment policy, then, was to intensify the categorisa-tion of humanity that had existed under colonialism. Although in the end general conditions experienced by interned Europeans were similar, initially the treatment of colonial military and government officials and civilians, of men and women, of Europeans and Eurasians, and of Europeans and Asians was strictly differenti-ated.[14] While as a group, for instance, women generally were interned later than men, significant differences emerged even in this category. Some, as spouses of 'Nipponworkers', were able to maintain their family intact, and were allocated to special family internment centres. The rich, at least initially, fared better than the poor (De Jong, 1985: 772.). Indonesian partners of European men and women of mixed descent previously accepted within the European community were now confronted with the choice of resisting the newly imposed racial classification and opting for internment along with their European neighbours, or staying outside the internment camps; of defining themselves as either European or Indonesian. Such a decision was made all the more difficult given their sole responsibility for the welfare of their (European) children. A small number of women were subjected to, and a smaller number opted for, prostitution (Van Velden 1963: 277–9; De Jong 1985: 776–81).[15]

The establishment and administration of civilian internment camps

The process whereby designated 'protective areas' in occupied cities became prisons was a gradual one. Across the Indies, arrangements for the internment of civilians in designated 'camps' were not finalised till the end of 1943 and only in the course of that year were these residential districts gradually sealed off from intercourse with the rest of the city by barbed wire and *gedek* (plaited bamboo matting). Thereafter, a process of consolidation followed in which smaller camps were gradually closed and their inmates relocated to larger ones. This process that occurred in the course of 1944 and early 1945, in Java at least, involved the trucking or training of large numbers of Europeans, particularly of women and children, across Java in conditions reminiscent of the Nazi transportation of European Jews. It was this extensive consolidation into fewer and much larger internment camps that generally resulted in the extreme conditions of overcrowding, malnutrition and high mortality (Van Velden 1963: 369–75; De Jong 1985: ch. 9).[16]

Given the numbers involved, the process of internment of civilian urban inhabitants was more drawn out in the main centres of the European community in Java than elsewhere in the archipelago, although the process was the same (Wertheim 1958: 8–9).[17] The four key colonial cities, home to the colonial administrative, professional and financial establishment, were Batavia, Bandung, Semarang and Surabaya. Relocation of women in these cities to designated 'safe areas' was organised by 'European Contact Committees', committees of prominent Dutch women appointed by Japanese authorities responsible for allocating individual families to houses and streets within an internment complex. In Batavia, the process of interning women and children did not begin till September 1942, where they were eventually consolidated into two suburban residential areas, Kramat and Tjideng, which by 1945 housed 3400 and 10,500 respectively. In Bandung internment began in October (into three main districts accommodating 7,000, 6,000 and 1,200 women and children respectively); in Semarang in November (8,000 eventually accommodated in Lampersari-Sompok, 3,700 in Halmahera, and 7,000 in several camps outside the city in Ambarawa); Yogyakarta and central Java from December (10,500); Malang and environs by January 1943 (7,000); and Surabaya by June 1943 (6,000) (De Jong 1985: 348–51).

Figure 8.3 One of the few extant pre-war houses that formed part of the Lampersari-Sompok internment camp. (Source: J. Coté, 2007)

In each case, relocation followed announcements on radio and via newspapers and wall posters requiring women and children to assemble at a specified place to enter the 'camps' (or to assemble for transportation by truck or train). The relocated women came to occupy housing districts from which their original (Indonesian or Eurasian) inhabitants had first been evicted (as made clear in Art. 2 of the Regulation no. 33). Women who merely relocated from one part of the city to another (normally from wealthy to less salubrious housing) were permitted to bring as many personal belongings as they could manage including books, linen, clothing, kitchen ware and even furniture (Boissevain and Van Empel 1981). Better off, and better prepared, women were thus initially well cushioned, in terms of familiar furnishings, clothing supplies, basic medicines, jewellery and funds. Over time, however, as these items were gradually traded, removed by order of Japanese commanders, left behind as a result of being relocated to other camps, or simply thrown out to make room for the ever increasing numbers of individuals forced to reside in a single house, this 'cushion' gradually depleted and eventually for all inmates disappeared (Boissevain and Van Empel 1981).

Initially, while the boundaries of such residential districts were still relatively open, food could still be purchased from former Indonesian neighbours or travelling food-sellers, or brought by former Indonesian house servants. Early on, European children were also able to continue their education in impromptu schools taught by women inmates; illicit radios continued to keep internees informed about the course of the war; and permits were still obtainable to undertake visits outside the confines to, among other things, visit or arrange the sending of parcels

Figure 8.4 Extant building that housed the Lampersari-Sompok internment camp kitchens and administrative centre. (Source: J. Coté, 2007)

to menfolk in distant camps. But by the end of 1943, and certainly after the take-over of civilian camps by the Japanese military, all such 'privileges' were withdrawn, regular house searches were instigated, onerous agricultural duties assigned and formal POW-style morning and evening roll-calls were introduced.

Surviving copies of the minute camp rules and regulations reveal how internees' lives were carefully regulated during the later years. Under headings such as: 'organisation of internees', 'arrangement and maintenance of buildings', 'daily behaviour', 'inspection', 'health and hygiene', 'fire and other emergencies', 'internal camp administration', regulations determined a daily routine that came to dominate the lives of women and children (Van Velden 1963: 565–70 [Appendix 8]). Increasingly suffering from malnutrition, ill health and the composite psychological impact of the loss of freedom, lack of privacy, loss of loved ones and constant surveillance, such routines forced a modicum of 'eventfulness' and activity in an otherwise spiritually and physically enervating situation. Internally divided into groups based on groups of houses, these activities were administered by group leaders (*hancho*) appointed by a Committee of Administration headed by a Japanese (*bushensho*), who in turn was responsible for establishing a number of committees each of which in turn required a leader (*kuncho*). Each group had eleven such committees to oversee daily activities, such as collecting meals from the communal kitchens and distributing irregular provisions of sugar, flour and coffee; collecting special infant rations of milk; carrying out house maintenance, and hygiene; organisation of agricultural labour and street cleaning; physical exercise sessions; learning Japanese; and arranging night patrol (Boissevain and Van Empel 1981; Kanahele 1967).

Figure 8.5 Transportation of Dutch women internees through Indonesian Republican lines, c. late 1945. (Source: Antara News Agency archive, Jakarata, with permission.)

The heritage of internment camps

While the physical hardship of women civilian internees – mothers, grand-mothers, daughters and sisters – as well as infants under these conditions can be guessed at, space unfortunately prevents an elaboration here of the deeper psychological suffering these women and a generation of children and adolescents must have experienced. This becomes only too apparent when reading the diary annotations written at the time. The existence, apart from secondary source accounts, of a relatively large number of published and unpublished diaries and post-war recollections as well as a publicly accessible oral history collection of recorded interviews with survivors (Steijlen 2002) make it possible to retell the experience of camp life in extensive detail.[18]

In the specific case of the Lampersari-Sompok internment camp, one of the largest wartime women's internment camps in Java, at least five published contemporary accounts exist.[19] These make possible an accurate reconstruction of the public and domestic lives, the physical and the inner experience, of the women of this camp. As a potential heritage site, furthermore, the contemporary Semarang residential district of Lampersari-Sompok still provides a physical basis for a tangible reminder of that experience. Several of the pre-war domestic houses in which internees were accommodated remain and a number of public buildings that served as the former internment camp's main administrative and organisational centres. Currently they are totally mute however: they reveal nothing of their history. In the busy suburbs of Indonesia's postcolonial cities, there is no place for looking backwards to a painful past. The physical structures in which this wartime experience was contained now form part of the fabric of modern urban life and the memory of it that may have remained with an older generation of former Indonesian neighbours has been obliterated by a new history.

Reflection

Twomey (2008) argues in relation to Australia that the civilian internee as an individual and as an issue lacks 'gravitas', lacking the weight of comparable numbers, on the one hand, and the 'benefit' of the extreme post-war opprobrium that the Nazi internment and genocide of Jewish civilians during the European war has attracted. Japanese civilian internment did not equate with a 'plan to exterminate all Europeans', she argues, so that, '[t]here is no single, powerful word like holocaust to which a survivor of a Japanese internment camp can lay claim' (Twomey 2008). Moreover, for the colonial Dutch – *belanda* (Dutch), *belanda-totok* (European Dutch), *belanda-indo* (Indo) alike – as suggested at the beginning of this essay, the community itself has an ambiguous identity and standing within the Netherlands, Indonesian and Japanese contexts and is largely unknown outside the Netherlands and Dutch-language literature. And yet, as the above has shown, many aspects of their experience represent and impinge upon major national and global historical and humanitarian phenomena. Arguably it is this civilian experience, as much as, if not more dramatically than, the defeat of the colonial military, that marks the real victory of the Japanese over Dutch (and European) imperialism, firstly, and thus, secondly, the beginning of Indonesian national independence. This in itself does – or rather should – provide the 'gravitas' to which Twomey refers, which the heritage industry might require for the separate recognition of the civilian internment experience of Dutch East Indies settlers.

Further, this civilian community became the specific target of an Indonesian militia campaign to force the recognition of Republican goals on Dutch society. Thus, to recognise this experience in terms of heritage would require a more direct recall of a European imperial past in Asia now largely neutralised behind a discourse of battle zones and military victories and losses. To excavate this private pain from a largely forgotten past would be to revive the less than honourable events that surrounded the end of imperialism and the glorious history of a revolution, to ruffle history's convenient curtain. Moreover, it might be unreasonable to expect the Indonesian nation or the citizens of a contemporary, modern city to make available a space to remember someone else's history. As indicated, the city and nation has already shown its recognition and respect to the dead in the form of the scrupulously respected and maintained Dutch and Allied War graves.

In Indonesia there is no equivalent day for remembering World War II since, clearly, for Indonesia there was no war, merely another colonialism. The Indonesian war – as real and as bloody as any – was against the attempted re-imposition of colonial rule after 15 August. *Hari Palahwan Nasional*, the Indonesian national day of remembrance (10 November), recalls in the first place the fallen at the first major battle against the imperial return in Surabaya in November 1945. This was the very time that Dutch civilian internees were in many places still trapped inside internment camps, often protected now by Japanese military under orders from British command, from direct attacks by Indonesian Republican militia. For many European civilian internees this moment is remembered as the most terrifying period of their time behind wire.

Conclusion

While war and its related nationalist historiographies continue to dominate the construction of collective memory, and former Allied states continue to concentrate on Japanese atrocities, recent trends in scholarly history towards a more global perspective suggest such narrow constructions of public memory and memorialisation need to be reconsidered. A new generation of 'world historians' is ascribing significance to these wartime events that go well beyond those of traditionally chauvinist national or private narratives (Fujitani *et al.* 2001; Williams 2004; Baylis and Harper 2007). Williams has perhaps most provocatively argued for a reassessment of 'the scared assumption that the Second World War was a wholly right-minded crusade against fascism' (Williams 2004: 40). He has argued for the Asia-Pacific war to be seen in terms of the beginning of the demise of 'White global hegemony', a turning point in world history.

Heritage is about meaning – meaning embedded in the contemporary significance ascribed to past events. A consideration of the heritage of the experience of civilian women internees in Indonesia draws attention to how contentious this may be. While an emphasis on 'sites of pain and shame' in heritage discourse might well continue and confirm traditional perspectives, it also has potential to open up new questions by investigating more carefully whose 'pain' and whose 'shame' were involved. Private suffering has the potential to unsettle national narratives conventionally associated with the memorialising of the Asia-Pacific war that continue to overwhelm and obscure the memory of private pain and any sense of national shame. Celebration of tragic heroism and an overwhelming sense of the righteousness of war in the service of Western imperialism ignore the tendentious benefits gained for indigenous nationalism and carry the heavy accent of racism. The question is whether the 'heritage industry' is able to take account of such new historiographical directions.

Notes

1 This is evident in the growing 'ANZAC pilgrimages' by Australians and prominent visits to Yashukuni shrine in Japan. In the Netherlands Dutch pilgrimages to 'fields of honour' outside the Netherlands are organised annually by the Oorlogsgravenstichting – the Dutch War Graves Foundation. There were already more than 15,000 registered visits to the seven Dutch war graves sites in Indonesia in 1996.
2 The renovated Japanese Yashukuni War Museum, Yasukuni Jinja Yushukan, for instance has been criticised for failing to make mention of the existence of internment camps, the victims of the Burma–Thailand railway project or even the Nanking massacres.

3 The first community memorial commemorating the end of the Asia-Pacific war in the Netherlands was established in 1971 specifically to remember Dutch women victims of Japanese occupation.

4 These cemeteries are: in Java, Menteng Pulo and Ancol (Jakarta), Leuwogajah, Pandu (Bandung), Candi, Kalibanteng (Semarang), Kembang Kuning (Surabaya); in Molukku, Ambon. Apart from the Ambon cemetery administered by the Commonwealth War Graves Commission, these are overseen and maintained by the Oorlogsgravenstiching, the Netherlands War Graves Foundation. Other cemeteries commemorate Dutch war dead in Thailand, Burma and Japan.

5 A majority of camps were closed in the course of 1944–5 under a Japanese policy of camp consolidation. The full list is provided in Van Velden (1963) as an appendix.

6 A plaque on a sculpture representing two women and a child declares: *Hun geest heeft overwonnen* (Their spirit has won through). Another plaque states: *Ter eerbeidige nagedachtenis aan de vele ongenoemden die hun leven offerden en niet rusten op de erevelden* (In respectful memory of the many unknown [women] who gave their lives and are not lying in the fields of honour).

7 Apart from women resident in Semarang, the Semarang camps came to house women originally interned in women's internment camps in the cities of Yogyakarta, Surakarta, Malang, Surabaya and Magelang, each of which had earlier acted as collection points for local women from smaller nearby European settlements.

8 In 1944 the Japanese established two camps for young teenage boys between 10 and 17, in Cimahi (near Bandung) and Ambarawa (near Semarang).

9 Notably Balakpapan, the main oil field, captured prior to the Japanese landing in Singapore.

10 The two Dutch-language accounts of the civilian experience used here, Van Velden (1963) and De Jong (1985), are generally recognised as the most complete and objective sources for the Dutch experience. Space does not allow detailed reference to the two contemporary published diaries (Jansen 1988 and Boissevain and Van Empel 1981) used in the preparation of this discussion which confirm and supplement these accounts.

11 Van Velden (1963) concludes that arbitrary punishment was relatively rare, 'the great majority of internees were never personally punished [and] most only saw a Japanese once or twice a day during roll call' (p. 342).

12 Indonesians experienced lack of food, money or employment, physical maltreatment as forced labourers (*romusha*) or prostitutes, and were transported beyond the archipelago, to work on the Thai–Burma railroad and in Japanese coal mines.

13 Ironically this paralleled the colonial system of recognising nationality which formed the basis of the legal division between Europeans, Indonesians and Chinese. Indonesian clerks assisting Japanese administration in this process were all too familiar with the certificate which had excluded them from white privileges.

14 Self-defined Jews, in many cases recent refugees from fascist Europe, were often imprisoned separately though in some instances registered themselves as Asian, in which case they were not interned till the end of 1943 (Van Velden 1963:77 n. 4). Nationals of countries allied with Japan were initially exempted but pro-Nazi/Fascist Dutch (*NSB'ers*) were generally not recognised.

15 Van Velden asserts that Tokyo authorities specifically prohibited subjecting European female internees to prostitution. She also reports cases of women participating on a 'voluntary' basis in prostitution. Aside from forced female prostitution, De Jong notes the existence of paedophilic abuse in boys' camps by Japanese guards.

16 On the basis of Red Cross and Japanese figures Van Velden estimates that at least 10–13 per cent of the between 73,000 and 80,000 internees in Java died in the last year of internment and that the mortality rate increased dramatically after April 1945, particularly for the over 50s, for men more than women, and for non-Dutch Europeans than for Indies-Dutch internees.

17 According to the 1930 census, 76.67 per cent or 147,648 Europeans in Java (where the majority of the 200,000 Europeans in the Dutch East Indies at that time were) lived in

urban centres, more than half in six towns with a total population (including Indonesians and Chinese) of 100,000 or more. Only 6.35 per cent of an estimated total of 40.9 million Indonesians in Java were categorised as urban.
18 In the Netherlands the archival and published record of the war experience of Dutch military and civilians in Indonesia is undertaken by NIOD, the Netherlands War Documentation Institute. This functions in a similar way to the Australian War Memorial.
19 Boissevain and Van Empel (1981); Bouwman (2000); Klamer (1995); Kruisman (2001); Neytzell De Wilde (1987); Vermeer-Van Berkum (1980).

References

Baylis, C. and Harper, T. (2007) *Forgotten Wars: The End of Britain's Asian Empire*, London: Penguin/Allen Lane.
Boissevain, G. and Van Empel, L. (1981) *Vrouwenkamp Op Java. Een Dagboek*, Amsterdam/Brussel: De Boekerij.
Bosma, U. and Raben, R. (2003) *De Geschiedenis van Indische Nederlanders: De Oude Indische Wereld 1500–1920,* Amsterdam: Bert Bakker.
Bouwman, R. (2000) *Twee Moeders. Kampdagboeken En Bersiap*, Rotterdam: Indonet.
Coté, J. and Westerbeek, L. (eds) (2005) *Recalling the Indies: Colonial Memories and Postcolonial Identities*, Amsterdam: Aksant.
Dirlik, A. (2001) '"Trapped in History" on the way to Utopia: East Asia's "Great War" Fifty years later', in T. Fujitani, G. White and L. Yoneyama (eds), *Perilous Memories: The Asia-Pacific War(s)*, Durham and London: Duke University Press.
Fujitani, T., White, G. and Yoneyama, L. (2001) 'Remembering and dismembering the Asia-Pacific War(s)', in T. Fujitani, G. White and L. Yoneyama (eds), *Perilous Memories: The Asia-Pacific War(s)*, Durham and London: Duke University Press.
Jansen, L. (1988) *In Deze Halve Gevangenis: Dagboek van Mr Dr L.F. Jansen, Batavia/Djakarta*, Franeker: Uitgeverij Van Wijnen.
Jong, L. de (1985) *Het Koninkrijk der Nederlanden in de Tweede Wereldoorlog, Vol. 11b, Nederlands-Indië, Part Two*, 's-Gravenhage: Staatsuitgeverij.
Kanahele, G. (1967) *The Japanese Occupation of Indonesia: Prelude to Independence*, Ann Arbor, MI: University Microfilms, microform.
Klamer, I. (1995) *Kind In Een Japans Concentratiekamp*, Published by the author.
Kratoska, P. (ed.) (2005) *Asian labor in the wartime Japanese empire: Unknown histories*, Armonk, NY: Sharpe.
Kruisman, L. (2001), *Lampersari Nog Niet Voorbij*, Assen: Servo.
Locher-Scholten, E. (1999) 'Van Indonesische urn tot Indisch monument: Vijftig jaar Nederlandse herinnering aan de tweede Wereldoorlog in Azië', *Bijdragen en mededelingen betreffende de geschiedenis der Nederlanden*, 114: 2.
Neytzell De Wilde, C. (1987) *Een Mary-Gold Als Verjaardagscadeau. Aquarellen En Schetsen, 1942–1945*, Franeker.
Oorlogsgravenstichting (1999) 'De ereveld Kalibanteng te Semarang', 33–42. Available online at: http://www.ogs.nl.
Ruff-O'Hearn, J. (1994) *50 Years of Silence*, Sydney: Tom Thompson.
Sajor, I. (n.d.) 'The Women's International War Crimes Tribunal on Japan's Military Sexual Slavery: A Historical Landmark in Ending Impunity'. Available online at: http://www.aplconference.ca/speech/Sajor.htm.

Sato, S. (1994) *War, Nationalism and Peasants: Java under the Japanese occupation 1942–1945*, Sydney: Allen & Unwin.

Steijlen, F. (2002) *Memories of 'the East': Abstracts of the Dutch interviews about the Netherlands East Indies, Indonesia and New Guinea (1930–1962)*, Leiden: KILTV Press.

Steijlen, F. (2005) 'Remembrance of Dutch war dead in Southeast Asia, 1942–45', Paper to Kyoto workshop (typescript).

Taylor, J. (1983) *The Social World of Batavia: European and Eurasian in Dutch Asia*, Madison, WI: University of Wisconsin Press.

Twomey, C. (2008) 'Remembering War and Forgetting Civilians: The ambiguous position of civilian internees in Australian commemorations of the Pacific War', in K. Blackburn and K. Hack (eds), *National Memories and Forgotten Captivities: POWs, Internees and Colonial Subjects in Japanese Occupied Asia*, London: Routledge.

Velden, D. van (1963) *De Japanse Inerneringskampen voor burgers gedurende de tweede wereldoorlog*, Groningen: JB Wolters.

Vermeer-Van Berkum, C. (1980) *Dagboek Uit Japanse Kampen '44–'45. Kon Ik Maar Weer Een Gewoon Meisje Zijn*, Amsterdam/Brussel: Elsevier/Van Goor.

Westerbeek, L. (2007) 'Dutch Indonesians in Australia: Second Generation Identity in the Diaspora', PhD thesis, Deakin University.

Williams, D. (2004) *Defending Japan's Pacific war: The Kyoto School Philosophers and Post-White Power*, London and New York: RoutledgeCurzon.

Chapter 9

Difficult memories

The independence struggle as cultural heritage in East Timor

Michael Leach

This chapter examines the way difficult sites of imprisonment, trauma and resistance are being remembered in the newly independent nation of East Timor. While the difficult challenge of memorialising massacre sites, places of political imprisonment, torture and human rights abuses confronts many post-conflict societies, few represent as profound a loss as Timor-Leste, having suffered an estimated minimum 102,000 casualties during the Indonesian occupation from 1975 to 1999, along with forced population displacements and extensive non-fatal human rights violation through arbitrary detention, torture and rape (CAVR 2005: 43).[1]

In Timor-Leste, these difficult legacies are complicated by the distinct cultural and linguistic affiliations promoted by successive colonial regimes, political schisms within the former independence movement, a lack justice for the victims of human rights abuses during the Indonesian occupation, and the recent rise of regional tensions. These fissures have complicated the process of nation-building, and the articulation of a unifying postcolonial national identity. As such, they are critical to understanding the cultural heritage of the independence struggle and its conservation in Timor-Leste, which is itself an exercise in articulating cultural nationalism.

In examining East Timorese responses to these difficult issues since independence in 2002, this chapter discusses some of the challenging contexts of cultural heritage management in Timor-Leste, and surveys the colonial and postcolonial 'layers' of the cultural heritage landscape, examining their competing visions of East Timorese identity. It then focuses on East Timorese nationalist conservation of difficult sites in the struggle for independence, including key jails and interrogation centres, massacre sites, and recent monuments to the armed resistance movement Falintil (Armed Forces for the National Liberation of East Timor). With limited resources, East Timor has had notable success in the conservation of key sites, and memories of the liberation struggle, at both the national and the local levels. Nonetheless, it is argued that the cultural heritage landscape reflects a major 'fault line' in post-independence politics, in that the contribution of younger East Timorese nationalists in the struggle for independence remains relatively neglected.

Contexts

During the struggle for independence, a truly national sense of East Timorese identity and community arose from the collective experiences of suffering under the Indonesian occupation, which had a unifying effect across various ethnic and language groups under the 'colonial gaze' (Anderson 1993). Since independence, maintaining this unified sense of a common national identity has proven a more challenging task. Timor-Leste has witnessed intergenerational disputes over national identity and official languages (Leach 2003), and wider 'history wars' within the former independence movement over the symbolic 'ownership' of the independence struggle, and its core historical narratives (Leach 2006). One widely endorsed and popular narrative of East Timorese nationalism is that of *funu*: of a 450-year 'national' resistance struggle against consecutive foreign occupiers. However, this broadly unifying historical narrative is complicated by the more divisive cultural legacies of successive colonial eras. Beneath it, a complex and ongoing struggle over postcolonial cultural affiliations and national identity is evident.

Put simply, the distinct experiences and educational backgrounds of two generations of nationalists, respectively encountering Portuguese and Indonesian colonialism, have complicated the task of articulating a simple, unifying postcolonial national identity. Older nationalists have politically dominated the post-independence state, and it is clear that significant numbers of young people have felt misrecognised by some 'official' articulations of national identity embedded in the East Timorese constitution, and in the policies of the first government. As such, while the process of articulating the cultural components of nationalism may be metaphorically understood as one of 'imagining' a nation (Anderson 1983), in practice it may involve the universalisation of cultural and political values of a dominant nationalist grouping (Leach 2002: 45).

One touchstone issue is the choice of official languages, and the official cultural affiliations of the independent state. While the indigenous lingua franca *Tetum* is accorded a high degree of cross-generational endorsement, Portuguese has been less popular with the younger generation educated in Indonesian. The official use of the language, and the 'privileged ties' accorded to Portuguese-language countries – embedded as an 'official' conception of national identity in the East Timorese constitution of 2002 – made sense for an older generation of the political élite, literate in Portuguese, and instrumental in the rise of East Timorese nationalism in the 1960s and early 1970s. For this generation, Portuguese was important as a unifying language across the élite of local language groups (before the spread of Tetum in the 1980s), and as a language of the armed resistance. Its choice as an official language also acknowledged the critical diplomatic support of Lusophone countries during the occupation. For the younger generation educated in Bahasa and with little knowledge of the old colonial language, however, the choice of Portuguese raised fears of their exclusion from symbolic sources of power and cultural identity in an independent East Timor.

Another example of this 'fault line' is evident in intergenerational debate over nationalist historiography, and the nature of an 'authentic' postcolonial national identity. For an older generation of nationalists, emphasising the long history of *funu*, the Portuguese presence is critical to East Timorese nationalism: unifying different regions against a common occupier, bringing Catholicism, and marking the nation as a distinctive grouping not only in relation to Indonesia as a whole, but, equally, to the indigenous peoples of Dutch-colonised, Protestant-influenced west Timor.[2] Many nationalists in a younger generation look for what they see as a more authentic postcolonial identity, looking primarily to its Melanesian or indigenous roots, and more interested in the commonalties with west Timor. As one interviewee put it (Leach 2006: 232), 'I would prefer to study indigenous history, not related to colonialism. East Timor's history itself; the local things.'

With some 75 per cent of the population under thirty years of age – but the political élite still dominated by an older generation – these differences are important political fault lines. Indeed, two key background factors behind the political crisis in East Timor in 2006 were political divisions within the former independence movement and these well-documented intergenerational tensions. Among other things, the partial rejection of certain 'official' narratives of national identity and history by young people highlights the difficult legacy of cultural division in the wake of consecutive colonial eras in East Timor. These wider intergenerational divisions over national identity and history are an important context to understanding issues of cultural heritage management in the independent nation.

Inevitably, another critical context in Timor Leste has been one of limited resources for the maintenance and restoration of the built cultural heritage landscape, though the international community has donated money for several key projects such as UNESCO's support for the conservation of the *Uma Fukum*: the oldest Portuguese colonial building in Dili, a former barracks and future site of the national museum. In the UN transitional administration period, the Portuguese government also resourced reconstruction of many colonial-era buildings, including churches and government offices. The small number of major projects supported by the East Timorese government has generally been co-funded by external partners. I examine these further below.

'Layers' of cultural heritage

East Timor became the newest member of the UN upon independence in 2002, following 450 years of Portuguese colonial rule ending in 1975, and a 24-year struggle against Indonesian occupation between 1975 and 1999. As the future President and Nobel Peace Prize recipient Jose Ramos-Horta (1996) noted, 'East Timor is at the crossroads of three major cultures: Melanesian, which binds us to our brothers and sisters of the South Pacific region; Malay-Polynesian, binding us to South East Asia, and the Latin Catholic influence, a legacy of almost 500 years of Portuguese colonisation'. These influences have offered disparate resources for competing colonial and nationalist accounts of East Timorese history and identity

(Leach 2006: 224). During the twenty-four-year Indonesian occupation, these tensions became a site of symbolic struggle; with Indonesian neo-colonial historiography emphasising historical Malay connections, and East Timorese nationalists highlighting Melanesian affinities and the 450-year impact of Portuguese colonialism, by which East Timor could be identified as a nation distinct from Dutch-colonised west Timor.

Similarly, the various colonial and postcolonial layers of cultural heritage in Timor-Leste represent contested attempts to reinterpret the past in ways which suit, respectively, Portuguese, Indonesian and nationalist ideas of East Timorese identity. The built landscape of cultural heritage and monuments charts a changing history from 'heroes of the Portuguese empire', through neo-colonial 'integration' monuments of Indonesia; to the monuments of an independent state. As Wiley (1994: 145) notes, collective identities commonly interpret the past as the linear 'origin' of the present political self, or of a future self it is in the process of 'becoming' (see also Anderson 1983: 22–36). Each layer of the memorial landscape of Timor-Leste exhibits this process of remembering the past in ways which ideologically buttress 'contemporary' political projects of collective identity construction.

Timor-Leste still has many Portuguese colonial monuments, including memorials and statues to various 'heroes of the empire'. These are primarily dedicated to metropolitan Portuguese, but also prominently include monuments to loyal Timorese *Liurai* (kings) who fought or died '*por Portugal*'; either in helping to suppress indigenous rebellions, or as in the case Dom Aleixo Corte-Real of Ainaro, in fighting the Japanese occupation. Portuguese colonial historiography emphasised positive relations with the mother country and the progress of 'Portugalisation' – a colonial metaphor for a 'civilising' mission involving the spread of Catholicism, and the 'pacification' of periodic rebellions (Gunn 1999: 22–4). Of particular interest here are monuments remembering victims of the Japanese occupation, such as the prominent monument to the 1942 massacre of Portuguese troops in Aileu. With typical colonial myopia, these are primarily monuments to Portuguese soldiers and officials, not the estimated 50,000 Timorese who died during the occupation.

Indonesian-era monuments also reflect on the Portuguese colonial past. These typically seek to depict the forced integration of East Timor as a 'return to the fatherland', and portray elements of East Timorese nationalism against the Portuguese as consonant with Indonesia's own anti-colonial struggle against the Dutch (Gunn 2001:10). For example, most major towns in East Timor have Indonesian integration monuments, some of which depict Dom Boaventura, an anti-Portuguese rebel Liurai of the early twentieth century, in traditional dress, breaking free from the chains of Portuguese colonialism. In this way the Indonesian regime appropriated a key image of then-nascent East Timorese nationalism, and adapted it to an integrationist purpose, celebrating the forced integration as a triumph of Timorese anti-colonialism. Where East Timorese traditional houses have four pillars, the integration monuments often have five-sided platforms, reflecting the five Indonesian citizenship principles of Panca Sila. Importantly too, the Indonesian regime took pains to conserve certain sites such as the nineteenth-century Portuguese jail at

Figure 9.1 Indonesian Integration Monument, Dili, depicting a traditional Timorese warrior breaking loose from the chains of Portuguese colonialism. (Source: M. Leach)

Aipelo, preserved as a monument to the brutality of colonial era. Here, it is possible to witness the serial connections between the ideology of the successive colonial regimes, and heritage conservation practices in each era (Logan 2003).

Timorese nationalist cultural heritage

The final layer of cultural heritage consists of East Timorese memorials reflecting on the Indonesian era, and the pain and trauma of the liberation struggle. Prominent among these post-independence sites are the *Comarca Balide* (Balide Jail), a former jail and interrogation centre; the 'heroes monument' to Falintil resistance fighters at Metinaro; and memorials remembering the victims of massacres in the lead-up to and aftermath of the 1999 referendum on independence, such as those in the Suai and Liquica churches.[3]

These newer sites are central to the process of forging a postcolonial national identity. Some, like the 'heroes monument' at Metinaro are designated as sacred spaces of the nation, to be under permanent honour guard. Others, like the monuments to the victims of the Suai and Liquica massacres, recall traumatic events that took place in already sacralised spaces, honouring the memory of victims who died sheltering from TNI or their proxy militias in churches, or cemeteries. These difficult sites of cultural heritage are especially important in this process of articulating a nationalist view of East Timorese history and identity, as they are intimately tied in with wider processes of national reconciliation, and post-conflict justice in Timor-Leste. It is no accident that one of the key sites, the Comarca Balide, is now home to the records of Commission for Reception, Truth and Reconciliation (CAVR).

Comarca Balide: the Commission for Reception, Truth and Reconciliation

The most important repository of national memories of the Indonesian occupation is the Comarca Balide. A former Portuguese colonial jail built in 1963, the site was used as an incarceration facility by several regimes, including the short-lived unilaterally declared Democratic Republic of East Timor in late 1975. Employed briefly by Fretilin to house UDT and Apodeti prisoners after the civil war in 1975, the jail was then an Indonesian interrogation centre run by the notorious military police and intelligence organisations Kodim and Morem. The Comarca's importance as a site of pain and suffering under successive regimes made it a symbolically compelling choice for the headquarters of the CAVR after independence. Once the CAVR's primary testimony collection activities were wound down in late 2005, the site was designated as a permanent memorial and archive for CAVR documents, including the thousands of victim testimonies.

The initial proposal to rehabilitate the Comarca came from the association of ex-political prisoners (ASSEPOL) in 2000, and was adopted by the then-nascent CAVR as an appropriate site to house the 'human rights history' of Timor-Leste. In 2002, a memorandum of understanding determined that the Comarca would become the Dili office of the CAVR for its mandate period, then stand as an archive under a long-term objective to 'preserve the former Balide prison for future generations as a memorial to repression and as a centre for the promotion of human rights and reconciliation in East Timor'. These objectives were endorsed by the government of Timor-Leste.

Restored with the support of the Japanese and Irish Governments, the Comarca building was ready for the formal opening of the CAVR hearings in February 2003. The original ASSEPOL inspiration was not forgotten, with the publicity leaflet featuring a quote from one of the founding committee members: 'We will show that flowers can grow in a prison.' The restoration process was participatory and inclusive, with ex-prisoners strongly involved in landscaping and other features of the restoration, as a form of rehabilitative therapy. One woman who had spent her childhood there while her mother was imprisoned transformed the inner courtyards into gardens. Former political prisoners also built the furniture and lecterns in the courtyard meeting space area. Before the opening, another former prisoner conducted a traditional cleansing ceremony. In this way, the Comarca restoration project was actively conceived both as a site for personal recovery, and as a national historical repository.

On 20 December 2005, at the end of the CAVR mandate period, the Comarca became a permanent memorial for the victims of human rights abuses in Timor-Leste, and home to the post-CAVR technical secretariat, charged with disseminating the CAVR report and maintaining its permanent archives. The process of converting the Comarca site into a memorial and historical repository has been conducted in consultation with UNESCO, and other relevant international museums.[4]

The Comarca as a memorial

The Comarca houses both standing memorials to victims of human rights abuses, and other less conventional memorials, literally embedded in the architecture of the site. In the former category, the 'Santa Cruz room' is the archive for the thousands of CAVR records collected during its mandate, its name recalling the site of the 1991 massacre of students which put the occupation of Timor-Leste firmly back on the world stage. Another room houses the 'Suai Circle', a memorial to the victims of the Suai massacre during militia rampages in 1999, with photographs, traditional *tais*, and votive painted stones recalling individual victims.

One innovative method of preserving the memory of human rights abuses is through the conservation of prisoner graffiti. In total there are 65 graffiti, preserved in whole or part, including one from a future CAVR commissioner imprisoned during the Indonesian era. Most graffiti are in Portuguese, and many express the simple remembrances of prisoners, such as 'Here lay Zeca'. Others mark extended periods of arbitrary imprisonment in the early years of the Indonesian occupation, such as one scratching in which a prisoner laments: 'I spent my past in this cell.' Some show a sense of humour under adversity, such as one which declares: 'special cell for world leadership candidates'. Yet others are more disturbing, such as those found in the isolation cells under the main jail: 'You tortured my body in the fetters of your empire.' Some graffiti in the isolation cells record perhaps the last testament of political prisoners, such as one dated 10 August 1976, nine months after the Indonesian invasion, in which a list of names follows an etching on a wall: 'In this cell of death were ...'

The power of these graffiti lies in the fact that they are intensely personalised artefacts of a lived present of suffering, rather than abstract, general or reconstructed memories of the past. As the CAVR (2003) notes, these conserved graffiti remind the visitor of the wider function of the building as a memorial and historical repository of narratives:

Figure 9.2 Conserved prisoner graffiti, Comarca Balide. (Source: M. Leach)

The graffiti from the jail and the unrenovated isolation cells serve as stark testimony to the plight of political prisoners and the CAVR archives hold many written, audio and visual records to supplement the memory of this time and the story of what happened in the building.

While the internal rooms of the Comarca have been renovated, the prisoner graffiti are conserved under plastic frames, deeper under the modern paint layers, where many were inadvertently preserved in later Indonesian times. By contrast, the isolation cells have been left as they are, aside from the installation of lighting 'so that visitors can see for themselves conditions in these 'cells of death'' (CAVR 2003).

The Comarca also contains the legacies of other occupants, including graffiti and coarse artworks by TNI officers, such as one depicting a large number of Indonesian soldiers with a woman stripped of her clothes. The site also conserves the more recent graffiti of rampaging Aitarak and Mahidi militias in 1999, declaring Xanana Gusmão 'a mongrel'.

Cultural heritage and human rights

The connection between cultural heritage maintenance and human rights monitoring is made explicit in the Comarca management plan. As Jose Caetano Guterres (2005), coordinator of the CAVR archives team, notes, the primary role of the archive 'is to provide evidence of the violations ... on which the victims can base their request for reparations and on which the authors can be pursued'.

The CAVR records now consist of thousands of interviews, victim testimonies, and community profiles. Drawing heavily on the approach of the South African Truth and Reconciliation Commission, the Comarca Balide has adopted three principles defining the nexus between archive maintenance and human rights.

The first principle of 'prevention through preservation' sees archives as a critical means of preserving the history of human rights abuses, so that evidence is passed on to future generations, and such violations may be prevented in future. The second deals with issues of public accountability. By facilitating public access to these records, and entrenching the principle of openness in the relationship between citizenry and state, future governments will be kept accountable. The third deals with promotion of rights to information as both a democratic safeguard, and a barrier to attempts to rewrite history. As Joinet (2004) argues, drawing on UN Commission on Human Rights principles, the corollary of the individual 'right to know' – a legal right of victims – is a collective 'duty to remember' assumed by the state. Archives are critical to 'sensitising' governments to these principles.

The permanent presence of the CAVR archives is intended to ward against historical revisionism, but also to support the broader work of collective memory construction by providing 'a solid bedrock upon which to build true representations and interpretations of people and events'. Importantly, in the East Timorese context, these principles were explicitly linked to the process of reconciliation and post-conflict nation-building. The managers of the Comarca site hope the CAVR archives will facilitate unifying constructions of national history and collective memory in the light of the deep divisions and scars of colonial eras (Guterres 2005):

> Since memorials affect the ways in which we confront past, present and future, they, and … their associated archives, have the potential to play significant roles in democracy building, in the promotion of human rights, and in the pursuit of justice. Memorials may also serve as state-sponsored forms of symbolic reparation and may help promote other forms of reparation and reconciliation.

Interestingly, the Comarca philosophy draws an explicit contrast with the role of archives – as relatively open sites for democratic participation in the construction of collective memory – and the approach of colonial-era memorials, with their static monuments of a military nature, and their ideological rigidities, imposed by a distant state.

Despite these laudable ambitions, by 2005, the overall status of the CAVR and the recommendations of its report were cast in doubt by the *Realpolitik*-inspired Truth and Friendship Commission (TFC). This bilateral Indonesia/East Timor Commission was established to 'investigate the events of 1999', sidelining the recommendation by a UN panel of experts that an international war crimes tribunal be established if Indonesia failed to bring to justice those responsible for the post-referendum violence. It appeared that the CAVR report might be sidelined in favour of the TFC, which focuses more on diplomatic relations with Indonesia than justice. While it was clear that the task of pursuing Indonesian human rights violators was not one that could be pursued by East Timor alone and without international support and pressure, the crisis of 2006 exposed the raw core of unresolved post-independence tensions in East Timor. In particular, as the cycle of gang violence unfolded, it exposed an explosive legacy of resentment over the failure to bring the perpetrators of the 1999 violence to justice (UN 2006).[5] Equally, for many commentators, the rise of 'east–west' regional tensions in Timor-Leste was also related to the unresolved political legacies of the Indonesian occupation. Sparked by intergenerational conflict in the army between Falintil veterans from the eastern region, where the military resistance had been more sustainable, and younger, more junior western recruits, who felt discriminated against, the army dispute broadened into wider civil conflict between east and west, partly over which 'region' had contributed more to the resistance.[6] In this context, the critical importance of the CAVR's report and human rights archive to a nation-building agenda were starkly highlighted.[7]

While these recent developments may impact little upon the status of Comarca as a national memorial to suffering, it has a wider symbolic effect on the CAVR as an institution symbolising reconciliation, justice, and an archival 'safeguard' against future human rights abuses. Complicating the progress of the Comarca site as a CAVR memorial and archive, the building now also houses the Dili satellite office of the TFC. Tensions between the two bodies are evident, and include a lack of a formal memorandum of understanding on TFC access to CAVR records. At the time of writing, the CAVR had no clear ongoing mandate, aside from a technical secretariat charged with distributing the report *Chega!*. As such, no dedicated archival staff were assisting the public to access the records. Access was also limited by the absence of an archive law regulating public rights to information, and, more practically, by the lack of a thorough index of CAVR documents. In sum, there were evident tensions between the Comarca philosophy of openness and preserving historical memory in the interests of justice, and a new diplomatic process emphasising good international relations.

The Heroes Monument, Metinaro

At the top of the pantheon of East Timorese nationalist memorial sites, the impressive 'Heroes Monument' at Metinaro to the fallen Falintil soldiers is designed as a sacralised national site, to be under permanent honour guard. Built close the main East Timor Defence Force (ETDF) barracks, the centrepiece of the site is an open platform monument, designed to accommodate official ceremonies, with three flagpoles, facing the open sea. The site also comprises a national memorial garden and natural reserve – to honour all the victims of the struggle for the independence – a Chapel, and two ossuary houses containing the remains of several hundred Falintil fighters, at which visitors may pay their respects.

Built with the support of the United Nation Development Program, as well as USAID and other donors, the site was a major project of the Recovery, Employment and Stability Program for Ex-Combatants and Communities in Timor-Leste (RESPECT). Despite its success in establishing the Metinaro site, the program has been a controversial one, tarred by government's initial failure to adequately recognise and compensate former combatants for their sacrifices during the 24-year struggle for independence. Aside from those who joined the ETDF, a number of former veterans have since formed the backbone of various 'anti-system' political groups who reject the government and the new constitution.

The difficulties of nation-building are reflected in one minor controversy over the Heroes Monument site, with one of these veteran-dominated groups, the CPD-RDTL, arguing that their fallen comrades should be buried in their own districts.[8] Once again, this critique highlights a perennial tension in East Timor between nation-building projects and the ongoing strength of local and regional identities based on language and ethnic groups. These tensions, so evident in the crisis of 2006, touch the cultural heritage landscape just as they influence broader debates over national identity and history.

National Museum of the Resistance

Housed in the former Portuguese-era courthouse in Dili, the Archive and Museum of the East Timorese Resistance opened in early 2006. In a more conventional museum style, but with innovative exhibits, the museum differs from the CAVR in that its archives preserve contemporary documents, artefacts and photos of the resistance movement between 1975 and 1999, rather than subsequent victim testimonies. Supported by the Portuguese Government's Instituto Camões, and the Association of Resistance Veterans, the archives include the document collections of key resistance leaders and Falintil brigades, and those of the clandestine front operating in towns, along with exhibits such as Falintil leader Konis Santana's typewriter.

The key exhibit is a series of 52 life-size panels on the history of the resistance, with photos and interpretative text, ordered chronologically and thematically, with an accompanying catalogue in Tetum, Portuguese and English. As one of the curators, José Mattoso argues, in a country in which 54 per cent of the inhabitants are under 15 years of age, the collective history of the resistance in Timor-Leste 'will remain a fact expressed by a fragile memory' unless preserved and recorded quickly for future generations (Mattoso 2004). While an impressive exhibit, beautifully housed in the renovated court of justice, only three panels focus specifically on the key role of the youth and student-dominated civilian resistance. As I argue further below, this lower level of recognition accorded to the youth contribution to the independence struggle is a feature of the cultural heritage landscape, and one that reflects the broader intergenerational 'fault line' in post-independence politics.

Figure 9.3 Monument to the victims of the Suai massacre in 1999, Suai. (Source: M. Leach)

Massacre sites: Suai and Liquica

Some 2,600 East Timorese are estimated to have been killed by the TNI or their proxy militias in the violence leading up to and following the independence referendum in September 1999 (CAVR 2005: 44). The most notorious massacres of civilians took place in or around church sites, while the victims were seeking shelter. Some of have been honoured at the district level, normally with some outside assistance. For example, the monument to the 200 victims of the Suai massacre was built by people of Covalima district with support from the East Timorese government, the governments of Ireland and UK, and the UN Serious Crimes Unit.

In examining the post-independence cultural heritage landscape of East Timor, it is important to acknowledge different levels of memorialisation, and to look beyond the realm of 'formal' monuments. In the grounds of the Suai Church itself, local memorials, often family-made, offer simple remembrances of particular individuals killed on that day, including three priests. As these sites were already sacralised spaces, the church and local parishioners have exercised much of the responsibility for the less formal memorials of these tragic events.

Similarly, the small but moving monument to the 60 victims of the Liquica Church massacre was clearly designed and constructed at the local community and parish level by those closest to victims. Indeed, all over Timor-Leste, local memorials for those who died in the violence in 1999 may be found, organised at the village or community level. Indeed, there is scarcely a town above village size without one.

Other memorials and 'immanent' cultural heritage

These more informal memorials include locally made monuments in hiding places for Falintil resistance fighters, built by the proud community members who assisted them. The site of the Santa Cruz massacre in 1991 is itself commemorated informally with votive candles on the front gate. Though the informal memorial is very moving, to some of the younger generation, the lack of a more formal memorial appears a strange omission after five years of independence.

Other more difficult sites are partly remembered, recalled by one side of the brief but bloody civil war in 1975 between Fretilin and UDT (Timorese Democratic Union). For example, sites such as the *Armagem* (storehouse) in Aileu – used as a Fretilin jail during the early and difficult years of Indonesian occupation – still stir difficult and divisive memories in the town. Similarly, a small local memorial on the road to Same in central Timor commemorating two victims of the civil war 'barbarically assassinated by Fretilin' show small signs of local dissent from official narratives of the cultural heritage landscape. This 'whispered' remembering of a difficult era highlights the unresolved legacies of the civil war. Despite some genuine efforts at reconciliation, including the CAVR process which covered the civil war period, these sites highlight aspects of East Timorese history considered inimical to the nation-building task, if not to the wider process of reconciliation.

Other sites of suffering have been converted to more practical uses. In the wake of the 1999 referendum, when departing Indonesian troops and their proxy militias destroyed some 90 per cent of East Timor's infrastructure, buildings for civil purposes were at a premium. As a result, some imprisonment sites have been converted to novel uses. For example, the former jail at Aileu in central Timor now houses a primary school, with barbed wire and guard towers recalling the previous function.

The final level, and in some ways the most important, is the unintentional or 'immanent' cultural heritage landscape – consisting of the unrestored wreckage of houses and buildings burned or damaged by departing TNI and their militia in 1999. Alongside these ubiquitous sites, invariably festooned with militia graffiti, are other unforgotten but abandoned sites, such as the Indonesian interrogation centre in Baucau, which lies boarded up immediately behind one of the key tourist attractions of the area, the colonial era Baucau Pousada.

Cultural heritage as recognition

Memorials and repositories of difficult national memories, like the Comarca, seek to make sense of the collective experiences of a people in ways that foster a sense of national unity, and valorise the pain and trauma of all those who suffered in the struggle for liberation. An essential element of 'nation-building', more broadly, is the cultural production of *unifying* narratives of collective identity and history. For

Figure 9.4 House destroyed by militia in 1999,Venilale. (Source: M. Leach)

these reasons, a certain level of popular legitimacy must support 'official' (constitutional, or state-endorsed) narratives of cultural nationalism. However, as I have argued above, the 'national' values and culture of the 'imagined community' may in fact privilege those of a dominant nationalist grouping, and contribute to cultural and political conflict after independence. Below, I employ a recognition approach to examine the way the nationalist cultural heritage landscape in Timor-Leste has valorised some contributions to the independence struggle more than others.

Broadly speaking, a recognition approach examines the way distorted or inadequate forms of recognition may become important sources of motivation for political mobilisation and resistance (Honneth 1995: 138–9). Perceived 'disrespect' to a group's sense of self, to its traditions and values, or a perceived 'misrecognition' of its contribution to shared and valued social goals, such as national independence, may create the conditions for political conflict (Honneth 1995: 121–43). As noted above, young people clearly feel misrecognised by some aspects of East Timorese cultural nationalism after independence.

With these intergenerational tensions in mind, it is useful to review Timor-Leste's cultural heritage landscape on a 'recognition' basis. Broadly speaking, the success of East Timor's independence struggle was due to a unique combination of three forces: the armed resistance of Falintil (the armed wing of Fretilin, and later of CNRT, both of which were dominated by first-generation nationalists); the underground civilian resistance (dominated by youth and student groups); and the diplomatic front and international solidarity networks.

While the political leadership of Fretilin and CNRT fared well in post-independence government, the armed resistance of Falintil has had some serious problems with recognition, with many former veterans feeling inadequately reintegrated into society, and inadequately compensated for their sacrifices. There has been some progress since 2005 in the form of veteran registration processes, pensions and retraining programmes, and in cultural heritage terms, the Heroes Monument at Metinaro and the National Museum of the Resistance strongly highlight this first key element of the resistance in the memorial landscape.

By contrast, the youth-dominated civilian resistance remains comparatively neglected in the nationalist cultural heritage landscape. While the 12 November anniversary of the Santa Cruz massacre is now a public holiday, dedicated to the victims of the massacre (National Youth Day), it is surprising that there is still no formal monument on or near the Santa Cruz site, or elsewhere in Dili, despite some parliamentary discussion of the idea when the public holiday was declared in 2004. The significance of this site to the East Timorese independence struggle cannot be overstated, as it was the footage of the massacre in 1991 that put East Timor's plight firmly back on the world stage. In sum, there is to date comparatively little recognition in the nationalist memorial landscape of the youth contribution to the liberation struggle. This misrecognition forms part of a broader set of intergenerational tensions over postcolonial political settlements in Timor-Leste, which together represent key background factors contributing to the crisis of 2006.

The third force – that of the diplomatic front and international solidarity campaigns, including thousands of diaspora Timorese – has also been relatively neglected in nationalist memorials. In 2002, an International People's Park commemorating the role of international solidarity in securing the referendum for independence was created in a prominent beachside park at Lecidere, in Dili. By 2005, the original memorial had been mysteriously sidelined by a new and larger monument commemorating the UN, and various international governments' peacekeeping contributions since 1999. This resulted in a sail-sculpture in the original park being removed, and a small original monument and plaque being physically sidelined by a new structure and large signs emphasising the corporate and governmental sponsors of the monument. Rather than finding a new site to acknowledge the important role of state-based internationalism since 1999, the prior site – recognising broader notions of the international 'people-to-people' solidarity so critical to the independence struggle – was simply displaced.

By the 2007 elections, some of these gaps in the heritage landscape were being acknowledged by key opposition figures from the older generation, signalling a growing awareness of intergenerational tensions as a potent issue in East Timor's politics. Perhaps responding to the Fretilin government's neglect of these issues, President Gusmão, then running for Prime Minister with a new opposition party, awarded 'clandestine resistance' medals in the presidential election campaign period, honouring many former activists, including victims and survivors of the Santa Cruz massacre. Heritage issues have also been spoken of as part of the agenda of the newly elected president, Jose Ramos-Horta, including a memorial to the victims of the massacre at Santa Cruz, and – again reflecting the links between ideology and cultural heritage, and a shift in power to a new government closer to the Catholic Church[9] – a new memorial on the site of Pope John Paul II's visit in 1989.

Conclusion

A patchwork of cultural heritage sites, authored by several generations of colonial and nationalist elites, serves as a reminder of Timor-Leste's long and difficult history of occupation, resistance, and ultimately, of national liberation. These different historical 'layers' of cultural heritage offer competing visions of the past in Timor-Leste – visions which still echo in the memorial landscape, recalling the distinct political projects of successive regimes. For the Portuguese colonial era, with a visual narrative of 'Portugalisation' evident in monuments and grand churches, a typical *mission civilitrice* colonial discourse of progress from animist 'backwardness' to 'civilisation' was emphasised. For the Indonesian era, with its integration monuments seeking to highlight imagined pre-colonial unities, the visual narrative is one of 'reunification', and of Asian resistance to European colonialism, subsuming the East Timorese struggle under the aegis of its own nationalist narrative. And for East Timorese nationalists, the broad narrative is one of *funu*, or the struggle of a united people against consecutive colonial occupations. Each offers competing visions of East Timorese collective identity, its origins, and history.

Behind the visual competition between layers, each layer has its own contradictions – and the East Timorese nationalist project is no exception. It has been argued that while key sites in the nationalist heritage landscape have succeeded, with few resources, in preserving difficult national memories for future generations, more could yet be done to valorise all participants in the struggle for independence equally; and in particular, the youth- and student-dominated civilian resistance. Secondly, it has been argued that this pattern of misrecognition relates strongly to other cleavages in post-independence politics, which contributed directly to the crisis of 2006. These include broad intergenerational tensions, but also the 'east–west' conflict, itself linked to unresolved legacies of the occupation and 'recognition' disputes over contributions to the resistance struggle. Finally, as ongoing uncertainty over the Comarca site demonstrates, cultural heritage policy is also linked with other political problems of the independent state: of reconciling good relations with neighbours with a pressing national need for post-conflict justice.

Perhaps inevitably, then, the difficult issues of cultural heritage management mirror the larger challenges of nation-building in Timor-Leste: of recognising different generations' experiences in the liberation struggle, and accommodating the ongoing power of local and regional identities in presenting a unified national story. In light of recent upheavals the East Timorese state needs to demonstrate its wider and official recognition of all those who participated in the struggle for independence: young and old, east and west.

Notes

1 CAVR's estimate of the minimum total number of conflict-related deaths is 102,800 (+/-12,000). This figure includes both killings and deaths due to privation. The often cited figure of 180,000 is CAVR's upper estimate of total conflict-related mortality.
2 As Jose Ramos-Horta put it, 'If you take away Portuguese language and religion, there is no such thing as East Timor' (cited in Chesterman 2001).
3 The section draws upon site visits between 2005 and 2007 and interviews with personnel responsible for managing the sites.
4 Including the Famine Museum in Ireland, Hiroshima Peace Memorial Museum, and the Port Arthur Museum in Tasmania.
5 As the subsequent report of the UN Secretary-General noted 'The resurfacing of divisions that pre-dated 1999 has highlighted the need to address the past as part of the nation-building process. The assessment mission found that the demand for justice and accountability for the serious crimes committed in 1999 remains a fundamental issue in the lives of many Timorese.'
6 Many of the 'east–west' tensions in the ETDF were in fact intergenerational. Only some 200 of the 600 'petitioners' had signed the petition alleging discrimination against westerners, the majority being younger soldiers aggrieved over the mistreatment and secondary status in relation to older, former Falintil veterans.
7 According to one of the CAVR report's authors, Reverend Vasconselos, *Chega!* would offer an important antidote to the unprecedented politicisation of regional identity. Countering the perception that 'east–west' divisions were determined by different experiences under the Indonesian occupation, the report demonstrated that 'violations were indiscriminate and not related to the ethnic identity of victims or where they were born'. See Scott 2006.
8 Interview with Aitahan Matak, CPD-RDTL (Committee for the Popular Defence of East Timor) spokesperson, 8 November 2005.
9 The Catholic Church had been critical of the former Fretilin government, and protested its strong opposition to compulsory religious education in government schools.

References

Anderson, B. (1983) *Imagined Communities: Reflections on the Origin and Spread of Nationalism*, London: Verso.
Anderson, B. (1993) 'Imagining East Timor', *Arena Magazine*, 4 (April–May): 23–7.
CAVR (2003) 'Comarca: From colonial prison to centre for reconciliation and human rights', Dili: CAVR.
CAVR (2005) *Chega!: The report of the Commission for Reception, Truth and Reconciliation in Timor-Leste*, Executive Summary, Dili: CAVR.
Chesterman, S. (2001) 'East Timor in Transition: From Conflict Prevention to State-Building', *International Peace Academy Reports*, May.
Gunn, G.C. (1999) *Timor Loro Sae: 500 Years*, Macau: Livros do Oriente.
Gunn, G.C. (2001) 'The Five-Hundred Year Timorese Funu', in R. Tanter, M. Selden and S. Shalom (eds) *Bitter Flowers, Sweet Flowers: East Timor, Indonesia and the World Community*, Sydney: Rowman & Littlefield.
Guterres, J.C. (2005) 'Human Rights and Archives', paper presented to the DTP Human Rights Training, CAVR, Dili, 11 February.
Honneth, A. (1995) *The Struggle for Recognition: The Moral Grammar of Social Conflicts*, Cambridge: Polity.
Joinet, L. (2004) 'The Administration of Justice and the Human Rights of Detainees',

Report to the Sub-commission on Prevention of Discrimination, Commission on Human Rights, UN.

Leach, M. (2002) 'Valorising the Resistance: National Identity and Collective Memory in East Timor's Constitution', *Social Alternatives* 21(3): 43–7.

Leach, M. (2003) 'Privileged Ties: Young People Debating Language, Heritage and National Identity in East Timor', *Portuguese Studies Review* 11(1): 137–50

Leach, M. (2006) 'East Timorese History after Independence', *History Workshop Journal* 61(1): 222–37.

Logan, W. (2003) 'Hoa Lo: a Vietnamese approach to preserving places of pain and injustice', *Historic Environment*, 17(1): 27–31.

Mattoso, J. (2004) 'The resistance archives and national identity', *Timorese Resistance in Documents*, Dili: Mario Soares Foundation.

Ramos-Horta, J. (1996) *Nobel Lecture*, Stockholm.

Scott, C. (2006) 'East Timor: CAVR report sees the light of day', 3 August. http://www.progressio.org.uk/Templates/Internal.asp?NodeID=93131 (accessed 3 June 2007).

UN (2006) 'Report of the Secretary-General on Timor-Leste pursuant to Security Council Resolution 1690', 8 August.

Wiley, N. (1994) 'The Politics of Identity in American History', in C. Calhoun (ed.) *Social Theory and the Politics of Identity*, Cambridge: Blackwell, 130–49.

Part III

Civil and political prisons

Chapter 10

Port Arthur, Norfolk Island, New Caledonia
Convict prison islands in the Antipodes

Jane Lennon

The European settlement of Australia was based on convict transportation which influenced the social evolution of the nation. Australia, the only nation occupying a whole continent, was founded on the sweat, sorrow and suffering of felons forced to migrate across the seas to another hemisphere, a new world. The French, exploring in the South Pacific, perceived this forced migration as successful and copied it half a century later in their overseas territory of New Caledonia. As well as geographical proximity, each of these 'prison islands' illustrates the view of the metropolitan governments of Great Britain and France that unwanted people should be sent to the 'ends of the earth'. This chapter examines the history of convict transportation and its administration in the South Pacific, its social impact and physical heritage and provides case studies of three 'prison islands', places of incarceration of body and spirit.

Transportation

Convict transportation to Australia is considered as part of the global migrations, a major feature of the last three centuries leading to the creation of new nations (Pearson 1999: 4). While convicts form only a small proportion of all migration in this period (involving less than one million convicts), their contribution to the colonisation process was disproportionately great. Australia, French Guiana, New Caledonia and Singapore could not have been developed without such a labour inflow initially, and the growth of Gibraltar, Bermuda, Cuba, Puerto Rico, Penang, Malacca, Mauritius and Siberia would have been retarded without convict labour (Nicholas 1988: 37).

The following themes underpin the history of global convictism:

- the use of convict labour to develop colonies for the economic benefit of the home nation, or as strategic tools in global politics;
- the use of transportation of convicts to relieve the home state (and sometimes its colonies) of unwanted people, and as a deterrent to others;
- changing ideas regarding punishment and reform of convicts; and
- the role of convicts in nation-building (Pearson and Marshall 1996: 39, 57).

The forced migration of people involves punishment. Conversely, its outcome was often a broader free migration and the development of independent nations. In the case of convict transportation, the convicts usually went on to live as free people with opportunities not available to them in their home land.

Australia witnessed a new colonial experiment: an unexplored continent would become a gaol walled by the Pacific Ocean. The Crown shipped more than 160,000 men, women and children in bondage to Australia – the largest and furthest forced exile of citizens ordered by a European government in pre-modern history (Hughes 1988: 1–2). Motives for this migration included strategic naval purposes, assisting English trade expansion into the Asia-Pacific region and providing a dumping-ground for convicts from the overflowing penal hulks of England. Botany Bay, which indents the east coast at 34°S latitude, was chosen as the site in 1786 following adoption of Lord Sydney's plan (Macintyre 2004: 29–30).

To preclude French and Dutch expansion from the East Indies, Britain decided to use convicts to build a new base that would protect the empire's far eastern establishments and operate as a resupply depot. Penal exile had been a provision of English law from Tudor times and contractors were paid to ferry those sentenced to 'transportation beyond the seas' to the West Indian and North American colonies, but the American War of Independence in 1776 closed this option. The Botany Bay settlement was a positive response to Britain's situation in Europe in the mid-1780s and the removal of convicts was a secondary accompaniment (Frost 1980: xi–xv). Nevertheless, it was hoped the severe punishment would also deter crime: Botany Bay was practically at 'the end of the earth' (McMichael 1988: 58).

From 1793 until the defeat of Napoleon at Waterloo in 1815, the pressing demand for military manpower meant that the numbers of convicts transported fell from 4,500 in the first four years to only another 6,000 from 1793 to 1810 (Macintyre, 2004: 34). By 1800 there were 5,000 British residents of New South Wales (NSW) divided evenly between Sydney and Parramatta, indicating the balance between mercantile and agricultural pursuits in the open-air prison, with another 1,000 on Norfolk Island. Further strategic settlement outposts were made at Risdon Cove–Hobart in 1802 and Launceston on the Tamar estuary in 1803.

Administering the convict system

The first phase of 'primitive transportation' occurred from 1787 to 1810. To clear the English hulks and prisons and to establish a British strategic presence in the Pacific involved about 9,300 men and 2,500 women, seven per cent of the total number of transported convicts (Hughes 1988: 161). The State was responsible for supervising convicts, whether employed in public works or assigned to work for private settlers. Even while serving his time, the male convict was not a pariah. He was a 'government man', the term itself symbolising the difference in his status from incarcerated felon. This change arose out of private use of convict labour crucially important in the expansion of private trade and agriculture in transforming the colony after 1792 (McMichael 1988: 57–9).

The convict was deemed 'emancipated' upon the expiry of his sentence, or by earlier pardon, and in 1800 most of the 3,000 colonists were former convicts and their status was not easily expunged. They were known as 'emancipists' in contrast to the 'exclusives' who arrived free. This division troubled all aspects of public life in the confined new colony until the numbers of native-born on both sides, and their attitudes, finally prevailed in the 1830s when the emancipist 'currency lads and lasses' challenged the 'pure merinos' in a popular movement for equal rights for all colonists (Macintyre 2004: 42, 72–3).

The 'building phase' followed from 1811 to 1830. England's population nearly doubled during these years and unemployment resulting from mechanisation and rural land enclosures caused a crime wave ensuring an increased supply of felons. Simultaneously, the growth of the Australian pastoral industry created a ravenous demand for convict labour. This phase accounted for 44,100 male and 6,100 female convicts from England and Ireland, about 31 per cent of the total number of transportees (Hughes 1988: 161). From 1815 to 1820 there was a rapid increase in the arrival of convicts – more than 11,000 in NSW and 2,000 in Van Diemen's Land (Macintyre 2004: 46). Governor Macquarie favoured incarceration for controlling labour, and convict barracks and Female Factories were constructed as well as orphans' schools. Pastoralists received assigned labour but the increasing convict numbers swamped the system and expenditure increased so that Macquarie's local critics joined London officials in condemning the cost of public works. These included the first real application of Georgian design styles to convict buildings (Kerr 1984: 40–1).

Debate raged as to whether transportation was an effective punishment and deterrent of crime, or whether it had become a form of assisted migration to a new colony. In 1819 Commissioner J.T. Bigge investigated the convict system in NSW. He called for stricter supervision, more severe conditions for labour resulting in an elaborate convict work gang system for public works, no land grants or admission to public positions on expiry of sentences, removal of large numbers of convicts, from Sydney to more distant establishments so that Norfolk Island was re-settled in 1825 and Maria Island and Port Arthur were established. His recommendations defined the future development of the colony where land was owned by free men, worked by convicts and grew wool. Free migrants arrived in NSW in increasing numbers – 8,000 in the 1820s, 30,000 in the 1830s and 80,000 in the 1840s (Macintyre 2004: 53–4, 73).

The 'peak phase' was from 1831 to 1840. The convict system was working at its most efficient in 1830, after which it declined. In this decade 43,500 male and 7,700 female convicts landed, about 32 per cent, and more than the previous two decades (Hughes 1988: 162). By the 1830s 'Botany Bay' came to be a symbol in the English language of 'desolation, loneliness and cruelty' rather than its original naming for the bounty of nature (Blainey 1994:26). This infamous reputation stirred evangelical Christians who were campaigning against transportation on the grounds that the convict system was immoral and 'unnatural', fostering homosexuality. English humanitarians thought it strange that in the very decade when slavery was abolished in distant colonies of the empire, another form of cruel servitude was practised on their own race in the convict colonies (Macintyre 2004: 75).

Jeremy Bentham was the most vocal anti-transportation critic and argued instead for incarceration in England using a circular prison, a panopticon, based on an 'all-seeing' principle of reform (Hirst 1983: 9). The Molesworth Committee established by the British House of Commons in 1837 found the assignment system to be inefficient and inhumane. Britain 'now disowned what it had established, the colonists argued that a coerced convict labour force was 'unBritish.' Native-born Australians had come to hate the stigma of convictism – and the competition from assigned labour – and in 1840 the government suspended transportation to New South Wales (Hirst 1983: 27; 216–7).

The 'last phase' ran from 1840 to 1868. Some 26,000 convicts were poured into Van Diemen's Land in the 1840s, resulting in 34 per cent of the population being convicts under sentence in 1847 (Hughes 1988:162). The assignment system that had been phased out between 1838 and 1843 was replaced by a probation system, which had a set sequence of steps, each with greater freedoms, as the convict was gradually 'redeemed' (Brand and Sprod 1990). At least 85 probation stations were established between 1841 and 1853, but the pastoral gentry and reformers demanded the removal of the criminal element and a new start. The gold rushes finally undermined forced immigration as punishment. In 1853 transportation was abolished and Van Diemen's Land was renamed Tasmania (Blainey 1994: 59). In 1855 the last convicts were transferred from Norfolk Island to Tasmania, where the dwindling numbers served out sentences until Port Arthur was closed in 1877. Meanwhile the embryo colony of Western Australia, cut off from Sydney by 3,000 miles of desert and bush, sought convicts as free labour in 1850 and 9,700 felons were transported, the last being a group of Irish Fenians in 1868.

Social impact

Of the 162,000 convict migrants to Australia, men outnumbered women six to one, and about 60 per cent had previous convictions. Although comparatively few convicts were transported for political offences, transportation was an important tool in the machinery of English state repression dealing with Scottish Jacobeans, representatives of most English protest movements, industrial upheaval and agrarian revolts and with the Irish following the rebellion of 1798. Irish dissidents formed Australia's first white minority and saw themselves as a doubly colonised people (Hughes 1988: 163, 175, 181).

Anglicanism was the official religion, but a large proportion of convicts were Irish Catholics. The tensions between the two in both religious observance and human interaction is present throughout the convict era and beyond, and formed a major cultural component of Australian life for 150 years until the influx of middle Europeans to Australia after World War II (Hughes 1988: 195).

The convicts were representative of the workforce in Britain and Ireland – ordinary working men and women and not, as later popular image would have it, an unskilled urban criminal underclass. Of those transported to New South Wales, approximately 60 per cent were born in England, 5 per cent in Scotland, 1 per cent in Wales and 34 per cent in Ireland – roughly in proportion to their composition in the United Kingdom population. While the pain of imprisonment and transportation may have been traumatic, the long-term outcomes of the experience of migration may not have been (Nicholas 1988: 53–4).

Initially, Botany Bay was defined as the antithesis of English pastoral and social happiness for people exiled at 'the furthest limits of the world'. The convict and free were alienated from the institutions and standards which had shaped their lives. The two influences of British heritage and Australian experience merged in their response to the new land. Gradually the grim garrison and strange land abounding with 'perpetual disappointments' depicted by the First Fleet diarists faded from view. Glowing images of Australian salubrity gained credence simply because of the effect on imaginations of the distance between Australia and Britain – at such 'unreal' remoteness, an 'unreal' world could be envisaged (Gibson 1984: 70).

Over 95 per cent of convicts never saw Britain or Ireland again (Nicholas 1988: 58). Soon what had been a place of exile and pain became a location of choice with the gold rushes of the 1850s, but the shame of the convict past lingered on in the developing national psyche. Moreover the convict migration had set in train irreversible consequences for the natural environment and for the original inhabitants. In theory and law, if not in fact, Aborigines had full legal status[1] and were superior to the convicts, who resented this bitterly and who, galled by exile, needed to believe there was a class lower than themselves. Consequently racism began with the convicts and was the first Australian trait to percolate upwards from the working class (Hughes 1988: 95).

Norfolk Island

The Norfolk Island garrison established in March 1788 was significant as an extension of the New South Wales penal settlement aimed at securing access to the island's timber and flax resources, which were considered vital to Britain's strategic positioning in the Pacific region. It was one of the first European settlements in the South-west Pacific, with a population of about 1,000, until its first abandonment in 1814. The archaeological remains reflect this first settlement history. The wreck of HMS *Sirius*, shipwrecked on a reef off Kingston in March 1790, illustrates the fragility of the initial convict system: the only communication between Norfolk Island and Sydney was one 170 ton brig.

Norfolk Island was one of two places of secondary punishment of particular infamy for its treatment and degradation of convicts. (The other was Macquarie Harbour on the New South Wales coast.) In 1827 Governor Darling established the second settlement as 'a place of the extremist Punishment short of Death' for twice convicted 'incorrigibles' who were under martial law and had to quarry stone and build every structure on the island. In 1833 the first major rebellion resulted in mass punishments and 14 of the 137 convicted being hanged in the presence of clergy. William Ullathorne was present and later became a major witness in the inquiry which led to abolition of transportation to New South Wales (Hughes 1988: 470–9).

The reforming Captain Alexander Maconochie was appointed governor in 1840 and, appalled by the brutality, introduced a 'mark' system whereby prisoners could reduce their sentences by good behaviour and hard work. He also gave prisoners their first free day – a public holiday to honour the Queen's birthday, and introduced Bible studies. His specially designed barracks at Longridge still remain. Of the 920 prisoners he released, only two per cent were reconvicted, but his reforms puzzled authorities and he was recalled in 1843 (Clay 2001: 245–9). His replacement was the harsh disciplinarian, Major Childs of the Royal Marines, whose control ended with the 'Cooking Pots' riots and the execution of twelve men in October 1846 (Hoare 1999: 61). The next commandant was John Price who remained as 'one of the most durable ogres of the Australian imagination' for over a century as the brutal commandant in Marcus Clarke's great Australian novel, *For the Term of His Natural Life*. Price's rule until 1852, when Bishop Willson exposed his tortures, was 'the last paroxysm of the System's cruelty' (Hughes 1988: 543, 551).

The second settlement of Norfolk Island, centred on the Kingston and Arthur's Vale Historic Area, is the best-conserved large-scale convict settlement in Australia. Its significance is enhanced by the continuing use of the landing pier, beach store and boat shed from the 1840s and the lack of subsequent development, making the design features of the settlement very obvious. It has the longest heritage conservation works programme in Australia, operating since 1976.

The landscape of the convict settlement at Kingston presents the paradoxes of the convict era – the neat and ordered row of civil and military officer's housing in Georgian style, two walled military barracks, the two-storeyed Commissariat Store and the Government House are consciously and strategically separated from the surviving walls of the prisoners compounds, the gaol, the works areas and the crank mill, the sites of convict punishment and labour. The pines that covered the site were felled to allow close scrutiny of the convicts, and so the landscape remains open today (Australian Heritage Database – AHD).

The historical and emotional impact of the site is heightened by the post-convict settlement of the island by the community of descendants of the *Bounty* mutineers, transferred from Pitcairn Island in 1856. They lived in the convict area, mined it for building materials, and their horror of the inhumanity of the convict system underpins the stories that are passed down to the present day and reinforce the understanding of Kingston as a place of beauty and sorrow. The story of the *Bounty* descendants eventually settling on Norfolk Island is itself another expression of the theme of migration in the South Pacific.

Arthur's Vale and Cascades cultural landscapes contain the footings and furrows of some of the earliest European agricultural activity in Australia, dating

Figure 10.1 Kingston, Norfolk Island, January 2005. (Source: J. Lennon)

from 1788. Quality Row is the most extensive street of surviving pre-1850 penal settlement buildings in Australia, which give the place the unique character of an early nineteenth-century government village. The Norfolk Island pines are a distinctive element in the picturesque landscape, whose aesthetic qualities have been acknowledged since the first settlement in an artistic record continuing to the present.

Port Arthur

Port Arthur operated from 1830 to 1877 and was actively promoted by the colonial and imperial authorities and subsequent historians, novelists and dramatists as a 'hell on earth'. This response is reinforced by the structures reflecting much of the evolution and change in British penal practices during the nineteenth century, including the system of silence and isolation in the Separate Prison, that are today regarded with abhorrence. The surviving fabric at Port Arthur includes a variety of residential buildings, ranging from the Georgian stone housing of the Commandant and civilian staff, the cottage occupied by famous Irish political prisoner Smith O'Brien, to the Penitentiary and the Separate Prison, representing the severe interpretation of the Pentonville penal system. A number of surviving industrial buildings and archaeological sites demonstrate the work of convict labour, including the dockyard and associated buildings, a limekiln, mill remains and the boy's prison on Point Puer. These were deliberately arranged in the landscape to reflect the division of convict housing and punishment, labour, hospital, church, and civilian and military accommodation, and the need to maintain control at all times (AHD).

Port Arthur was the centre of a large-scale penal and industrial enterprise encompassing the whole of the Tasman Peninsula. It was important in the economic development of Van Diemen's Land, providing saw-milling, ship-building, manufacturing, coal mining and brick-making. The Coal Mines outstation operated from 1833, providing the most severe form of punishment for re-offending convicts, short of capital punishment. It is the only surviving penal coal mine in Australia, with evidence of the earliest pit top workings installed in 1845. The experience of convicts sentenced to the mines is powerfully evoked by the remains, particularly the main mine shaft, quarries, convict-built jetties and set of alternating underground cells. These cells were an ingenious method of isolating convicts at night from even the most minimal contact with their fellow prisoners.

After the convict-era Port Arthur became a holiday destination in its new guise as the town of Carnarvon, from which the 'stain of convictism' had to be expunged aided by a series of bushfires. Despite this, much of the convict fabric survived, especially stone and masonry, to be re-valued as an historical asset as early as 1917, when part of the site was legally protected and the earliest conservation works began. Each of these phases illustrates the impact of the convict experience on the developing Australian national consciousness. The landscape itself is both an historical document and an aesthetic record of the town planning of convictism. It shows 170 years of landscaping and gardening associated both with convictism and the subsequent attempts to first eradicate that memory by renaming it Carnarvon and developing a township, and then to reinforce its historical significance. The picturesque setting of Port Arthur features the Church and the Penitentiary both with landmark and symbolic value in vistas within the historic site. Its ruins and formal layout, and the care with which this is maintained, symbolise a transformation in Australia from 'hated stain' to recognition of a convict past.

The parkland of Port Arthur is, in part, both an accidental and a deliberate artefact of park management practices in the context of ruined buildings and mature English trees. These were a function of deliberate design, now projecting an idealised notion of rustic contentment contrasting dramatically with Port Arthur's penal history. This paradox is a very important part of the place's significance. Port Arthur is a symbol of modern heritage practice in Australia – an expression of changes in attitude to our heritage (AHD). Port Arthur is a major Tasmanian tourist destination as a highly revered icon of Australia's convict past that symbolically represents Tasmania's place in Australian history. For some Australians of Anglo-Celtic background, Port Arthur has enabled rediscovery of personal links with convictism. It has also become a particularly poignant place

Figure 10.2 Tourist seaplane, Port Arthur, November 2004. (Source: J. Lennon)

following the April 1996 massacre of 35 visitors and staff by a lone gunman – 'Port Arthur' is now understood worldwide to represent the case for new policies for gun reform, which has added a powerful new layer to the national meaning of the place (Lennon 2002: 38–47).

Australia's convict sites share patterns of environmental and social colonial history, including classification and segregation; dominance by authority and religion; provision of accommodation for the convict, military and civil population; amenities for governance, punishment and healing; and the elements of place building, agriculture and industry. These patterns can be read in the surviving heritage of these places today.

New Caledonia's convict history

In 1852 as the British system of transportation of convicts ended, the French system began, initially to French Guiana. Within France this anachronistic venture had already a long history of debate about the most suitable type of penal establishments going back to 1788, when Lapérouse on his voyage of scientific research also sailed into Botany Bay. James Cook had sighted Grand Terre and named it New Caledonia in 1774 while Dumont d'Urville charted the coastline in 1827. Forster (1996: 4) believes that Australian historians have not adequately appreciated the wider impact of Botany Bay on the European consciousness, and French historians have not recognised its pivotal role in the establishment of their own penal transportation system. This role was influenced by the first scholarly history of Australia by Ernest de Blosseville in 1831 and Alexis de Tocqueville's critiques of the transportation system and its impact on Australian society.

Debate continued during the 1830s and 1840s on the lower costs of transporting criminals rather than imprisoning them in France and on the merits of the American penitentiary system versus the English 'deportation'. In France deportation was only for political prisoners, but supply of such prisoners was limited (Forster 1996: 53). De Tocqueville, famous for his study of American democracy, believed that separate confinement was the penal panacea, because making transportation a credible deterrent by increasing the ferocity of corporal punishment – citing the extraordinary British use of flogging – must fail as the result was not workable in the recipient society, as well as being morally unacceptable (Forster 1996: 103–17).

Increased crime and recidivism caused Louis-Napoleon in 1851 to propose changes in penal policy and in March 1852 hard labour convicts detained in the naval *bagnés* [penal works in dockyards] were dispatched to French Guiana to undertake cultivation, forest exploitation and public works. In 1853 the Navy raised the French flag on New Caledonia and took possession of it as a future penal settlement – 'the Sydney of France in Oceania' (Forster 1996: 161–8).

In 1864 the first convicts arrived in the administrative base, Nouméa, and were kept on Île Nou while building the colony's public works, including Nouméa's St Joseph's Cathedral and most of the roads. The Île Nou Penitentiary was the most important penal establishment and a transit centre for convicts allocated elsewhere in the colony. The Communards, deported after the collapse of the revolutionary Paris Commune in 1871, included many professionals and Parisian artists. These were sent to the Île des Pins, while the more dangerous were incarcerated on the Ducos peninsula across the harbour from Nouméa. After an amnesty in 1880, most Communards returned to France. Also in 1871, Arab warriors in Algeria revolted against 40 years of French colonisation and the Berber leaders were deported for 50 years to New Caledonia (Logan and Cole 2001: 16–17).

Good conduct and repentance could bring assignment to private employers or even a land grant following the Australian example. Convicts were classified into three general categories – 'transportation' for convicted criminals, 'deportation' for political prisoners, and from 1884 'relegation', by which habitual petty criminals were transported. Convicts also worked on prison farms such as that at Bourail or in the nickel mines at Thio (Lyons 1986: 71). Convicts transported for civil crimes had to remain in New Caledonia after completion of their sentence for a period equal to the duration of the sentence, and if their sentence was for eight years or more, they were never to leave (ibid).

The colony was heavily dependent on convict labour. For example, in 1877 immediately before a Kanak uprising, the European population of about 16,000

Figure 10.3 Ruined cells, Ducos, New Caledonia, August 2007. (Source: J. Lennon)

was made up of 4,000 deported Communards and their families, 6,000 transported criminals, 2,700 military and guards, and 3,000 free settlers (Nicholas
1988: 35). Overall New Caledonia received 20,000 transported convicts, about
4,250 deportees and a significant number of people relegated to the island. This
included about 1,000 women.

In the 1870s aided by the discovery of nickel, large tracts of Kanak land were
taken over for French settlement and in 1878 a revolt started at La Foa and spread
along the coast – 200 French and 1,200 Kanaks were killed and 800 Kanaks were
exiled to the Île des Pins. In 1887 the French introduced in its colonies the *Code
de l' Indigénat*, a set of laws for governing indigenous people such as the Kanaks.
This imposed subordinate legal status on the Kanaks, forced them into mountainous reservations, restricted their movements and traditional trading routes
and required them to work for settlers and the colonial authorities. Towards the
end of the penal colony era, free European settlers (including former convicts)
and Asian contract workers out-numbered the population of forced workers. The
indigenous Melanesian populations declined drastically in that period.

Transportation to New Caledonia ceased in 1897 as a 'French Botany Bay'
proved to be a mirage due to factors including a demographic imbalance (there
being hardly any female convicts) and a poor economic base for a colony (Forster

1996: 174–5). However, the penal colony did not close until 1922 (Nicholas 1988: 35). In 1931, New Caledonia was declassified as a place of exile.

There are many places on the islands associated with the penal colony and the following are designated as historic monuments: in Nouméa, the Penitentiary (1867) and Camp Est (1864) at Île Nou, Old Hospital of Marais, Saint Joseph's Cathedral (1876–90); Fort Téremba, Moindou (1871); Chapel of Nemeara, Bourail (1878); and the Cemetery on Île des Pins for those deported from the Paris Commune (Province Sud 1995). Heritage legislation exists at the provincial government level but few places are protected, especially privately owned places. Professional expertise and conservation building skills are limited and changes just happen. The convict story is part of the interpreted history of New Caledonia and features in tourism marketing. The fort complex at Téremba was reconstructed as a result of community effort from 1984 and is now run by a management committee as a museum with guided walks and theatre performances, whereas evocative ruins at Ducos and Île des Pins are crumbling away without any effort at stabilisation or interpretation. Some Kanaks have mixed feelings about convict history as another privileging of colonialism over proper respect for their culture.

Today the Melanesian Kanaks constitute 42.5 percent of the total population while European settlers make up 37 percent. The smaller minorities number about 15 per cent and tend to support France. Indeed two-thirds identify themselves with the 'Caldoche' community, that is, whites who have lived in New Caledonia for several generations and who are often descendants of the convicts. Growing awareness of their dispossession led the Kanaks to form an independence movement in the 1980s. Following a decade of civil unrest and assassinations, including that of the Kanak leader Jean-Marie Tjibaou in 1989, the Centre Culturel Tjibaou dedicated to Kanak culture opened in Nouméa in 1998. Architect Renzo Piano's design of the Centre echoes Kanak traditional houses and reflects the rights of colonised indigenous populations in shaping their destiny, emphasising 'a cultural politics-of-becoming rather than a politics-of-origins' (Murphy 2002). For the whole community a transformative approach to heritage conservation appears necessary.

A hidden past

Australians were generally reluctant to acknowledge the convict past. In folklore and popular song the brutality of the system was emphasised by the gothic horrors of Macquarie Harbour, Port Arthur and Norfolk Island. For many decades Australians acquired a vivid picture of the convict era from Marcus Clarke's novel, *For The Term of His Natural Life*, which had originally been printed as a newspaper serial from 1874. As the post-gold-rush generation moved for federation of the colonies into the Commonwealth of Australia, the convict era was regarded as an important part of a national past:

I was the convict
  Sent to hell,
To make in the desert
    The living well:

I split the rock;
   I felled the tree-
The nation was
    Because of me.

Dame Mary Gilmore,
Old Botany Bay, 1918

In 1988 Robert Hughes's evocative history, *The Fatal Shore*, was probably the most popular Australian history book, but its likening of nineteenth-century convict Australia to the twentieth-century Gulag Archipelago of the Soviet Union was inappropriate given the divergent economic and social histories of the two nations. However, following the Bicentenary of European settlement of the east coast of Australia, also in 1988, it became fashionable to claim convict ancestry, to announce one's belonging to a long line of Australians.

Transformation of convict ruins into scenic attractions, which are the picnic spots and recreation areas of local residents, has effectively disguised the pain, suffering and brutality of the convict years. In Tasmania this denial of connection still permeates today (Goc 2002: 26), while tourism programmes are seen as 'trivialisers and parasitic feeders upon the real sufferings of real men in the real past' (Hay 1996: 68). The professional conservation industry has been accused of surrendering the difficult quest for meaning to the 'queasy realm of cultural silence' and the quarantining of gothic ruins in their convict past as an end point compared to seeing them as a beginning for modern Australia (Young 1997: 33).

Attempts to destroy evidence of the pain and shame of the convict inheritance took many forms and began early with Edward Lord's destruction of Tasmanian records in 1810. This was followed by burning of convict buildings at Port Arthur and Sarah Island in the 1880s and the Chief Justice's advocacy in the 1890s of destruction of convict buildings to obliterate the 'convict stain' (Daniels 1998: 241). Remains of the original settlement at Sydney Cove are found in the fragile footings of Governor Phillip's house and its later additions, now preserved *in situ* in the Museum of Sydney forecourt. This seat of British authority in the colonisation of Australia from 1788 to 1845 is now in the form of a buried archaeological deposit – a hidden past exposed only to the inquiring gaze of passers-by. The edifices of the convict system were considered an obstacle to moral and political progress and physical reminders of the convict system were an embarrassment to a socially upwardly mobile Anglo-centric middle class.

Similarly, in New Caledonia there is a general silence about the convict origins of the white or Caldoche society which is in an uneasy reconciliation with the Kanak culture. Yet the very layout of settlements, farms and transport routes reflects the convict system.

Celebrating convictism

Over 200 places with existing convict-built features of heritage significance remain in Australia along with collections of artefacts associated with major prison sites and a rich archive of meticulous records. Convict sites generally mean visible men's sites, while women convicts' sites are almost all invisible, either archaeological remains as at the female factories or part of the grand Georgian mansions that dot the rich pastoral landscapes of the countryside.

It is ironic that Norfolk Island and Port Arthur on the Tasman Peninsula, the two largest convict sites in Australia associated with convict incarceration and the cruellest punishments, are located in landscapes of great scenic beauty. These places became celebrated as tourist attractions and have been conserved as part of Australia's heritage, both being among the seventy iconic places now on the National Heritage List (http://www.environment.gov.au/heritage/national/index. html – accessed 1 May 2007).

The Australian Government, in partnership with relevant state and territory governments, submitted in 2008 a nomination for World Heritage listing of eleven of Australia's convict sites as an exceptional example of the global story of forced migration. These include Port Arthur and Norfolk Island as well as, in New South Wales, Old Government House (Parramatta, now in suburban Sydney), Hyde Park Barracks (Sydney), Cockatoo Island Convict Site (Sydney), and the Great North Road (near Wiseman's Ferry); in Tasmania, the Cascades Female Factory Site (Hobart), Darlington Probation Station (Maria Island), Coal Mines Historic Site (via Premadeyna) and Brickendon-Woolmers Estates (near Longford); and, in Western Australia, Fremantle Prison.

Presenting the history and interpreting its significance to visitors is part of modern heritage conservation practice. All three 'prison islands', offer tours and brochures to guide visitors around the sites where interpretive panels with explanatory text and historical photographs are located. Port Arthur has a visitor centre where visitors are given a coded entry card, which determines their fate in the convict system, and they follow that route through the historical displays, a very effective history lesson. All three places have museums of artefacts excavated from or used there by convicts and their guards.

It is easy to fossilise the past to keep it safe in museums, but heritage managers must act as 'advocates for the future of heritage places while respecting and recognising the desires and decisions of the present'. In this context Eleanor Casella (1997: 78) asked how best to manage material and cultural landscapes that gain their primary significance from hideous histories, and whether retention of these sites glorifies inhumanity or acts as a physical warning to future generations in providing them with places of pilgrimage.

Convict histories are commemorated in the reconstructed Fort Téremba and the Communard Cemetery on the Île des Pins, but the once large convict complexes at Ducros and Nouville are being redeveloped, while many ruins remain hidden under tropical growth waiting for study, conservation and a voice.

Reflection

Painful historical associations of incarceration and exile seem out of place in these remote and beautiful places, now modern tourist attractions. Interpretation of this difficult heritage has also changed over time: shame at our convict heritage has now given way to considerations of the treatment of indigenous minorities, the first inhabitants of these places.

David Lowenthal has described five tactics to deal with 'heritage that hurts' in sites of sorrow: ignoring, erasing, celebrating, transmuting, commemorating; none is totally effective but all have some merit. Each generation is increasingly removed from the eyewitness traumas and monuments proliferate to tell the tales – lest we forget (Lowenthal 2003: 4–6). In interpreting convict places, meanings have always collided despite their 'human essence' (Hay 1996: 68).

New approaches are required to keep the historical memories alive but 'interpreting the evidence through the distorting filters of marketing expediency, romantic embellishment and irrelevant ideological theories' can effectively erase the convict heritage (Kerr 2002: 6). Dramatic performance portraying the social and emotional intersection of meanings about debates and events that occurred within the walls of convict buildings is a current favoured approach (Clark 2002: 37). Interpretation needs to recognise both the tensions of using our cultural heritage on site and the historical amnesia of many visitors about the depth of our stories and their linkages into a much wider world. In a postmodern age where visitors choose 'some of this and some of that' as a result of deconstructed messages used in advertising, the solid foundations for systematic enquiry are often missing (Lennon 2006: 56). Thematic frameworks provide an opportunity to identify and record multiple stories associated with a place often lost or forgotten in this generation.

As the convict heritage is both tangible in the celebrated ruins, solid buildings and archives, and intangible in the idiom of language and attitudes, finding new approaches is a challenge for both educators and conservation practitioners trying to balance preservation of the old and adaptation to accommodate contemporary uses and meanings.

Acknowledgements

Dr Christophe Sand, Director of Archaeology, Museum of New Caledonia, generously critiqued an earlier version of this paper and also took me to the convict ruins on Ducos peninsula.

Notes

1 Aborigines in 1788, under Governor Arthur Phillip's instructions from the British Colonial Secretary, were regarded as free people with full legal protection; this changed after Phillip's departure and they did not have the same level of citizenship as non-indigenous Australians until the referendum on the matter in 1967.

References

Australian Heritage Database (AHD) Entries for Port Arthur and Kingston-Arthur's Vale – http://www.environment.gov.au/heritage/national/.
Blainey, G. (1994) *A Shorter History of Australia*, Milsons Point, NSW: Vintage.
Brand, I. and Sprod, M. (ed.) (1990) *The Convict Probation System: Van Diemen's Land 1839–1854*, Sandy Bay, Tasmania: Blubber Head Press.
Casella, E.C. (1997) 'To enshrine their spirits in the world: heritage and grief at Port Arthur, Tasmania', *Conservation and Management of Archaeological Sites*, 2: 65–80.
Clark, J. (2002) 'Talking with empty rooms', *Historic Environment*, 16(3): 34–7.
Clay, J. (2001) *Maconochie's Experiment*, London: John Murray.
Daniels, K. (1998) *Convict Women*, St Leonards, NSW: Allen & Unwin.
Forster, C. (1996) *France and Botany Bay*, Carlton: Melbourne University Press.
Frost, A. (1980) *Convicts & Empire, A Naval Question*, Melbourne: Oxford University Press.
Gibson, R. (1984) *The Diminishing Paradise, Changing Literary Perceptions of Australia*, Melbourne: Sirius.
Goc, N. (2002) 'From convict ruins to the Gothic ruins of tourist attraction', *Historic Environment*, 16(3): 22–6.
Hay, P.R. (1996) 'Port Arthur: where meanings collide', *Island*, 57: 67–76.
Hirst, J.B. (1983) *Convict Society and its Enemies, A History of Early New South Wales*, Sydney: George Allen & Unwin.
Hoare, M. (1999) *Norfolk Island, A Revised and Enlarged History, 1774–1998*, Rockhampton: Central Queensland University Press.
Hughes, R. (1988) *The Fatal Shore*, London: Pan.
Kerr, J.S. (1984) *Design for Convicts: An account of design for convict establishments in the Australian Colonies during the transportation era*, Sydney: Library of Australian History.
Kerr, J.S. (2002) 'Islands of vanishment, islands of emergence', *Historic Environment*, 16(3): 3–6.
Lennon, J. (2002) 'The Broad Arrow Café, Port Arthur, Tasmania – using social values methodology to resolve the commemoration issues', *Historic Environment*, 16(3): 38–47.
Lennon, J. (2006) 'Gothic Silence or postmodern deconstruction? Presenting the values-based stories of heritage places of national significance', *Historic Environment*, 19(2): 52–6.
Logan, L. and Cole, G. (2001) *New Caledonia*, Melbourne: Lonely Planet.
Lowenthal, D. (2003) 'Tragic traces on the Rhodian shore', *Historic Environment*, 17(1): 3–7.
Lyons, M. (1986) *The Totem and the Tricolour: A Short History of New Caledonia since 1774*, Kensington, NSW: New South Wales University Press.

Macintyre, S. (2004) *A Concise History of Australia*, Melbourne: Cambridge University Press.

McMichael, P. (1988) 'Brutalized, Beggared and Bought', in V. Burgmann and J. Lee (eds), *A Most Valuable Acquisition, A People's History of Australia since 1788*, Melbourne: McPhee Gribble Penguin.

Murphy, B. (2002) 'Centre Culturel Tjibaou: a Museum and Arts Centre Redefining New Caledonia's Cultural Heritage', *Humanities Research*, ANU, Canberra, 9(1).

Nicholas, S. (ed.) (1988) *Convict Workers: Reinterpreting Australia's Past*, Melbourne: Cambridge University Press.

Pearson, M. (1999) 'Convict transportation – Australia in a global context', *Historic Environment*, 14(2): 4–10.

Pearson, M. and Marshall, D. (1996) *Study of World Heritage Values, Convict places*, Report for Department of the Environment, Sport and Territories, Canberra.

Province Sud (1995) *Sites et Monuments Historiques de la Province Sud Nouvelle-Calédonie*, Nouméa: Direction de la Culture de la Province Sud.

Young, G. (1997) 'Isle of Gothic Silence', *Island*, 60/1: 31–5.

Chapter 11

Hoa Lo Museum, Hanoi
Changing attitudes to a Vietnamese place of pain and shame

William Logan

Vietnam is a country more scarred than most as the result of centuries of inter-mittent civil war and frequent foreign intervention. It has, therefore, many places that bear witness to past episodes of pain and injustice and that also reflect the ambivalence that present-day societies often feel towards these episodes. This paper deals with Hoa Lo, the former prison located in central Hanoi, the capital of the Socialist Republic of Vietnam. Here successive groups of prisoners expe-rienced extremes of suffering but the pain felt gives way to other emotions over time, not excluding shameful regret on the part of some perpetrators of suffering. The fact that the punished and the punishers swapped roles at several points shows the complexity of dealing with places of pain and shame, both by societies in general and by heritage professionals in particular.

Constructed by the French colonial regime as its main security headquarters and jail – or *Maison centrale* – the jail took in its first prisoners in 1899. It passed into the hands of the communist regime installed in North Vietnam in 1955 and for a time held as prisoners of war a number of American pilots downed during the Vietnam War. At the Sixth Communist Party Congress in 1986, Vietnam decided to re-join the world economy with a set of economic liberalisation policies known collectively under the tag *doi moi* ('renovation') and economic development has been rapid thereafter. Indeed, by the early 2000s Vietnam's rate of growth was second only to China's, although admittedly starting from a lower base. By the early 1990s, therefore, the question inevitably arose of what to do with this old and out-moded prison, sitting as it did in the heart of Hanoi on land that was becoming a prime target for commercial redevelopment. Resisting calls to remove the prison totally, the Vietnamese turned this place of pain and shame into a new museum, which opened to visitors in 1997, alongside a high-rise business centre. I have told this story in detail elsewhere (see Logan 2003); here the focus is on what Hoa Lo represents and whose voices are being heard in the interpreting.

The chapter also focuses on the way that publicly funded museums, such as Hoa Lo, respond to changing attitudes towards the painful and shameful elements in the community's past. It particularly explores the way in which the perceived political and economic needs of the society and the status of host city, both desired and perceived, play a key role in this process, leading to shifts in museum

Figure 11.1 The French colonial Maison Centrale, restored and re-used as the Hoa Lo
Museum. (Source: W. Logan)

exhibition policy. In the case of Hoa Lo, the permanent exhibition was primarily
conceived and designed in order to memorialise the incarceration of political
leaders in the period of struggle for national independence, and in this way the
exhibition policy reflected the ideological basis of national identity formation in
Vietnam. But the Hoa Lo museum has also had to deal with the imprisonment
of American POWs and, at a time when increasing numbers of Western tourists,
including American, are visiting the museum, there has been a move towards
telling this part of the story more fully. The chapter argues, however, that more
than the tourism dollar is involved and that the museum continues to serve the
political interests of the state, which are changing as Vietnam's place in the world
changes. Consequently Hoa Lo's role becomes more complex as it tries to reflect
the new political and economic needs of the Vietnamese state and yet maintain
its role as a community memorial.

Hoa Lo: place of pain and shame

It is now commonplace in the heritage discourse to view museums, at least those
supported by the public purse, as manifestations of the ideologies underlying
national identity and state formation. In Vietnam, as elsewhere, this is true and

nowhere more clearly seen than in its numerous war museums (see Logan 2000; Schwenkel 2004; Bleakney 2006). The way in which the ideology is manifested, however, is variously interpreted. Sutherland, for instance, in her study of a selection of Hanoi museums, sees the colonial conflict as being 'generally downplayed in favour of other periods, such as the Vietnam–American war and Vietnam's successive attempts at repelling northern invaders' (2005: 153). By contrast, the focus in Hoa Lo is mostly on the nationalist conflict, beginning with the early colonial resistance and uprisings and moving on to the open conflict with the French in the First Indochinese War of 1946–54. Certainly Hoa Lo deals with the Vietnam War ('American War' or Second Indochinese War) of circa 1964–73, but, as Bleakney and Sutherland concede, Hoa Lo has been maintained as a sacred site of memory principally for the Vietnamese rather than Americans.

Much of the writing about Hoa Lo and other Vietnamese war museums has been from an American standpoint. Bleakney (2006: 163–8) provides a picture of how US veterans remember and revisit Hoa Lo, highlighting the 'distorted view of the treatment of POWs at this prison'. Her overall aim is to 'examine the new meanings of the [Vietnam] war produced through American veterans' memorializing practices at various sites of memory in the United States and Vietnam' ; that is, she is essentially answering to American needs. However the voice of the Vietnamese authorities is also clearly heard at Hoa Lo, both representing the pain and shame of those nationalists who suffered under the French and giving a partial interpretation of the pain the Vietnamese meted out to the American prisoners of war. By contrast, the French voice is largely absent, the French colonial regime being painted in wholly negative terms as the perpetrators of injustice.

Hoa Lo was built in 1896–9 in the centre of the French quarter of Hanoi, rather than isolated as most other colonial prisons in Vietnam were. Sitting alongside the Court of Justice and the Intelligence Department, it completed a 'triad of suppressing tools against the patriotic movement of the Vietnamese' (Le Van Ba 2004: 6). Like much of the construction work done by the French, the prison broke with traditional Vietnamese custom. As Zinoman (2001: 27) observed, before the French conquered the Indochinese territories in the nineteenth century, incarceration was not a usual way of dealing with offenders. In a Confucian society such as Vietnam it was considered that it was best to leave punishment to the family and village. But the colonial authorities needed a prison to deal with those Vietnamese who refused to accept the forced military 'pacification', and the chief government architect of the time, Auguste-Henri Vildieu, was engaged to design the prison on the site of the razed Phu Khanh village – houses, *dinh* (communal house), pagodas and all. According to Vietnamese architectural historian Dang Thai Hoang (1985: vol. 2, 24), the prison's architecture was especially formidable: with its walls of stone 'making it look so strong, [and] by puncturing the surrounding ... walls with iron-barred portholes, the French must have sought to create, especially for those outside, a most terrifying impression of life within'.

The prison's bland name of *Maison centrale* obscured the brutal reality. Originally designed for 450 prisoners, by 1954, when the French regime collapsed

Figure 11.2 Contemporary bas relief depiction of heroic Vietnamese prisoners suffering under the colonial authorities. (Source: W. Logan)

with the rout at Dien Bien Phu, it held more than 2,000. Many early resisters and rebels were incarcerated in its dark cells. They called it Hoa Lo – literally meaning 'furnace with coal' (referring to the kilns of the original Phu Khanh village), but figuratively meaning 'Hell's Hole'. An upsurge of anti-colonial activity in the 1930s led to a rapid increase in the number of communists, nationalists, secret society members and radicalised workers and peasants held in Hoa Lo and other Vietnamese prisons (Zinoman 2001: 200). The roll call of revolutionary and later communist government figures incarcerated in Hoa Lo includes Nguyen Thai Hoc, leader of Yen Bay Mutiny 1930, who was imprisoned and executed in 1930, and Dang Thi Quang Thai, the first wife of North Vietnamese army leader, General Vo Nguyen Giap, who was tortured and died in Hoa Lo. Three luckier inmates survived and rose to become General-Secretary of the Vietnamese Communist Party: Truong Chinh (General-Secretary 1941–56), Le Duan (1960–9; later President), Nguyen Van Linh (1986), and Do Muoi (1991–97).

Thus, far from repressing the nationalist movement, the imprisonment of key leaders in Hoa Lo made it one of the main centres for revolutionary education and the instillation of nationalist fervour. Even a revolutionary newsletter, *Lao tu tap chi* ('Prison Review'), was published monthly without discovery. Many inmates were able to rise above their pain and suffering to engage in poetry and singing, political discussions and plays. Some of the memoirs used by Zinoman (2001: 131–5) refer to the liberation from the rigid feudal class divisions that was made possible by living at such close quarters and taking part in activities that under normal social circumstances would have been regarded as shameful, such as sharing the same prison food, experiencing the coarse informality of communal nudity, primitive and public toilets, and the inversion of the rigid Vietnamese pronominal system.

In 1945 and again in the mid-1960s the type of prisoner held in Hoa Lo changed dramatically. During the period of Japanese control (1940–5), the French colonial authorities had been left to run Vietnam's civil administration under Japanese observation, including the prison system and Hoa Lo (Marr 1995: 66–7). Some nationalists were released, being replaced, after the *coup de force* in 1945. At the same time several hundred French civilians were rounded up by the Japanese Kenpeitai, on suspicion of aiding or being likely to aid the Allies. Then, in 1955, another reversal of incarcerated and incarcerator occurred when Hoa Lo passed into the hands of the communist regime then assuming power in North Vietnam. Subsequently, during the 'American War', Hoa Lo held American pilots shot down and taken prisoner in and around Hanoi.[1] These men dubbed Hoa Lo the 'Hanoi Hilton', a name that has become part of the heritage of the place despite the fact that a real Hanoi Hilton opened to business in 1999 half a kilometre away. The most famous prisoners included Senator John McCain and Lt Everett Alvarez Jr of San Jose, California. The former, a Republican from Arizona and US presidential candidate in 2000 and 2008, was shot down over Hanoi's West Lake and spent six years in captivity there. Alvarez was the first pilot shot down (in 1964); he was kept in Hoa Lo until the Paris Peace Agreement was signed eight years later (Karnow 1994: 389). Another noted prisoner, Pete Peterson, who had spent much of his six years as a POW in a dark, cramped cell in Hoa Lo, became US ambassador to Vietnam in the late 1990s. Much of the American press in the 1960s reflected the passions aroused in the United States by the humiliating imprisonment of their downed pilots in Hoa Lo.

From prison to museum

Places of pain and shame hold different values for the different sets of people involved. In the case of Hoa Lo, the Vietnamese are themselves divided. There are many older Vietnamese, notably in the South and in *Viet kieu* (overseas Vietnamese) communities, notably in the US, France and Australia, who have an ambivalent attitude towards the prison's symbolism for this period in the 1960s and early 1970s, tied as it was to the communist regime installed in Hanoi. A few such people may even view negatively the prison's role in incarcerating French officers after the 1954 Dien Bien Phu defeat. For most residents of Hanoi and former North Vietnam, however, the issues are more straightforward: while it might be argued that the French were doing no more than was expected of colonial powers in the nineteenth and early twentieth centuries, this is no justification and colonial times are remembered with bitterness.

When the 1986 *doi moi* policies began to transform the urban landscape of Hanoi and other Vietnamese cities (Logan 1995, 2000), the question about what to do with the prison, located in the French Quarter, which was becoming a prime target for redevelopment, brought the ambivalent attitudes on the Vietnamese side plainly into the open. There were, of course, some calls to expunge totally the prison's physical presence from the city because it represented a bitter past that was now over and best forgotten. Against this pro-demolition and redevelopment attitude were ranged the pleas of war veterans, from both the Vietnamese and American sides, to keep the whole complex as a memorial. For the current Vietnamese government, the Hoa Lo prison stood out as one of the most obvious symbols of French oppression and because of the significant part it played in the revolutionary struggle. Since the Vietnamese ultimately won their battle for national sovereignty, for the victorious regime Hoa Lo has become the symbol of actions to be commemorated rather than erased or ignored. In this respect it is different from many other prisons where suffering has not been mitigated by better times. Hoa Lo is seen as a symbol of transcendence – both at the personal level for those political prisoners held there who now have heroic status, and at the national level.

Nevertheless the economic potential of the site could not be totally ignored. In the end, the controversy worked itself out in a way that demonstrates the distinctively pragmatic side of the Vietnamese character (Logan 2000: 9). The prison site was completely re-worked, turning this place of sorrows into a new museum for the citizenry and foreign tourists to visit, but opening the rest of the site up to commercial redevelopment. The public debate highlighted, however, a strength of emotion that was perhaps surprising in a society that had learned over the millennia to accept without question directions from above. The campaign to save the 'Tree of Love' – an almond tree whose nuts, leaves and bark were used by prisoners for medicinal purposes – particularly highlighted the emotional fervour. Located originally in a prison courtyard but falling in the 1990s on the boundary line of the proposed commercial redevelopment site, the support of hundreds of witnesses eventually forced the authorities to excise eight square metres from the commercial site in order to have the tree saved.

In September 1993, a prime ministerial decision awarded the contract to a Vietnamese–Singaporean joint venture company to build a US$60 million 24-storey complex comprising a luxury hotel, apartments, a conference centre and offices, known as Hanoi Towers (now Somerset Grand Hanoi). The same decision approved the conservation of part of the prison as a museum. In May 1994 the prison was transferred from the Hanoi Police Department to the Hanoi People's Committee Cultural and Information Department. The detailed project 'Investment, repair, conservation and effective improvement of the Vestige Hoa Lo Prison' was approved in 1997 by the Hanoi People's Committee. A few months later, the building was registered by the Ministry of Culture and Information as an historic vestige. From the Vietnamese government's point of view, the total redevelopment of the site sought to make the most of both the past and the future. The Hanoi People's Committee entrusted the restoration of the gaol and the creation of a historical museum to the Ministry of Culture and Information in January 1994 and work began in 1995.

Figure 11.3 The 'Tree of Love' in its plot of land excised from the commercial site. (Source: W. Logan)

At the ground-breaking ceremony in November 1994, Dinh Hanh, Vice-Chairman of the Hanoi People's Committee, underlined the official interpretation of the place as having 'a historical position in the struggle against foreign aggressors of the Vietnamese nation'. The dominance of this symbolism meant that the subsequent development of the museum focused on the French treatment of Vietnamese nationalists. By contrast, the high-rise hotel/business centre complex makes no concession to the existence of the prison; no attempt has been made to mark the former building's footprint, nor display related artefacts or photographs. Hoa Lo has now been reduced to the main two-storey entrance block and opened to the public as a museum under Vietnamese government management. Phase 1 of the project, focusing on repair and conservation work, was completed in October 1997 and the prison museum was opened to the public, as were Hoa Lo's research and educational facilities. Phase 2, leading to the creation of the precinct commemorating patriots and revolutionary soldiers, was completed in February 2000.

How successful is the Hoa Lo museum at capturing the meaning of the place? The initial observation is that most of the horror of the place has disappeared. The museum is antiseptically clean; the smells and cries of prisoners are long gone. This muting of the historical reality is probably inevitable; although 'soundscapes' and other interpretative techniques can sometimes make past experiences and sensations 'come alive' to modern visitors, Hoa Lo, like most Vietnamese museums, is under-resourced and such high-tech approaches are currently out of the question. There is also little historical, political and cultural context-setting. For the Vietnamese visitor, of course, the background is often known through personal memories and family reminiscences or through the public education system. Whether the education system with its continuing highly ideological content attracts young Vietnamese to explore their recent past by visiting museums such as Hoa Lo or in fact turns them off is an issue worthy of further consideration. But most non-Vietnamese tourists seem at a loss when trying to understand the place. They observe the Vietnamese prisoners' narrow cells, with black walls and tiny windows set too high for the prisoners to see anything but a patch of grey or blue sky according to the passing seasons. Two guillotines are on display. The area where the American airmen are said to have been kept is clean and bright. Interpretation panels provide little detail and the English – the only tourist language used – is often poorly written. Outside, the sense of colonial oppression has been totally swept away, to be replaced, perhaps, with a new kind of economic control represented by the new twin tower business complex. The creation of the Hoa Lo museum effectively turned history into heritage, serving contemporary needs rather than attempting to reflect the past in a more scholarly or objective way. There is enough to remind but not completely offend French tourists, and a deliberate effort is made to counter the expectations American tourists have that the harsh treatment meted out to their pilots should be at the forefront of the presentation.

Serving the people: memories and memorialisation

In recent years the museum has begun to attract larger numbers of visitors, reaching more than 20,000 domestic and international visitors in 2007. It has a staff of 20, including eight qualified curators and conservators and four guides. Its greatest strength lies in the rich combination of its status as a registered heritage building and its artefact collection. The building itself relates to what is being remembered and it serves both memorial and civic education functions as well as being a museum. In her 2004 doctoral dissertation on the politics of memory and representation in Vietnam, Christina Schwenkel considers how Vietnamese museums confront the need to cater for both domestic and international audiences. In fact, we need to go further and distinguish between the need to cater for both Hanoian and other Vietnamese visitors and for both those with direct family or other personal connections with the prison and those other Vietnamese for whom the prison is simply a generalised symbol of the nation's past.

Like other nation states, Vietnam seeks to acknowledge the sacrifice made by its many citizens who laid down their lives to protect the state's integrity or whose lives were drastically altered by physical injury or pyschological trauma. In Hoa

Lo, a national memorial function is intentionally maintained as a 'memorial to the revolutionists who devoted their life for the Fatherland' (Le Van Ba 2004: 31). National leaders make an official visit on three occasions during the year: on 3 February to mark the formation of the Vietnamese Communist Party; on 27 July, the 'Day of Wounded Soldiers'; and on 12 March, commemorating a heroic attempt by prisoners on that day in 1945 to break out of the jail, an event which helped to trigger the August Revolution later that year. For those who personally experienced incarceration in Hoa Lo, and their immediate families, there is a natural desire that their personal sacrifice, experience and memories are recognised by younger generations. This is particularly urgent in countries where the population is rapidly growing, as in Vietnam where more than half the current citizens were born since the end of the Vietnam War and for whom the war is often relegated to the distant past of history books. According to the Hoa Lo Director, Dr Nguyen Thi Don, the families of internees now dead want to see their relatives' names on official lists displayed in the museum. Some families went further and requested that lifelike faces of their relatives be used on museum display models, a suggestion resisted by the museum in favour of using merely 'typical faces'.

In order to encourage local Hanoians to visit Hoa Lo they are not required to pay an entry fee. The state also funds visits by groups of schoolchildren with the aim of propagating and perpetuating its official version of national history, already well entrenched in school curriculum. Hoa Lo thus is seen as playing a major role as

> a place to educate the young generation of Vietnam in the revolutionary tradition, the spirit of national pride and the responsibility to the Fatherland in the new era of peace and development toward a society of wealthiness [sic], fairness, democracy and civilization.
>
> (Le Van Ba 2004: 31)

Researchers are encouraged to use the large collection of official records and personal dossiers of 'stronghearted and loyal communists ... struggling in prison to make the glory of Vietnamese heroism' (Le Van Ba 2004: 31). The Hoa Lo management makes an effort to give life to the museum by allowing ex-prisoners associations access to the building and about 15 currently hold meetings and run events there. The question arises, however, whether there will be a change in the nature of museum and exhibition policy after witnesses die out. The Director is conscious of imminent change but believes that Vietnamese people, by comparison with the more individualistic Westerners, are very strongly family- or clan-oriented, with respect for ancestors. Grandparents bring their children to tell them about their past and this passing on of the stories, it is thought, will minimise impact of the witnesses dying out. Then, after a witness dies, his/her family will come to the museum each year on the anniversary day of the death to remember. In short, while the living memories may disappear, the memorial role will continue, alongside the museum function.

Figure 11.4 The memorial to revolutionary martyrs and heroes, overshadowed by the Hanoi Towers. (Source: W. Logan)

Serving the state: shifting exhibition policy

As outlined, to the current Vietnamese government it is the incarceration of political prisoners during the colonial period that must be kept uppermost in the collective memory. Official project documents as well as tourist booklets such as the *Hoa Lo Prison Historic Vestige* (Le Van Ba 2004) focus on the period 1896–1954 and contain only very brief discussion of the US pilot prisoners held during the Vietnam War. This emphasis on French injustice, the determination to overcome pain and humiliation, and the transcendent message that out of sufferings great things can arise serves the modern Vietnamese state well. Since the museum was designed in the mid-1990s, however, there have been signs of a shift in the original interpretative emphasis. A new set of displays was installed in 2006, significantly giving greater importance to the Vietnam War but seeking to impress upon visitors that large proportions of the French and US population supported the Vietnamese nationalist struggle.

Why and how has this shift occurred? In one sense it represents a more complete picture of the Cold War period, challenging the simple East/West binary that is common in museum interpretations of that period. But does the shift reflect an increasing maturity of interpretative policy, perhaps in response to a liberalising of the political scene within Vietnam? Is the motivation a desire to 'reframe, inform and enable society's conversations about difference' – as Sandell describes the new role for museums (2007:173) – or is it simply to reaffirm the Hanoi ideological position of victim turned victor? If museums are to take on Sandell's new role and use their cultural authority, in their 'capacity to determine and authoritatively communicate meaning' to challenge stereotypes about cultures and help to produce new understandings of cultural differences, museum curators play a key role in developing new collections and revising displays. A key issue in understanding the evolution of Hoa Lo, and perhaps of governance in Vietnam more generally, is the extent to which the museum professionals were able to modify their practice free from political dictation by the Party or Hanoi People's Committee.

The current Director, Dr Don, was responsible for the design of the new set of interpretative exhibits. Although a Scientific Board comprising the directors of other Hanoi museums – the Revolutionary Museum, Ho Chi Minh Museum and the National History Museum – must approve the general outline of all exhibition proposals, Dr Don claims that the Hoa Lo curators, like curators in other Vietnamese museums, have the power to make detailed decisions about exhibition design and content. In the Hoa Lo case, a primary intention was to correct some of the earlier restoration and interpretation errors made by the previous Project Management Board and to take advantage of this in order to extend the Vietnam War component. Planning is under way for further changes to the exhibitions over 2008–9, and the Ministry of Culture, Sports and Tourism (formerly Ministry of Culture and Information) had already by early 2007 approved a proposal to show more of Hoa Lo's collection relating to the US interventions. Dr Don's aim has been to take into account the visitors' reactions to the episodes of pain and shame represented by and in Hoa Lo, in particular to respond to the comments of French and US visitors and to take advice from former prisoners/witnesses. In her experience, foreign visitors are almost invariably respectful, many of the ex-military men coming with their wives with the hope that the experience will help their wives to understand them better and some volunteering information about the work they are doing for Vietnam back home in the US. This conforms with Bleakney's generalisation (2006: 154) that

> When veterans visit memorial sites on their return trips to Vietnam, ... they visit their own heritage – memories from their previous time in Vietnam, or experiences shared with other veterans. Their goal is not to retreat into the past but to re-imagine it in the present and reconstruct it for the future; the healing and closure elements of veterans' return journeys imply progression not regression.

It appears, nevertheless, that Vietnamese curators and their scientific committees also respond to the needs of the state as they understand it. This may not come as a set of publicly announced directives but is more likely to emerge from backroom consultations and corridor discussion (McCarty 2001; Logan 2002). Vietnam does not have a tradition of public debate on community issues. Consequently, as Hue-Tam Ho Tai (2001: 9) notes,

> Lacking a sanctioned outlet for debating political and cultural differences, Vietnamese public discourse often has an oblique quality; it is full of hidden meanings and allusions. Since substance so often must be presented in oblique fashion, the stylistics of commemoration are an important marker of meaning.

One such key need of the Vietnamese state that had been much discussed in the Vietnamese media was completion of the trade normalisation process with the US and membership of the World Trade Organisation, and there is no doubt that pressure comes from the Ministry of Foreign Affairs, as well as from the Vietnam–America Friendship Association, one of the largest friendship and cultural exchange programmes permitted by the Vietnamese government, for Vietnam to move on and become friends with its former enemies. Eventually US Congress authorised the granting of Permanent Normal Trade Relations with Vietnam in December 2006 and Vietnam became a member of WTO on 11 January 2007, its twelve-year campaign to gain entry fulfilled. Another major factor that cannot have escaped the Scientific Board is the growth of international tourism, especially from the United States. An aviation agreement between the US and Vietnam in December 2003 has allowed American carriers to fly directly between the two countries for the first time since the end of the Vietnam War (Hotel Online 2004). American Airlines opened daily flights from Los Angeles in April 2004 and United Airlines followed later in the year with a flight from San Francisco (*Vietnam Economic Times* 2005: 238). Out of the ten international tourism markets on which Vietnam is particularly focused, the US holds huge potential and has already become the second-largest market after Japan. The number of US tourists rose from 189,000 in 1995 to 272,000 in 2005, though the US market is dominated by *Viet kieu* and therefore more closely linked with Ho Chi Minh City than Hanoi. In terms of international visitor numbers at Hoa Lo museum, the management estimates that 40 per cent of visitors come from the US compared with 20 per cent from France and negligible numbers from Japan and China.

Another factor experienced in most nation states is the expectation placed on museums and other cultural institutions located in the capital city to provide a showcase for visiting dignitaries and a backdrop to major political ceremonies. Since Hanoi is the symbolic heart hub of the Vietnamese political territory and nation (Logan 2007b: 51), the government and the people generally expect the capital to represent them – that is, to reflect their achievements, not just to themselves but, on the international stage, to the governments and peoples of other countries. In particular, it is important that foreign diplomats, media representatives, donor organisations and tourists relay positive messages about the country and its people. The cultural role of the capital city is also essential in nation-forming, underlying the efforts by national governments to form and reinforce a national sense of identity and to use this to tie the citizenry together into a more cohesive and cooperative entity. Heritage, of course, performs a major part in this, with cultural elements from the past being selected by the government and the dominant or élite group in society, added to heritage registers of one kind or another, and held up as the 'official' heritage of the people's achievements. Museums provide a venue to display national achievements and reinforce the status acquired by the government in hosting international meetings, such as the 2006 APEC meeting held in Hanoi, or other big events.

Thus, while the well-educated Western visitor might have wished for more incisive interpretation in the Hoa Lo museum, the focus on cleanliness – on 'clean history' – was and continues to be seen as meeting both Western and Vietnamese requirements. David Lowenthal's admonition (1985: 346) that 'The past's worst horrors are beyond the power of replication' also suggests the impossibility of providing anything but a cleaned-up version of places of pain and shame such as Hoa Lo. From the point of view of the current Vietnamese regime, the museum continues to provide a valuable opportunity to spread its message of endurance and survival against the greatest of odds, a message that remains relevant to today's Vietnamese struggling still to achieve reasonable living standards. Increasingly, the museum seeks to tell the prison story in a way that does not offend tourists and in line with the ideological spin that the authorities demand.

In the nature of public museums worldwide

When I first began researching Hoa Lo in the late 1990s, I arrogantly thought that cultural heritage professionals working in public museums in the West, in contrast to their counterparts in Vietnam, were allowed considerable independence in the way that they mount exhibitions to interpret national stories. I believed that in Vietnam museum professionals were restricted by ideology and government requirements and unable to develop a more objective 'warts and all' interpretation approach. What has become clear over the past decade, however, is that public museums everywhere serve to some extent the ideological interests of the governments that fund them and curators everywhere can confront restrictions on their ability to interpret the national past freely, whether these restraints are imposed directly by governments in power or indirectly (and often sub-consciously) through self-censorship. Indeed, recent history has shown that such restrictions are not unusual, even in the Western democracies. The pressure always exists for museums to show visitors the nation at its best – especially for the ever-growing numbers of international tourists, as Davison points out (2006: 91), but also domestic visitors and perhaps especially schoolchildren whose minds are particularly open to formation. Since governments support public museums through legislative provisions and funding, it follows that they will take an interest in what is shown – and often will want their ideological values reflected, rather than those of opposition parties and groups.

We are used to sneering at the manipulation of public opinion and exploitation of 'history' and heritage in totalitarian regimes, including the communist ones. Vietnam today is no longer a full-blown totalitarian state, nor is it a total democracy (Hue-Tam 2001: 9); it is experiencing 'creeping pluralism' (Logan 2000: ch. 8). Events over the decade have shown that even the 'enlightened' Western democracies can revert to political processes of censorship and media manipulation that are very little different from those we criticise elsewhere. In the United States, France and Australia, 'culture wars' have occurred in which governments have rejected critical interpretations of the nation's past as demeaning and have sought to impose their own more 'positive' visions of the past onto school programmes and textbooks as well as public museums.[2] Museums are not self-sufficient in any country. As Mayr (1998: 463) points out:

> The efforts of museums are subject to certain basic limitations that lie in their very nature. For the most part, these limitations stem from the obligations of museums to society, their dependence upon financial supporters, and the sources of their intellectual authority. Museums are not financially self-sufficient; they survive only with the help of large, regular subsidies (often three-quarters or more of their annual budgets), usually from the public. In return the institutions are understood to serve the public. … In return for indispensable financial support, museums give up some autonomy.

Museums in socialist countries, like Hoa Lo in Vietnam, are therefore less different from Western museums than we in the West have liked to think. The ability to act as social agencies helping, as Sandell advocates (2007: x), to 'negotiate, constitute and communicate' social understandings of cultural difference is limited everywhere that governments are locked tightly into ideological positions. In this light, the managers of Hanoi's Hoa Lo museum deserve respect and support for their efforts to tell the complex and still acutely sensitive story of pain and shame that is encapsulated in the building's physical structures and its collections.

Acknowledgements

I am especially grateful to Dr Nguyen Thi Don, Hoa Lo Director, and Mrs Tran Thi Nhi, curator at the Revolutionary Museum in Hanoi, for their generous assistance during my last visit to Hoa Lo (April 2007). Their valuable insights into the operation of museums in Vietnam supplemented observations made during previous visits and analysis of policy framework documents and exhibition briefing papers translated by Nguyen Thanh Binh. Fiona Erskine, my research assistant at Deakin University, helped in the collection of other relevant documents.

Notes

1 Estimates of the numbers held in Hoa Lo are unclear. For the total number of US airmen captured during the entire Vietnam War, the number varies from nearly 600 (Karnow 1994: 389) to more than 700 (Maclear 1981: 361). Most of these were held in the 14 or so prisons in and around Hanoi.
2 For a discussion of recent museum controversies in Europe, United States and Australia, see Casey (2006), Davison (2006), Kohn (1995), Lagerkvist (2006) and Logan (2007a). The Enola Gay exhibition fiasco at the Smithsonian Institution came back to the public's attention with the death of the Hiroshima bomb pilot in late 2007. Ganley (2005) outlines the French textbook controversy.

References

Bleakney, J. (2006) *Revisiting Vietnam: Memoirs, Memorials, Museums*, New York and Abingdon, UK: Routledge.
Casey, D. (2006) 'Reflections of a National Museum Director', in M. Lake (ed.) *Memory, Monuments and Museums: The Past in the Present*, Carlton, NSW: Melbourne University Press.
Dang Thai Hoang (1985) *Hanoi's Architecture in the Nineteenth and Twentieth Centuries*, Hanoi: Nha Xuat Ban Xay Dung, Hanoi, 2 vols (in Vietnamese).
Davison, G. (2006) 'What Should a National Museum Do? Learning from the World', in M. Lake (ed.) *Memory, Monuments and Museums: The Past in the Present*, Carlton, NSW: Melbourne University Press.
Ganley, E. (2005) 'France orders positive spin on colonialism', Associated Press, 2 November 2005. Available online at: http://www.imani.fr/component/option,com_content/task,view/id,87/Itemid,18/ (accessed 15 June 2007).
Hotel Online Special Report (2004) *Hotel Performance Heats Up in Hanoi and Ho Chi Minh City*, November. Available online at: http://www.hotel-online.com/News/PR2004_4th/Nov04_VietNamHotels.html (accessed 4 September 2007).
Hue-Tam Ho Tai (ed.) (2001) *The Country of Memory: Remaking the Past in Late Socialist Vietnam*, Berkeley, CA: University of California Press.
Karnow, S. (1994) *Vietnam: A History*, London: Pimlico.
Kohn, R.H. (1995) 'History and the culture wars: the case of the Smithsonian Institution's Enola Gay Exhibition', *The Journal of American History*, 82(3): 1036–63.
Lagerkvist, C. (2006) 'Empowerment and anger: learning how to share ownership of the museum', *Museum and Society*, 4(2): 52–68.
Le Van Ba (2004) *Hoa Lo Prison Historic Vestige*, Hanoi: Administration Board of Hoa Lo Prison.
Logan, W.S. (1995) 'Heritage planning in post-*doi moi* Hanoi: the national and international contributions', *Journal of the American Planning Association*, 61(3): 328–43.
Logan, W.S. (2000) *Hanoi: Biography of a City*, Sydney: UNSW Press; Seattle: University of Washington Press; Singapore: Select Publishing.
Logan, W.S. (2002) 'Golden Hanoi, Heritage and the Emergence of Civil Society in Vietnam', in W.S. Logan (ed.), *The Disappearing Asian City: Protecting Asia's Urban Heritage in a Globalizing World*, Hong Kong: Oxford University Press.
Logan, W.S. (2003) 'Hoa Lo: a Vietnamese approach to preserving places of pain and injustice', *Historic Environment*, 17(1): 27–31; republished in N. Garnham and K.

Jeffery (eds) (2005) *Culture, Place and Identity*, Dublin: University College Dublin Press.

Logan, W.S. (2007a) 'Reshaping the "Sunburnt Country": heritage and cultural politics in contemporary Australia', in R. Jones and B.J. Shaw (eds), *Geographies of Australian Heritage: Loving a Sun-burnt Country?* Aldershot, UK: Ashgate.

Logan, W.S. (2007b) 'The cultural role of capital cities: Hanoi and Hue, Vietnam', in K.C. Ho & H.-H.M. Hsiao (eds), *Capital Cities in Asia-Pacific: Primacy and Diversity*, Taipei, Taiwan: Center for Asia Pacific Area Studies, Academia Sinica.

Lowenthal, D. (1985) *The Past is a Foreign Country*, Cambridge, UK: Cambridge University Press.

Maclear, M. (1981) *Vietnam. The Thousand Day War*. London: Thames Methuen.

Marr, D.G. (1995) *Vietnam 1945: The Quest for Power*. Los Angeles: University of California Press.

Mayr, O. (1998) 'The "Enola Gay" fiasco: history, politics, and the museum', *Technology and Culture*, 39(3): 462–73.

McCarty, A. (2001) *Governance Institutions and Incentive Structures in Vietnam*, paper presented to the Building Institutional Capacity in Asia (BICA) Conference, Jakarta, 12 March.

Sandell, R. (2007) *Museums, Prejudice and the Reframing of Difference*, Abingdon, UK, and New York: Routledge.

Schwenkel, C.L. (2004) *Iconographies of War: The Transnational Politics of Memory and Visuality in Contemporary Vietnam*, unpublished PhD dissertation, University of California, CA.

Sutherland, C. (2005) 'Repression and resistance? French colonialism as seen through Vietnamese museums', *Museum and Society*, 3(3): 153–66.

Vietnam Economic Times (2005) 'Viet Nam. Opportunities for Investors', Hanoi: Vietnam Economic Times.

Zinoman, P. (2001) *The Colonial Bastille: A History of Imprisonment in Vietnam, 1862–1940*, Berkeley, CA: University of California Press.

Chapter 12

Places of pain as tools for social justice in the 'new' South Africa

Black heritage preservation in the 'rainbow' nation's townships

Angel David Nieves

Over a decade of democracy has brought massive reforms and advances across the heritage industry of South Africa, while bringing little change or understanding of the cultural significance of Black heritage resources in the country's still isolated townships. Despite ten years of massive reform by the African National Congress (ANC), and the emergence of new political discourses of nation-building and Black self-empowerment, these race-based inequalities are growing. Although the Mandela and Mbeki governments have attempted to build an inclusive national identity, grassroots community-based organizations remain marginal to the heritage process required for a complete and responsible accounting of the history and legacy of apartheid.

This chapter examines efforts to recognize historic places, such as sites of political unrest, as a means to enhance citizen participation in late or newly developing democracies. Much of the history of the anti-apartheid movement takes place in the townships in what many heritage professionals would consider to be "the mundane" and ordinary structures and environments of the poor. Therefore, it is necessary to develop a different set of criteria and strategies for documenting and preserving these important sites. It is particularly critical to pose the following two questions: Can a community-based museum model help to establish a culture respectful of human rights only a mere decade after apartheid? Can these heritage sites begin to foster a set of political values and attitudes favoring human rights through civic engagement for all South Africans, regardless of race, class, gender, or sexuality? The chapter focuses on the heritage museum recently developed at the Langa Pass Court and Office Building in Cape Town by members of the Langa Heritage Foundation and the Hector Pieterson Memorial and Museum in Johannesburg.

Cape Town 1994: the Langa Pass Court and Office Building

In 1982, when Nelson Mandela (prisoner 488/64) was transferred from his jail cell on Robben Island, to the Cape Town mainland, he could never have imagined that some seventeen years later (in 1999), he would return to inaugurate Robben

Island Museum, one of South Africa's first three UNESCO World Heritage Sites (Shackley 2001: 356; Gouws 1994: 18). Robben Island has become South Africa's most famous cultural tourism attraction – an international symbol of freedom and liberation (Nanda 2004: 380–1). The maximum-security island prison was home to key leaders of the African National Congress (ANC), the so-called "Rivonia Trialists" of 1964 who included Nelson Mandela, Ahmed Kathrada, Walter Sisulu and Govan Mbeki (Strange and Kempa 2003: 370). Mandela spent nearly twenty years imprisoned in its "B Block" where political prisoners accused of plotting against the apartheid government were kept between 1960 and 1990 (Shackley 2001: 356). Shortly after Mandela's release in 1990, proposals began to circulate suggesting new uses for the island, among them that it be converted into a "university" – South Africa's own version of the Open University. The site, renamed Robben Island Museum (RIM) in 1997, is today heralded as the locus for civic engagement in the "new" multicultural South Africa. The museum was formed to "contribute to the economic development of South Africa by attracting international tourism, and to contribute to the transformation of South African Society and the enrichment of humanity" (Nanda 2004: 397; Allen and Brennan 2004: 12).

From gulags in the former Soviet Union, to the Slave Forts on Ghana's Gold Coast, communities are struggling with their long ignored and hidden histories of state torture, terror, and mass genocide (Coombes 2003: 69). With the rise in the 'prison tourism' phenomenon across the globe, new heritage management strategies require an important re-envisioning of sites of "dark tourism". Can these sites of tragedy and "dissonant heritage" be used as models for community-based education and renewed political and social inclusion? (Mason 1994: 49; Duffy 2002: 303–6). Marginalized urban communities across South Africa are also questioning state-sponsored "national narrative" efforts, like the Truth and Reconciliation Commission (TRC), that sought to investigate human rights abuses while granting amnesty to those accused of crimes against humanity (Gibson 2004: 6). As art historian Annie Coombes has argued in *History After Apartheid* (2003: 4),

> difficulties have arisen in South Africa, as elsewhere, since the rhetoric of "community" is the result of a genuine attempt to incorporate a more representative multicultural diversity in many aspects of public life, but can also be a slipshod way of 'managing' the more contradictory and potentially troublesome aspects of cultural and political diversity.

In particular, this essay examines efforts to establish historic places, like these sites of the former "prison industrial complex," and of political unrest as potential alternative educational and community-based museums for enhancing citizen participation. I will argue that these sites can be seen as viable "tools for social justice" and human rights through a renewed process of civic engagement in grassroots community-based museums (Hirzy 2002: 9). Can a community-based museum model help to establish a culture respectful of human rights only

Figure 12.1 Langa Pass Office after renovation, Cape Town, South Africa. (Source: A.D. Nieves)

a mere decade after apartheid? Can these heritage sites begin to foster a set of political values and attitudes favoring human rights through civic engagement for all South Africans? I am focusing on two sites in my larger research project – the Langa Pass Office and Court Building in Cape Town (Fig. 12.1) and the Hector Pieterson Museum and Memorial Precinct in Soweto, Johannesburg (Fig. 12.2). Both cities have invested numerous resources in developing new initiatives encouraging domestic and foreign visitors to reflect on the country's non-white population – an examination of heritage resources within former all-Black townships that, unfortunately, has been deferred until recently (L. Kaplan 2005, pers. comm., 17 May). The "township tourism" movement continues to grow, heavily impacted by day-tours into the townships with scheduled visits that include "shebeens" (unlicensed bars), schools, community centers, and traditional faith healers (or "sangoma") (Allen and Brennan 2004: 12).

As curator Christopher Du Preez has suggested, "The past decade has seen democracy actively dislodging the 'singularity' of South Africa's apartheid history and heritage" (Du Preez 2006). A decade of democracy has brought massive reforms and advances across the heritage industry, while changing little the understanding of the cultural significance of Black heritage resources in South Africa's still isolated townships. Despite ten years of massive reform by the ANC, and the emergence of new political discourses of nation-building and Black self-empowerment, these inequalities are growing. I maintain that while the Robben Island Museum offers an acceptable (or more easily palatable) vantage point for "collective memory-making" for the ANC in a "new" democratic South Africa, it is the sites in the former all-Black townships which highlight the many continued injustices and social ills faced by residents still victimized by a legacy of segregation (ie. poverty, the AIDS pandemic, etc.). What are the necessary steps to be undertaken if an informed model for sustainable tourism that engages the complex social, economic, and environmental issues facing these long-ignored townships is to truly take hold? (Department of the Environment and Heritage 2004: 6). Perhaps historian Jean Comaroff is correct when she characterizes the democratizing spirit of history in the postcolony by suggesting that "local traditions are [being] reinvented, long-silent ancestors speak once more. Organic intellectuals offer 'struggle tours' in which mundane urban spaces express vocal counter-histories; so much so that public life has been overtaken by a growing cacophony of testimonies" (Comaroff 2005: 125). Despite attempts by the government to build an inclusive national identity, grassroots community-based organizations remain marginal in the creation of a national narrative that exposes the history and processes of apartheid more fully. In heritage work, community ownership is an essential part of transformation, but a recent study that gives an overview of the entire heritage sector in South Africa admits that, to date, community involvement and participation have received very little attention (Wells 2004). Clearly, massive post-apartheid upheavals were reined in at the same time as the ANC began efforts to acknowledge the country's atrocities and human rights violations, and to commemorate the decades-long liberation movement that began in the 1950s.

It is important to note that before 1994, much of South Africa's cultural tourism product was largely dominated by sites connected with European heritage, including the legacies of the Anglo-Boer and Anglo-Zulu wars (Shackley 2001: 357). Since 1985, museum professionals in South Africa have begun a process of self-critique and analysis that has led them to recognize that their institutions, too, played a part in the oppression inflicted by the ruling white minority since the early nineteenth century. Many of the country's museums were founded by the settler élite, while museum culture itself was a product of the forces of colonialism and racial apartheid which were to dispossess huge numbers of colored and indigenous peoples from Southern Africa (Webb 1994: 20).

A major result of the explosion in cultural and heritage tourism activities across South Africa since the first all-free elections in 1994 is a growing interest on the part of foreigners in the former all-Black townships adjacent to most major metropolitan centers. Tours for whites curious about the living conditions of "primitives" and "exotics" in the "Bantu townships" had already been taking place outside cities like Johannesburg as early as the late 1960s. By 1976, with the rise in Black consciousness, and the growing turmoil caused by student protests against Soweto's government officials, many of these early tours to the townships ended (Dondolo 2001: 1).

In Cape Town, township tours emerged sometime in the late 1980s as a kind of "field trip" model for white Capetonians who wished to see the "other side" of Cape Town through controlled and orderly means without threatening their fragile domination of Black South Africans. By the late 1980s townships were being incorporated into the more mainstream South African tourism industry. Many of the early township tours were initiated by local white government officials curious about the "Black areas," about which they knew so little because of the strictures of the apartheid state (Dondolo 2001: 3).

Townships throughout the country have become major tourist attractions and destinations in recent years. Townships were historically at the forefront in the struggle against apartheid, and township tours resurfaced after 1994. The images emerging from the 1960s Anti-Pass Laws Campaign in Langa, the 1976 student uprising in Soweto, and the 1980s massive reform movements against apartheid had all originated from within the bounded spaces of the local townships. Some heritage professionals argue that with their depictions of, "... 'real' history, 'real' people and the 'real' South Africa ... township tours are presented as an alternative to cultural village performances as tourists are invited to see the local residents in the townships as more authentic and in non-performative environments" (Dondolo 2001: 4; Witz, Rassool, and Minkley 1999: 17; Kirshenblett-Gimblett 1998: 47–8). Despite any claims that township tours are truly "non-performative," local residents perform for tourists in different ways – allowing visitors to enter their homes and businesses, and to photograph their once private traditional healing practices. As Barbara Kirshenblatt-Gimblett (1998: 48) has argued,

> The everyday lives of others are perceptible precisely because what they take for granted is not what we take for granted, and the more different we are from each other, the more intense the effect, for the exotic is the place where nothing is utterly ordinary. Such encounters force us to make comparisons that pierce the membrane of our own quotidian world, allowing us for a brief moment to be spectators of ourselves, an effect that is also experienced by those on display.

When the African National Congress first took office a decade ago, it proposed a new policy framework entitled the Reconstruction Development Program (RDP). The RDP is considered an "integrated, coherent socio-economic policy framework that seeks to mobilize South Africans and its resources toward the final eradication of apartheid and the building of a democratic, non-racial and non-sexist future." Its six basic principles linked together make up the political and economic philosophy that underlies the work of the ANC. Those principles most significant to developing a more pluralistic and democratic society include: (1) a people-driven process; (2) nation-building; (3) link reconstruction and development; and (4) the democratization of South Africa. Subsequent policy development has grown out of the RDP – particularly concerning cultural heritage conservation and economic development through the growing tourism industry.

For many community leaders and local government officials, tourism – perhaps more than any other sector – has the potential to achieve the varied objectives of the RDP (Department of Arts, Culture, Science and Technology 1996).

The continued growth of "township tourism," similar to the "ghetto tourism" that is commercially successful in cities like Harlem, New York, or Watts in Los Angeles, requires urban and heritage planners to re-examine the tools for documenting and preserving sites reflective of the larger liberation struggle (Ashworth 2004). Unfortunately, much of the physically extant heritage does not easily lend itself to the traditional standards of what is considered "architecturally significant" or visually impressive. Much of the history of the anti-apartheid movement took place in the townships among what many heritage professionals would consider to be "the mundane" and ordinary structures and environments of the poor. Therefore, it is necessary to develop a different set of criteria and strategies for documenting and preserving these important sites (Davies 2003: 32–4).

The City of Cape Town has recently developed new community-based tourism initiatives that support skills development, job creation, and enterprise that reflect the city's cultural diversity and promote cultural pluralism. The township of Langa, outside central Cape Town is significant as a site of protest and self-determination, where in 1960, 6,000 marched in protest against apartheid pass laws. The South African police fired on the protestors, killing four people at Langa, as well as 69 others in Sharpeville, thereby catalyzing the subsequent Black liberation movement. The Langa Heritage Foundation, in partnership with the City of Cape Town's Heritage Resources Section, has been working to conserve the site of the Langa Pass Office and Court Building and to develop a model program for sustainable tourism through a new community-based museum site. Local residents are now witnessing the creation of tourism-related jobs as concrete benefits of cultural heritage management, increasing public support for further heritage projects.

Langa was founded in 1927 and is the oldest surviving formally planned township of its kind in South Africa, the very first township established under the Natives (Urban Areas) Act of 1923. Many of its residents were forcibly displaced from Ndabeni. Ndabeni was set up at the turn of the twentieth century in response to fears of Africans spreading diseases. The Act was designed to enforce racial segregation, control Black access to cities, and control the development of residential housing in the urban Apartheid City. The township's population of over 47,000 comprises only 7 percent of the total number of Blacks living in Cape Town. Langa was considered the primary housing option for the former residents of Ndabeni. The township was planned as a model "native urban village" under the 1923 Act on a segregated site on the urban periphery of Cape Town's Central Business District (Theberge 2004: 4).

Residence in Cape Town among Blacks could only be legally attained by having proof of being born in the city, or proof of employment. A pass, indicating the status of each person, had to be carried at all times and renewed regularly under penalty of law, and the threat of subsequent reprisal from local police. The handling of passes and cases related to pass laws was located within the Administration Block in Langa and the Pass Office and Court Building – a timber frame structure built in the early 1950s. The Pass Office and Court Building were constructed directly in front of the Administration building, in the centre of the Administration Block. Initially there were two structures: the main building housed the magistrate's office, administration offices, holding cells and the court room, and a secondary building was used as a holding cell, initially for men and later for female prisoners. Pass administration involved daily queues of people coming to have their passes renewed and to get new passes issued, as well as court proceedings against those found in violation of the Urban Areas Act – that is, not carrying an up-to-date pass. Those arrested for pass violations would be charged and fined or sentenced to time in Pollsnor prison – with an average sentence of one month in prison for not having a pass. Residents from across the Cape region who lived during the 1950s and 60s through the early 1980s, had some experience with the pass hall either in acquiring a pass book or through forms of protest against the state. By the 1980s, the structure, built of untreated wood, was deteriorating from disuse. Although not considered "architecturally significant" by most traditional conservation practitioners, the Pass Office has great historical value as the only extant pass office in South Africa. Many former pass offices were burned down as a result of the liberation struggle.

A multiracial group of heritage leaders and residents began meeting in 2000 to discuss the site's potential. Funds for the restoration of the building and the initial museum were primarily garnered from the local government with volunteer support from the community. The partnership between the government and community representatives was initiated with a proposed large-scale documentation project, completed in 2003, of significant heritage sites throughout Langa. The proposed museum would address a number of important issues. Its purpose would be:

- to provide recognition of the significant value of Langa's heritage;
- to provide an opportunity for Langa's residents who suffered repression under the Apartheid governments to be documented and for their experiences to be heard by interested people and succeeding generations;
- to provide a place where oral histories may be recorded and historic artifacts be donated/loaned to the museum's archives;
- to provide a public venue where visitors and locals can listen to identified residents' stories of historic events;
- to act as a tourist destination that depicts the political and social heritage of an important historic area in a variety of media; and
- to initiate the development of economic opportunities for local residents through the creation of a museum shop, tour routes and theater performances.

The building opened amid some controversy in its adoption as a local community museum. Resident attitudes toward the site were in direct conflict with what "the state" and its conservation architects had envisioned (Theberge 2004: 4).

Community representatives wanted the Pass Office to closely resemble their previous experiences under apartheid while obtaining passes. The backless wooden benches, dim lighting, and poor ventilation would help visitors reflect on the history of South Africa while recreating its role as an artifact of apartheid. The city of Cape Town believed that the Pass Office should instead act as a more traditional museum with the necessary exhibition space for memorializing the past (Deckler, Graupner, and Rasmuss 2006). Ultimately, and through much negotiation, some of which is ongoing even today, community representatives were able to achieve their goals for a more grassroots-based (and even culturally sustainable) conceptualization of museum-making.

The ANC has, over the past decade, faced an enormous challenge in creating a new national identity that embraces the past while still allowing for a framework that incorporates all of its many diverse groups from across the African diaspora and its transnational borders. While myriad cultural and civic institutions are now involved in "collective memory-making" in South Africa, heritage sites are recognized as among the best equipped to document the nation's challenges.

In complex postcolonial societies seeking to reconcile different viewpoints within a new political order, heritage becomes a highly political and contentious arena where decisions are made about its conservation, presentation and current usage against a background of various and even competing interpretations. The role of the archive in museum-making throughout South Africa has been discussed by numerous scholars and practitioners. The most publicized of those venues has been the District Six Museum in Cape Town, which sees as one of its central missions the repatriation of lost property as a result of apartheid law. Other museums have now begun to look at their role in not only repatriation, but the more complex challenge of providing reconciliation through the museum-making process. The Hector Pieterson Museum, in Johannesburg's Soweto, provides another example of the ways in which a community-based museum model can help to establish a human rights agenda only a mere fourteen years after apartheid rule.

Soweto 1976: the Hector Pieterson Memorial and Museum

Numerous public, private, and international initiatives at museums and commemorative sites are now challenged to represent the legacy of apartheid and the struggle against its brutality and degradation. For example, the District Six Museum in Cape Town, the Apartheid Museum and Constitution Hill, both in Johannesburg, and the Red Location Museum of Struggle in Port Elizabeth all embody the strong social justice agenda of the "new museology." Thus, one hallmark of the newly elected government in post-apartheid South Africa was its steadfast commitment to the ideal that public institutions were to be made more accessible to a broader multi-racial, multi-ethnic audience. Public institutions across South Africa, including its national museums, could now respond to

Figure 12.2 Hector Pieterson Museum Square. (Source: A.D. Nieves)

societal needs and pressures as a way of restoring justice. However, questions remain as to what moral ends might actually be achieved through public state funded institutions such as the museum.

Museums and organizations, motivated by community groups, have recently been formed to coordinate and share their "best practices" between "sites of conscience" around the world. Organizations now link together such diverse sites as former slave housing, death camps, tenements, work prisons, and torture chambers in order to jointly institute a global space of "human rights" and "citizenship" through "critical dialogue with the past." The Hector Pieterson Museum has been grappling with the social and political challenges of the HIV/AIDS pandemic in Soweto and works with demobilized former cadres of the military wings of the ANC and Pan Africanist Congress (PAC). Community organizations in Soweto, like *Asikhulume*, have used the Hector Pieterson Museum as a platform to raise unresolved issues about those people who have "disappeared" as a result of the former apartheid state's systematic killing of ANC leaders.

On the occasion of the 30th anniversary of the uprisings, the memorial was used by the National Youth Commission as a platform to debate the current state of the country's youth by representatives of diverse political organizations mobilizing to enact change. The Hector Pieterson Memorial and Museum as an emerging "site of conscience" already critically engages in dialogues of redemptive survival, recovery and restorative justice as it offers visitors choices between admissible and inadmissible memory. As historian Leslie Witz has argued, a collective national past was crafted by the government, "presented as a national inheritance and labeled as heritage … this past was to be utilized as a powerful agent for cultural identity, reconciliation and nation building" (Witz 2007: 107).

The Hector Pieterson Memorial and Museum, and in particular the building itself, can be seen as a direct result of the TRC's long-term mission of promoting healing through redemptive public acts. The TRC's political project of healing and reconciliation through the making (or progeniture) of new cultural forms and institutions, that bear witness to accounts of racial violence, remains contested because of its overtly normative and moralizing effects on the human rights narrative. In and of itself the building's architecture acts as a container, housing contested or even conflicting narratives of the events surrounding June 16 1976, and allowing the site to act as a platform for new social justice practices at the museum through its policies, exhibitions, collections and public outreach efforts. Although the building can be seen as a product of institutional cultures of witnessing, it functions in many ways as both a medium and an artifact in the historical narrative of the Uprisings – disrupting the possibility of amnesia and national collective memory-making. The building maintains historical resonance through its emancipatory potential and acts as a conduit for "instituting dialogical forms of historical consciousness between testimony donors and communities of witness" (Feldman 2004: 164). In many ways the Hector Pieterson Memorial and Museum refuse to accept a final state-sponsored narrative because it would necessarily subject the politically deleted and absent to a kind of biographical closure and even permit the state certain freedoms from its ongoing accountability (Feldman 2004: 166).

Historian James E. Young has argued that commemorative museums and projects can be seen as redemptive sites as long as one understands how they engage with the memories of those events they seek to honor while still engaging with the present – i.e. how they engage in a kind of "memorial uncanny." Young writes,

> By extension, the *memorial uncanny* [emphasis added] might be regarded as that which is necessarily anti-redemptive. It is that memory of historical events which never domesticates such events, never makes us at home with them, never brings them into the reassuring house of redemptory meaning. It is to leave such events unredeemable yet still memorable, unjustifiable yet still graspable in their causes and effects.
>
> (Young 2000: 3)

The Hector Pieterson Memorial and Museum in Johannesburg, South Africa is at once a redemptive site where past injustices are confronted through civic engagement, and also a "site of memory," where one is allowed to engage with a complex present and a still developing democracy through still untold and incomplete narratives (Ndlovu 1998; Brink *et al.* 2001; Hlongwane *et al.* 2006).

The Hector Pieterson Museum, designed by the Johannesburg-based architectural firm of Mashabane Rose Associates (MRA), with design principal Jeremy Rose as the project's lead designer, officially opened its doors to the public on National Youth Day, June 16 2002, marking the 26th anniversary of the political unrest and infamy that accompanied the 1976 Soweto Uprisings. The Museum – named for twelve-year-old Hector Pieterson, one of the first victims of the Uprisings – is now regarded globally as a symbol of the radical transformation that has distinguished South Africa's museums and cultural institutions in the decade since the dismantling of apartheid. The Memorial and Museum are located on the corner of Khumalo and Pela Streets in Soweto's Orlando West township. Within sight of the museum, about 100 metres away, is the location of Orlando West Junior Secondary School and Orlando West High School on Vilakazi Street – those schools that housed the majority of students who were to march before police began shooting, violently disrupting what was to be a peaceful protest (Pohlandt-McCormick 1999: 5). Just two blocks away Zolile Hector Pieterson (Pitso), a youth who would later become a symbol of the student freedom struggle against apartheid that culminated with the first democratic elections of 1994, was killed at the intersection of Moema and Vilakazi Streets. His death – and the subsequent murder of 575 other protestors in the Uprisings – are memorialized at this National Heritage Site. Together, they contribute to our understanding of student involvement in the anti-apartheid and liberation struggles.

Parents working as day laborers, house-maids, and at other jobs in nearby Johannesburg on the morning of June 16 1976 were still unaware of the events in their community that would catapult consciousness of the liberation struggle across the globe. Students estimated to be about 10,000 in number were gathering along Vilakazi Street, next to the junior secondary and high schools, to protest against Bantu education in general and, specifically, the imposition of Afrikaans as a medium of instruction. Township residents had long regarded education as a means of empowering their children, and, as such, the students' grievances were also allied against apartheid and other racially based government policies.

The exact details of the day remain highly contested and debated despite the many first-hand accounts available in local archives, repositories and research centers across the country and abroad. One account suggests that the students remained in steadfast order despite attempts by police forces to disrupt the protestors with threats of violence, incarceration and torture. In *Whirlwind Before the Storm* (1980), Brooks and Brickhill, write,

> Despite the tense atmosphere the huge crowd [of students] remained calm and well ordered … Suddenly a white policeman lobbed a teargas canister into the front of the crowd. Pupils ran out of the smoke dazed and coughing. The crowd retreated slightly, out of the range of the teargas smoke, but remained facing the police, waving placards and singing. A white policeman drew his revolver. Black journalists standing by the police heard a shout: "Look at him. He's going to

shoot at the kids." A single shot rang out. There was a split second's silence and pandemonium broke out. Children screamed. More shots were fired. At least four pupils fell, and others ran screaming in all directions (1980: 8–9).

At the end of the day, some twenty students died, according to "official" state records, although many more were seriously injured and wounded.

The Museum that commemorates these shameful events is an impressive flush-jointed red-brick and galvanized steel building, three storeys high, with irregularly shaped windows cut into the fabric of the building in what appears to be a random pattern (MRA Architects 2003: 33; Allen and Brennan 2004: 12; Rogerson and Kaplan 2005: 214). The museum functions as an elevated platform helping visitors establish connections to significant sites across Soweto's heritage landscape. Moving along a series of ramps, visitors can look through strategically placed windows taking in views of, among others, the Orlando Stadium and the police station. The nearby community requested that the building contextualize with the local vernacular houses surrounding it – small red-brick, semi-detached houses with iron metal sheeting roofs, built in the 1940s. The edge of the museum square is defined by several dry-stack black-slate walls of increasing height, known as "the wall of memory." In the museum's glass-walled atrium, hundreds of marble bricks, each inscribed with the name of a victim, are strewn on a carpet of gravel.

For some, the initial impression of the museum is that of a cathedral or religious sanctuary, with its double height ceilings, tall thin-banded windows, stripped wood floors, concrete columns and tall red-brick walls. The architects, Mashabane Rose Associates, "wanted the building to establish a physical presence on the site, to memorialize the hundreds of students that died and to be a reminder of the deep impact of this turning point in South African history." They also wanted a "building that connected with the community" (Castle 2003: 52).

The site, where the community suggested "a [commemorative] board should be posted" is now marked with a bench, a piece of dry stacked wall, and a short description of the events leading to Hector Pieterson's death. In Sam Nzima's now famous photograph Pieterson is cradled in the arms of Makhubu, who alongside Antoinette Pieterson, rushed the dying twelve-year-old youth to a car belonging to journalist Sophie Tema (Fig. 12.3). From there he was taken to the nearby Phomolong clinic and certified dead on arrival. From the shooting site, a line of trees used to symbolize a firing line draws the visitor to the memorial site. Through this visual link and the surrounding physical context, the visitor can begin to piece together the events as they might have happened.

Today the memorial and museum precinct is a public gathering space where the cenotaph, furnished by the ANC Youth League and dedicated by then President Nelson Mandela, is now installed. The cenotaph has the following inscription:

> To honor the youth who gave their lives in the struggle for freedom and democracy. In memory of Hector Peterson [sic] and all other young heroes and heroines of our struggle who laid down their lives for freedom, peace and democracy.

Figure 12.3 Hector Pieterson Memorial exterior, Soweto, Johannesburg. (Source: A.D. Nieves)

This memorial is surrounded by a square using road kerbs, cobbles and grass block paving "to recall the material quality of the streets" where the uprising began and then spread to other parts of Soweto and the country (Reilly 2003: 14). The cenotaph, originally laid in 1992, has been redesigned and now lies in a lowered space with a small "weeping" water feature. The memorial ground within the public square is described by its designer as follows:

> framed by a large, dry stacked black slate wall, recalling the thousands of students who rose up against Bantu education … [it] incorporates a robust indigenous landscaping to root the building in its context. The gardens are patterned and shaped with road kerbs, gravel and concrete recalling the textures of the roads upon which all the activity took place.
>
> (Rose 2006)

As one walks away from the "dry stacked black slate" wall the visitor sees and interacts with "a line of indigenous grass [native rooigras] between two rusting steel plates … drawn over one kilometre from the memorial across Khumalo Road to the actual shooting site indicated earlier as marking the beginning of the journey and storyline. This signpost takes you inside the museum building" (Rose 2006). This section of stacked slate is further conceptualized as "the central void." The architects write, "The central void [open to the sky], empty and austere, remembers the missing stories and individuals. The route around the centre permits glimpses of the void as a reminder of the missing individuals and their stories" (Rose 2006).

One of the challenges that faced the curatorial team in the making of the Hector Pieterson Museum was the development of a comprehensive narrative surrounding the events of June 16 1976, integrating the use of relevant material and cultural artifacts from the period. Among museum professionals across South Africa it has been observed that there is a trend to develop historical narratives that seek to tell the "entire story." The most widely accepted approach among museum and heritage professionals has been to condense the whole story in one brief, uncomplicated narrative. This was constantly an area of debate and discussion among those who participated in the making of the Hector Pieterson Museum. Though the narrative and exhibitions at the Hector Pieterson Museum are focused around the story of the 1976 Uprisings consultants, museum professionals, and local community members grappled with the question: "Where to begin and where to end?"

In an article entitled "Between Room 307: spaces of memory at the National Civil Rights Museum," architect and historian Mabel Wilson makes the following observations that may be relevant to the creation of new museums in post-apartheid South Africa, particularly in light of the struggle to end apartheid through grassroots mobilization. Wilson notes: "by trying to 'tell the whole story' … the museum unwittingly denies its public the possibility of articulating their own meanings and associations of [a given] complex history" (2001: 17). Thus, according to Wilson, "the endeavor to memorialize encourages, albeit unintentionally, a static interpretation" (2001: 17). The Hector Pieterson Museum attempts to grapple with this challenge by mixing researched narratives with sometimes conflicting first-hand oral testimonies and memories, offering the public enhanced possibilities of articulating their own meanings and associations. Thus:

> The integration of the narrative, museum space and the physical landscape outside is the most potent and memorable aspect of the museum. The museum becomes a device for viewing and unpacking the township, the physical landscape and the spaces in which 16 June's events unfolded.
>
> (MRA Architects 2003: 33)

The memorial site plays an important spiritual role for visitors and those who experienced the uprisings first-hand. It is a place of contemplation and remembrance, as well as a site of reminiscence of that fateful day, and figures as part of a larger healing process. The memorial design recognizes the needs and "voices of those who are marked by loss and suffering and who are concerned with mourning rather than celebration" (Rioufol 1995: 15). It is a unique space where contemporary South Africans and future generations can contemplate memories both painful and problematic, providing its visitors with multiple and even conflicting narratives that allow for a more complex understanding of our role in shaping the future.

Social justice and social inclusion are both closely related concepts, and still remain largely missing in much of the current debates concerning township heritage and urban redevelopment across South Africa. In the late 1980s the concept of sustainable development was introduced into the environmental debate as an expression of the interdependence between the three systems identified as basic to development: the economic system, the social system, and the biophysical system. Across South Africa, cultural heritage is seen as a primary vehicle for new forms of economic development – one able to contribute financially to broader issues of resource management for marginalized communities. However, the demands of foreign tourism on South Africa may also paradoxically contribute to the destruction of the natural and cultural environment, and it is therefore essential to find ways to protect these environments for present and future generations – particularly in former all-Black townships. Interestingly, Scotland may serve as an example here, as it made important inroads in social justice and social inclusion through massive social policy development and constitutional reform in the early 1990s. Since 1999, with the re-establishment of the Scottish Parliament, social justice has become a focus of much development work across local government agencies and policy frameworks. South Africa could similarly develop a clearly stated heritage framework based on social justice initiatives (Duffy 2002: 303).

I have argued that it might be possible to begin seeing these former prisons and sites of protest as repositories for national histories, which at the same time embrace a new form of community-based civic engagement. Elsewhere, in Argentina for example, the Topography of Memory Program of *Memoria Abierta* (Open Memory) begins to link civic engagement with cultural sustainability through the work of architect Gonzalo Conte (Sevcenko 2004). Through an alliance of eight Argentine human rights organizations and local citizens, clandestine detention centers and other urban spaces once used for purposes of state terrorism now work to explore the reconstruction of history and memory. I maintain that understanding the cultural significance of historic sites in South Africa's former all-Black townships requires an intersectional framework that both cuts across a long-held "tourist's gaze" based on white supremacy and challenges our assumptions about power, authority, race, class and gender in our globalizing world.

References

Allen, G. and Brennan, F. (2004) *Tourism in the New South Africa: Social Responsibility and the Tourist Experience*, New York: I.B. Tauris.

Ashworth, G. (2004) "Tourism and the Heritage of Atrocity: Managing the Heritage of South African Apartheid for Entertainment," in T. Singh (ed.), *New Horizons in Tourism: Strange Experiences and Stranger Practices*, London: Oxford University Press.

Brink, E., Malungane, G., Lebello, S., Ntshangase, D. and Krige, S. (2001) *Recollected 25 Years Later: Soweto 16 June 1976 – It All Started with a Dog*, Cape Town: Kwela Books.

Brooks, A. and Brickhill, J. (1980) *Whirlwind Before the Storm*, London: International Defence and Aid Fund for Southern Africa.

Castle, E. (2003) "Textured Ground," *Art South Africa*, 2(2): 48–53.

Comaroff, J. (2005) "The end of history, again? Pursuing the past in the postcolony," in S. Kaul, A. Loomba, M. Bunzl, A. Burton, and J. Esty (eds), *Postcolonial Studies and Beyond*, Durham, NC: Duke University Press.

Coombes, A. (2003) *History After Apartheid: Visual Culture and Public Memory in a Democratic South Africa*, Durham, NC: Duke University Press.

Davies, R. (2003) "Black Heritage Areas in South African Cities: Issues and Dilemmas," in *Langa Heritage Study*, Heritage Resources Section, Cape Town: Environmental Management.

Deckler, T., Graupner, A. and Rasmuss, H. (2006) *Contemporary South African Architecture in a Landscape of Transition*, Johannesburg: Double Storey.

Department of Arts, Culture, Science and Technology (1996) "New Policies and Institutional Frameworks," in *All Our Legacies, Our Common Future – White Paper on Arts, Culture and Heritage*, Pretoria: Department of Arts, Culture, Science and Technology.

Department of the Environment and Heritage (2004) *Steps to Sustainable Tourism: Planning For a Sustainable Future for Tourism, Heritage, and the Environment*, Canberra: Department of the Environment and Heritage.

Dondolo, L. (2001) *Depicting History at Sivuyile Township Tourism Center*, Paper presented to the "Mapping Alternatives: Debating New Heritage Practices in South Africa" conference, Centre for African Studies, University of Cape Town, Cape Town.

Duffy, T. (2002) "Exhibiting Human Rights," *Peace Review*, 12(2): 303–9.

Du Preez, C. (2006) *Curator's Statement*. Available online at: http://www.freewebs.com/redlocationmuseumarchives/curator.htm (accessed January 15 2008).

Feldman, A. (2004) "Memory Theatres, Virtual Witnessing, and the Trauma-Aesthetic," *Biography*, 27(1): 163–202.

Gibson, J. (2004) "Truth, Reconciliation, and the Creation of a Human Rights Culture in South Africa," *Law and Society Review*, 38(1): 5–40.

Gouws, A. (1994) *Report of the Robben Island Political Feasibility Study as Commissioned by Peace Visions*, Cape Town: Peace Visions.

Hirzy, E. (2002) "Mastering Civic Engagement: A Report From the American Association of Museums," in *Mastering Civic Engagement: A Challenge to Museums*, Washington, D.C.: American Association of Museums.

Hlongwane, A., Ndlovu, S. and Mutloatse, M. (eds.) (2006) *Soweto 76: Reflections on the Liberation Struggles, Commemorating the 30th Anniversary of June 16, 1976*, Johannesburg: Mutloatse Arts Heritage Trust.

Kirshenblatt-Gimblett, B. (1998) *Destination Culture: Tourism, Museums, and Heritage*, Berkeley: University of California Press.

Mason, R. (1994) "Conflict and Complement: An Exploration of the Discourses Informing the Concept of the Socially Inclusive Museum in Contemporary Britain," *International Journal of Heritage Studies*, 10(1): 49–73.

MRA Architects (2003) "Hector Pieterson Museum, Soweto," *The Digest of South African Architecture*, February: 32–3.

Nanda, S. (2004) "South African Museums and the Creation of a New National Identity," *Museum Anthropology*, 106(2): 380–1.

Ndlovu, S. (1998) *The Soweto Uprisings: Counter-memories of June 16, 1976*, Johannesburg: Raven Press.

Pohlandt-McCormick, H. (1999) *I Saw a Nightmare …, Doing Violence to Memory: The Soweto Uprising, June 16, 1976*, Ph.D. Thesis, University of Minnesota.

Reilly, C. (2003) "A Powerful Piece of Interpretive Space," *Planning*: 12–15.

Rioufol, V. (1995) "The University of Resistance to Apartheid," *Lesedi: IFAS-Research Newsletter, French Institute of South Africa*, May 12: 15.

Rogerson, C. and Kaplan, L. (2005) "Tourism Promotion in 'Difficult Areas: The Experience of Johannesburg Inner City," *Urban Forum*, 16(2–3): 214–43.

Rose, J. (2006) "Site," in A. Hlongwane (ed.), *Hector Pieterson Memorial Museum and The June 16 1976 Trail, General Management and Conservation Plan*, Johannesburg: Hector Pieterson Memorial and Museum.

Sevcenko, L. (2004) *Sites of Conscience: Using the Past to Shape the Future*, Paper Presented at the "Using the Past to Shape the Future: Addressing Civic Issues at Historic Sites, Museums, and Cultural Centers" Conference, University of Illinois, Chicago.

Shackley, M. (2001) "Potential Futures for Robben Island: Shrine, Museum, or Theme Park?," *International Journal of Heritage Studies*, 7(4): 355–63.

Strange, C. and Kempa, M. (2003) "Shades of Dark Tourism: Alcatraz and Robben Island," *Annals of Tourism Research*, 30(2): 386–405.

Theberge, S. (2004) *Everywhere But the Ground: The Spatial Politics of Memory in Cape Town*, Paper presented at the "History Matters: Spaces of Violence, Spaces of Memory" Conference, New School University, New York.

Webb, D. (1994) "Winds of Change," *Museums Journal*, 94(4): 20–24.

Wells, J. (2004) *Who Owns Heritage? Developing Powers to Local Government and Traditional Leadership in the East Cape of South Africa*, Unpublished paper in author's possession.

Wilson, M. (2001) "Between Rooms 307: Spaces of Memory at the National Civil Rights Museum," in C. Barton (ed.), *Sites of Memory: Perspectives on Architecture and Race*, Princeton: Princeton Architectural Press.

Witz, L. (2007) "Transforming Museums on Postapartheid Tourist Routes," in G. Buntinx, C. Rassool, C. Kratz, L. Szwaja, T. Ybarra-Frausto and B. Kirshenblatt-Gimblett (eds) *Museum Frictions: Public Cultures/Global Transformations*, Durham, NC: Duke University Press.

Witz, L., Rassool C., and Minkley, G. (1999) *Tourism in African Renaissance*, Paper presented at the conference entitled "Public History, Forgotten History," University of Namibia, August 22–23.

Young, J. (2000) "Daniel Libeskind's Jewish Museum in Berlin: The Uncanny Arts of Memorial Architecture," *Jewish Social Studies*, 6(2): 1–23.

Chapter 13

Negotiating places of pain in post-conflict Northern Ireland
Debating the future of the Maze prison/Long Kesh

Sara McDowell

Remembering and forgetting sites of pain

Material remnants of the past, according to Till (2005: 7), 'haunt our imaginations and performances by materializing social relations'. The physical remnants of conflict haunt many contemporary societies, evoking the saliency of past hurts and divisions in the present. There are those, as Till suggests, who feel the *need* to be haunted by the past: to return there; to re-enact their experiences; to sanctify a place to remember; for what is potentially visible, as Lowenthal (1985: 238) reminds us, is omnipresent. There are others, however, who wish to forget and exorcise painful memories from the present. Goodfellow (2002) suggests that there are always silences and absences within narratives of memory. Silence is often necessary, particularly within political cultures in which certain groups work to banish hauntings or dark memories into the realm of the taboo (Schreiner 2002: 57). The word 'taboo' can be understood to constitute something too painful or shameful to discuss (or remember), something which is hidden or banned from the public, often for their own protection (Rudas, cited in Schreiner 2002: 57). Physically obliterating sites of painful memories from the landscapes of the present can, for many, be psychologically liberating. Yet attempts to forget or deny the past may also prove futile. Many academics have argued that to forget, one must first remember (Edkins 2003). Roth (1995: 5), for example, writing about trauma, suggests that memories of the event that occasioned the trauma only disappear whenever they become part of the historical consciousness. Referring explicitly to acts of preservation or commemoration, Schreiner (2002: 63) notes that: 'what never has been inscribed also may never be forgotten, because it is not accessible to forgetfulness'. Acknowledging and demarcating the past can then arguably serve to alleviate the 'burden of memory' (Assman, cited in Schreiner 2002: 64).

In the aftermath of conflict questions invariably arise over the fate of sites that occasion(ed) hurt. The struggle over memory and meaning reveals how both individuals and society come to terms with the imprints of violence and division (Petkovic 2005: 40). The material residue of Northern Ireland's turbulent past haunts the political, economic and cultural landscapes of the transitional present. Spanning three decades and costing approximately 3,700 lives, ethno-nationalist

Figure 13.1 The prison entrance. (Source: S. McDowell)

violence in the region imparted a tangible and intangible heritage of loss, pain and division. Littered across the rural and urban landscapes is the fabric of conflict: memorials, murals, defunct military installations and prisons emptied of the 'political prisoners' they once housed. The inception of peace marked by the paramilitary ceasefires of 1994 and ensuing peace negotiations has triggered a rigorous debate surrounding the fate of such sites and what they might mean for the present and future of Northern Ireland. Through the negotiation of these sites, we try, as Till notes, to 'localize meaning about what we think the past is' (Till 2005: 13), or, perhaps alternatively, what it should be.

One of the most enduring debates of late concerns the site of the now redundant Maze/Long Kesh Prison once labelled 'a microcosm' of the conflict (Jarman 2000: 283). Closed in October 2000 following the contentious release of the remaining political prisoners under the terms of the 1998 Belfast Agreement, which sought to draw a line under a particularly fraught period of ethno-nationalist conflict, the 360-acre site on the outskirts of Belfast is a gaping reminder of a painful past and disputed present. The imperative to address the site's future (and thus its meaning) was hastened by the government's decision in 2002 to transfer military sites to the public, as a symbolic gesture. This chapter follows the post-conflict debates and dilemmas of negotiating and representing a site that directly and indirectly administered, facilitated and perpetuated pain on multiple levels.

The historical context

Northern Ireland has been embroiled in conflict and division since its inception in 1921. Created as a response to the Irish problem, which had dominated the political landscape in Britain for much of the nineteenth century, the partition of the island occasioned much resentment manifested in successive waves of violence. Social unrest was particularly acute in the North, intensifying throughout the 1960s to become the period which became known colloquially as the 'Troubles'. The communal divide between Catholic–Protestant, Nationalist–Unionist and Republican–Loyalist, appeared to characterise the seemingly sectarian nature of the conflict. Nationalist ideology, for example, focuses on the unification of Ireland through constitutional means. Republicanism shares this objective but has, at times, embraced an armed struggle. Both ideologies see themselves as politically, culturally and historically Irish. Unionists want to maintain the link with Britain and consider themselves as politically, culturally and historically British. Loyalism, which is an inherently working-class ideology, is beginning to push for an independent Northern Ireland and distance itself from Unionism. There is also a religious dimension to this division with many Catholics seeing themselves as Nationalists and many Protestants seeing themselves as Unionists (this is not, however, absolute) (see Hennessey 1997: 1).

The Maze's place in the history of the Troubles dates back to the morning of 9 August 1971 when the then Northern Ireland Prime Minister, Brian Faulkner, with the support of the British government, introduced internment without trial in an attempt to deal with escalating violence. Northern Ireland, he believed, 'was simply at war with the terrorist' (BBC On This Day [9 August 1971]). Internment was first implemented for Republican detainees in 1971 and subsequently extended to Loyalists in 1972. The first internees were housed in a collection of dilapidated Nissen huts at Long Kesh, formerly a World War II Royal Air Force base. Both Republican and Loyalist internees immediately began agitating for political status, arguing that they were not the 'terrorists' that the state had deemed them to be. Rejecting the notion of criminalisation, they believed their crimes to be politically justifiable and valid (Irwin 2003: 472). After much external and internal pressure Special Category Status was conceded in 1974 by the then Secretary of State, William Whitelaw, which not only separated prisoners of war from ordinary criminals but permitted free association within the compounds along religious and ideological lines. It also allowed prisoners to avail of extra visits, food parcels and the right to refuse prison uniform. This move signalled a significant realignment of power within the prison as political prisoners took ownership of their environment and of their respective groups. They unilaterally, as Ryder (2000: 115) contends, imposed their own segregation, establishing exclusive territories for affiliates of the Ulster Defence Association, Ulster Volunteer Force, Ulster Freedom Force, Irish Republican Army and the Irish National Liberation Army.

By 1976, however, Special Category Status had been revoked following recommendations by Lord Gardiner. The Gardiner Report marked a departure in government policy and was met with much contestation. The criminalisation

Figure 13.2 The Nissen huts of Long Kesh. (Source: S. McDowell)

of paramilitary prisoners was part of a strategic change in policy which included the Ulsterisation of the security forces. This entailed putting the police force, the Royal Ulster Constabulary (RUC), on the 'front-line' primarily imagined to dissuade external observers from looking upon the conflict in Northern Ireland as anything other than an internal dispute between two 'Irish' factions (Arthur 1997: 165). As one Republican ex-prisoner noted:

> You can chart the attempts made from 1975 to de-politicise the whole conflict … it was aimed at Republicans … The British government was removing themselves as a party to the conflict. They were handing it back and creating confusion … to say that it was two tribes fighting.
> (Cited in Shirlow *et al.* 2006: 28)

Stripping prisoners of their political status illustrated the government's wishes to completely disengage with the territorial nature of the conflict. Criminalisation, as Foucault (1991) suggests, is a form of depoliticisation. Edkins (2003: 228) argues that it is a form of internal exclusion where the enemy (any anti-state group) becomes the criminal and dissent or disagreement is prohibited. This strategy dispelled any opportunities for dialogue and thus paved the way for yet more protest. Prisoners were subsequently moved from the temporary Nissen

Figure 13.3 One of the infamous H-Blocks. (Source: S. McDowell)

huts at Long Kesh into eight new 'H-Blocks' (due to the shape of the cells) and the prison was renamed Maze Cellular Prison. Republican prisoners responded by launching a series of campaigns to regain political status such as the 'blanket protest' (inmates wearing bed coverings instead of prison uniforms), the 'dirty protest' (during which prisoners refused to wash and smeared their own excrement over cell walls) and finally, the hunger strike in which ten men died (see O'Malley 1990). The martyrdom of these volunteers in 1981 resulted in the rise of Sinn Féin and reified the role of the prison within Republican hagiography, indelibly investing the makeshift infrastructures with (Republican) meaning. The escape of 38 prisoners in 1983 further contributed to the prison's infamous status, again aligning the site with Republican narratives. Loyalist prisoners, as 'pro-state paramilitaries' were often deterred from staging similar protests to their Republican counterparts following criticisms from the wider Unionist community (Shirlow *et al.* 2006: 26).

Drawing on case studies from South Africa and Taiwan, Buntman and Huang (2000: 43) argue that political imprisonment often develops political leadership. This is certainly true of the Maze. Throughout the Troubles the prison spawned a generation of new political leaders and, consequently, events within the prison were often directly connected to the conflict outside. Both Republican and Loyalist prisoners were instrumental in deliberating the cessation of violence in

1994, marking the beginning of the peace negotiations. So central to the advent of peace was the prison that Marjorie (Mo) Mowlam the then Secretary of State visited it in 1998 to negotiate Loyalist support for the peace process. Moreover, an integral clause of the 1998 Belfast Agreement (signed by over 71 per cent of the population in Northern Ireland) was that prisoners whose organisation was on ceasefire would be released. On 28 July 2000 one of the last groups of prisoners were released from the Maze under the prisoner release scheme. Among them were those responsible for atrocities such as the Shankill Road bomb, which killed nine people, and the Docklands bomb in England, which killed two:

> No one meant to be triumphalist. But there were neither apologies nor regrets, and the air rang to the sound of hundreds of cheers. The ex-prisoners departed defiantly in convoys, horns blaring, bound for homecoming celebrations, believing that they had defeated a jail which they said was built to break them.
> (Mullin 2000: 1)

The Maze as a place of pain and shame

Prisons as places of incarceration are synonymous with pain and shame at multiple levels. Physically and psychologically prisons are designed to control the minds and motivations of prisoners. They are constructed to segregate offenders from society. Inmates are disciplined, deprived of their liberty and subject to constant surveillance (Edkins 2003: 50). They must conform to internal power structures and often adhere to codes of silence and loyalty. These 'deprivations and frustrations', termed the 'pains of imprisonment' by Sykes (1958), come to constitute a serious psychological assault upon the self. Prisoners within the Maze both Republican and Loyalist cited beatings and strip searches as additional 'pains of imprisonment' (Crawford 1999; O'Raw 2006). Riley (2002: 451) suggests, however, that for political prisoners the psychological suffering of incarceration may be somewhat mitigated. In rejecting the moral authority of the dominant society, prisoners can resist the self-defining implications of confinement and continue to assert identity claims that are consistent with self-respect (Riley 2002: 451). While this may have been true for some prisoners within the Maze, there can be little doubt that as a political prison the Maze embodied a place of injustice and shame. Prisoners were tried and convicted in no-jury (Diplock) courts for 'scheduled' or 'terrorist-type' offences, while hundreds of innocent men were interned there during the early 1970s due to inaccurate ethnic and religious 'profiling'.

The Maze was constructed to quell and control a conflict that would eventually cost some 3,700 lives. The architecture of the site conformed to the prison's oppressive objective: its grey prefab structures and 17-foot-high perimeter wall measuring some two and a half miles, all lending to the psychology of confinement and repetition. Purbrick (2004) suggests that the H-Blocks marked an attempt to create a physical solution to a war situation; their penal design was intended to reproduce suppressive power thus shaping the forms of physical and political resistance. According to Coiste na n-Iarchimí (2003: 3), the umbrella organisation for Republican former prisoner groups (during their joint history), the prison housed some 25,000 Republican and Loyalist prisoners and its effects were particularly pervasive in certain communities. De Rosa (cited in Irwin 2003: 472), for example, estimates that over 11 per cent of the adult population (which is predominantly Nationalist/Republican) in the Springfield area of Belfast was imprisoned at some point. For the families of those imprisoned, the Maze was also a site of pain. The incarceration of a father, son or brother disrupted family life, transformed gender roles and often irreparably damaged relationships. Kennedy believes (cited in Irwin 2003: 472) that 1 in 3 of the population of the Lower Falls has experienced the effects of imprisonment in their immediate family. As one Republican woman notes:

> I've been going to that prison for my whole life. First to visit me da, then to visit my husband, then to see me daughter, that was hard because I had her young'uns while she was in Armagh. Now my grandson is in The Kesh. I've been in the prison for each generation of my family. I've done my whack five times over. I've done more whack then any of these men around. They just think I'm a nice old lady.
>
> (cited in Dowler 1998: 165)

Many of the prison staff and their families also remember the prison negatively. Many prison officers were intimidated and injured because of their association with the site, while a further 29 lost their lives both through suicide and murder. One officer, Patrick Kerr, was shot by masked men as he left Mass with his two young children in February 1987 (Ryder 2000: 303). His murder followed a series of attacks on his home which had resulted in the family moving only two years earlier. Another officer, Leslie Jarvis, was shot only a month later in his car outside Magee University College. He had been attending night classes. Two police officers who were called to the scene were also killed by a car bomb which had been placed under Jarvis' car (Ryder 2000: 304). The pressure on prison officers and the fear of retaliation on the outside was too much and a number of prison officers took their own lives, while others experienced severe psychological trauma. As one prison officer recalled:

> A good officer wary of his own security would try and avoid doing anything that would highlight him to prisoners – something that would lead to him being targeted on the outside. But the threats were there – and the death lists existed. If the prisoners wanted you to know that you were being targeted they had various means of doing it. Sometimes you would be told directly by the RUC that they had intelligence. Sometimes they would talk within earshot of an officer and reveal details about a colleagues' life – who his wife

was, what car he drove, where he went for a drink – and then you'd know that they were really serious … And so you would be immediately taken off shift, you'd be offered a degree of police protection in terms of home visits and other advice – and then you'd sit up all night from midnight until five in the morning, sitting with your official weapon in your hands, knowing that if they're going to come, it would be now.

(BBC Newsline 2000)

The many victims of those imprisoned and their families would also undoubtedly equate the prison with pain. As previously noted, the Maze's centrality to the peace negotiations has exacerbated this pain, as approximately 500 prisoners whose organisations were on ceasefire were released, as part of the 1998 Belfast Agreement, without serving their full sentences.

The interpretation of the Maze as a site of shame is particularly prevalent within Loyalist/Unionist communities. As pro-state paramilitaries, Loyalists considered themselves to be an extension of the state forces, a role deemed unnecessary by the majority of the community. Their imprisonment, unlike their Republican counterparts who were largely praised for their actions, was a source of embarrassment. For Unionist communities, prisoners and former prisoners are, as Gormally (cited in Shirlow *et al.* 2006: 24) suggests, the most obvious ex-combatants. In Northern Ireland they are the 'visible concentration of everything people feel about the conflict … they are the perpetrators of numerous atrocities, the enemies of democracy and civilization incarnate' (Gormally, cited in Shirlow *et al.* 2006: 24). That their place of confinement should evoke similar hurt, for many, is perhaps unsurprising. The pain associated with the prison reverberates far beyond those who came into immediate contact with it. A place where the memories of the state, combatants and civilians intersect, the prison has emerged as one of the most potent symbols of a particularly violent and dark episode of Northern Ireland's turbulent past. Precisely because of this, its fate in peacetime is of interest to many stakeholders.

Negotiating the site

In May 2002 the Maze complex was transferred to the Office of the First Minister and Deputy First Minister (OFMDFM) under the Reinvestment and Reform Initiative, the idea being that sites of conflict could help underpin the peace process in a practical and meaningful way. Not only did the site which constitutes some 360 acres (five per cent of all available publicly-owned regeneration land in Northern Ireland) represent the single largest investment opportunity in the region, but it was entrusted (at least in official rhetoric) with the responsibility of symbolising the transition of the region from conflict to peace, becoming an 'internationally recognised beacon'.

Crucially the representation of the Maze site became entwined with official plans to reconstruct and represent post-conflict Northern Ireland as a shared and neutral society, a considerable task in Shirlow's (2006) opinion given the continued saliency of segregation and ethnic division. Indeed a number of state agencies including the museum sector (Crooke 2005) have shied away from any real interpretation of Northern Ireland's turbulent past and have yet to designate it and its physical remnants as 'heritage'. The economic and political imperative to fully exploit the site's commercial value did not allow for any period of reflection, despite the conflict's rawness. Tasked with the responsibility of finding a flagship representational form that would achieve both, a consultation panel including representatives of the four main political parties – Democratic Unionist Party (DUP); Ulster Unionist Party (UUP); Social Democratic and Labour Party (SDLP); and Sinn Féin (who represented the interests of former Republican prisoners) – was established in March 2003 to solicit ideas from the public and deliberate the regeneration of the site.

Preserving the Maze

In 1972 the leader of the paramilitary organisation the Provisional Irish Republican Army (PIRA), Billy McKee, predicted that 'the war would be won in prisons' (Von Tangen Page 2006: 202). The 'armed struggle' to forcibly remove Britain from Ireland predated the recent conflict, as did Republican imprisonment, which dates back to the early twentieth century. Of all of those interested in the Maze's fate, only Republicans advocate preserving the site as a place of remembrance: as heritage. Events within the Maze are crucially important within Republican hagiography and for many the site constitutes 'sacred ground' (Linenthal 2001). Sacred ground does not, as Jackson and Henrie contend, 'exist naturally', rather it is 'assigned sanctity as man defines, limits and characterizes it through its culture, experience and goals' (1983: 94). It is then a reflection of an individual or group's emotional connectivity with a particular place or an expression of their 'societal arrangements' (Durkheim, cited in Azaryahu 1999: 482). Republicans are inexorably morally and politically committed to the site through the deaths of the ten hunger strikers.

In 2003, Coiste na n-Larchimí, supported by Sinn Féin, launched a sophisticated campaign to explore the possibility of, and measure support for, an 'inclusive' museum at the site. The Republican movement see the site, as Murray Brown (2004: 12) believes, as a 'key part of its propaganda arsenal, a reminder to younger republicans of the sacrifices made in a self-styled war with the British' and has even gone so far as to label it as 'Britain's Guantanamo Bay', as a place of pain, shame and injustice. Thus it must be understood as a political resource in the competition to narrate Northern Ireland's malleable past in the transitional present. Prisons, as Dewar and Fredericksen (2003: 46) note, separate offenders from mainstream society through the use of perimeter walls, internal fences, cellblocks and other physical barriers, thus creating a society within a society. In a museum context this 'creates a visually impressive fabric' that complements and enhances 'both interpretation of the nuances of prison life and public dialogue about that life' (Dewar and Fredericksen 2003: 46). Republicans are clearly aware of the benefits of using the site in a museum context and thus are acutely aware of the 'power dynamics embedded in the construction of heritage' (Crooke 2005: 131):

> Just as men and women can be made into heroes through their imprison-ment, so can their spaces of confinement be exalted by their presence. In this way more places of detention for criminals are transformed into powerful symbols of political freedom.
> (excerpt from Kilmainhaim Gaol guidebook, cited in Coombes 2003: 77)

In terms of importance Republicans rate the prison as 'one of the most impor-tant twentieth century historic buildings in Europe' (Murray Brown 2004: 5). Astonishingly they cite Robben Island and Auschwitz as possible analogies for the Maze. Republican ex-prisoners have frequently visited the former to explore and expose the possible similarities between the two prisons. Yet it is universally agreed that Robben Island is 'heritage'. The prison is credited as the 'founda-tional cornerstone of the new national image of South Africa' (Coombes 2003: 83) and was inscribed as a World Heritage Site by UNESCO in 1999, because it symbolised 'the triumph of the human spirit, of freedom, and of democracy over oppression'. Conversely, the meaning of the Maze is contested, as is its heritage status. The Auschwitz parallel is simply wrong on many, many levels. Despite the degradations that occurred within the Maze, comparisons pale in significance. An estimated 1.1 million people were murdered at Auschwitz-Birkenau in south-west Poland between 1941 and early 1945. It was also inscribed accordingly as a World Heritage Site in 1979, on the basis of its symbolic importance as 'a place of outstanding universal significance'. As argued elsewhere, the Maze is 'but a statis-tical footnote in the global heritage of pain' (Graham and McDowell 2007: 358).

Obliterating the site

The painful memories associated with the prison have led many to call for the site's complete destruction or obliteration. Obliteration, as Foote (2003: 7) contends, occurs whenever all trace of the past is removed or covered up from a site, causing the memory attached to that place to be elided, denied and erased. Such sites, he believes, are associated largely with shameful or dark events such as mass murders or notorious 'characters'. Victims of former prisoners and their families are particularly haunted by the Maze's presence and believe it has no place in Northern Ireland's future, a perspective shared by those who worked in the prison. A memorial located within the prison compound commemorating dead prison officers was removed following Republican demands for a museum. This symbolic move 'speaks volumes about the representational chasm between protagonists in a still unresolved and bitter ethnic conflict' (Neill 2006: 117).

Unionists are largely in favour of the prison's obliteration for a number of reasons, the most pressing of which is the fear that its preservation could lead to the sanctification of the Republican narrative, glorifying the armed 'struggle'. As one Unionist politician noted:

> It represents a very negative part of our history, some of the worst of the last 35 years. I am very much of the view that while we should not forget what happened there, we should not glorify it and turn it into a shrine.
>
> (Reg Empey cited in McKay 2000:13)

While Empey's comments exhibit at least an appreciation of the site as a significant part of Northern Ireland's heritage, however undesirable, he and the UUP believe that obliteration and regeneration is necessary to move forward. Likewise, Loyalists, despite their historical connections to the site, display little empathy or identification with its future, stemming perhaps from their paradoxical relationship with the prison. One of the few Loyalist ex-prisoners to voice an opinion on the site's fate, former UVF prisoner and then leader of the Progressive Unionist Party, David Ervine (1953–2007), also called for the site's effacement and challenged Republicans to 'build a shrine elsewhere' (Murray Brown 2004: 5).

The Maze 'masterplan': a lesson in dealing with difficult heritage?

The search for a development form to construct a shared narrative from a contested past on a site of shared pain ended in February 2005 after a long and arduous consultation process. The Consultation Panel's Final Report (the details of which were clarified in the 2006 Maze/Long Kesh Masterplan and Implementation Strategy) amounted to a compromise solution advocating the mixed use of the site. The regeneration proposals included plans for a 40,000 seat sports stadium; a rural excellence and equestrian zone; office, hotel and leisure facilities; a light industrial zone; the development of iconic artwork and landscaping and, interestingly, an International Centre for Conflict Transformation (ICCT).

Using a primarily pedagogic approach, the ICCT retaining some of the key buildings of the prison will somehow prophetically promote a 'shared society' and 'transform conflict' not just in Northern Ireland but internationally. Such a vision, while arguably commendable in intent, is, to some extent, sanctimonious and displays a certain lack of understanding. Moreover the details of how exactly this is to be achieved are vague, perhaps deliberately so (Graham and McDowell 2007). Fundamentally different from conflict resolution, conflict transformation advocates transforming the nature of conflict from violence to some other means. A concept first coined by political mediator, John P. Lederach (1995), conflict transformation is based on the premise that short-term resolutions or 'fixes' to conflict are largely unsuccessful, as divided or disputant communities do not understand their mutually destructive relationships which led to the conflict in the first instance. Rather, such communities should seek to transform or modify those relationships through what Folger and Bush (2001: 2) term 'empowerment and recognition'. This process has been interpreted by many people as a means of transforming and reshaping their own ideas about the origins, realities and consequences of the Troubles thus prohibiting an exploration or an understanding of the narratives of others (McDowell 2006).

The ICCT will consist of: one of the H-Blocks; the prison hospital where the ten hunger strikers died; the administration building and emergency control room; a section of the perimeter wall; a watchtower; a cage (Nissen hut); and the World War II aircraft and other structures still on site, a proposal criticised by archaeologists who believe that the relocation of certain sites will 'create a collection of isolated artefacts' thus undermining the archaeological impact of the prison as a whole (McAtackney 2005: 40). Officials are at pains to suggest that the centre is not a museum, despite the fact that it will house a number of buildings which are perceived (mainly by Republicans) to be symbolic. This immediately resonates with similar practices in Nuremberg when a building at the Nazi Party rally ground was preserved as a 'Documentation Centre' rather than a museum; 'the cultural assumption being that museums play a sacralising role' (McDonald 2006: 20). As undesirable heritage, stakeholders believed that the narratives should not be celebrated. Yet the naming of both centres appears to be little more than nomenclature as the general public are finding difficulty in differentiating between educational 'centres', which preserve artefacts from the past, and museums. It is also possible to argue that the narrating of the ICCT will undoubtedly raise similar representational issues to a museum (Graham and McDowell 2007). Many believe that the ICCT represents a victory for Republicans, endorsing their calls for a museum. Finlay Spratt, the chairman of the Prison Officers' Association, vehemently opposed the retention of any of the buildings arguing that the prison should be 'erased from the map':

> They are making a laughing stock out of us with an International Centre for Conflict Transformation. Millions of pounds are going to be spent glorifying this place. It's a total disgrace and it is just appeasement to terrorism on both sides.
>
> (Gordon 2005b: 1)

Implicit to the preservation of these buildings is then a general consensus (however contested) that they constitute a form of heritage and therefore should be protected, a point accepted by Northern Ireland's Department of the Environment. Only two months after the report was launched, the Environment and Heritage Service granted those buildings earmarked for retention listed status because of their 'heightened historical interest' (Gordon 2005a: 1). Heritage is widely accepted as the use of the past as a resource for the present (Ashworth and Graham 2005: 3). It conjures notions of a collective identity, something that has existed over time and commonly confers legitimacy (McDonald 2006: 10) (this of course is entirely congruent with the Republican movement's ideological objective).

Also controversial are the plans to construct a multi-use sports stadium which will, for the first time, as a symbolic shared space facilitate sporting events from across the cultural divide, including the Gaelic games, rugby and soccer. Sport as a popular cultural expression is invariably connected to political allegiance in Northern Ireland. This differential sports affiliation originates in segregated education, which promotes a segregated games curriculum (Sugden 1995). Yet Neill (2006: 117) argues that the viability of an out-of-town stadium, 10 miles from Belfast's centre, is sorely under-researched. A white elephant, he warns, would be a poor post-conflict beacon. Indeed the general public appears largely against the proposal. This issue has occasioned a major split: the united front of the New Belfast Group tasked with regenerating the post-conflict city aligned with central government interests propagating the stadium proposal, while the city of Belfast, with the support of the Tourist Board, and along with most soccer fans (Moulton, cited in Neill 2006: 117), prefer an in-town location. In January 2006, Northern Ireland soccer fans overwhelmingly voted against government plans to relocate their present stadium at Windsor Park to the Maze site (McKinley 2006: 1).

Despite these reservations, the Maze Consultation Panel is confident that it has found a symbolic representational form for the site, a platform to achieve the elusive 'shared society'. The DUP representative on the panel, Edwin Poots, believes the entire development if successful will acknowledge Northern Ireland's shared past but will build firm foundations for its collective future, while Paul Butler, the Sinn Féin representative, has every confidence that the site will 'turn swords into ploughshares'. On 2 April 2007, six months into the site's reconstruction, work began to dismantle the two-and-half-mile perimeter wall around the prison site. The timing of this particular act was strategically symbolic, designed to coincide with the establishment of a devolved assembly for Northern Ireland which for the first time witnessed power-sharing between the DUP and Sinn Féin. As Direct Rule Minister David Hanson noted:

> Last Monday a political wall came down, bringing with it a new start to life in Northern Ireland with a new Assembly and power sharing Executive. Today we are taking down a physical wall that will open the way to an iconic development that will also be shared by all the people here.
>
> (McAdam 2007: 1)

Conclusion

The struggle over memory and meaning reveals how both individuals and a society come to terms with the physical remnants of violence and division (Petkovic 2005: 40). Negotiating and restructuring these sites of pain in the aftermath of violence is, as Arif (2006) suggests, more than mere rebuilding; rather it is about architectural and emotional mediation between estranged or contested pasts and desired futures. It is, she argues, an act of healing, the mending of fissured social relationships in a material environment. These issues were echoed in the negotiation of the Maze site, as officials attempted to build a shared narrative of a disputed past on one of the most potent symbols of the Northern Ireland conflict. The contestation over the prison's fate reinforces McDonald's argument that the past is not simply subject to processes of remembering and forgetting, but that a range of stakeholders are also profusely aware of its potential (whether it is desired or not) in the present (2006: 12). The re-imagining of such difficult heritage has been undoubtedly painful. It has reopened old wounds, divided society, occasioned hurt and, at times, threatened to undermine the move forward. Yet for all its criticisms, the Maze/Long Kesh debacle has been successful in opening up the painful debate about Northern Ireland's violent past and its implications for the post-conflict future. So much lies with the prison's fate: a new future; economic prosperity and the elusive shared society: 'in the appreciation and commemoration of history, there is no substitute for standing in the footsteps of the past, even when that past is painful' (Cohoon McStotts 2007: 285).

Acknowledgements

I would like to thank Professor Brian Graham at the University of Ulster for his constructive comments on this chapter.

References

Arif, Y. (2004) 'The New Past: Remaking Downtown Beirut', Paper presented at The Politics of Cultural Memory Conference at Manchester Metropolitan University, 4–6 November.

Arthur, P. (1997) '"Reading" Violence: Ireland', in D. Apter, *The Legitimization of Violence*, London: Macmillan.

Ashworth, G. and Graham, B. (eds) (2006) *Senses of Time, Senses of Place*, Aldershot, UK: Ashgate.

Azaryahu, M. (1999) 'McDonald's or Golani Junction? A Case of a Contested Place in Israel', *Professional Geographer*, 51: 481–92.

BBC Newsline (2000) 'The Maze: The Prison Officer's Story', 27 November. Available online at: http://news.bbc.co.uk/1/hi/northern_ireland/854665.stm.

BBC On This Day [9 August 1971] 'NI enacts internment law'. Available online at: http://news.bbc.co.uk/onthisday/hi/dates/stories/august/9/newsid_4071000/4071849.stm.

Buntman, F. and Huang, T. (2000) 'The role of political imprisonment in developing and enhancing political leadership: A Comparative Study of South Africa and Taiwan's Democratization', *African and Asian Studies*, 35: 43–66.

Cohoon McStotts, J. (2007) 'Internment in the Desert: A Critical Review of Manzanae National Historic Site', *International Journal of Heritage Studies*, 13 (3): 281–87.

Coiste na n-Iarchimí (2003) *A Museum at Long Kesh or the Maze? A Report of Conference Proceedings*, Belfast: Coiste na n-Iarchimí.

Coombes, A. (2003) *Visual Culture and Public Memory in a Democratic South Africa*, Durham and London: Duke University Press.

Crawford, C. (1999) *Defenders of Criminals? Loyalist Prisoners and Criminalization*, Belfast: Blackstaff Press.

Crooke, E. (2005) 'Dealing with the Past: Museums and Heritage in Northern Ireland and South Africa', *International Journal of Heritage Studies*, 11: 131–42.

Dewar, M. and Fredericksen, C. (2003) 'Prison Heritage, Public History and Archaeology at Fannie Bay Gaol, Northern Australia', *International Journal of Heritage Studies*, 9: 45–63.

Dowler, L. (1998) '"They think I'm just a nice old lady": Women and the War in Belfast', *Gender, Place, Culture*, 5: 159–76.

Edkins, J. (2003), *Trauma and the Memory of Politics*, Cambridge: Cambridge University Press.

Folger, J.P. and Bush, R.A. (eds) (2001) *Designing Mediation: Approaches to Training and Practice with a Transformative Framework*, New York: Institute for Conflict Transformation.

Foote, K. (2003) *Shadowed Ground: America's Landscapes of Violence and Tragedy*, Texas: University of Texas Press.

Foucault, M. (1991) *Discipline and Punish*, trans. Sheridan, A., London: Penguin.

Goodfellow, R. (2002) 'Forgetting what it was to Remember the Indonesian Killings of 1965–6' in K. Christie and R. Cribb (eds), *Historical Injustice and Democratic Transition in East Asia and Northern Europe*, London and New York: Routledge.

Gordon, D. (2005a) 'H-Block is granted listed status', *Belfast Telegraph*, 16 May.

Gordon, D. (2005b) '"Erase prison from map" call; Prison Officers' leader slams Sinn Féin claim', *Belfast Telegraph*, 20 May.

Graham, B. and McDowell, S. (2007) 'The Future Past of Long Kesh', *Cultural Geographies*, 14 (3): 343–68.

Hennessey, T. (1997) *A History of Northern Ireland*, New York: St Martin's Press.

Irwin, T. (2003) 'Prison Education in Northern Ireland: Learning from our Paramilitary Past', *The Howard Journal*, 42: 471–84.

Jackson, R. and Henrie, R. (1983) 'Perceptions of Sacred Space', *Journal of Cultural Geography*, 3: 84–107.

Jarman, N. (2000) 'Material Remnants: Dealing with the remains of conflict in Northern Ireland', in J. Schofield, J. William Gray and C.J. Beck (eds) *Matériel Culture: The Archaeology of 20th Century Conflict*, London and New York: Routledge.

Lederach, J. (1995) *Preparing for Peace: Conflict Resolution across Cultures*, Syracuse: Syracuse University Press.

Linenthal, E. (2001) *Sacred Ground: Americans and their Battlefields*, Urlana: University of Illinois Press.

Lowenthal, D. (1985) *The Past is a Foreign Country*, Cambridge: Cambridge University Press.

McAdam. N. (2007) 'New Assembly will have final say on future of former jail grounds', *Belfast Telegraph*, 3 April.

McAtackney, L. (2005) 'Long Kesh/Maze: An Archaeological Opportunity', *British Archaeology*, 85.

McDonald, S. (2006) 'Undesirable Heritage: Fascist Material Culture and Historical Consciousness in Nuremberg', *International Journal of Heritage Studies*, 12: 9–28.

McDowell, S. (2006) 'Commemorating the Troubles: Unravelling the representation of the contestation of memory in Northern Ireland since 1994', Unpublished thesis: University of Ulster.

McKay, N. (2000) 'Unionist anger as mayor releases terrorist', *The Sunday Herald*, 30 July.

McKinley, S. (2006) 'No! 86.7% reject move to Maze: 42,500 seater gets thumbs down', *Belfast Telegraph*, 16 January.

Mullin, J. (2000) 'Symbol of a painful peace: Largest one-day exodus in 30 years sees 78 freed from prison', *The Guardian*, 29 July.

Murray Brown, J. (2004) 'Challenge of finding a way forward for the Maze', *Financial Times*, 12 October.

Neill, W.J. (2006) 'Return to the Titanic and Lost in the Maze', *Space and Polity*, 10: 109–120.

OFMDFM (2005) *Maze Consultation Panel Final Report*, Belfast: OFMDFM.

O'Malley, P. (1990) *Biting at the Grave: The Irish Hunger Strikes and the Politics of Despair*, Boston: Beacon Press.

O'Raw, R. (2005) *Blanketmen: An Untold Story of the H-Block Hunger Strike*, Dublin: New Island.

Petkovic, N. (2005) 'Officers and Gentlemen: The Impress of Tragedy and Violence', *Neohelicon*, 32: 35–41.

Purbrick, L. (2004) 'The Architecture of Containment: The H-Blocks of Long Kesh/Maze and the Representation of Conflict in Northern Ireland', paper presented at the *Politics of Cultural Memory Conference* at the University of Durham, 4–6 November.

Riley, J. (2002) 'The Pains of Imprisonment: Exploring a Classic Text with Contemporary Authors', *Journal of Criminal Justice Education*, 13: 443–61.

Roth, M. (1995) *Ironist's Cage: The Memory, Trauma and the Construction of History*, New York: Columbia University Press.

Ryder, C. (2000) *Inside the Maze: The Untold Story of the Northern Ireland Prison Service*, London: Methuen.

Schreiner, K.H. (2002) 'Remembering and Forgetting at Lubang Buaya: The Coup of 1965 in Contemporary Indonesian Historical Perception and Public Commemoration', in K. Christie and R. Cribb (eds), *Historical Injustice and Democratic Transition in East Asia and Northern Europe*, London and New York: Routledge.

Shirlow, P. (2006) 'Belfast: The Post-conflict City', *Space and Polity*, 10: 99–107.

Shirlow, P., Graham, B., McEvoy, K., Ó hAdhmail, F. and Purvis, D. (2006) 'Politically Motivated Former Prisoner Groups: Community Activism and Conflict Transformation', Belfast: Community Relations Council.

Sugden, J. (1995) *Sport and Community Relations in Northern Ireland*, Coleraine: University of Ulster/Community Relations Council.

Sykes, G. (1958) *The Society of Captives: A Study of a Maximum Security Prison*, Princeton: Princeton University Press.

Till, K.E. (2005) *The New Berlin: Memory, Politics, Place*, Minnesota: University of Minnesota Press.

Von Tangen Page, M. (2006) "A Most Difficult and Unpalatable Part": The Release of Politically Motivated Violent Offenders', in M. Cox, A. Guelke and F. Stephen (eds), *A Farewell To Arms? Beyond the Good Friday Agreement*, Manchester: Manchester University Press.

Part IV

Places of benevolent internment

Chapter 14

Beauty springing from the breast of pain

Spencer Leineweber[1]

Wild seas crash onto lava rocks spit long ago from the peninsula's volcano; the devil-winds of Pelekunu bend trees to the ground; a cataclysmic landslide formed 2,000-foot cliffs from the sloping tableland of the rest of the island. It is a place set apart by nature, the perfect place to isolate those with the separating sickness. From 1866 until 1969, people afflicted with leprosy or Hansen's disease[2] were quarantined for life at Kalaupapa (lit. flat leaf in Hawaiian), the remote northern peninsula of Molokai, an island roughly in the center of the Hawaiian Islands chain. Two Catholic religious from their community have been beatified and today 30 patients, sent to the settlement as young children, still call the National Historic Landmark of Kalaupapa their home. It is a place where human nature has created a community of both extraordinary and ordinary people, and where "beauty springing from the breast of pain" can be clearly seen in both (Stevenson 1889: n.p.).[3] The conservation work at Kalaupapa has had to adjust in the last twenty years to the active nature of the settlement in order to provide for continuing care of the patients and to interpret a resource like no other.

This disfiguring disease first arrived in Hawaii in the early 1830s from Chinese sailors jumping ship in the port of Honolulu; the disease still bears the name in the Hawaiian language of *mai pake,* or Chinese sickness. The disease was rampant by the 1850s, when Honolulu was a community of divergent interests; it was foreign traders versus pious missionaries. At the time, leprosy was considered incurable, a disease of licentiousness and inflicted on sinners; it was only proper for a newly Christianized monarchy to control the spread by passing a law of isolation to the government lands of the Molokai peninsula; there was not much initial thought for long term care. At first the settlement was established on the eastern or windward side of the peninsula at Kalawao, since an existing Hawaiian community, growing sweet potato and taro, occupied the more habitable leeward side at Kalaupapa. The patients were thrown roughly into the sea from the transport ships to swim to shore. Many did not make it; those that did were forced to grow their own food and build their own homes. Early days of the settlement were lawless; tales of rape, murder and painful death spread to Honolulu. Parents hid children who contracted the disease with the result that the disease spread quickly among closely related families. Although the disease is highly communicable only 5% per cent of the typical population has the genetic disposition for the disease. Today the graves bear witness to the death of more than 7,000 people afflicted with the disease and forced into exile to die on this isolated peninsula.

In 1980 the United States Federal government passed legislation to create the Kalaupapa National Historical Park to "preserve the only intact historic institutional settlement in the United States created for the sole purpose of isolating Hansen's disease (leprosy) patients from the rest of society" (United States Government 1980: 96–565). The Park includes 15,645 acres of land and water only 23 acres of which are owned by the federal government. The Park is managed through several cooperative agreements with different State of Hawaii agencies. The area defined by the Park boundaries is under the control of many State Departments, including Hawaiian Home Lands (DHHL), Health (DOH), Land and Natural Resources (DLNR), and Transportation (DOT). The Department of Hawaiian Home Lands manages a land trust of former Crown Land as future homesteads for native Hawaiians, a total of over 200,000 acres statewide. The health and subsistence of the remaining patients is the responsibility of the Department of Health. The natural and heritage resources are the concern of the Department of Land and Natural Resources and the airport is controlled by the Department of Transportation. These cooperating agreements give the long-term preservation and interpretive management of the settlement to the National Park Service which operates several other Parks statewide with resources that are at times much easier to manage than the issues at Kalaupapa. The Park's Kalaupapa mission includes a comprehensive view of the cultural landscape including the prehistoric and historic settlements, the marine habitat of the Hawaiian monk seal, and extensive valleys of endangered native plants.

Initially the patient community was not enthusiastic at this new federal intervention despite its good intentions. In 1909 the US Leprosy Investigation Station (USLIS) had been built on the peninsula with $300,000 and a complete lack of understanding of the psychology of patient care. Two barbed wire fences, ten feet apart, "protected" doctors from contact with patients and only nine patients were treated in just over four years (Hanley 1991: 385). "To people accustomed to ministrations by devoted missionaries such as Father Damien, Brother Dutton, and Mother Marianne ... who had no qualms about mingling with the patients, the sterile atmosphere, locked gates, and unfamiliar equipment of the station held no attraction" (Greene 1985: 290). There was no desire among the late twentieth century patients to be another federal experiment. The patients perceived the collapsing buildings around them as a triumph as it signaled the end of a tragic chapter in the history of Hawaii (Law and Wayne 1989: n.p.).

Since the requirement for isolation ended in 1969, today the patients come and go, and it is the outsider who is restricted, as permission to enter must be by invitation from the State, the National Park Service or a patient. Most visitors come as part of a patient-run mule ride down the steep cliffs from top-side Molokai. The desire is to see the settlement neighborhoods and especially the structures associated with Father Damien and Mother Marianne, the two beatified nine-

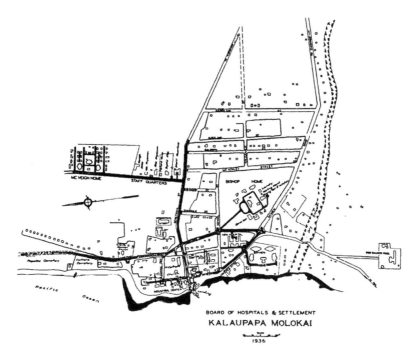

Figure 14.1 Western side of the Kalaupapa Peninsula, Board of Hospitals and Settlement 1936. McVeigh Home is in the upper left, Bishop Home in the middle and Bay View Home in the lower right. (Source: Hawaii State Archives).

teenth century Catholic caregivers to the community. Damien's St Philomena was restored in 1989 to mark the 100th year celebration of Damien's death; the McVeigh and Bay View neighborhoods were conserved in 2005, and Marianne's Bishop Home was repaired in 2007. Each of these locations has had a slightly different conservation approach and treatment illustrating the changing demands of preservation within the settlement during this nearly twenty-year period.

The Belgian priest who gave his life caring for the patients at Kalaupapa was Joseph de Veuster of the Congregation of the Sacred Hearts of Jesus and Mary, or Father Damien. He was sent from Belgium as a novitiate to replace the position secured by his own brother, Auguste, or Father Pamphile, SS.CC, who had contracted typhoid fever. Father Damien was ordained in the Cathedral of Our Lady of Peace in Honolulu in 1864. He spent several years in the island parishes of Hawaii and Molokai until he accepted the call to minister to the exiled patients at Kalaupapa in 1873. As Gavin Daws wrote in his book, *Holy Man*, "Damien was an unusual man living in a turbulence of holiness. ... He emerged as a trouble maker in the eyes of his superiors, who knew him as a person, and as a hero in the eyes of the world, where he was known by what he did" (Daws 1973: 249).

When Damien arrived most patients were dying from the poor living conditions and scarce food. They were living "pell-mell, without distinction of ages or sexes, old or new cases, all more or less strangers one to another, those unfortunate outcasts of society" (Damien 1886: 2). He was able to bring the needed focus to the settlement to improve conditions for all the patients, as well as to provide them with religious solace. The church where Father Damien ministered to these spiritual needs was St Philomena.

St Philomena has had several changes to respond to the needs of the Catholic patients. Initially, in 1872 Sacred Hearts Brother Victorian Bertrant SS.CC had a wooden chapel pre-cut in Honolulu and transported to the site in pieces; in 1876 Father Damien added a new wooden transept to form a cross with the original construction; in 1888 Damien tripled the size of the building with a masonry addition to serve his expanding congregation (Greene 1985: 577). Damien filled the space for mass three times on Sundays. (Daws 1984: 85) Although initially buried with his people next to the Church, Damien's remains were exhumed in 1936 at the request of King Leopold III and reburied at St Joseph's Church in Louvain, Belgium. He was beatified in June 1994.

Although the Church was the number one priority for restoration within the settlement, St Philomena could not be repaired by the National Park Service or the State of Hawaii. The building was in a catch-22 situation: the structure was owned by the Roman Catholic Diocese of Honolulu but no longer a consecrated church; the land was owned by the Department of Hawaiian Home Lands but kept in trust for native Hawaiians; the patients who wanted it preserved were "indigent wards of the state"; and the management was to be by the National Park Service but not for possibly forty plus years. Due to the separation of Church and State, no government agency could expend any funds for capital improvements. Led by patient Bernard Punikaia, a non-profit group was organized to protect and repair St Philomena. The patients invited a representative of each interested group to be a member of the executive committee and the "Friends of Father Damien" was formed. This Friends group raised the funds and oversaw the conservation construction for nearly a three-year period.

The type of conservation work to be undertaken at St Philomena was initially under debate. The National Park Service had recommended that the building be stabilized; i.e., just repaired, with no restoration to any previous period. This decision had been made because at the time of the Park Service investigation, minimal documentary evidence had been found concerning the interior of the building. Restoration to the Damien period was not possible. Damien had died before the bell tower had been completed, and an ornate entry portico constructed by Damien had no remaining physical evidence. The patient group felt quite strongly that the Church should be restored to 1932, the date that the settlement had moved to the other side of the peninsula from Kalawao to Kalaupapa; 24 December 1932 was the last time daily services had been held within the building. There were several patients still alive who remembered the Church in this period and they put out a call for photographic documentation. Dozens of

Figure 14.2 St Philomena Church, Kalawao, Kalaupapa Settlement, 2004. (Source: S. Leineweber)

time-worn photographs of weddings and funerals appeared from family albums. With the exception of emergency carpentry work by the US Marines to replace the rear façade after Hurricane Ewa in 1982 and many coats of paint, the Church was remarkably intact to the 1932 period.

The success of the construction was largely dependent on the respect of the carpentry crew for the complexity of the job to be undertaken. The project was competitively bid in the public sector using a list of pre-qualified contractors familiar with conservation work. Each was notified of the restrictions concerning living within the community and the difficulty of material access to the site. These restrictions were imposed on the living conditions of the workers due to the sensitive nature and privacy concerns of the patients in the settlement. For a year the construction company lived in a Quonset Hut as temporary housing, worked an eight-day work-week, and then traveled back to Honolulu for six days. All of the food and supplies needed to be brought in to the peninsula as only patients were permitted to purchase food at the State run store. With the exception of the settlement staff, they were the first significant group of "outsiders" to stay within the community since the building of the USLIS in 1909.

Material and travel access to the Kalaupapa peninsula is severely limited. There are no roads to the peninsula from top-side Molokai; many travel to the site by means of a three-mile foot trail which descends the cliffs in 26 switchbacks or by the twice daily light commuter plane when weather permits. The once a year material delivery barge is only possible in late August or early September due to the rough seas the rest of the year.

The contractor recognized the importance of the preservation of the original fabric at St Philomena even in its deteriorated state and a careful measured approach was taken for the construction. In most restoration projects the quality of the craftsmanship is paramount for preservation; at Saint Philomena, it was the lack of craftsmanship, the obvious physical struggle in joinery that was important to be preserved. The conservation decision was made to repair all structural wood by leaving the Damien construction intact and adding new clearly marked members adjacent to the original construction.

The first task was to secure the roof trusses to the top of the masonry walls. Archival research noted three letters from Father Damien to Bishop Herman Koeckemann SS.CC. in Honolulu asking for guidance on how to secure the roof trusses to the tops of the lava rock walls. Damien was a knowledgeable carpenter; he had built churches on the island of Hawaii and on top-side Molokai before he permanently moved to the settlement. However, all of these churches had been simple wood framed structures. There was neither archival record of the answer to Damien's request nor any physical evidence in the field that he ever received one. Only gravity kept the roof structure in place, there was no permanent attachment of any kind to the top of the walls. Before the onset of the next hurricane season the existing trusses were strapped and bolted onto the masonry walls without damage to the existing framework. Another immediate repair was new support for the large bronze bell in the church tower. The bell had broken away from its wooden frame and was lodged precariously on the uneven rocks of the inner walls of the tower just fifteen feet above the main entry to the Church used by the tour groups every day.

For exposed millwork, epoxy was used to preserve the damaged millwork, which had colorful painted finishes. The epoxy was donated by a Belgian company, de Neef Chemie, who were interested in being part of the conservation work after its President visited the Church. Not only did they supply the materials free of charge but they provided a two-week on site training to the carpentry crew in the correct use of their materials. Without this assistance it would not have been possible to keep the Damien materials intact as only a layer of paint remained for wood long ago eaten by drywood termites.

These historic paint finishes were at first difficult to analyze. Oral histories indicated the colors were very bright due to the reduced vision of many patients. Yet microscopic paint analysis provided mixed results, since the wood particularly in the 1876 addition had seen several previous lives in other buildings. Due to the scarcity of building materials on the peninsula, it was common practice to disassemble one building to build another more useful one. So there were multiple layers of paint already on the wood when it was first used within the Church structure. An elderly patient who came most days to "supervise" the restoration finally admitted he was an altar boy in 1930; he picked out very specific colors from the Munsell color chips. This was later re-confirmed when these colors were found as the base color for new elements known to have been added in 1930.

A great debate within the Friends group ensued over another finish, the re-painting of the irregular block lines on the interior of the church walls. Photographic documentation confirmed that the lines had been added in 1909. Members of the Friends group who were not patients wanted the pristine quality of the white plaster to provide a relief next to the wild greens and blues of the woodwork. The patients wanted the blood-red lines as their nature told of the hardship and pain of the painting. Punikaia would not compromise, insisting the lines were part of who he was as a person. The lines were a trial for the painter as well as it took him five times longer than he had originally estimated to repaint the lines; none of the lines were straight or in any regular pattern. The most recent layer of lines was also different than the underneath 1909 layer. The visiting altar boy had a daily tease with the Korean painter. He joked with him saying that since the painter was a Buddhist and not a Catholic, he required a much longer time in meditation when in the presence of God. The original Catholic painters, he said, had done it in no time at all.

Another substantial hurdle in the restoration of St Philomena was the difficulty in material and equipment delivery. While the drawings delineated the work to be done with a certain amount of precision, often the length of members needed to be "just a little bit longer" than what was ordered before the project began. This was a tremendous problem with no lumber yard down the road. Every additional wood member needed to be flown in on the twice-weekly air cargo service at tremendous cost. The lumber was limited to the size of the hold in the light aircraft, just under 20 feet in length. When the project was threatened with a shut down due to a lack of materials making the project "miss" the intended one-hundred-year memorial service, the US Marines came to the rescue and flew in the needed items. In order not to compete with any private commercial interests, the materials were first barged to the Molokai harbor at Kaunakakai on the opposite side of the island, trucked to the top of the cliff, and then air-lifted by the Marines in huge cargo nets down to the site.

The US Army Reserves also became an essential part of the project when they scheduled a training exercise to re-grade the dirt road to the site. They were able to bring a landing craft to one of the beaches despite the heavy seas, and their small bulldozer and road grader assisted in changing the slope of the road to the site. A build-up of dirt on one side of the road had made flooding of the road quite common; in the heaviest rains the only outlet to this mile long surface was the entry path and doorway to the Church. The result was mud in the Church after a heavy winter rain; the high water mark on the interior walls was just under 30 inches. The Army Reserves scraped down the road in a two-week reserve duty period to create a swale in the opposite direction to make the storm water flow away from the Church.

A problem at St Philomena has been the continued maintenance of the building. Repairs to the building have been made over time with the best of intentions but not with the best of results. In 1995 a sacred relic comprising the remains of

Damien's right hand was returned to the original grave at Kalawao. In preparation for this ceremony, portions of the interior of the building were painted; this time with a latex paint without the proper undercoat. This coat of paint blistered the layers put on in 1989 with a result that was less than satisfactory. Not horrified at all with the problem, one of the patients touched his arm and said that the ceiling now matched the rest of them. Water continues to seep in through hairline cracks in the exterior wall causing significant efflorescence on the interior. The block lines were painted on gypsum plaster, which is highly hydroscopic, so any water in the wall soon appears as efflorescence on the interior.

The 1932 date for the St Philomena restoration was an important milestone in the settlement's history. Most of the community moved from the windward side at Kalawao to Kalaupapa because substantial expansion needed to be made to the settlement. A false sense of a cure for leprosy had been created by faith in chaulmoogra oil. Chaulmoogra treatment was undertaken at the US Leprosy Investigation Station in Honolulu rather than at Kalaupapa. No new patients were isolated on the peninsula for nearly five years in the mid 1920s. "A few paroled patients going to their homes and describing the therapeutic and administrative methods of the station, has had a greater effect in inducing sufferers from leprosy to seek treatment than all the legal requirements or scientific discussions that can be invoked" (US Government 1921: 79). Unfortunately, these "paroled patients" thinking themselves cured had spread the disease to their families and produced a problem of epidemic proportions. Chaulmoogra treatment, despite the perceived success, was not a cure.

Many of the buildings that remain today on the leeward side of the peninsula are a result of this need to expand the settlement for the isolation of the many new patients sent to Kalaupapa in the 1930s. The Kalaupapa side of the settlement was organized into distinct neighborhoods or "Homes" each with a slightly different purpose. The National Park Service has undertaken the conservation work on three of these neighborhoods, Bay View Home, McVeigh Home, and Bishop Home.

Bay View Home was built as a series of large dormitory buildings and a central dining hall for the aged and blind male patients. The original Bay View Home of 1901 was destroyed by fire in 1914, a perpetual problem in the settlement, and a new Home was constructed in 1917 for 96 patients, and then improved in the 1930s expansion. The neighborhoods were tight communities of patients who depended on each other. As Helen Keao, a resident of Kalaupapa since 1942, said: "The old timers used to line the walkway of Bay View Home in the afternoon. They were the worst cases. Half were blind. The others who could see would give the others a running description, in Hawaiian, of everything they were seeing" (quoted in Law and Wayne 1989: n.p.). Bay View Home is still used for patients today, for the Volunteers in the Park program of the Park Service, and for offices. One patient in the building did not want to move as he had been in the same room for nearly fifty years. Conservation work on these buildings, due to difficulties in the removal of asbestos and lead paint with existing patients in

Figure 14.3 St Elizabeth Chapel, Bishop Home, Kalaupapa Settlement, 2005. (Source: S. Leineweber)

the buildings, included only new roofing, structural repairs, fire sprinklers, and touch-up painting.

A special neighborhood, McVeigh Homes, was built for "white foreigners" with leprosy. The neighborhood was constructed in 1908, re-built after fire in 1928, and then again improved in the 1930s expansion. The Caucasian patients had a difficult time in the settlement as they were not accustomed to the standard diet used for the native Hawaiian patients. Fourteen cottages were built to house one, two or three patients, as well as two eleven-room dormitories with a common eating hall and kitchen. The patients still reside in the small cottages, federal workers live in the dormitories, and the eating hall continues to be used for parties and other community activities.

These residences at McVeigh Homes were adaptations of plantation homes constructed by the sugar industry in the 1920s. The Hawaii Sugar Planters Association had issued standardized plans to all sugar plantations to improve the living conditions of sugar workers in 1919. These plans needed to be approved by the Territorial Department of Health. Later this same Department adapted these plans for their own housing problem at Kalaupapa.

The conservation problems found in the active settlement side of the peninsula are slightly different than those found at St Philomena. Saint Philomena was isolated from the active community and work could be undertaken without seriously impacting the life of the community. The St Philomena contractor lived in temporary housing, and drove over every day to Kalawao to undertake the work. However, the influx of new daily workers, mostly sub-contractors who were not familiar with the settlement etiquette, created a very unsettled feeling for many patients; they felt there were too many outsiders wandering around their community. A new method of delivery for undertaking the construction work was required.

Recent conservation work for the Homes has been undertaken as a special training project for the National Park Service's Historic Preservation Training Center (HPTC) based in Frederick, Maryland. The National Park Service has twelve training centers throughout the United States dedicated to developing specific skills for Park Service employees. The HPTC trains National Park Service employees in the skills needed to preserve the historic structures within the Park system. In addition, they develop partnerships with other Federal, State, and local agencies responsible for the stewardship of historically significant cultural resources.

A distinct advantage of the HPTC work within the Kalaupapa National Historical Park is the ability to cross-train local Park employees, as well as local construction workers in the special skills needed for conservation work. Three types of workers are used on the HPTC projects within the Park: park maintenance workers, exhibit specialists, who have completed the three-year training program offered by HPTC in Frederick, and one- or two-year contract employees from the local construction labor pool of top-side Molokai. Several times during each of the recent projects shorter term assignments have been made to send HPTC personnel from other Parks to Kalaupapa to undertake specialty training, such as putty-glazing of windows or shaping decorative millwork. Another advantage of this system is that the workers are Park Service employees wearing NPS uniforms familiar to the patient community. The repairs to the Kalaupapa neighborhoods have brought the construction workers to live within the settlement and become a part of the community. Many lose in the weekly card games, bring special food to the patients in the hospital, or practice hula on mid-week evenings. Personnel assigned from other parks undertake the smaller sub-contractor tasks, such as electrical and plumbing always wearing the Park Service uniform.

The conservation process also had to be approached slightly differently. With a dedicated long term construction crew, it was possible to order the materials for use in much larger shipments. Since there is a standard size lumber used during each building period within the settlement, the exact takeoffs were not as tightly controlled, as wood not used on one building can be used to repair the next. It was possible to order enough wood, roofing shingles, and paint to accomplish the work on many buildings with delivery by the more efficient barge system. With the HPTC crew working regular weekly shifts rather than on a "get it done as fast as possible" basis, the quality of the work has improved as workers became more familiar with the unusual construction materials, such as single board bearing walls.

The presentation of the construction documents was also done in a different manner to improve the efficiency of the repairs and accuracy of recording of the actual work undertaken. The conservation work was delineated in the plan view of the architectural drawings and the quantity more fully by a very detailed material estimate. The construction team recorded the members actually replaced on the elevation drawings of each building. This allowed for an appropriate record of the treatment process, recording the exact work accomplished in this year of the settlement's history.

At all times the conservation product was approached with a clear knowledge that the Park is still in its period of significance. Interpretation of the settlement must be secondary to patient care. The Church was isolated from the active community and can be interpreted without infringing on the everyday lives of the patients. The work at McVeigh is done carefully so that it can be a resource for later interpretation of the settlement, as well as be maintained as a fully functioning part of the community. To allow the breadth of interpretation at Kalaupapa, a few buildings within the McVeigh neighborhood have had a different kind of treatment, stabilization and moth-balling.

These buildings are associated with specific "ordinary" patients such as the studio of artist Ed Kato. This house will not be re-used to house settlement patients or State or NPS employees. Work accomplished included a new roof, new windows, fire sprinklers, exterior painting, and structural repairs but no other changes were made. Kato's personal belongings were packed away by the NPS curatorial staff. Left for future interpretation will be the adaptations made by him to open a window or the marks he made to turn the front door knob. His changes are part of the sad story of his life within the building; yet, this sadness is balanced by the absolute joy of paint splashes on the interior walls. Ed Kato was not a famous artist; he was not even a very good artist; but he loved to paint, and he painted everything, from the towering cliffs of the cultural landscape to faces on rocks left on the porches of friends. The last rocks he painted were happy faces near the grave of Mother Marianne at Bishop Home.

The complex known as the Bishop Home has had several very different configurations throughout its long history that impact its interpretation and future use. It is difficult to perceive the dense former development on the site from the four existing buildings that remain today. Honolulu banker Charles Reed Bishop donated $5,000 to establish a home for orphaned girls in Kalaupapa in 1889. The context statement written by Linda Greene in the Historic Resources study for Kalaupapa, *Exiles in Paradise*, notes, that "historically, the Bishop Home is important to the development of the settlement as one of the earliest humanitarian attempts to care for young girls and women sent to the settlement. ... The home became a model of institutional living as the Bishop family and the state continued to pour money into its improvement over the years ... its creation is one of the earliest chapters in the development of Kalaupapa settlement" (Greene 1985: 621). It is also the home of the work of another much loved member of the community, Mother Marianne Cope.

King Kalakaua of Hawaii approached the Catholic Church to provide nurse-sisters to care for those with leprosy in the monarchy's hospitals. The only group willing to undertake this difficult task was the Sisters of St Francis from Syracuse, New York. At the age of 45, the Reverend Mother Marianne Cope, the Provincial of the Mother House came with six sisters in November 1883. Their main task was to manage the monarchy's Kakaako Branch Hospital on Oahu, which served as a receiving station for patients gathered from all over the islands before they were sent to Kalaupapa. In 1888 the Hospital closed and Mother Marianne volunteered with two sisters to go to Kalaupapa to run the new Bishop Home for Orphaned Girls and continue the Baldwin Home for Orphaned Boys begun by Father Damien. "She was modest and shunned publicity of any kind, very few people beyond the limits of the Leprosarium knew about the Franciscan efforts in Hawaii. The world, having discovered, admired, and lost Father Damien went on believing that he was the only one who gave up his life for the lepers" (Hanley 1991: 375). Mother Marianne Cope spent thirty years in the settlement and died there in 1918.

Mother Marianne provided a different kind of care than Father Damien to the patients at Kalaupapa. Both genuinely cared about the patients and improved their livelihood. Mother Marianne made a real home for both her charges and for her fellow sisters. Her love for the patients can be understood in this quote by Robert Louis Stevenson:[3]

> As for the girls in the Bishop Home, of the many beautiful things I have been privileged to see in life, they, and what has been done for them, are not the least beautiful … The dormitories were airy, the beds neatly made; at every bed-head was a trophy of Christmas cards, pictures and photographs, some framed with shells, and all arranged with care and taste. In many of the beds, besides, a doll lay pillowed.
> (Balfour 1910: n.p. as quoted in Law and Wayne 1989: n.p.)

Even today, Sisters of St Francis provide care for the infirm at Kalaupapa living in the convent at Bishop Home; no Franciscan sisters have ever contracted Hansen's disease. In 1974 procedures were begun also to promote Mother Marianne to sainthood and in January 2005 her body was exhumed from her grave and removed to the Sister House in Syracuse, New York. She was beatified in May 2005.

The National Park Service generally does not repair a building until it has been released to them for Park use. Often when that happens the building has become so deteriorated it is almost beyond repair. Fortunately, an agreement was made on the repairs required to Bishop Home while the building was still used by the sisters. New electrical systems, weatherproofing including new wood shingle roof and wood windows, as well as a fire sprinkler systems were added to the building with the provision that when it is no longer needed by the Convent it will be turned over to the Park Service. In addition two small sister cottages have been repaired.

These buildings are constructed using canec, a fiberboard made from bagasse a by-product of sugar manufacture. These two buildings are the only known buildings in Hawaii constructed of this material as a structural exterior wall.

The conservation work at Bishop Home also presented a different problem because the site has changed substantially as it continues to be used by the Sisters. There is only a portion of the original chapel that remains from the Mother Marianne period. While the best preservation philosophy is to respect a site through time, consideration must also be given to how best to tell the entire story. There is a strong associative value with the cultural landscape of the site, particularly trees and landscape planted by Mother Marianne. However, there are no complete buildings from the strongest period of significance and no dormitory buildings for the period when it was used as an orphanage. None of the large orphanage buildings remain at Kalaupapa when there have been three in its history where at one time hundreds of orphaned children were cared for.

This is the greatest preservation dilemma for the entire settlement. As a site still in its original use, the highest priority still must be given to patient care. However, there is an unfortunate corollary to this that is also true. As the patient numbers diminish, the State has fewer funds to spend on repairing buildings, so the buildings that it controls are deteriorating rapidly. The harsh winds and sea air accelerate the deterioration. When the NPS signed the cooperating agreements in 1980 there were more than 400 buildings inventoried as part of the historic resource; now there are less than 200 (Soulliere and Law 1979). As the groups with an interest in the settlement make claims for their "own" such as the exhumation of both Father Damien and Mother Marianne, or even the removal of patients effects by family members, the site will change and the ability to interpret the entire 150-year story becomes more problematic. The bubbled paint, rocks with smiling faces, irregular block lines, and empty gravesites are there to remind one not to focus just on preserving the buildings. The people are essential to the complete story. The story of leprosy at Kalaupapa is a sad one, and as the settlement evolves into a National Park and the last patient is placed silently into the final grave, it must be remembered that Kalaupapa is a place about people who were sent away from their families to live in isolation in a very desolate place. They made that place not only a home but also a family where both laughing and crying could occur at the same time.

Notes

1 Spencer Leineweber FAIA has been the historical architect for all the architectural work discussed in this chapter.
2 Leprosy, is now legislated in Hawaii as Hansen's disease in an attempt to eliminate this centuries-old stigma. Hansen's disease was named in honor of the Norwegian physician, Gerhard Armauer Henrik Hansen, who in 1873 discovered the bacillus, *Mycobacterium leprae*, the first microbe found to be the causative agent of any human disease.
3 Robert Louis Stevenson visited Kalaupapa for eight days in May 1889 and wrote a letter to Reverend Sister Maryanne [sic] Matron of the Bishop Home on the day he met her, May

22. The letter contained the following poem:

To see the infinite pity of this place,
The mangled limb, the devastated face,
The innocent sufferers smiling at the rod,
A fool were tempted to deny his God.
He sees, and shrinks; But if he look again,

Lo, beauty springing from the breast of pain!
He marks the sisters on the painful shores,
And even a fool is silent and adores.

A facsimile of the poem is reproduced in Emmet Cahill (1990: 87).

References

Balfour, Graham, Sir (1910) *The Life of Robert Louis Stevenson*, 5th edn, London: Methuen.

Cahill, E. (1990) *Yesterday at Kalaupapa*, Honolulu: Editions Limited.

Damien, J. (1886) *Special Report from Rev. Father J. Damien, Catholic Priest at Kalawao. Personal Experience During Thirteen Years of Labor Among the Lepers at Kalawao*, MS., Hawaii State Archives, Honolulu, March 1.

Daws, G. (1984) *Holy Man: Father Damien of Molokai*, Honolulu: University of Hawaii.

Greene, L.K. (1985) *Historic Resource Study: Exiles in Paradise*, Denver: NPS, Denver Service Center.

Hanley, Sister Mary Laurence, OSF and Bushnell, O A. (1991) *Pilgrimage and Exile: Mother Marianne of Molokai*, Honolulu: University of Hawaii Press.

Law, A.S. and Wayne, L. (1989) *Kalaupapa + A Portrait*, Honolulu: Bishop Museum Press.

Soulliere, L.E. and Law, H.G. (1979) *Architectural Evaluation, Kalaupapa – Hawaii*, San Francisco: NPS, Western Regional Office.

Stevenson, Robert Louis (1889) *Letter. "To Reverend Sister Maryanne,"* Archives of the Sisters of St Francis of Syracuse, May 22.

United States Government (1980) Legislation: *Public Law 96– 565*: sec. 101, 102.1, 102.2, 105.2, 105.4.

United States Government (1921) *Annual Report of the Surgeon General of the Public Health Service of the United States.*

Chapter 15

'No less than a palace'
Kew Asylum, its planned surrounds, and its present-day residents

Keir Reeves and David Nichols

The image – like a memory – is evanescent and incomplete, but at the same time exudes a strong emotional resonance.

(Schacter 1995: 27)

Bentham's panopticon penitentiary is a project full of contradiction and ambiguity; a prison that is at the centre of philosophical disquisition, managed by a gaoler who has been depicted both as a ruthless capitalist entrepreneur and as a personification of the utilitarian state.

(Semple 1993: 1)

The buildings, archaeological sites and cultural landscapes of these sites are physical reminders of a regime of forced labour that evokes a strong emotional response.

(Port Arthur Historic Site Plan 2001: 47)

This chapter's objective is to move beyond standard understandings of places of pain and shame in the existing body of literature. It introduces a multidisciplinary heritage approach, focusing on the Kew Lunatic Asylum in Melbourne. This vast, impressive and prominent building highlights the level of government and public focus on benevolence, and benevolent incarceration, prevalent in Victorian era colonial society. When it opened, the Kew Asylum was among the largest such complexes in the world, its creators aspiring to bring forth a model institution that was not only an exemplar of colonial Victorian society[1] but also of the British Empire.

For the purposes of this chapter we use close reading of the specific site and past attitudes towards it in order to provide a more general set of observations about interpreting and understanding sites of benevolent incarceration as places of pain and shame. Strategies for evaluating the interpretation and conservation are provided in this case study of the asylum and its cartilage, which now comprises two housing developments, with a third on the grounds of a comparable institution, Kew Cottages, just beyond its borders.

Pain and shame permeate the cultural fabric of every society, leaving a legacy of tragedy. Such situations often occur as a result of involvement in conflict or adherence to a belief system based on intolerance. The most immediate physical reminders of painful and shameful events of the past in the present day are former places of incarceration and imprisonment. Many prisons, detention centres and hospitals are now heritage buildings, and each site is usually associated in the popular memory with at least one specific tragic historical circumstance. In the case of the Melbourne Asylum the impress of tragedy is not as readily evident as it would be at, say, a massacre site; nonetheless it is regarded as a place typified by broader societal fears regarding madness.

A key factor in the emergence of the modern prison between 1730 and 1850 was the transition from corporal punishment directed at the body to the imposition of discipline directed at the mind. One result of this has been the reformative ideal that functioned, Michael Ignatieff (1978: xiii) states, as a 'vision of humane moral reclamation that has obscured its function as a legitimation for an intensification of carceral power'. He goes on to suggest that during the nineteenth century 'the extension of popular sovereignty was accompanied by the elaboration of institutions and the deployment of philanthropic strategies designed to implant the inner disciplinarians of guilt and compunction' as a means of social control. The inherent paradox in the rise of the modern penal system has also led Ignatieff to investigate 'why it came to be considered just, reasonable, and humane to immure prisoners in solitary cells, clothe them in uniforms, regiment their day to the cadence of the clock, and "improve" their minds with dosages of scripture and hard labour' (Ignatieff 1978: xiii). In this respect the interpretation of sites of imprisonment represents a present-day reflection on the moral boundaries of different societies in previous eras.

Conjecture over the symbolism of sites of imprisonment is not a new phenomenon. During the early modern era in France the Bastille was a key site of incarceration and also the symbol of political imprisonment during the eighteenth century when it was used to confine a number of well-known dissenters. Despite its original function as a prison its enduring historical legacy has been as a place of political dissent, occupying a key place in French national memory into the present day. Likewise, as Neier (1995) has observed, the Tower of London, now a key tourist attraction and cultural heritage site, was once regarded as a place of incarceration but also of dissent. The challenge for heritage practitioners in determining usage strategies of these sites in the present day is to formulate an interpretive framework that communicates the role of what was essentially a prison when it was an active institution while also addressing stakeholders' present-day concerns.

The interpretation, conservation and management of former places of pain and shame presents a particular set of challenges for heritage practitioners. Analysing heritage sites of significance and the way their usage is conditioned by memory provides one way of understanding former sites of imprisonment. Such analysis also provides a multidisciplinary cross-cultural technique in which heritage sites of imprisonment can be interpreted as part of a cohesive heritage management strategy.

Spencer Leineweber in this book notes that Molokai, Kalaupapa, Hawaii, the former site of a leper colony and hospital, was declared a National Historical Park in 1980. Once there were 1,000 patients at Kalaupapa; today its graves outnumber the patients by 200 to 1. When the final patient dies or moves away, the National Park Service will administer the peninsula. The stigma attached to the site and the resultant ostracism towards its inhabitants is still remembered. The pejorative connotations of the term 'leper' are still a delicate matter for the last remaining patients, one of whom commented that 'even after you're cured, society will not let you heal yourself because of the "L" word. "Leper" as a term is similar to a racial epithet' (Yong 2003). The shame surrounding leprosy and the fear it induces has historical precedents; as Foucault commented 'the leper was caught up in the practice of rejection, of exile enclosure' as a result of the extension of disciplinary power throughout the nineteenth and twentieth centuries (Foucault 1977: 198).

Similarly, the political symbolism of Hoa Lo's, or Robben Island's, heritage are often symbolic political statements that address themes and issues beyond these sites' original penal functions (Anon. 1883; Logan 2003; Robben Island Museum 2002). The idea of contested memory provides one way of explaining interpretations of the past and management of these sites in the present. In practical terms this means that management strategies for former sites of imprisonment are often intricately linked with political concerns that revolve around culturally sensitive matters. In turn government policy can find expression in the decision-making processes that determine the significance of a particular site and its interpretation for heritage tourists.

The question of what has and has not been culturally marked is important (Foote 1997: 33). As Foote has argued when discussing the impress of tragedy on the American landscape, it is important not to overlook those that are not readily marked as they are just as informative in spelling out the values a society does not wish to remember (Foote 1997: 7–8). By identifying the historical background of heritage sites and evaluating ways in which they have been interpreted, it is possible to disclose the contested nature of their understanding by present-day observers.[2] This is a process that demonstrates how groups and individuals struggle to shape the past to their own ends (Gillis 1994).

This can also happen at a relatively mundane level; Bridget Franklin has observed of a conversion of a former mental hospital in provincial England that people can resist 'the notion of total denial of the building's past' (2002: 30). In the case she cites, a local councillor and former employee at the hospital made the request that there should be an interpretation centre on the site; this was acceded to.

Historical context to a heritage site

The Kew Asylum building has had a contentious history from its inception. While, as mentioned above, it may have initially been regarded as an exemplar of Victorian-era civic planning, it was also seen by nearby residents as a monolith inappropriate to a burgeoning bourgeois suburb or, in the words of one journalist writing in the late nineteenth century, 'a huge dreary barracks' (*Australasian Medical Gazette* 1883: 44). Such sentiments were to be echoed for a century as various bodies' reports advocated site redevelopment. Redevelopment eventually did take place in the mid-1990s as part of a broader 'heritage-ization' process, a practice that is becoming increasingly central to reinterpreting imprisonment sites (Lennon 2002).[3] Yet we contend that the key role of memory in determining public policy occurs, in cases such as this, by design rather than default.

In 1950 a Melbourne University architecture student visited the Kew Asylum. It filled her with awe:

> This dank and dismal building, the most impressive in Melbourne, has the distinction of being the most complete and costly flop in the city's history. Many things add to its sinister appearance – the dark spotty walls, the slate roof, the long shadows, and most of all the hundreds of black green trees which infest the place. Yet it is a grand and simple building, a fine piece of work; but not as an asylum. It is too prison-like, too monumental. The endless screeching and wailing of the women seems strangely in keeping with this grim environment.
> (McIntosh 1950: 1)

This writer was adding her voice to the many critics of the building's use as an asylum, though many had advocated demolishing the building entirely. When John Cain's state Labor government announced its decision to close the facility in 1988, the proposal to retain and reuse the building was widely supported. As a bold and imposing edifice with a large central tower, it had achieved iconic status early in the twentieth century, if not earlier, and calls for its destruction – which began soon after its erection, due less to the building itself and more to its perceived ill-fit with the institution it housed – had become rare.

The recycling of the building as the central element of upmarket housing was, however, contentious and, the authors argue, should have been more so. The Kew Lunatic Asylum (known since 1960 as Willsmere) was, not unnaturally, seen by many as haunted by a history of the horror, cruelty, fear and misery of both mental illness itself and the often inhumane treatments associated throughout the nineteenth and twentieth century with its cure. Willsmere as it stands today can be regarded – much like Pentridge Gardens in Melbourne's northern suburbs, on land formerly occupied by a notorious maximum security prison – as a 'heritage' development which denies, rather than countenances (much less celebrates), the site's past. This paradoxically reiterates the largely middle-class residents of Kew's attitude to the Asylum – the suburb had always 'turned its back' on or otherwise chosen to ignore it – yet it does a disservice to the Asylum's cultural heritage.

Building the Asylum

The Asylum was first mooted very early in Melbourne's existence: the few people of Kew, at this stage a sparsely populated outer suburb of a Melbourne just entering its third decade, were ambivalent about the proposed establishment on their north-western edge. From the early twentieth century this ambivalence often became direct protest. In 1905, locals' objections led Victorian Premier Bent to announce the buildings' removal, though in fact it was only the abutting Yarra Bend Asylum which was removed (*Kew Advertiser* 1927). State politician W.S. Kent-Hughes, advocating a plan for redevelopment of the Asylum site as a combination of park-land and residential subdivision – the latter to pay for the former – announced:

> The main difficulty with the Kew Asylum is the cost of removal, but its trans-ference to a more suitable site is an urgent necessity for more reasons than one. The buildings are old, very badly constructed, and out-of-date. The sun never reaches certain portions and the general lay-out considerably hampers the work of the doctors.
>
> (*Kew Advertiser* 1927: 2)

Yet only three years later, to the chagrin of Kew's civic fathers, the Depression saw such schemes set aside; when one councillor suggested that the City could expect a windfall from the sale of the Asylum grounds, the laughter from the chamber was ironic – as was, perhaps, the statement that invited it (*Kew Advertiser* 1930).

Graeme Tuer, an architecture student writing in the 1960s, suggested the Kew residents' attitude was the result of 'aesthetic snobbery' relating to the distaste (and fear) felt towards the mentally ill, though perhaps blended with an aesthetic reaction to the structure. Tuer adds that 'as late as 1952, when the Government planned to spend £500,000 for the modernization of the building', thus extending the institution's life, 'public protest was strong' (Tuer 1962:1).

Protestors' ire may well have been magnified in the previous decade as the pros-pect of the Asylum's replacement with another facility at Macleod, Mont Park, was mooted in the 1940s; Mont Park then became merely *another* facility, and Kew remained. Sylvia Morrissey, in her Honours thesis studying the relationship between the Asylum and the surrounding district, suggests that the Asylum never had a direct connection with Kew's residents (Morrissey 1988), though it is notable that a gift of the old Asylum gates was made to the City in the 1940s; stripped of any signifiers, they were installed at the northern end of Victoria Park.

The original 1856 plan for the Asylum by George Vivian, the Public Works Department's Chief Architect, was held in abeyance for some years. Two gate-keepers' houses were built in accordance with the original plan, which underwent redesign eight years later in collaboration with Frederick Kawerau. The 1856 'lodges' have been identified by Miles Lewis, Jenny Carew and Angela Roennfeldt as derived from the book *Villa Rustica* (1848) by Charles Parker, 'regarded as one of the major formative influences in the rise of the domestic Italianate style about the middle of the century' (Lewis *et al.* 1988: 98). One of these buildings was demol-ished in the late 1960s; the other remains the oldest mental health-related building in Victoria (op. cit.: 12). Most commentators are in agreement that for the grand building that stands Vivian 'simply copied plans of existing English asylums'. The

Figure 15.1 Willsmere's isolation from the rest of Kew remains, as this photograph from the west of the buildings demonstrates. (Source: D. Nichols)

British asylum Colney Hatch is most commonly cited as the prime influence for Vivian, whose preference was for a monumentally grand façade (Tuer 1962: 3); this institution was sufficiently familiar to those investigating Kew Asylum in the mid-1870s as to be a yardstick for comparison in matters of economy (Board of Inquiry 1876: 63). Kew Asylum is typified by Morrissey as following 'an anglicized second Empire scheme' externally while starkly utilitarian inside (Morrissey 1988: 33).

Colney Hatch and Hanwell, another British asylum often cited as an influence on Vivian, were planned along the E-plan barracks type, a model already losing favour in Britain by the mid-1850s. Lewis *et al.* suggest that one of the main reasons for Colney Hatch and Hanwell's influential nature in the design of British Empire asylums was their proximity to major cities as much as their architecture or design. It may well be that, as institutions regularly visited by interested and/or professional parties, it was necessary for authorities to present them (or even to conceive them) as world's best practice in ways that would not be necessary for other, more remote, institutions. It should perhaps be countenanced that from Vivian's point of view, an impressive and recognisable *example* of an asylum was what was required for Victoria: his primary concern was, surely, to please his client/employer, the Victorian colonial government's bureaucrats and politicians. Certainly it had to be an ostentatious and grand building, and Morrissey suggests that the prime motivation for the siting of the Asylum derives 'from the proximity of the heights of Studley Park, to the low ground of Yarra Bend' (Morrissey 1988: 26).

Figure 15.2 Graeme Tuer's image of the main Asylum building in the early 1960s. (Courtesy of G. Tuer)

In 1864, Vivian prepared designs for institutions at the rural towns of Ararat and Beechworth as well as for a revised version of the still-unbuilt asylum at Kew. In this last, the ultimate responsibility for the design was given to Kawerau, 'a German architect on the staff of the Public Works Department, who had assisted Vivian with the original scheme' (Lewis *et al.* 1988: 17). After further controversy and accusations of poor workmanship against builder John Young, the building was opened in 1872. Lewis *et al.* tell us that it shortly came to be felt, among the wider and the professional community, that 'the colonial government [had] backed the wrong horse' (Lewis *et al.* 1988: 21) in opting for such an epic construction at a time when smaller, cottage-style accommodation was becoming more fashionable – an example of this, for a different purpose, being the Old Colonists' Association at North Fitzroy set up by Melbourne theatre-owner George Coppin (Barrett 1971).

While the asylum functioned well as a symbol of the new colony's wealth (trumpeting what Morrissey calls a 'grand imperturbable statement of colonial bombast' (Morrissey 1988: 73) and described locally in 1876 as no less than 'a palace' (Day 1998: 19)) and its philanthropic and progressive nature, this particular building could justifiably also be seen as 'a gigantic exercise in an outmoded and inappropriate scheme of asylum design' (Lewis *et al.* 1988: 17). Indeed, many similarities can be seen between the Asylum and the short-lived but highly expensive Outer Circle railway line which ran close to it in the early 1890s, and which was roughly contemporaneous

– it was conceived in 1873, the year after Kew Asylum opened, though the section incorporating Willsmere station ran only between 1891–2 (Beardsell and Herbert 1979: 1). Indeed, in 1891 the *Daily Telegraph* noted wryly if cruelly that the railway would be useful only to 'the inmates of the Kew Asylum, and they travel very little, except in fancy' (Beardsell and Herbert 1979: 110–14).

Of course, the imperfect Asylum having been built, it would have been an act of greater folly to then quickly dismantle it. What is, perhaps, surprising is that it remained in its role as a place of incarceration and/or rehabilitation for the mentally ill for the ensuing 110 years, despite a prevalent belief over most if not all of that period that it was unsuitable for such a purpose.

The building and its grounds

Prior to its conversion to its present-day use, Lewis *et al.* dispassionately detailed the condition of the Asylum and the historic importance of its various features. The windows in the building, they said, were 'reasonably large' by the standards of the time, and the purposes for which they were built, but 'today they look mean' (*Lewis et al.* 1988: 89).

In the continuing catalogue of meaningless expense incurred by colonial and state governments long gone, it was noted that half of the six brick-and-cement water tanks built underground at the Asylum were inherently useless. The ornate towers contained 65 large water tanks, formerly shipping containers, which were difficult to draw water from and remained disused for most of the twentieth century (Board of Inquiry 1876: 69; Lewis *et al.* 1988: 109; Tuer 1962: appendix).

Of the grounds themselves, Lewis *et al.* noted:

> Within the perimeter of the main compound Vivian provided on each side three 'airing grounds', which were landscaped, and three 'airing courts', which were not; twelve enclosures in all, apart from the large yard area at the rear of the building ... The larger courts were quite featureless but for a long sun shed along one side of each, the adjoining pairs being back to back.
>
> (Lewis *et al.* 1988: 120)

The rationale for these spaces, Lewis *et al.* deduce, can be gleaned from Connolly's influential 1847 text *The Construction and Government of Lunatic Asylums*, which prescribes an improving landscape of summer-houses, lime-trees, gravel walks, sporting facilities, shaded seating and shallow duck ponds. The airing courts and other external features, such as sunshades evoked, for Lewis and his colleagues, 'the nature of asylum life more tellingly today than the interiors of the building', yet they felt this was more clearly seen in remnant garden areas at the smaller Ararat institution of the same vintage, and was therefore not a key element of the Kew Asylum's appeal or value (Lewis *et al.* 1988: 11–20). The open space at Kew was, therefore, configured as space to be repackaged or filled, rather than retained.

The significance of Kew Asylum to Melbourne

In 1988, Lewis *et al.* paid homage to the importance of the Asylum in Melbournians' lives. They noted that the idea of the Asylum had caught the imagination of the city, to 'become the very symbol of madness in Victoria'. Additionally, they suggested:

> Few Melbournians have visited the Kew Asylum but, conversely, almost all have seen it from a distance. The surprising and almost exotic quality of the towers glimpsed from various angles, but recently most of all from the Eastern Freeway [constructed in the 1970s], has become almost a part of the Melbourne experience as the Yarra River and the clocks at Flinders Street Station. But in strictly visual terms there is only one comparison, and that is with Government House [close to Melbourne's central Botanic Gardens]. Both are sited on hills, the towers of both rise out of green trees … both are known better from a distance than close at hand …
>
> (Lewis *et al.* 1988: 163)

To Lewis *et al.*, however, the building's former use was of minor significance. The towers, for instance – which architecture students from the University of Melbourne in 1959 had assumed were for Benthamite observation (Goss, Woodford and Mason 1959: n.p.) – 'have had little but ornamental use' and were, in effect, 'huge waste spaces' (Tuer 1962: appendix). They added that an enquiry held 'several years after the completion' of the facility disclosed that patients barely used the outdoor spaces. While of course this does not account for (or discount) any use in the ensuing century, it nevertheless adds to the picture of a building ill-suited to the purpose for which it was ostensibly built, but filling perfectly its '*true*' role: a grand edifice celebrating the philanthropic possibilities of the people of Victoria (Tuer 1962: appendix). Ultimately, Lewis *et al.* concluded, only the 'external fabric' of the building was genuinely important, including the 'architecturally pretentious administration block' and its 'atypical … German influence', the towers, as landmarks, the surviving landscaping, and a handful of additional elements (Lewis *et al.* 1988: 12).

In the second volume of the report (completed without Lewis or his co-authors), Best Overend Partners wrung further issues from the premise that the Asylum building had no intrinsic value as a monument to mental health, asking:

- How much of a monument to man's misfortune is needed for posterity?
- How is this 'complex' to be seen in relation to the two other such institutions within this state, at Beechworth and Ararat?
- Does the state need more than one? And/or does the metropolis of Melbourne need one?
- Can a developer overcome the possible stigma of history and re-use of any Lunatic Asylum Buildings?

- How could a developer overcome the penitentiary-like appearance of these
  buildings due to small secure windows within large wall areas?'
  (Best Overend and Partners 1988: 5)

Best Overend assumed that educational and/or institutional use was the most
likely for the site, though 'multi-unit accommodation' – that is, a hotel – was also
mooted, while light industrial use was thoroughly discouraged (Best Overend and
Partners 1988: 9), presumably in great part because this was not in keeping with
most land use in Kew. In discussing the overall site, Best Overend and Partners
canvassed the likelihood of new buildings being erected in the redeveloped proximity of the Asylum; they conceded that 'there is clearly a need to allow the historic
significance of the site to determine some limitations that should be imposed on
the construction of these new buildings', including the retention of the main axis
relating to the original Lodge (Best Overend and Partners 1988: 8–9). This axis
was reinforced in an unusual and arguably unsympathetic way, as seen below.

Willsmere today

A.V. Jennings, the original purchasers of the Willsmere site, sold it to Central
Equity in 1992. It was announced that Willsmere and its grounds would be used
for housing projects combining the central asylum buildings with new residences.
Willsmere as it exists today is a 'gated community' of apartments, some within
the shell of the original institution, and others included as additional two-storey
semi-detached housing completing what had previously been only partial enclosure of the open 'courts' by the original buildings. Beyond this, new detached
housing and one older building, the original Lodge, are situated outside the walls
to the Asylum's north.

Central Equity's advertising for Kew Gardens, as the development external to
the Asylum building and wall became known, omitted the Asylum from both
its text and images. Rather, it relied heavily on rarity and exclusivity: 'Not in 50
years has such a prestigious inner suburban location been available in a unique
parkland' (*Melbourne Weekly* advertising supplement 1994) along with images of
the Fairfield Boat House at Studley Park, a golf course, and the exclusive Catholic boys' school, Xavier. Drawings of the new houses of the development were
blended into a photograph of Studley Park, suggesting that houses backed onto
native bush (rather than each other, as is the reality). A more unusual sales pitch
was the claim that the development had been '12,000 hours in the planning'
(*Melbourne Weekly* advertising supplement 1994).

As a condition of the development permit by the Historic Buildings Council,
(novice) heritage practitioners were engaged by the site developer to provide
a blueprint for the Kew Asylum Museum and Archives (Cianci and Morgan
1998). During a series of fieldtrips to the site the present authors were unable
to locate the Museum, and believe that the most striking element of Willsmere
in its present state is the deliberate detachment from its original purpose despite

emphasising its heritage significance. The online Kew Asylum/Archives report triumphantly that:

> almost every trace of the building's past has been eradicated – after all, who would want to live with constant reminders of the asylum and the unfortunate inhabitants that came before?
>
> (Cianci and Morgan 1998)

This, to us, is the crux of the problem presented by a site such as Willsmere – just as it is presented by the numerous international examples aforementioned, by 'Pentridge Village', and by sites at which relative isolation has become an attraction rather than a device for control, such as the former Rottnest gaol, now a hotel. To attach 'historical' meaning to a place without further elaboration is as simplistic and meaningless as to proclaim it 'evocative'.

Problems and fears

Within Willsmere's gates, tennis courts and other recreation facilities are available; the only true common areas are, however, the gardens themselves. Residents have, in some instances, sectioned off areas of the wide verandas for their own use, though the barriers used are impermanent.

In traditional suburbia enclosed recreation space has often been seen as problematic in terms of safety, access and utility. In a gated community such issues may, at very least, be more open to community negotiation. The construction of the Asylum building to facilitate surveillance – even if, in practical terms, this is only achieved informally today – also might negate some of the safety issues (which are, in any case, usually only issues of perception – itself nevertheless a powerful driver).

While it would not be entirely true to say that the Town Planning Movement – as much as it did espouse a particularly paternalistic bent – was prescriptive in its aims and actions in ways comparable to the administration of an asylum, it is certainly true that the Kew Asylum and Town Planning have some common environmental determinist ancestors, and that Willsmere as it is today and urban planning are unusual, but not entirely unfeasible, bedfellows. Commonalities include nineteenth-century understanding of social engineering, belief in the calming and inspirational effect of the shaped landscape, and notions of the self-monitoring community. Some of these mindsets can be twinned with the assumptions that come with the construction of the Kew Asylum, most notably the apparently Benthamite conceptions of the 'airing courts' overlooked by the building, allowing all activities to be observed from within; and more broadly, belief in the restorative nature of a natural environment. The nature of life at Willsmere today – close-living apartments, narrow doorways (many cut from windows) and communal open space – represents to a great degree the kind of lifestyle that Australians have long been told, and have told each other, was

Figure 15.3 The verandahs of the residential areas at Willsmere are subtly sectioned off so that each resident has a kind of 'front yard' space. (Source: D. Nichols)

anathema to this particular strand of Western society (Freestone 2000; Davison, Dingle and O'Hanlon 1995).

This was an issue faced by town planners of the 1920s and 30s as they sought to introduce an innovative feature – the 'internal reserve' – into suburban design (Freestone and Nichols 2004). Though there were a number of factors involved in the general failure of these features, perhaps the most pertinent of which is the way in which the developments in question were gradually populated. Planners of the early twentieth century, and historians since, have often tended to assume the real issue with the internal reserve is the resistance, in a society in which private land ownership is so central, to the idea of common land, which attempts to blend the public and the private (as opposed to park land, which is unproblematically and visibly public). A similar example, morphed from the internal to the external – and therefore apparently more easily monitored – is the swathes of open space surrounding the high-rise apartment buildings built by the Victorian Housing Commission in the 1950s and 60s, to a template often ascribed to Le Corbusier. The difference between living in a high-rise flat in inner-city Melbourne and in an apartment carved from the ancient (for Melbourne, which was founded in 1834) grandeur of an ostentatious asylum might seem self-evident, though differing degrees of investment and ownership, in the literal or social sense, are plainly key. In both cases, however, one is often 'on display', must negotiate, communicate and compromise with neighbours, and must take a responsibility for one's wider environment.

As with so much of the Willsmere residential complex, this element of inbuilt 'institutional-ness', problematic for most private homeowners – not to mention residents of institutions! – is apparently here seen as a benefit, or simply ignored. Certainly, it is in the interests of residents to minimise the disadvantages in such an arrangement. There is also, it has to be assumed, a factor which architects, builders and, to a certain degree, urbanists arguing for a limitation of 'sprawl', have sought to nurture in Australian society: the idea that apartment living, which necessitates much less privacy and much more sharing of space, is both chic and practical.

The arrangement and construction of Kew Gardens, the estate outside the former Asylum's walls, was completed in 1995, the year after Willsmere. In 1858 when the Asylum was announced, Morrissey tells us, a number of Kew residents who had bought land in the vicinity were incensed – they had been under the impression that the government reserve on which the Asylum was to be sited had been 'intended for a village' (Morrissey 1988: 36). A village – of sorts – was eventually forthcoming 140 years later, arguably as a result of the semi-rural nature of the expanse of land at the north of the Asylum proper and the way in which it had been 'peninsularised' by the Eastern Freeway and Willsmere Road to its north and west. Kew Gardens' planners appear to have hoped to evoke a 'village' atmosphere for the nine streets outside the gated residences, with curvilinear, nominally 'organic' street patterns. These are calculated in two instances (Cremin and Hutchison Streets) to present a tree-lined avenue highlighting the Asylum's central tower as an endpoint in the way early twentieth-century plans might maximise the importance of a church or other local civic building. Few plans, however, would go to such lengths to highlight the relatively featureless *back* of a tower, behind a high wall.

The remainder of the street pattern, redolent of the 'dead worm' so despised by new urbanists (Duany, Plater-Zyberk and Speck 2000: 34), is in keeping with neither the Asylum's nor Kew's origins. The nineteenth century, the era in which most Australian cities developed, was the era of the 'grid pattern'. As they stand, the curved streets to the Asylum's north serve simply to confuse anyone wishing to understand the original Asylum grounds. In this the design is comparable to the aforementioned 'Pentridge Village', which does not reference the area's century-and-a-half history as a penal institution and indeed relies on an ignorance of (or disregard for) history for its success.

In fact, the present authors posit, this is a site that requires ongoing consideration as part of a broader landscape. It is a cultural landscape, originally conceived to intersect with another mental health-related facility, Kew Cottages, since redeveloped; the Eastern Freeway (highly controversial during its time of construction); and the adjoining Studley and Yarra Bend Parks, a large tract of natural and cultivated parkland on Melbourne's central river. Willsmere retains significance in the present day as a cultural marker and as a point of reference to many who

260 Keir Reeves and David Nichols

see it, standing apparently passively on a rise like a stentorian lion, formally delineating the inner and outer eastern suburbs as effectively as the Yarra itself. Within such a landscape, replete with a significant built environment that can only be understood in a broader context, it requires not only a lifting of the blanket denial of its former use and history, but also ongoing reassessment and imaginative acknowledgement of its past incorporated into its present and future.

Conclusion

The importance of memory and the need to interpret these sites with community memory in mind is particularly pronounced in the case of former imprisonment sites as they intimately related with culturally potent and politically sensitive matters.

No doubt other hospital, prison, school and cemetery sites around the world pose similar issues to planners, developers, and would-be users on a daily basis. In Melbourne, another former mental health facility, Royal Park, was redeveloped for the 2006 Commonwealth Games village – to later be sold as 'Parkville Gardens' – the original Edwardian buildings retained among new, high-density pre-cast concrete terraces. Residents of Willsmere and Royal Park in their earlier incarnations, part of a group not normally considered appropriate candidates for consultation in ordinary circumstances just as many of them were not entitled to vote, were not able to put forward their own opinions on the future use of the site – which, in any case, was considered for redevelopment once it had been vacated and former tenants relocated to other places. An experimental musical group called Willsmere, featuring ex-residents of the institution, haunted Melbourne's airwaves and performance spaces for a brief period in the mid-1980s; they left no lasting recordings, and their existence was the last gasp of the old, negative connotations of the institutional name.

In Australia, and many other Western nations, the retention of large and/or iconic public buildings has come to be seen as a public concern. If buildings outgrow or are no longer suitable for their original purpose, new purposes must be found – a condition, in many cases, of their retention, and understandably so. Clearly in some cases the recycling of a heritage structure for a new use requires an understanding, on the part of those who would reconfigure the building and those who would use it in its altered form, of the building's former uses and history. When such understandings are limited to an aesthetic appreciation of a structure and/or place, new users are unable to appreciate local community dynamics, politics and, of course, history. Communities of whatever stamp require a sense of place, identity, an association with the local area, and an understanding of cultural patterns and the ways they change over time.

Of course, it is highly unlikely that any residents of Willsmere are unaware of their home's former purpose. It can only be assumed that the consolations of the development's cost and exclusivity cushion them from what otherwise might be oppressive or sinister associations with madness and its treatment. What is perhaps more disturbing is the denial of the international significance of Willsmere as a singular example of a large-scale site associated with benevolent incarceration, as ignorance of its complex past is encouraged.

Acknowledgements

The authors wish to thank Professor Miles Lewis of the Faculty of Architecture, Building and Planning, University of Melbourne, for providing access to the otherwise unavailable *Kew Lunatic Asylum: A Conservation Analysis of the Willsmere Mental Hospital* volumes in his possession. They would also like to acknowledge the invaluable research assistance from Kirsty Marshall.

Notes

1 That is, society in the Colony of Victoria (1851–1901).
2 See also Schacter (1995: 25): 'One example is that strong memories – well encoded or frequently rehearsed information, for example – are less likely to exhibit distortion than are "weak" memories. Stated in slightly different terms, when a stored representation or engram is held together by strong connections among its constituent features, it may be less susceptible to distorting influences than when the connections are weak.'
3 For a description of the 'heritage-ization' of the Port Arthur site, see also Jane Lennon's chapter in this book and Eleanor Conlin Casella (1997).

References

Anon. (1883) 'Victorian Lunatic Asylums', *Australasian Medical Gazette*, November: 44–5.
Australasian Medical Gazette (1883) November.
Barrett, B. (1971) *The Inner Suburbs: Evolution of an Industrial Area*, Carlton: Melbourne University Press.
Beardsell, D. and Herbert, B. (1979) *The Outer Circle: a History of the Oakleigh to Fairfield Railway*, Windsor: Australian Railway Historical Society (Victorian Division).
Best Overend and Partners (1988) *Kew Lunatic Asylum: A Conservation Analysis of the Willsmere Mental Hospital. Volume 2: Options for the Future*, Melbourne: Best Overend and Partners Architects and Dr Miles Lewis.
Board of Inquiry (1876) *Report from the board appointed to inquire into Matters relating to the Kew Lunatic Asylum*, Melbourne: John Ferres.
Casella, E.C. (1997) 'To enshrine their spirits in the world: heritage and grief at Port Arthur, Tasmania', *Conservation and Management of Archaeological Sites*, 2: 65–80.
Cicanci, L. and Morgan, H. (n.d.) 'Kew Asylum Museum/Archives', Available online at: http://www.asap.unimelb.edu.au/pubs/articles/asa97/KEWA.htm (Accessed 3 October 2006).
Davison, G., Dingle, A.E., O'Hanlon, S. and Monash University Department of History (eds) (1995) *The Cream Brick Frontier: Histories of Australian Suburbs*, Clayton, VI.: Monash Publications in History, Department of History, Monash University.
Day, C. (1998) 'Magnificence, Misery and Madness: A History of the Kew Asylum 1872–1915', PhD thesis, University of Melbourne.
Duany, A., Plater-Zyberk, E. and Speck, J. (2000) *Suburban Nation: The Rise of Sprawl and the Decline of the American Dream*, New York: North Point Press.

Foote, K.E. (1997) *Shadowed Ground: America's landscapes of violence and tragedy*, Austin: University of Texas Press.

Foucault, M. (1977) *Discipline and Punish: The Birth of the Prison*, New York: Pantheon.

Franklin, B. (2002) 'Monument to Madness: the Rehabilitation of the Victorian Lunatic Asylum', *Journal of Architectural Conservation*, 3: 28–39.

Freestone, R. (2000) 'Planning, Housing, Gardening: Home as a Garden Suburb', in Troy, P. (ed.), *A History of European Housing in Australia*, Cambridge: Cambridge University Press.

Freestone, R. and Nichols, D. (2004) 'The rise and fall of the internal reserve', *Landscape Research*, 29 (3 July): 293–309.

Gillis, J. (1994) *Commemorations: The Politics of National Identity*, Princeton, NJ: Princeton University Press.

Goss, I., Woodford, B. and Mason, I.G.R. (1959) *The Older Buildings of the Kew Mental Asylum*, History of Architecture IV Essay, University of Melbourne.

Ignatieff, M. (1978) *A Just Measure of Pain: The Penitentiary in the Industrial Revolution, 1750–1850*, New York: Pantheon Books.

Kew Advertiser (1927) 'Playground for the North. Ambitious Kew Scheme. Five-Mile Lake would fill Yarra Valley', 13 January: 2.

Kew Advertiser (1930) 'A New Recreation Reserve for Kew: Proposal Shelved for Twelve Months on Account of Financial Depression', 27 March: 1.

Lennon, J. (2002) 'The Broad Arrow Café, Port Arthur, Tasmania – Using Social Values Methodology to Resolve Commemoration Issues'; paper presented at Australian ICOMOS National Conference, Port Arthur.

Lewis, M., Carew, J. and Roennfeldt, A. (1988) *Kew Lunatic Asylum: A Conservation Analysis of the Willsmere Mental Hospital Volume 1: The Text*, Melbourne: Best Overend and Partners Architects and Dr Miles Lewis.

Logan, W.S. (2003) 'Hoa Lo: a Vietnamese approach to preserving places of pain and injustice', *Historic Environment*, 17(1): 27–31.

McIntosh, M. (1950) *Kew Asylum*, Bachelor of Arts (Honours) thesis, University of Melbourne.

Melbourne Weekly (1994) 'Kew Gardens' advertising supplement, 18 January.

Morrissey, S. (1988) *The Asylum and the Community: The Relationship between Kew Asylum and the suburb of Kew, 1854–1879*, Bachelor of Arts (Honours) thesis, University of Melbourne.

Neier, A. (1995) 'Confining Dissent in the Political Prison', in N. Morris and D.J. Rothman, *The Oxford History of the Prison: The Practice of Punishment in Western Society*, New York: Oxford University Press.

Port Arthur Historic Site Management Authority (2001) *PAHSMA Interpretation Plan*, Port Arthur: PAHSMA.

Robben Island Museum (2002) *Annual Report 2001–2002*.

Schacter, D.K. (ed.) (1995) *Memory Distortion: How Minds, Brains and Societies Reconstruct the Past*, Cambridge, MA: Harvard University Press.

Semple, J. (1993) *Bentham's Prison: A Study of the Panopticon Penitentiary*, Oxford: Clarendon Press/Oxford University Press.

Tuer, G. (1962) 'Kew Lunatic Asylum', Bachelor of Architecture thesis, University of Melbourne.

Yong, J. (2003) 'Last days of a leper colony'. Available online at: http://www.cbsnews.com/stories/2003/03/22/health/main545392.shtml (accessed 22 March 2003).

Chapter 16

Between the hostel and the detention centre

Possible trajectories of migrant pain and shame in Australia

Sara Wills

Since the late 1980s, Australia has maintained a series of immigration detention centres to accommodate those deemed to have arrived or remained in the country 'unlawfully'. While a number of the sites have been closed or 'mothballed', many remain places of incarceration. More recently dubbed 'immigration reception and processing facilities', these sites gained national prominence from late 1999 onwards as their capacity to contain 'unlawful non-citizens' was challenged by increased numbers of asylum-seekers arriving from Central Asia and the Middle East; and by a government concerned to emphasise in the heat of an election campaign that '*we* will decide who comes to this country and the circumstances in which they come' (Howard 2001). While not without controversy, including many detailed reports about the pain and shame inflicted in and by these centres, the 'facility' provided by detention has been broadly supported across the mainstream political and public spheres in Australia. Both the Liberal–National Party coalition in government and the Australian Labor Party in opposition have argued that detention maintains the integrity of Australia's migration and humanitarian programmes (Wills 2002). Yet opposition to elements of the detention regime has been consistent and strenuous in some quarters, and many of those campaigning on behalf of refugees have argued that the mandatory detention of asylum-seekers has betrayed the 'proud tradition' of 'an Australia that made people in genuine need feel welcome, safe and able to contribute to the nation and community' (see Wills 2005a). Some state that they now feel ashamed of the nation, and one could argue indeed that immigration detention centres are slowly being recognised by a growing group of Australians as 'places of pain and shame'.

It seems legitimate to ask, therefore, what kind of basis such feelings provide for the possibility of 'remembering' places such as the now closed but once notorious Woomera Immigration Reception and Processing Centre? Some clues were provided when in May 2003, the Australian Broadcasting Commission aired a documentary 'About Woomera' as part of its flagship *Four Corners* investigative series. The programme followed the troubled history of this remote South Australian centre, which opened in 1999 and at its peak housed 1400 detainees in facilities built to accommodate less than a third of that number. It graphically detailed how this detention site had traumatised not only detainees, but also many of the security guards who worked there (ABC 2003a). At the end of the programme, viewers

Figures 16.1 and 16.2 Woomera Immigration Reception and Processing Centre, South
    Australia: opened in November 1999 and closed in April 2003, now 'moth-
    balled' but available as a contingency centre. (Source: S. Wills)

were invited to respond to an online forum, and in a long list of postings, 'pain' and particularly 'shame' were persistently broached in the discussions:

> From: Guest   19/05/2003 9:33:34 PM
> Subject: Shame ... shame ... shame!
> Thanks for a very good report. I feel so ashamed as an Australian that we would let such a thing happen. Where are the Govt. controls and standards ... what are we paying public servants to do? We expect that they should make sure this sort of thing does not happen. Shame Philip Ruddock.

> From: Simone   19/05/2003 9:41:44 PM
> Subject: Pain
> It hurt me so much to see how people fleeing persecution can be treated with such a lack of humanity in our country, how this will impact on the rest of their lives, how outrageous it is that a private company could operate in such a manner without being pulled up by our govt, how frightening that we could be living in a time when there is so little respect/concern for humanity in our government policies ... where the only tool people in detention feel able to protest with is their own bodies. Without doing something I feel in a small way responsible for allowing this to happen in our country (ABC 2003b).

While acknowledging that there is value in the emotion and immediacy of these responses, I find them also indicative of potential problems with the memorialisation of detention centre sites as places of pain and shame. 'Guest' seeks to express shame and anger, but then shifts the burden of shame elsewhere (to the government and Minister for Immigration, Philip Ruddock). 'Simone' focuses initially on the pain that *she* felt watching the programme (as opposed to that of the detainees), then distances herself from the 'impact' detention might have 'on the rest of *their* lives', returning to her own fright, back to the pain of detainees bodies and finally 'in a small way' to her own responsibility. I shall return later to such expressions of pain and shame and particularly the way they tend to circumscribe the potential of Woomera as a 'site of memory' (Nora 1989).

Yet following the 'Shame, shame, shame!' thread, another viewer of 'About Woomera' responded:

> From: Dobro   19/05/2003 11:50:53 PM
> Subject: re: Shame ... shame ... shame!
> I found the report more frightening and harrowing to watch than practically anything I have seen before, in the media; except perhaps the Nazi death camps. In 1950, my parents arrived in this country with nothing except a two year old baby – me. Over 50 years later, we have made a life, we have contributed to our neighbourhood and our society. My children have been born here and they are now the third generation of our family to call Australia home. We were refugees. We were reviled by some and welcomed

by others. But, in the end it worked. There seemed to be a will back then to make this country an example of how a democratic and a civilized society treats those who flee from tyranny and hopelessness… (ABC 2003b).

Like others, 'Dobro' wants to return to the 'proud tradition' of refugees being able to make a life in Australia, and quickly passes over the gap between arrival and 'success' in a manner that is no doubt designed to emphasise in this context the 'contribution' of refugees. But there is also an articulation and 'flash of memory' that although brief opens up more productive space than the hurt or shame of 'Guest' and 'Simone', or the idea of 'contribution'. 'Dobro' mentions the 'Nazi death camps', places from which some of Australia's post-war refugees were drawn. Detention centres are indeed a kind of camp, and this connection to other forms of incarceration has been suggestively explored (Birch 2001, Perera 2002, Pugliese 2002b).

But there is another gap here that interests me. 'Dobro' was probably too young to remember much about the 'reception and processing facilities' of the 1950s, but I want to argue here that Australia's post-war migrant hostels – places where several hundred thousand refugees and migrants were received, processed and accommodated between 1947 and 1986 – offer a 'pre-history' to detention centres, and a place to reconfigure the nation's pain and shame. This is a mixed history and not one that offers a simple recovery from shame through pride in the nation's past. While cited by some activists as a viable 'alternative to mandatory detention' (Stephen 2002), such histories do not always yield all that is required or desired by the 'shamed' contemporary rememberer seeking to recover pride (Neumann 2004).

Yet by returning us to other specific histories – and other gaps between the ethics and the politics of hospitality (Derrida 2000) – hostel sites offer a model for thinking about the kinds of remembering and heritage-making that might be possible at Australia's detention centres. In what follows I briefly recall this history and offer contexts that develop an archive of migrant feeling for understanding the place of immigration detention centres: historical understandings of the nation as a place of refuge; an awareness of what has been 'held' and 'facilitated' by forms of detention; a brief glimpse at the work of migrant memory at one hostel site; and, drawing on Sara Ahmed's work on the 'sociality of emotions' (2004), a consideration of national attempts to deal with shame and the politics of pain. These contexts are not the only ones possible for understanding such sites, but they contribute to an overall argument that remembering at such places may best be enacted in terms of ambivalence as much as contingence, and should resist the temptation to produce sites of pain and shame where the unitary national subject can sanctify the past or 're-cover'.

Holding centres of migrant memory

As an official offshoot of empire founded in 1901, and with a history stretching back only as far as the eighteenth century, Australia is a migrant nation built on the reality of continuous arrival: of over nine million people undertaking an often long and arduous journey to begin a new life here, more than half a million of whom have been refugees. While this is a circumscribed history, with Indigenous sovereignty magically conjured away, it reflects one reality in Australia today: that two-thirds of the population were either born overseas or have at least one parent born elsewhere. With over six million arrivals since the Second World War alone, following a post-war immigration boom that drew initially on refugees from Europe, Australia thus has a substantial history of providing forms of refuge for those who have chosen or been forced to flee their homeland (Jupp 2002). What kind of history has this produced? What kind of memories does Australia have of being a migrant nation? What kind of memorial consciousness has arisen; what kind of migrant history and heritage?

Like all imagined communities, Australia has a myth model of nationhood that selects and incorporates stories insofar as they fit into a coherent narrative of nation-building and become part of the 'national symbolic' (Berlant 1991). Migration history in Australia has largely contributed to this project, with migrant stories included for their 'contribution' to national history – a paradigm familiar to other migrant-receiving nations (Gabaccia 1999) – and allowing a positive rendering of a progressive, and ultimately multicultural state where 'many' have come together 'as one'. In this formulation, the various racisms of the *Immigration Restriction Act* of 1901 get washed away by the tide of (white) multiculturalism (see Ang and Stratton 2001) – even though the social, cultural and racial anxieties of a never-quite-dead White Australia still clearly affect Vietnamese refugees (Mellor 2004; Thomas 1997), and have most recently been expressed in relation to Sudanese arrivals (*Media Watch* 2007).

Such are the 'memories' which inform policy-making about migrant incorporation in Australia today, with the current emphasis on skilled and business immigration reflecting how we value newcomers for the way in which they contribute to this national growth (Hage 1998, 2003). In other words, the contribution model of migrant history retains very real power in Australia, and what Foucault (1980: 82) called 'subjugated knowledges' are still frequently 'disqualified as inadequate to their task or insufficiently elaborated: [as] naïve knowledges, located low down on the hierarchy beneath the required level of cognition or scientificity'. Thus in the wake of the *MV Tampa* and 'children overboard' incidents of 2001–02 (see Marr and Wilkinson 2003), Immigration Minister Ruddock (2002) was at pains to emphasise that 'Australia has a very proud record … of assisting people in great humanitarian need', and that it is 'vital that unfounded and patently incorrect claims are not used to form judgements that erode the pride we as a nation are entitled to feel about the hand we extend to those in such great need'. National historians argued that our migration programme had been 'the great Australian success story' (Hirst 2001), and voices or un-legitimised sources that tangled with this story were largely unavailable to debate a memorial migrant consciousness that could inform the nation in different ways. Thus the mnemonic role of histories *not* constructed around pride and nationhood were largely unavailable. As I have argued elsewhere (Wills 2004a), arousing and arranging memory to suit a (White) nation's needs left us resorting often to the realms of fantasy (see also Hage 1998; 2003; Neumann 2004).

Until recently, migrant hostels have had almost no role in this national story (Sluga 1994), with hostel histories coming to light only in local and site-specific acts of remembrance (e.g. Moss 1997; Synan 2002). Yet hostels offer a possible archive for understanding a heritage of migrant detention and a reconfigured national historical consciousness. Migrant hostels – also known as migrant reception and training centres, dependents' holding centres, and migrant workers' hostels – were established after the Second World War to provide initial accommodation for government-assisted refugees and immigrants to Australia. Both the war and the preceding Depression had left Australia with a severe shortage of housing and building materials (Greig 1995), and government provision of temporary accommodation for migrants was deemed practically and politically necessary (Jordens 1994: 1997). Thus over the next three decades, around thirty reception, training and holding centres and workers' hostels were adapted from army camps or constructed using largely prefabricated components, with management of the various types of hostels undertaken by the Departments of Immigration and Labour and National Service, state governments and a private company (Jordens 1997). The distinctions between facilities are important: as a rule, British migrants – considered to be only in need of accommodation – were housed in the better-equipped urban hostels; while non-British migrants – considered to be in need of 'reception', education and training – were sent to the more spartan rural and remote migrant centres or workers' hostels. This differential treatment of British and non-British migrants was a significant feature of the programme, as was family separation, and training and work-related experiences (Jordens 1997; Jupp 1966; Panich 1988; Kunz 1988). Nevertheless, for many post-war immigrants, hostels and holding centres provided an experience of being hosted by the state, and some kind of refuge (if not much hospitality).

What was 'held' by these centres is worth exploring. They 'held' of course the workers required to help build post-war Australia, accommodating them in strategic locations close to agriculture, infrastructure and industry. But they were also sites that held together or 'centred' notions of Australianness and helped to define and transmit a national 'way of life' in the post-war period. They were frontiers of assimilation, of the policies, procedures and practices that directed the cultural and national re-education of non-British migrants, and helped to delimit what it meant to become a 'new Australian'. English classes, the ministrations of the visiting Good Neighbour Councils and official welcoming pamphlets echoed the arguments of the Citizenship Conventions held throughout the 1950s, that the: 'assimilation objective is not just to ensure that the newcomer is contented, comfortable and well occupied – but that he [*sic*] is indeed finding his comfort and well-being in a community which is distinctively Australian' (Boyer 1957). The reality, as Sluga (1988; 1994) has argued, is that hostels were for many places of material and cultural *discomfort*, and sometimes little or even 'no hope'.

Indeed resident complaints, rising expectations among migrants and fears that Australia would not be able to attract and retain sufficient numbers of immigrants forced changes in the standard and type of accommodation in the mid-1960s

(Jordens 1997), and in the 1970s there was a shift from hostel accommodation to self-contained 'clustered units' and 'transitory flats' as economic recession saw the Government reduce assisted migration (Junankar *et al.* 1993). International developments in the mid–late 1970s, however, marked a new phase of hostel accommodation, as refugees from South America and South East Asia moved into 'migrant centres' (ELO Scheme 1980, Viviani 1984). While not without significant problems, the hostel programme of this era, and specifically its reception, processing and settlement of refugees (see for example ELO 1980; McCoy 1996), provides a direct contrast with current practices, and this contrast is all the more apparent given that some of these sites were converted to detention centres in the 1980s.

Thus hostels potentially evoke memories of being both more and less hospitably 'settled' by the nation. Moreover in the last decade there have been signs that hostel accommodation has begun to loom larger in the national consciousness, with one result being the development of a cultural heritage site at the former Bonegilla Migrant Reception and Training Centre in the south-eastern state of Victoria. Suggesting a possible model for the future remembrance of detention centres within the nation, this site is worth exploring.

Sites for epic memory, or the 'sociality of emotion'?

Bonegilla Migrant Reception and Training Centre was the largest and longest running of Australia's migrant hostels, accommodating more than 300,000 migrants between 1947 and 1971. Situated on the site of a large but remote army camp, it provided initial reception, accommodation, education, training and holding facilities for those coming as refugees from a war-torn Europe and seeking a new life for their families in Australia. In its almost quarter-century of operation, it housed refugees and migrants from over thirty nations. Consequently it is arguably the most 'remembered' of Australia's migrant hostels, and was the subject of a small but important monograph in the 1980s that explored also some of the 'national dreams that conjured the possibilities for its existence', and 'the way it changed the lives of those who were meant to live that dream' (Sluga 1988, xii).

In 2005, almost 35 years since its closure, these former residents were invited to return to the site. In 2002, the State Minister for Major Projects in Victoria had allocated $2 million 'to recognise and celebrate the site', and to enable 'Bonegilla migrants and their descendants ... to rediscover their family's Australian beginnings' (Batchelor 2002). Subsequently Block 19 – one of 24 similar accommodation complexes that spread over the 130 hectare site – was redeveloped, with the Victorian Multicultural Commission contributing $70,000 to assist with marketing and promotion, and Tourism Victoria allocating $20,000 for a two-day launch. This launch went ahead in December 2005, marking the culmination of a place-making process that has now designated the site as a 'heritage park' where visitors are invited to 'reminisce' about 'a rich period in Australia's history that strongly contributed to the multi-cultural fabric of today's Australia' (Parklands Albury-Wodonga 2006); and to understand it as 'a focus point for all post-war

Figures 16.3 and 16.4 Bonegilla, Victoria: site of Australia's largest post-war migrant reception and training centre between 1947 and 1971, and since 2005 of 'the migrant experience' interpretation centre. (Source: S. Wills)

migrants and families who wish to remember and, in most cases, celebrate their roots' (BME 2000).

The focus of this park is a new interpretation centre, 'The Beginning Place', located to the side of the remaining accommodation blocks. A permanently open and un-staffed facility, this new centre includes a number of multimedia features as well as information panels on the history of the site. In many ways a sophisticated and well-designed installation, it is sensitive to various elements of the post-war migrant experience, providing examples of positive and negative 'memories' for those who now wish to visit this 'beginning place'. Documentation available at the centre and elsewhere underlines the potential for the site to be 'significant to the whole nation as a host society', and to 'invite exploration of the mixed community responses to newcomers, prompting examination and exploration of the expressions of feelings such as wariness, hostility, compassion, neighbourliness and indifference associated with "taking in strangers" (Pennay 2006: 2). More emphasis, however, is placed on its function as a site that commemorates the 'bravery' and 'courage' of all post-war migrants who 'came and settled here'. Its primary place-making energy, therefore, is to mark it as 'the beginning place' in a history that moves forward for these migrants, in some respects sidelining the 'original' experience, or making it at least an inhabitable memory for migrants and their descendants today.

In this specific transformation of the space of the migrant hostel into an elaborated place, we see evidence certainly of the emergence of a form of post-war migrant 'epic memory' that seeks to join the national story (Vitelli 2006). One feature of such 'epic memory' in Australia is its 'extension and transformation of colonialism' (Vitelli 2006: 9), and much emphasis on post-war migrant experience can be seen as a type of defining moment in the assumption of Australian identity and culture predicated on becoming complicit in the reproduction of colonialism. This is a significant 'act of memory' (or forgetting) outlined well in a recent call for a 'decolonising migrant historiography' in Australia (Pugliese 2002a).

More broadly I would argue, in the rush to be Australian, the pressure to forget other histories often renders migrants (the) only qualified rememberers (in both senses of 'qualify'), developing a 'heritage' and 'pride of place' in Australia that amounts to a 'park life' of migrant memory. While underlining sympathetically the fact that hostels like Bonegilla were places where the displaced were once 'allowed no identity except that arising from their lack of place and their usefulness as workers', Sluga (1994: 195–200) also noted that the history of such places has subsequently been 'constructed to represent a period of assimilationist immigration history' that is past, and to serve many other needs. In particular, Sluga argued, such places could serve as the locus of a 'migrant dreaming' that provides 'an antidote to the rootlessness of the exile' (p. 203), with migrants, their children and now grandchildren able to locate in places such as Bonegilla a 'beginning place', an originary place that is in Australia.

I would argue also that this is what is marked in the local histories of individual migrant hostels produced in the last ten years, often as collected oral histories that 'celebrate' and settle hostel stories: that mark a later stage in a journey that seeks first accommodation by the state and then accommodation in the state. Not all perform this journey (e.g. P O 1982), and nor is this to dismiss such works or the energies expended on them. One value of such accounts indeed is that they avoid the tendency of some academics to ride roughshod over these histories in their haste to make an ideological point. While their form and meaning still prompt questions about the specific work of memory's cultures, they force us to consider how 'memories are ... active symbolic presences and "agents" in the urban and social landscape that reveal as well as mask and conceal' (Vitelli 2006: 9). What such memories clearly reveal also, for example, are practices, policies, experiences and outcomes of migrants getting helped. These are important histories for these sites that could act today to remind us of the idea of 'holding' the vulnerable with care (Fung 2007), and the value of more extensive settlement services. The 'lost art of the national cuddle' has been noted in other contexts (Hage 2003), and we seem to have been left with either the vice-like grip of detention or, with the broader dismantling of social welfare and services, a perception that any form of 'holding' is no longer needed. Under new regimes of 'mutual obligation', hostels are derided simply as places that 'spawned many of the ghettos in our mainland capital cities', and as reflecting mistakes in settlement policies because they did not 'address our economic and defence vulnerabilities' (Hurford 2006). Hostel rememberers could be agents of an ethics of care for the newly arrived in Australia.

But it is still important to examine 'site myths' and monument-making – to address the mythic retellings of hostel experience – that amount to a refusal by many to address less 'caring' processes of arrival, gathering, exchange and dissipation – including attempts to resist some forms of 'help' or 'domestication' that may have occurred on these sites. In the works of 'rememberers' such as the poet P O (1982), for example, we are provided with an alternative 'migrant dreaming' that functions: to reveal the desire to be accommodated but not contained; to see the energy, anger and violence of a 'multicultural real' that rejects assimilationist hospitality; and to see where there were ways of negotiating, avoiding and resisting what has been called 'the wagging finger of the hostel gate' (Skrzynecki 1985). We may hear not of efficient 'reception and processing', but circumstances of protest and revolt. At Bonegilla in 1952, for example, Italians lured to Australia by promises of work were frustrated to find none:

> We started to revolt. We burned two or three huts and set fire to the church, not because we didn't like the church, but because the Italian priest there used to say, 'Have patience, God is on your side', and we were fed up with him ... We just wanted to show the authorities we mean business, give us a job or send us home. We marched towards the main office to plead with them to give us jobs but before we got to the administration block we saw four tanks with machine guns on top in front of us ... Some of us ran, I was one of them ... Soon after this the Italian consul arrived, and people went to hear him. The first thing he said was, 'You are fortunate to be in a country like Australia'. After three months unemployed! No sooner he finished these

words than people rush on the stage and nearly killed him. His car was burned, the hall where he spoke was destroyed and the police had to come and rescue him through the back door.

(Loh 1980: 19)

Providing room for critical memories – and noting how they might (or already) activate present and possible future spaces that challenge the relationship between hospitality and domestication – allows us also to make links with contemporary detention practices and processes of temporary migrant accommodation that no simple story of arrival and 'beginning' can achieve. It allows us to think about much more contemporary proposals to 'host' Kosovar refugees at the still remote Bonegilla site – never realised at this location, but fulfilled in other remote military barracks (Mares 2001). It allows us to make connections between past and present practices of 'ethnic caging': that what one sees caged in detention centres is 'ethnic will', a 'mode of categorising and dealing with national otherness in the process of defending the nation from external threats [which] is intrinsically linked to the way national otherness is categorised and dealt with internally' (Hage 1998: 105–16).

Yet while there are certainly continuities between the training and holding facilities of hostels and what has been facilitated by detention centres, it is necessary to emphasise that the contemporary detention regime cannot be linked easily to the practices of accommodating migrants and refugees in hostels. It is necessary to underline the stark difference between those who, in however much discomfort, usually spent no more than a few months waiting to find accommodation in the broader community as part of the road to citizenship, and those who are detained involuntarily behind razor wire and are entirely uncertain whether they will *ever* begin a path to some kind of belonging in Australia. While some migrants may have been disappointed or felt culturally insulted by conditions in the post-war hostels, Australian detention practices breach *any* understanding of a just and 'proud record' of migration to Australia, and of treatment of refugees. Since the mid-1990s, innumerable problems have emerged in association with the contemporary detention regime (see for example ACHSSW 2006; CO 2001; Flood 2001; HREOC 1998; 2004; 2007; Mares 2001); detention centres have become the new lynch-pin of an ongoing 'defend, deter and detain' mentality (Cronin 1993) in which, it has been argued, the trauma of detention has become a *feature* of migration policy (Mitropoulos and Rozensweig 2000, Mitropoulos 2001).

So the principle and practice of hostel accommodation and detention should be linked only cautiously. While some hostel sites have been transformed into detention centres – thus linking the 'facility' of detention and what the Department of Immigration itself calls the 'immigration presence' on these sites (Fung 2007) – the layering of these cultural landscapes of migrancy on and in these sites in Australia should only be explored in a way that does not return us to national pride. We can do it by creating suitable archives of feeling around such sites, which recognise not only the effects of divergent forms of contact, but what I want finally to elaborate as an appropriate 'sociality of [national migrant] emotion'.

Finishing with shame, and the politics of pain

In her thoughtful exploration of 'the cultural politics of emotion', Ahmed (2004: 8) reminds us that:

> If the object of feeling both shapes and is shaped by emotions, then the object of feeling is never simply before the subject. How the object impresses (upon) us may depend on histories that remain alive insofar as they have already left their impressions. The object may stand in for other objects, or may be proximate to other objects. Feelings may stick to some objects, and slide over others ... [F]eelings do not reside in subjects or objects, but are produced as effects of circulation. The circulation of objects allows us to think about the 'sociality' of emotion.

Places of pain and shame are by definition sites, or 'objects', of feeling, and as we saw with 'Guest', 'Simone' and 'Dobro', detention centres are sites to which feelings of pain and shame currently 'stick'. Yet, following Ahmed, our potential for feelings of pain and shame in relation to detention centres are produced as impressions and effects of circulation: as a product of the 'sociality of emotions' in Australia, and thus the way certain histories remain alive to us.

In her analysis of aspects of the expression of national shame in Australia, Ahmed underlines the essential relation between recognition and shame, and suggests that in the context of Australian politics, the process of being moved by the past seems better than the process of remaining detached from it, or assuming that it has nothing to do with us (2004: 102). Yet Ahmed proceeds to outline how collective shame often conceals as much as it reveals and may restore or reconcile the nation to itself, without effectively addressing those whose pains are supposedly recognised. Ahmed demonstrates how this has often been the case in expressions of national shame in Australia regarding the treatment of Indigenous peoples, and how in the face of Indigenous demands for an apology, saying sorry should not be something the nation addresses to itself, should not return the nation to itself, but should address an 'other'. In this respect, Ahmed concludes, we need to find ways of expressing shame before others without finishing the act, without converting shame to pride; it needs to remain an act that is for and can only be received or finished by others (pp. 101–20).

Over-emphasising or mis-recognising the nature of the relationship between migrant hostels and detention centre sites potentially risks performing such a narrative of recovery in a gesture that fails to move towards others. So no legitimate comparison of hostel and detention sites should forget the *politics* of pain, or the uneven effects of holding practices in a migrant nation. To link these sites of refugee and migrant 'accommodation' risks flattening out the differences between the two histories and turning it into a kind of national experience held in common, and contributing to the national or epic memory outlined above. As noted already, it would be a mistake to make a simple connection between 'understanding' the experiences of those in detention based on an earlier national or even personal experience or memory of accommodation in hostels. Although I want to make this a possible trajectory for understanding, it is necessary to bear in mind Ahmed's warning about fetishising pain: about transforming the wound of pain into an identity for the nation that fails to effectively address other histories. These need to be remembered: histories of the particular transnational routes of migration, refuge and asylum, and thus today of what Appadurai (1990) calls the 'complex, overlapping disjunctive order' of the new global cultural economy. This 'fetishisation' of the wound of detention into an identity for a 'wounded nation' would assume an equivalence between what have to be recognised as very different injuries.

The different injuries of detention have emerged very clearly in published accounts of individual refugee stories published in the last five years in Australia. They remind us of national disjuncture around stories of migration. But reading testimonies of injury from any period involves rethinking the relationship between the past and the present, and the inclusion of the past does not necessarily mean an entrenchment of the past or the priorities formed through it. As Ahmed explains, citing bell hooks, 'the task is "not to forget the past but to break its hold"', and

> in order to break the seal of the past, in order to move away from attachments that are hurtful, we must first bring them into the realm of political action. Bringing pain into politics requires we give up the fetish of the wound through different kinds of remembrance. The past is living rather than dead; the past lives in the very wounds that remain open in the present.
>
> (2004: 33)

An acknowledgement of the pain and shame of hostel sites 'returns' us ultimately to detention centres; and to the pain of those in detention:

> Since the moment we arrived in the detention centre, we have forgotten what happiness and laughter means, and scenes of suicides, death and terror make us more depressed … I am talking about a true prison, where thoughts are killed and death is always knocking at the door … We feel like all the world is unaware of us. Hail Australians! You should open your eyes and be aware of what is being done in your name … Certainly this injustice done to innocent people will form a dark spot in Australian history and Australians cannot escape from it.
>
> (Amor and Austin 2003: 38–9)

Representing the vague terrains of our otherness

Much of what I have argued implicitly challenges the idea of the nation or national frameworks as appropriate or capable places for feeling pain and shame in the contexts discussed here. But as the quote above illustrates, the appeal to the national subject remains important, and if we reformulate the idea of Australia as a migrant nation with multiple histories of arrival and contact, then it may allow us some latitude and hope in this regard. To return to the idea of a possible 'site of memory' (mindful of Nora's negative connotations), and my original question about what forms of remembrance and heritage-making might be possible at Australia's detention centre sites, representing pain will mean both re-presenting 'our' otherness and the other-ness of others. It is a way of getting close, but 'we' do not become the same.

At the moment, the kind of work performed by many published first-hand accounts of life in detention may be a necessary 'listening' phase for the nation to come to terms with this lack of 'sameness'. This will not be a work of mourning that 'lets go' of pain and loss (Freud 1934), or takes the other inside to perform a self-serving kind of melancholy. But in Australia it could be about the way and extent to which we remember that we might actually be 'with others' as refugees or migrants before we are defined as 'apart from' them. To be touched or moved by another's pain does depend on the sociality of being with others, of getting close enough to touch. Pain surfaces in relationship to others who can bear witness to it and authen-ticate it. We all carry impressions of those others as part of the dynamic process of identity-making. The creation of the subject depends on the impressions of others, others who exist within and apart from 'us' at the same time. To preserve an attach-ment is not to make an external other internal, but to keep one's impressions alive, as aspects of us that are more than us, as a sign of our debt to others (Ahmed 2004: 159–61): in Australia, as impressions and signs of arrival and unsettled migrancy.

So we cannot claim the *wound* of detention as 'our' own – in the sense that for a broader history of a migrant nation, which could easily slide into a national appropriation of pain for the collectivity – which could then be 'mourned' at a site of remembrance as a form of national recovery. The issue becomes how we can respond to pain that we cannot claim as our own: how we respond in a way that does not take the testimony away from others as if it were only about our ability to feel the feelings of others. It becomes, to use Ahmed's phrase, about 'the contingency of pain' (2004: 20). And in Australia, similarly to the issues confronted in the case of Aboriginal pain, the experience of pain has to be bound up with a recognition of loss – the loss of a 'we' – the loss of the possibility of a certain kind of national body or community. Recognising the pain of others calls for a different kind of inhabitance and moves the story on – on to a 'politics based not on the possibility that we might be reconciled, but on learning … that we live with and beside each other, and yet we are not as one' (Ahmed 2004: 39).

So, not forgetting 'Guest' and 'Simone' and 'Dobro', I argue for the necessity of national and even migrant shame in Australia as part of the necessary work of iden-tifying and 'dealing' with detention centres as potential heritage sites of the future. I argue for this shame to be tied to a history of migrants 'hurting' in Australia, but in addition I make claims for a *productive* sadness arising from a form of melan-cholic community (Caluya 2006), which could attain nevertheless some degree of national prevision. Through the consideration of currently expunged archives of feeling that are offered by sites of migrant arrival, we find possible trajectories for interpreting the pain and shame of detention sites. But remembering Woomera or any of Australia's detention centres should perform 'memory work' that produces 'memory as praxis rather than text' or elegy (Frazier 1998: 108). In the process we could re-work also Australian migrancy not as a finished identity but something that happens: that has happened, and continues to happen.

As I have argued elsewhere, I feel such unfinished-ness at unmarked and unremembered migrant hostel sites in Australia – at 'vague terrains', like the old 'Wiltona' hostel, now largely a self-storage facility in Melbourne's industrial west – resists the production of too easily 'epic' memories and might remind us how tough the process of negotiating a new place can be (Wills 2006; Solà-Morales Rubió 1995). Moreover, the 'beginning place' is not so much necessarily a memory that can be easily invoked as it is hospitably settled. Even as we seek to resist a 'narrative [that] scoops up others on its own terms and within its own self-understanding' (Rose 2004: 21) we might also recognise that 'nations rest on such historical consciousness – on a chain of connection between "them" and "us"' (Attwood and Foster 2003: 26). This contemporary 'praxis' should focus on establishing ethical connections between contemporary narratives of nationhood and the histories, experiences, sites and vague terrains of migrant temporary accommodation, if only to facilitate exploration of the hiatus to which Derrida (2000) drew our attention: between an *ethics* and a *politics* of hospitality. Between the hostel and the camp, there is possibly space for an ethical national conversation.

References

Ahmed, S. (2004) *The Cultural Politics of Emotion*, New York: Routledge.

Amor, M. and Austin, J. (2003) *From Nothing to Zero: Letters from Refugees in Australia's Detention Centres*, Melbourne: Lonely Planet.

Ang, I. and Stratton, J. (2001) 'Multiculturalism in crisis: the new politics of race and national identity in Australia', in *On Not Speaking Chinese: Living between Asia and the West*, London: Routledge.

Appadurai, A. (1990) 'Disjuncture and Difference in the Global Cultural Economy', *Public Culture*, 2(2): 1–24.

Attwood, B. and Foster, S.G. (eds) (2003) 'Introduction', in *Frontier Conflict. The Australian Experience*, Canberra: National Museum of Australia.

Australian Broadcasting Commission (ABC) (2003a) 'About Woomera', *Four Corners*, 19 May, Sydney.

Australian Broadcasting Commission (ABC) (2003b) 'About Woomera Forum Archive'. Available online at: http://www2b.abc.net.au/4corners/forum/archives/archive14/default.shtm (accessed 26 September 2007).

Australian Council of Heads of Schools of Social Work (ACHSSW) (2006) *We've Boundless Plains to Share: The First Report of the People's Inquiry into Detention*. Available online at: http://www.peoplesinquiry.org.au (accessed 2 October 2007).

Batchelor, P. (2002) 'Albury Wodonga architect to design Bonegilla Commemorative Centre', media release, Minister for Major Projects, State Government of Victoria, 13 September, Melbourne.

Berlant, L. (1991) *The Anatomy of National Fantasy*, Chicago: University of Chicago Press.

Birch, T. (2001) 'The last refuge of the "un-Australian"', *UTS Review*, 7(1): 17–22.

Bonegilla Migrant Experience (BME) (2000) Bonegilla Migrant Experience home page. Available online at: http://www.bonegilla.org.au/ (accessed 8 July 2007).

Boyer, R. (1957) *The Australian Good Neighbour Movement—Past and Present*, Melbourne: Government Printer, pp. 7–11.

Caluya, G. (2006) 'The aesthetics of simplicity: Yang's Sadness and the melancholic community', *Journal of Intercultural Studies*, 27(1–2): 83–100.

Commonwealth Ombudsman (CO) (2001) *Report of an Own Motion Investigation into the Department of Immigration and Multicultural Affairs' Immigration Detention Centres*, Commonwealth Ombudsman. Available online at: http://www.ombudsman.gov.au/commonwealth/publish.nsf/AttachmentsByTitle/reports_2001_dima_statecorrectional.pdf/$FILE/Correctional+facilities.pdf (accessed 1 October 2007).

Cronin, K. (1993) 'A culture of control: an overview of immigration policy-making', in Jupp, J. and Kabala, M. (eds) *The Politics of Australian Immigration*, Canberra: Bureau of Immigration Research.

Department of Immigration and Ethnic Affairs (DIEA) (1986) *Don't Settle for Less*, Canberra: AGPS.

Derrida, J. (2000) *Of Hospitality*, Stanford: Stanford University Press.

Ethnic Liaison Officer Scheme (ELO) (1980) *Report on the Effectiveness of Commonwealth Services at Migrant Centres*, Melbourne: ELO.

Flood, P. (2001) *Report of Inquiry into Immigration Detention Procedures*, Canberra: AGPS.

Foucault, M. (1980) *Power/Knowledge*, ed. Colin Gordon, trans. Colin Gordon, Leo Marshall, John Mepham and Kate Soper, New York: Pantheon.

Frazier, L.J. (1998) 'Subverted memories: countermourning as political action in Chile', in M. Bal, J. Crewe and L. Spitzer (eds) *Acts of Mourning: Cultural Recall in the Present*, Hanover: University Press of New England.

Freud, S. (1934) 'Mourning and Melancholia', *Collected Papers*, vol. 4, ed. E. Jones, trans. J. Riviere, London: The Hogarth Press.

Fung, P. (2007) *Alternatives to mandatory detention: studies of the Maribyrnong/Midway Hostel*, Postgraduate Work-in-Progress paper, 31 May, Australian Centre, University of Melbourne, Melbourne.

Gabaccia, D.R. (1999) 'Is everywhere nowhere? Nomads, nations and the immigrant paradigm of United States history', *Journal of American History*, 86(3): 1115–34.

Greig, A. (1995) *The Stuff Dreams Are Made Of: Housing Provision in Australia 1945–60*, Melbourne: Melbourne University Press.

Hage, G. (1998) *White Nation: Fantasies of White Supremacy in a Multicultural Society*, Sydney: Pluto Press.

Hage, G. (2003) *Against Paranoid Nationalism: Searching for Hope in a Shrinking Society*, Sydney: Pluto Press.

Hirst, J. (2001) 'More or less diverse', in H. Irving (ed.), *Unity and Diversity: A National Conversation: The Barton Lectures*, Sydney: ABC Books.

Howard, J. (2001) Address at the Federal Liberal Party Campaign Launch, Sydney, 28 October. Available online at: http:www.pm.gov.au/media/Speech/2001/speech1311.cfm (accessed 30 October 2007).

Human Rights and Equal Opportunity Commission (HREOC) (1998) *Those Who've Come Across the Seas: Detention of Unauthorised Arrivals*, Sydney: HREOC.

Human Rights and Equal Opportunity Commission (HREOC) (2004) *A Last Resort? The National Inquiry into Children in Immigration Detention*, Sydney: HREOC.

Human Rights and Equal Opportunity Commission (HREOC) (2007) *Summary of Observations following the Inspection of Mainland Immigration Detention Facilities*, Sydney: HREOC.

Hurford, C. (2006) 'Silver lining to Hilali', *The Australian*, 2 November: 10.

Hutchison, M. (2004) 'Accommodating strangers: Commonwealth Government records of Bonegilla and other migrant accommodation centres', *Public History Review*, 11: 63–79.

Jordens, A.-M. (1997) *Alien to Citizen: Settling Migrants in Australia, 1945–75*, St Leonards, NSW: Allen & Unwin.

Jordens, A.-M. (1994) *Redefining Australians: Immigration, Citizenship and National Identity*, Sydney: Hale & Iremonger.

Junankar, P.N., Pope, D., Kapuscinski, C., Ma, G., and Mudd, W. (1993) *Recent Immigrants and Housing*, Canberra: AGPS.

Jupp, J. (1966) *Arrivals and Departures*, Melbourne: Cheshire-Lansdowne.

Jupp, J. (2002) *From White Australia to Woomera: The Story of Australian Immigration*, Cambridge: Cambridge University Press.

Kunz, E.F. (1988) *Displaced Persons: Calwell's New Australians*, Canberra: Australian National University.

Loh, M. (1980) *With Courage in their Cases*, Melbourne: FILEF.

Mares, P. (2001) *Borderline: Australia's Treatment of Refugees and Asylum Seekers*, Sydney: UNSW Press.

Marr, D. and Wilkinson, M. (2003) *Dark Victory*, St Leonards, NSW: Allen & Unwin.

McCoy, D. (1996) *From hostel to 'home': immigration, resettlement and community – the ethnic Vietnamese in Australia, 1975–1995*, unpublished PhD thesis, University of New South Wales.

McMaster, D. (2001) *Asylum Seekers: Australia's Response to Refugees*, Melbourne: Melbourne University Press.

Media Watch (2007) television programme, Australian Broadcasting Commission, Sydney, 8 October.

Mellor, D. (2004) 'The experience of Vietnamese in Australia: the racist tradition continues', *Journal of Ethnic and Migration Studies*, 30(4): 631–58.

Mitropoulos, A. and Rozensweig, B. (2000) 'With intent: death and suffering as policy', *xborder*. Available online at: http://www.antimedia.net/xborder/xb_suffering.php (accessed 12 April 2007).

Mitropoulos, A. (2001) 'A chapter in the political management of protest', *xborder*. Available online at: http://www.antimedia.net/xborder/xb_ombud.php (accessed 30 October 2007).

Moss, M. (1997) *Taking a Punt: First Stop Bonegilla: Stories by Darebin Residents*, Preston, Victoria: City of Darebin.

Neumann, K. (2004) *Refuge Australia*, Sydney: UNSW Press.

Nora, P. (1989) 'Between memory and history: *les lieux de mémoire*', trans. Mark Roudebush, *Representations*, Spring.

Panich, C. (1988) *Sanctuary? Remembering Postwar Immigration*, St Leonards, NSW: Allen & Unwin.

Parklands Albury-Wodonga (2006) 'Block 19 Bonegilla Migrant Experience'. Available online at: http://www.parklands-alburywodonga.org.au/parks/Block19Bonegilla.htm (accessed 4 June 2007).

Pennay, B. (2006) 'Bonegilla Block 19: a site of national significance', *Bonegilla Update*, July.

Perera, S. (2002) 'What is a camp…?', *Borderlands e-journal*, 1(1), <http://www.borderlandsejournal.adelaide.edu.au/vol1no1_2002/perera_camp.html> (accessed 2 October 2007).

P O (1982) 'A documentary impression of the history of the Bonegilla Migrant Camp', *Doubletake*, ABC Radio National, 3 August, Melbourne.

Pugliese, J. (2002a) 'Migrant Heritage in an Indigenous Context', *Journal of Intercultural Studies*, 23(1): 5–18.

Pugliese, J. (2002b) 'Penal asylum: refugees, ethics, hospitality', *Borderlands e-journal*, 1(1). Available online at: http://www.borderlandsejournal.adelaide.edu.au/vol1no1_2002/pugliese.html (accessed 15 October 2007).

Rose, D.B. (2004) *Reports from a Wild Country: Ethics for Decolonisation*, Sydney: UNSW Press.

Ruddock, P. (2002) 'Distortions malign a compassionate country', *The Sunday Age*, 13 January.

Skrzynecki, P. (1985) *Joseph's Coat*, Sydney: Hale & Iremonger.

Sluga, G. (1988) *Bonegilla: A Place of No Hope*, Melbourne: Department of History, University of Melbourne.

Sluga, G. (1994) 'Bonegilla and migrant dreaming', in K. Darian-Smith and P. Hamilton (eds), *Memory and History in Twentieth-Century Australia*, Oxford: Oxford University Press.

Solà-Morales Rubió, I. de (1995) 'Terrain vague', in C. Davidson (ed.), *Anyplace*, Cambridge, MA: MIT Press.

Stephen, S. (2002) 'There are alternatives to mandatory detention', *Green Left Weekly*, 13 March.

Sturken, M. (1997) *Tangled Memories: The Vietnam War, the AIDS Epidemic, and the Politics of Remembering*, Berkeley: University of California Press.

Synan, A. (2002) *We Came With Nothing: Story of the West Sale Migrant Holding Centre*, Sale, Victoria: Lookups Research.

Thomas, M. (1997) 'The Vietnamese in Australia', in J.E. Coughlan and D. McNamara (eds) *Asians in Australia: Patterns of Migration and Settlement*, Melbourne, NSW: Macmillan.

Tyler, H. (2003) *Asylum: Voices From Behind the Razor Wire*, Melbourne, NSW: Lothian.

Vitelli, F. (2006) 'Epic Memory and Dispossession: The Shrine and the Memory Wars', *Mongrel*, 1 (April): 8–21.

Viviani, N. (1984) *The Long Journey: Vietnamese Migration and Settlement in Australia*, Melbourne NSW: Melbourne University Press.

Wills, S. (2002) 'Un-stitching the lips of a migrant nation', *Australian Historical Studies*, 33(118): 71–89.

Wills, S. (2004a) 'Losing the right to country: the memory of loss and the loss of memory in claiming the nation as space', *New Formations*, 51: 50–65.

Wills, S. (2004b) 'When neighbours become good friends: the Australian embrace of its millionth migrant', *Australian Historical Studies*, 35(124): 332–54.

Wills, S. (2005a) 'History('s) re-turns', *Cultural Studies Review*, 11(5): 208–11.

Wills, S. (2005b) 'Migrant hostels', in A. Brown-May and S. Swain (eds), *The Encyclopedia of Melbourne*, Cambridge: Cambridge University Press.

Wills, S. (2006) 'Possible spaces of everyday hospitality: hostels, migration and memory', paper presented at Everyday Multiculturalism Conference, Centre for Research on Social Inclusion, Macquarie University, 28–9 September, Sydney.

Index